FROM SUMMITS
TO SOLUTIONS

FROM SUMMITS TO SOLUTIONS

Innovations in Implementing the Sustainable Development Goals

Raj M. Desai, Hiroshi Kato, Homi Kharas, and John W. McArthur

EDITORS

BROOKINGS INSTITUTION PRESS
Washington, D.C.

The Brookings Institution is a private nonprofit organization devoted to research, education,
and publication on important issues of domestic and foreign policy. Its principal purpose
is to bring the highest quality independent research and analysis to bear on current and
emerging policy problems. Interpretations or conclusions in Brookings publications
should be understood to be solely those of the authors.

Library of Congress Cataloging-in-Publication data are available.
ISBN 978-0-8157-3663-9 (pbk : alk. paper)
ISBN 978-0-8157-3664-6 (ebook)

9 8 7 6 5 4 3 2 1

Typeset in Adobe Garamond Pro

Composition by Cynthia Stock

Contents

Part III. UPDATING GOVERNANCE

Acknowledgments

This volume is the outcome of a collaborative project between the Brookings Institution and the Japan International Cooperation Agency Research Institute (JICA-RI).

The editors would like to thank the following individuals for their contributions to the Authors' Workshop: Magdi Amin, Shaida Badiee, Daniella Ballou-Aares, Manish Bapna, Ani Dasgupta, Steve Davenport, Jessica Fanzo, Haishan Fu, Amanda Glassman, Jeff Gutman, Christine Hogan, Chris Jochnick, Danny Leipziger, Daniela Ligiero, Keith Martin, Bruce McNamer, Paul O'Brien, Rajul Pandya-Lorch, Tony Pipa, Sudhir Shetty, Kathy Sierra, Marilou Uy, Aleem Walji, and Sam Worthington. They extend their gratitude to Gordon McCord for reviewing chapter one.

The editors would also like to acknowledge Marjorie Pannell and Janet Walker from Brookings Institution Press for providing invaluable editorial support, and Jenn Cohen, Tyler Ditmore, and Madelyn Swift for coordinating the preparation of the final manuscript.

Brookings is grateful to JICA-RI for its financial and intellectual support of this project. Brookings recognizes that the value it provides is in its absolute commitment to quality, independence, and impact. Activities supported by its donors reflect this commitment, and the analysis and recommendations contained in this volume are not determined or influenced by any donation. The chapters reflect the views of the authors and not the official position of any specific organization.

CHAPTER ONE

The Need for Innovations to Implement the Sustainable Development Goals

Raj M. Desai, Hiroshi Kato, Homi Kharas, and John W. McArthur

On September 25, 2015, 193 countries adopted a set of goals to end poverty, protect the planet, and ensure prosperity for all people, under the auspices of the UN's 2030 Agenda for Sustainable Development. These Sustainable Development Goals (SDGs) represented a historic breakthrough in multilateral cooperation. As stated in the summit agreement:

> This Agenda is a plan of action for people, planet and prosperity. . . . All countries and all stakeholders, acting in collaborative partnership, will implement this plan. We are resolved to free the human race from the tyranny of poverty and want and to heal and secure our planet. We are determined to take the bold and transformative steps which are urgently needed to shift the world onto a sustainable and resilient path. As we embark on this collective journey, we pledge that no one will be left behind. (United Nations, 2015)

The agreement on the SDGs was followed in December by the Paris Agreement on climate change and preceded by adoption of the UN's Addis Ababa Action Agenda at the July 2015 Third International Conference on Financing for Development.

In 2015 the three agreements were considered a triumph of international cooperation. The pathway had been complicated. Differing visions of the appropriate number of goals and targets, the potential costs, and the means of implementation led to protracted negotiations lasting more than three years, from 2012 to 2015. In 2014 even the holding of a Financing for Development conference was questioned, with many arguing there was little political appetite for more aid commitments. Success in Paris was also far from assured, with the history of the failed 2009 Copenhagen climate summit still a vivid memory in the minds of many people.

So it was with a sense of relief that all national governments reached the agreements with support from so many other stakeholders—civil society, the business community, academics and scientists, young people, and indigenous groups. But the ambitions had been laid out with few specific overarching action plans. A simple question—What happens next?—remained unanswered.

The universal, inclusive, and integrative nature of the SDGs, coupled with their broad scope—seventeen goals and 169 targets—poses specific challenges for implementation. At its core, Agenda 2030 is about stimulating change, because everyone agrees that a business-as-usual approach will not suffice. Moreover, shifts in technology, finance, and global politics are occurring too rapidly for anyone to imagine that a simple continuation along historical pathways will deliver the right results. There is an imperative to articulate new approaches that will alter the trajectories so as to achieve every goal. What needs to change, whose actions need to change, and how can change be organized?

Our purpose in compiling the essays in this volume is to offer practical suggestions for innovations that could and should be adopted to bring about necessary change. Without such change, there is a risk of active inertia, of bureaucracies in governments and companies recognizing limitations in their traditional approaches but finding themselves unable to react with sufficient forcefulness and purpose to alter outcomes.

Where Are We? SDG Trends and Gaps

The optimism that lay behind the decision to set the SDGs as ambitious global targets stemmed from the considerable gains realized under the Millennium Development Goals (MDGs). Many of the poorest countries registered major accelerations in progress on measures of health and education in particular, even in cases where targets were not explicitly met. At least 20 million and as many as 30 million additional lives were saved compared to pre-MDG trends, the majority in sub-Saharan Africa (McArthur and Rasmussen, 2018).

A starting point for the SDGs is the final stretch in ending extreme poverty. In 2015, around 700 million people were living on less than $1.90 per day (in 2011 U.S. dollar purchasing power parity terms). By 2030, even under current trajectories, that number is slated to be closer to 440 million people, or 5 percent of the world's population. However, after falling by roughly one percentage point per year over a generation, the global trend of progress is on course to slow. That is because an increasing share of the world's remaining extreme poverty is becoming concentrated in countries with slow rates of progress and fast-growing populations.

Notably, Nigeria is beginning to represent the foremost concentration of the global poverty challenge. As India continues to enjoy rapid progress in reducing extreme poverty, Nigeria's estimated numbers continue to grow. By the end of 2018, India will likely drop below 80 million people living in extreme poverty, while Nigeria's figure is expected to be higher. Of course, the challenges of extreme poverty are not limited to any single country. At least thirty-one countries are "severely off track" with respect to the goals of ending extreme poverty (Gertz and Kharas, 2018). Among 123 countries with data to assess 2030 trajectories across measures of access to water, access to sanitation, undernourishment, and primary school completion rates, only seven countries are on track to meet all four relevant SDG targets (updated calculations based on McArthur and Rasmussen, 2016). Change is needed everywhere.

Among developing countries, the challenges of extreme poverty and basic needs are closely related to the SDG challenge of ending preventable child and maternal deaths. Target 3.1 calls for the world to reduce the maternal mortality ratio to 70 deaths per 100,000 live births, down from around 216 per 100,000 live births in 2015, and target 3.2 calls for every country to reduce the child mortality rate to no more than 25 deaths per 1,000 live births. A recent study (McArthur, Rasmussen, and Yamey, 2018) estimated that approximately forty-two countries are currently off track for both maternal and child mortality. If every country achieves both targets, an additional 11.8 million lives will be saved compared to current trends, including 10.2 million children and 1.6 million mothers. Here, Nigeria accounts for around a third of the lives at stake. When the Democratic Republic of Congo and Pakistan are included, these three countries alone account for more than half the lives at stake.

Many of the countries facing the deepest poverty challenges also have fragile public institutions. A generation ago, those contexts were considered too difficult for long-term development programming, but recent evidence suggests there are opportunities for progress. For example, Schmidt-Traub (2018) finds evidence suggesting that, among country proposals submitted to the Global Fund to Fight AIDS, Tuberculosis, and Malaria (GFATM), there is no difference in technical quality between proposals prepared by fragile states and those prepared by non-fragile states. Nnadi and others (2017) show that with the right strategic and operational tactics, direct interventions like vaccinations can be effective even in diverse conflict situations. In a similar vein, Gertz and Kharas (2018) show that World Bank project evaluations have found increasingly similar success rates in countries that are severely off-track with respect to extreme poverty trajectories. It is not clear that state fragility or a recent lack of progress necessarily inhibits progress toward an SDG target.

At the other end of the economic spectrum, the sustained expansion of many fast-growing countries is driving a realignment of the world economy and its geopolitics. For the past decade, Asia has been the engine of more than half the world's annual aggregate economic growth, even when Japan is excluded. This marks the first time in the modern era that emerging Asia has been the leading driver of the global economy.

In this context, the challenge of sustainable development is universal. Many advanced economies have experienced a slowdown in labor productivity growth, relatively stagnant median wages, and deepening concern over the concentration of economic gains among the very wealthy. Across high-income countries, the share of people reporting inadequate income to buy food throughout the year has been stagnant (Gertz and others, 2017). A study of Canada's domestic trajectories with respect to SDG targets showed that even such an advanced economy is not yet fully on track for any of the first sixteen goals (McArthur and Rasmussen, 2017). This is not because Canada cannot achieve the goals by 2030 but rather because a significant population or set of issues is getting left behind in each policy domain. Thus the global reference points for defining economic success are shifting.

Recouple Economic Growth and Social "Good": The Case for Inclusion

One distinguishing feature of Agenda 2030 is that it calls for inclusion. It speaks to the growing global resonance of arguably the foremost SDG theme—to leave no one behind. Whether the issue is gender, indigenous status, ethnicity, religion, sexual orientation, geography, class, migration status, or some other aspect of identity, every country in the world is grappling with the policy challenges of inclusion and with political tensions resulting from exclusion. In some countries, these tensions are generating constructive public reckonings about groups and communities that have been left behind, with social media technologies providing new forms of public debate. The international #MeToo movement's illumination of long-standing gender inequities highlights the speed at which political transformations can arise. In other countries, governments have taken a more authoritarian or restrictive stance and used the same technologies to limit public discourse. There is constant tension between the benefits and costs afforded by the expanding array of digital tools.

This difference in governments' reactions reflects a central contrast in the world. On the one hand, the SDGs can be interpreted as an effort to promote the successful expansion of the global middle class. From this perspective, the outlook is good. One of the most fundamental structural changes in the world economy is the unprecedented growth of the number of people living on around

$11 to $110 per day. In 2000, fewer than 2 billion people lived in this income band. Today the corresponding number is more than 3 billion, and the world is about to become, for the first time, majority middle class. By the SDG deadline of 2030, there will likely be more than 5 billion middle-class people, with most of the expansion coming in Asia (Kharas, 2017).

On the other hand, these new middle-class people will need an unprecedented expansion of infrastructure to support their livelihoods, including energy, transport, and housing infrastructure, all of which present a challenge to achieving the environmental sustainability goals. These same people will also change the politics of distribution in their own economies, often pushing for more social insurance programs as opposed to social assistance programs from which the poor also benefit (Desai and Kharas, 2017).

Few countries in recent years have been able to achieve economic growth along with a distribution perceived as fair to all. Calls for "inclusive growth" or to "leave no one behind" are heard, but there is less clarity on what this means in practice: probably some combination of more equal access to opportunities through getting the right skills and education, less discriminatory labor markets that reward men and women equally (among other inequities), and stronger public safety nets. There is nothing about how market economies operate that inevitably leads to a deterioration in income distribution, at least in terms of the consumption opportunities of the poorest. As an empirical matter, there was no systematic relationship between growth and distribution in the postwar period. Looking across countries at changes in the Gini coefficient—a measure of inequality—over ten-year periods since 1950 shows that the mean change is zero. Just as many countries saw improvements in their Gini coefficients as saw a deterioration. The same result holds in the period since 2000, when digital technologies and winner-take-all companies have emerged. Of 146 countries that have two surveys separated by about a decade since 2000, thirty-seven have had a worsening of the Gini coefficient by more than 1 percentage point, eighty-one have shown an improvement, and the remaining twenty-eight have had no change.[1]

Nevertheless, the size of changes in top incomes suggests that some growth pathways and policies deliver better distributional outcomes than others. In this book, much of our discussion of targeting places and updating governance has implications for the distributional aspects of opportunities and outcomes.

---

1. Authors' calculations, based on Gini coefficient data published in the World Bank's PovcalNet database.

Decouple Economic Growth and Environmental "Bads": The Case for Ecology

One stark feature of the current global economy is the dramatic strain humanity is placing on Earth's natural assets. Climate change is the most prominent of these, with greenhouse gas (GHG) emissions still growing year over year as of 2017. Based on the current trajectory, emissions will reach roughly 60 gigatons (GT) per year by 2030, rather than decline to around 40 GT, as required by the Paris Agreement on climate (UNEP, 2017).

For most of the twentieth century, economic growth was fueled by growth in energy use and a corresponding increase in GHG emissions. As the scientific evidence mounted of a link between human-driven carbon emissions and climate change, efforts began to decouple economic growth from these negative environmental consequences. In the United States, for example, GHG emissions peaked in 2007. In the following years up to 2016, overall gross domestic product grew by more than 12 percent, while greenhouse gas emissions declined by 11 percent, which translates to a greater than 20 percent decline in emissions per unit of GDP (EPA, 2018; World Bank, 2018). Globally, the onset of decoupling has been less pronounced, as aggregate economic growth rates have been much faster and the transition away from carbon-intensive energy systems generally slower, leading to ongoing increases in overall emissions.

Climate change is not the only environmental "bad" to be considered. A related challenge lies in the world's oceans, which cover 70 percent of the planet. Increasing GHG concentrations are altering their average temperature and acidity and thus severely affecting the nature of the oceans, which in turns affects life on land. SDG 14 helps to highlight that the oceans are also minimally protected, with increasing risk of mass extinctions, as a few countries' fleets push ever farther into the high seas, depleting fish stocks and biodiversity through overharvesting. Pollution amplifies the problems, as plastics and nutrient runoffs are dispensed from intensified industrial and agricultural production systems in mature and fast-growing economies.

To capture these and other challenges, Johan Rockström and colleagues (Steffen and others, 2015) have proposed a framework of nine planetary boundaries, of which biodiversity loss and the use of phosphorus and nitrogen (largely in fertilizer to boost global food production) are already at or beyond critical thresholds. These challenges draw attention to the need for better management of the global commons as a central element of the SDG agenda.

Overall, the evidence suggests that the adverse environmental consequences of existing growth strategies are not inevitable—rather they result from inertia and the absence of incentives to change. Agenda 2030 draws attention to the need for such changes. Its central thesis is that planetary stewardship can keep pace with economic progress if the right technology, financing, incentives, and cross-border cooperation mechanisms are all in place.

Structural Challenges at the National Level: Communication, Measurement, Coordination

The SDGs focus attention on all the above issues and more, adding up to a much broader set of topics than the main MDG concerns of alleviating extreme poverty and meeting basic needs.[2] But the comprehensive nature of the SDGs means the goals are difficult to explain in a single narrative framework. The story line takes on different emphases in different contexts. It requires governments to focus on issues at home and abroad. It requires them to think about all segments of their populations. It requires clarity across interlocking economic, social, and environmental problems. And it requires partnering among all sectors of society. Even if doing so may already be among the inherent responsibilities of any government, it would be naïve to downplay the challenge of motivating all countries to pursue the full set of issues concurrently.

A separate challenge lies in acquiring the appropriate data to inform that pursuit. In part, this is the challenge of building data systems in developing countries. SDG 2, for example, includes five outcome targets, having to do with undernourishment, malnutrition, smallholder productivity, sustainable agriculture, and biodiversity. As of early 2018 only three of these, SDG targets 2.1, 2.2, and 2.5, had any information included in the UN's SDG global database. Of those three targets, only one indicator, undernourishment, has trend data available for 165 (out of 193) UN member states. For the other two targets and embedded indicators, trend data are available for less than half of all countries. The world's data are insufficient to track meaningfully what is working and what needs to change. The gaps are further amplified when disaggregated data within countries are sought. Unless the relevant data systems are built with urgency, it is not clear how countries can forge needed progress toward these goals.

Policy leadership is essential to overcome inertia on both the narrative and policy integration fronts. To promote public understanding, advocates need to articulate salient priorities and describe specific pathways for action. At the operational level, leaders need to pioneer new forms of integrated insights across domains of expertise and levels of government.

---

2. MDG 7 concerned environmental sustainability, but that goal did not achieve significant policy traction relative to other goals (McArthur and Rasmussen, 2018).

For example, the global challenges of reducing rates of obesity and noncommunicable disease will only be successfully tackled through a combination of public awareness, private sector innovation, successful urban planning, appropriate policy incentives, and integrated public sector action. The last implies cooperation among traditionally siloed government functions in the arenas of health care, education, and infrastructure. Similarly, the promotion of sustainable food systems will require cooperative action across sectors, jurisdictions, and technical realms.

The SDGs are helpful in drawing attention to these types of structural interconnections. But attention amounts to only one of many necessary ingredients for success. In this respect, the UN has provided a framework. It is up to local leaders of the public and private sectors and civil society to forge the practical connections and solutions within their own geographic and operational domains. In turn, the leaders of international organizations need to craft incentives for disparate communities to cooperate and learn from each other.

Structural Challenges at the Global Level: Multilateralism Under Stress

During the MDG period, multilateral institutions played a central role in galvanizing new forms of international cooperation. At present, many constituencies' weakening commitments to multilateralism, a broad return to protectionism, shifts in the balance of global economic power, and the spread of nationalist politics all risk undermining the consensus on which Agenda 2030 rests. Emerging powers like China have responded to weakened multilateralism by accelerating efforts to fashion alternatives such as the Asian Infrastructure Investment Bank, multicurrency swap agreements with regional central banks, and the Belt and Road Initiative to build infrastructure linking China with western Asia, Europe, and Africa.

The gaps between those made prosperous and those left behind by economic and technological progress are widening and becoming more difficult to manage. In the early 2000s, after two decades of fiscal turmoil in developing nations, many argued that globalization was not working for the poorest countries. Since 2008, populist politicians have argued that it is not working for the richest countries either.

Ongoing political developments are heightening fears that an era of "deglobalization" is upon us (Saravelos and Winkler, 2016). In the United States, such fears have coincided with threats of trade wars and more pronounced anti-immigration postures. In Europe, anti-immigration parties have gained a new prominence. France's National Front, the Dutch Party for Freedom, and the Austrian Freedom Party all emerged as serious electoral contenders in their respective countries. Antiglobalists have also achieved breakthroughs in countries where they had previously failed to gain traction, such as Germany and Sweden, where the Alternative for Germany and the Sweden Democrats respectively have realized big electoral gains.

In the EU's east, Poland, Hungary, the Czech Republic, and Slovakia are now led by staunchly antiglobalist populists.

These political strains are contributing to three types of multilateral gaps: gaps in institutional assistance, gaps in collective action, and gaps in peer learning.

Gaps in Institutional Assistance

The political currents have affected the environment for global development financing. The Addis Ababa Action Agenda did not secure participation from many finance ministers of developed and emerging markets. No new development finance or implementation plans were connected with the new SDGs. And since the 2030 Agenda was adopted in 2015, rich countries' aid spending on the least developed countries has fallen each year despite international commitments to do the opposite. As table 1-1 shows, total official aid financing for development in 2016 was actually slightly lower than in 2014, even when measured in current dollars, and official lending for development was only slightly higher (and is far smaller in scale).

Nor has private capital stepped into the breach. Many developing countries objected to private sector participation in SDG deliberations, and the private sector was not brought to the negotiating table at Addis Ababa (Hearn, 2017). Basel III regulations aimed at restoring stability to the global financial sector have put a premium on short-term, safe lending. Banks have withdrawn from project finance in developing countries, and even private investment in infrastructure projects has fallen (see table 1-1).

Table 1-1. External Support for SDG Investments

Billions of current U.S. $

Type of Support	2014	2016
Net official aid	161.8	157.7
Net lending by official institutions	18.6	21.8
Private financing	275.3	180.7
Total	455.7	360.2

Sources: Data from OECD DAC2a (http://stats.oecd.org/Index.aspx?DataSetCode=Table2A); OECD 2016 Mobilization Survey; World Bank, World Development Indicators (WDI), Public and Publicly Guaranteed (PPG), private creditors; World Bank, International Debt Statistics: Net financial flows bilateral and multilateral; World Bank, WDI PPG, concessional and multilateral; World Bank, Private Participation in Infrastructure (PPI) Project Annual Update Reports.

Note: Private financing includes lending by the private sector to governments and public institutions; guarantees, syndicated loans, collective investment vehicles, and credit lines associated with official projects (2015 value used), as well as private participation in infrastructure (PPI). Net official aid covers concessional finance, whereas net lending by official institutions covers nonconcessional finance.

In developing countries, one implication of flat or declining traditional sources of international finance is that financing for the SDGs must come from "beyond aid," even though aid will remain especially important for low-income countries and a select range of sectors. Going beyond aid can shift the agenda in several ways. First and foremost, it means putting far greater emphasis on domestic resource mobilization. At the recently concluded pledging session for the Global Partnership for Education (GPE), donors committed $2.3 billion for the three-year period 2018–2020. This covers only a small share of the global education financing gap, but notably, the fifty-three developing country partners of GPE also agreed to raise their domestic contributions to education by $30 billion, to achieve a total spending level of $110 billion over the same three-year period.

Second, the private sector continues to innovate with SDG financing. Green bond issuance surpassed $150 billion in 2017, compared to just $10 billion in 2013. A target of $1 trillion by 2020 has been set. Of course, these figures do not necessarily represent increments to financing available for the SDGs, but they do suggest a keen investor appetite. The green bond market appears to tap into investors' desire for transparency, reporting, and accountability in financial investing. If that momentum continues, the whole shape of finance for sustainable development could change.

A third move beyond aid has to do with blending of official and private finance, often for infrastructure projects. Private and public capital play different functions in these efforts. The former brings scale, technology, and implementation expertise. The latter can strengthen institutions, bring complementary scale, help manage risks, improve domestic capacity, provide incentives for public goods, and build a solid pipeline of projects.

Gaps in Collective Action

Among established institutions, fragility in multilateral cooperation impedes reform at a time when renewal is essential. It cannot be overstated that the foremost breakthroughs during the MDG era were largely driven by new institutions, new resources, and new technologies, especially in the health sector. For example, the GFATM and the U.S. president's Emergency Plan for AIDS Relief were both launched in the early 2000s to scale up newly available technologies for the treatment and prevention of infectious diseases, accompanied by pioneering philanthropic investments from the Bill & Melinda Gates Foundation, among others, and major increases in official development assistance for health.

In considering the evolving frontiers of the world's SDG challenges, one needs to consider what new efforts are needed today. We may again need new institutions, new technologies, new policy incentives, and new forms of partnership among public and private actors. Recently launched entities such as the Asian Infrastructure Investment Bank, major transregional undertakings such as the Belt and Road Initiative, and the communities of action for the oceans will undoubtedly frame new contours for international cooperation. Legacy organizations will need to update themselves accordingly or else may not be able to cope.

Even the voluntary national commitments under the Paris Agreement on climate have been challenged in some quarters, leading many subnational players to forge their own international coalitions, sometimes in partnership with other sovereign states. Meanwhile, some major issues don't yet have a proper multilateral governance structure. For example, the world has established conventions for managing commerce conducted on top of the oceans, namely, the Law of the Sea. But the world does not yet have a clear system for addressing threats beneath the ocean surface, such as destructive fishing practices, marine pollution, runoff from improper land use practices, or overexploitation of fisheries. One of the primary difficulties that could hinder collective action on these fronts is that many such threats, while common to numerous countries, vary greatly in intensity and magnitude by location. Thus new forms of regional and global cooperation are essential.

Gaps in Peer Learning

Since many aspects of the SDG challenge will be confronted on domestic fronts, including among the advanced economies, international cooperation will be needed to bolster peer learning. In the wealthiest economies in particular, the challenge to leave no one behind will hinge on innovations in internal cooperation that reach the people in greatest need. Local governments and market players will need to collaborate to promote new forms of progress. A form of reverse technology transfer might also be needed to translate the lessons learned from community development strategies in low-income environments or to leverage low-cost market innovations taking shape on the frontiers of emerging markets. In these and other instances, the task for multilateral institutions will be to support accelerated rates of progress through knowledge sharing rather than providing financial resources, finding points of connection and collaboration among disparate countries that have common domestic aims but face different political and fiscal constraints.

Upgrading the SDG Action Plan: A Focus on Changing Trajectories

Against this background of new global goals and multilateral strain, it is urgent to put forward SDG action plans of appropriate scope and ambition at global, national, and local levels. Success will depend on changing trajectories in specific cases. Unpacking global averages to the level of individuals is at the heart of "leave no one behind." An illustrative example is global poverty. At the aggregate level, about 1.1 people per second are lifting themselves out of extreme poverty. That is not too far from the rate of 1.5 people per second that is required if all the nearly 630 million people estimated as poor around the start of 2018 (plus natural population growth) are to be helped above the extreme poverty threshold by 2030 (World Data Lab, 2018).

Looking at these numbers, it is tempting simply to encourage everyone to do a little more or a little better. But that would be a misreading of the situation. The issue is that in some places a lot more needs to be done, while in other places trajectories are more or less on track. In fact, in about seventeen countries today, the absolute numbers living in extreme poverty are projected to rise between now and 2030. In another forty-six countries, the number living in extreme poverty will come down but at a rate that still leaves many people in extreme poverty by 2030 (World Data Lab, 2018).

In considering implementation issues for the SDGs, then, it is important to go beyond a global overview to develop a granular picture of what is happening and where. Detailed data need to be made available by country, locality, and, often, community. Strategies, plans, and resource distribution must accord with the granular picture or else efforts will be dissipated over a variety of worthy but less impactful activities. For its part, SDG 1 cannot be achieved in the absence of explicitly funded strategies to address poverty in countries whose current trajectories need the most change.

The SDGs can be a powerful driver of change precisely because they lend themselves to exploring and comparing alternative trajectories. With the end point of 2030 defined and the starting point in 2015 known (at least baselines should be available relatively soon), alternative pathways for each goal can be constructed under different policy and investment scenarios.

Nonstate Actors

While it is true that the SDGs represent an intergovernmental consensus, it does not follow that implementation is solely the responsibility of government. Policymakers in each country can set the strategy and dedicate resources, but implementation will have to reach beyond governments. Private credit and capital markets, for example, will have a key role in financing investments that contribute to progress. Companies will need to provide core goods and services to support achievement of the SDGs while complying with economic, social, and governance standards. Many in the business community have individually embraced the goals, and far-sighted business leaders have recognized that considerable opportunity is implicit in Agenda 2030. The Business and Sustainable Development Commission (2017) identified $12 trillion in new market opportunities in just four economic systems—food and agriculture, cities, energy and materials, and health and well-being. The trick will be to get widespread business engagement in new leadership, new partnerships, new technologies, and new approaches.

Scientists and engineers will also need support to generate crucial technological breakthroughs while ensuring equitable access in low-income environments. Civil society and media will need to keep innovating to ensure citizens are engaged and informed, in a way that holds powerful interests accountable. Subnational and local governments may have to take a stronger role in investing in public goods where national governments are reticent. Various mechanisms for international cooperation that served the world well in the twentieth century might need to be reformed for the twenty-first.

Innovations for Breakthroughs

The contributors to this book look at frontier issues of implementation. The topics do not try to be comprehensive, and many crucial areas, such as the provision of basic education and health services, are not addressed. Instead, we asked experts in their fields to think about issues where breakthroughs are needed or where not enough attention has been given to a topic. The discussions in this book are squarely focused on new things that must be done to change global and country trajectories to meet the SDGs.

The contributors look at what our current economic system measures and cares about, and note that it fails to measure and capture full value, whether in the form of women's unpaid caregiving or as environmental and social sustainability. Without capturing value properly, economies systematically underinvest in these areas and create distortions, with undesirable consequences. But if maximizing value is to drive behavior, either it must be priced in in all its dimensions or a new generation of entrepreneurs must be persuaded that reputational effects, branding, mission-driven values, and employee retention are sufficient to encourage changes in how business is conducted.

The contributors also look at new approaches to targeting specific places. Thinking about the geography of where we need change is important. The oceans and high seas represent some of the least governed parts of the planet, with dire consequences for both terrestrial and marine life. To take another example, much is made of the need to distill the SDG goals so they are applicable to individual urban areas, but most cities today have a complex mix of municipalities, which makes horizontal coordination just as much a problem as the vertical coordination of cities with national governments to establish and pursue their own localized

SDG targets. And for all the discussion of cities, we should remember that nearly half the world's population—and a far greater fraction of poor people—still live in rural areas. How can SDGs be achieved there? Can we learn more about what places to target by improving our understanding of what is happening at local levels, using new techniques of geospatial observation and building up statistical capabilities within countries to generate spatially disaggregated data?

Ultimately, achieving the SDGs requires agreement among stakeholders on a governance system to address coordination gaps. Updating governance arrangements will be crucial in areas such as citizen participation, multilateral banking, the global commons, coordinating the proliferating partnerships in sectors such as global heath, and even in the way rich countries pursue the SDGs at home and abroad. Without improvements, it is unlikely the institutional structures aiming to support the SDGs will be able to carry out their task.

The authors offer innovative thinking in the three core implementation areas—capturing value, place-based targeting, and multistakeholder governance—addressed in this book.

Innovations in Capturing Value

"We treasure what we measure" is an old business adage. It applies equally to public policymakers and is perhaps the issue most salient to the discrepancy that has arisen between economic growth and sustainable development. Growth alone does not deliver sustainability precisely because it is driven by profit maximization while ignoring other social priorities. To succeed on the SDGs, mechanisms must be found to invest in the things that are valued by society but which private business does not yet necessarily measure or address on its own.

SDG 5, for example, calls for gender equality and the empowerment of all women and girls. Although these principles are critical to achieving inclusive growth, significant gender gaps in economic opportunity and political agency persist. Jeni Klugman and Laura Tyson in chapter 2 examine mechanisms that could narrow the gaps. They note that progress in narrowing the pay gap between women and men—which had been closing in recent years with rising levels of female education—has now slowed in most lower- and middle-income countries. It is still the case that, in addition to being overrepresented in the informal sector labor force and in low-wage occupations, much of women's work consists of (usually) unpaid child care or eldercare. Though some of this unpaid work may be a result of choice, evidence suggests that many women, especially younger adults and older teens, cannot look for paid work because of their unpaid responsibilities. Klugman and Tyson argue that public investment in care services for newborns, infants, and the elderly can reduce the burden of unpaid care on women and boost their labor participation. Extending women's access to financial services can also allow families to save for education and health, and to start small businesses. In addition, Klugman and Tyson call for private businesses and government agencies to help unleash women's potential in the workforce by addressing their own organizational biases in hiring, promotion, and contracting.

Looking at other forms of national-scale investment, there is much talk of the SDGs requiring "integrated" processes with respect to mobilizing resources that address a broad range of goals simultaneously. What do these look like? Amina Mohammed and Simon Zadek in chapter 3 provide firsthand insight into the process that led to Nigeria's first sovereign green bond issuance in 2017. Mohammed's perspective derives from her service as minister of the environment, a post she took up after serving as UN Secretary-General Ban Ki-moon's special adviser on the post-2015 development agenda, right up through the September 2015 SDG summit. Zadek was formerly co-director of the UN Environment's Inquiry into the Design of a Sustainable Financial System. Their chapter, written in their personal capacities, offers a unique account of their collaboration, told through a first-person narrative. When she took up the environment portfolio, Mohammed was looking for instruments to tackle Nigeria's interconnected challenges of poverty, insecurity, poor governance, and environmental degradation. She realized that green bonds could be a way to break down silos among diverse constituencies and called on UN Environment's Inquiry for help. Together they devised a way to harness the interests of influential economic actors, public and private, to deliver measurable progress on environmental outcomes. This approach offered new methods for capturing environmental and political value across constituencies.

The full breadth of SDG ambitions cannot be realized without large-scale contributions from private business, which can help both by innovating new solutions and by minimizing problematic actions. Jane Nelson in chapter 4 argues that common standards, goals, and metrics with respect to environmental, social, and governance indicators will be crucial for success. But any movement toward measuring market actors' contributions faces many technical and political challenges. Nelson therefore offers a framework for leapfrogging from a norm of celebrating standout business entities to mainstreaming business contributions to the SDGs. The personal commitment of individual business leaders forms one crucial piece of the puzzle. Business coalitions are also essential, within and across industries; and here financial institutions and capital market intermediaries play particularly important roles. Policymakers need to do their bit too, creating the policy and regulatory environment that encourages market actors to report the right metrics.

Partnerships of this sort between public and private sectors (along with non-profit players) are vital to implementing the SDGs. The track record of such collaborations, however, has not been sufficiently successful, according to Ann

Florini. In chapter 5 she argues that most partnerships tend to founder for reasons beyond financial constraints, chiefly skill shortages. Partnerships often do not attract professionals with the requisite expertise to manage and expand collaborations across multiple sectors, each with its own organizing principles, agenda, and culture. Florini explores some of the determinants of the success and failure of multistakeholder efforts even when partners share a common objective. Reviewing the cases of partnerships formed to achieve an important social or developmental goal (health, education, gender equality, and food security), she shows how mismatches between partners' priorities, communication platforms, or timelines can lead to coordination failures. She then outlines some of the skills, incentives, and mindsets that can increase the value of collaboration and gives some examples of programs that provide these ingredients.

SDG 9 addresses three important aspects of sustainable development: infrastructure, industrialization, and innovation. In chapter 6 Rogério Studart examines the unfolding of events in Brazil, which for many years successfully targeted public investments to build up its human capital and end poverty but at the expense of investing in infrastructure. Lack of infrastructure in turn led to private investment and job creation falling well short of desired levels. Studart analyzes Brazil's experience with creating a scaled-up program to invest in more sustainable infrastructure. This is easier said than done. The practical difficulties facing Brazil were considerable, from the need to develop a pipeline of projects with appropriate social and environmental safeguards to undertaking and financing infrastructure in an environment of high domestic interest rates. A platform approach developed by the National Development Bank held initial promise but ran into difficulty as domestic bond markets—the ultimate source of the long-term capital needed for infrastructure—never developed sufficiently. Studart concludes with a salutary reminder of the many complementary activities that are needed to move forward with sustainable infrastructure investments, including coordinated macroeconomic policies, financial market development, regulatory arrangements, innovations to bring in new players and financial instruments, and the effective use of public money to catalyze a program at scale. His takeaway message is that a domestic agency dedicated to sustainable infrastructure is a necessary but by no means sufficient condition for success.

Innovations in Place-Based Targeting

SDG implementation is not an abstraction. It involves making investments and policy choices that affect specific places. Often, however, the geographic elements are not considered, and explicit place-based targeting remains the SDG exception rather than the rule. For example, even though most of those being left behind reside in rural areas, there is no specific SDG target that focuses on the rural dimensions of development. Thanks to new technologies, however, the opportunity is at hand to change the trajectories of rural livelihoods. Bettina Prato in chapter 7 argues that directed public investment in infrastructure for agrifood corridors that connect rural and urban areas, along with improved access to public services, offers promise of accelerating the slow-moving transformation of traditional rural life through outmigration and the shifting of labor from agriculture to off-farm activities. She argues that public policies need to regulate and facilitate supply chain relationships that can link smallholder farmers, including women and youth, to urban areas. Doing so on a large scale requires empowering rural constituencies so that more of the value added from the agrifood system ends up in rural areas. Her key point is that rather than divide the world into rural and urban areas, policymakers should think in terms of spatial policies that connect these together.

If new approaches to spatial planning are to take root, policymakers will need tools to identify and visualize the spatial dimensions of economic and social data. Linda See, Steffen Fritz, Inian Moorthy, Olha Danylo, Michiel van Dijk, and Barbara Ryan in chapter 8 provide examples of the use of satellite remote sensing and call detail metarecords to help generate granular maps of where poor people reside, even in locations such as North Korea where little other evidence is available. These technologies have the considerable attraction of being scalable but lack the institutional base of a public-private partnership that could appropriately fund and catalyze activities to generate a database of evidence from across the globe. In recognition of the proliferation of small-scale attempts to demonstrate what can work, the authors also caution against "indicator fatigue," or the acceptance of reporting requirements and data generation as the end product rather than the input into real actions and impacts.

With 169 SDG targets, the burden of data collection and analysis in monitoring SDG progress can be substantial for all countries, rich or poor. For low-income countries, however, the onus is substantially greater because the statistical agencies have limited personnel and resources. Ryuichi Tomizawa and Noriharu Masugi in chapter 9 evaluate the modalities of technical assistance to help build capacity for statistical agencies in developing nations. Relying on the more than three decades' worth of experience of the Japanese International Cooperation Agency (JICA) in implementing statistical capacity-building programs, the authors conclude that expertise and institutional capabilities are established only by providing painstaking, on-the-ground support to official statistics agencies in the developing world. They refer to the absence of data collection in Cambodia, where no general census took place between 1962 and 1998. Another decade passed in training agency staff, implementing the population census, and preparing for an economic census scheduled for 2011. Tomizawa and Masugi use the lessons of the Cambodian experience to develop a blueprint for improving the ability of statistics agencies across the developing world to collect, use, and disseminate relevant data. They also provide tips on helping statistical agencies utilize "big data," data from the internet, and other sources for developmental needs.

Few demographic shifts will define the place-based contours of the SDG era as much as the growth of cities, especially in low- and middle-income countries. But as Reuben Abraham and Pritika Hingorani point out in chapter 10, the increasingly widespread recognition of cities' importance has not translated into a common understanding of cities, how to define them geographically, and how to ensure governments are responsive to rapidly shifting spatial realities. Taking India as an example, Abraham and Hingorani find the country to be considerably more urbanized than some official statistics suggest. As a result, urban governments need to increase horizontal coordination among neighboring urban areas to promote economies of scale, especially in areas such as transport. They also need to see themselves as systems integrators, providing place-based integration across vertical layers of government. As hosts to more than half of humanity, cities across the globe can serve as the front line for targeting SDG efforts on an extraordinary breadth of issues, ranging from reducing traffic deaths to mitigating the effects of climate change.

One of the major early SDG deadlines is for target 14.5, to conserve 10 percent of coastal and marine areas by 2020. In chapter 11, Enric Sala and Kristin Rechberger consider this target in the context of a growing body of literature suggesting that fully half the ocean needs to be protected. Along with an overview of the ocean's contributions to terrestrial life and the many ways in which humans are severely damaging ocean life through actions ranging from overfishing to acidifying and polluting the seas, Sala and Rechberger present a practical strategy for large-scale conservation. Marine reserves anchor the approach since they can serve as regenerative "fish banks" that promote the growth of ecosystems in neighboring areas. If 30 percent of all countries' exclusive economic zone and at least 80 percent of the high seas are targeted, the 50 percent global protection task can be achieved by 2050, if not sooner. This conservation objective should be accompanied by better regulation of the fishing industry, including dramatically improved regional fisheries management.

Innovations in Multistakeholder Governance

The third area ripe for innovation is governance, broadly defined. The global sustainable development agenda is increasingly defined by its complexity and interconnectedness. Suitable solutions can be found only if diverse players bring knowledge, information, and a commitment to act to the table. Doing so requires new systems of governance that define the roles of the actors, the rules by which they operate, and lines of authority and collaboration linking actors to each other. It also requires spaces in which new players can be integrated into existing trans-national networks of experts, stakeholders, and decisionmakers who set agendas, design policy solutions, and evaluate outcomes. We call this type of arrangement multistakeholder governance.

Multistakeholder governance starts with common understandings to inform collective action. One of the core—and novel—SDGs aims is to encourage developed country societies to reflect on their own domestic policies and perfor-mance, and to share in a common responsibility for delivering global outcomes. Margaret Biggs and John McArthur in chapter 12 examine these questions in the context of Canada, an advanced economy that is often praised both for its domestic successes and for its history of multilateral contributions. Building on a separate recent benchmarking assessment, Biggs and McArthur show how the SDGs can be adopted as a society's "North Star," a shared outcome framework to shed light on internal and external challenges, drawing attention to which people and issues are being left behind. The authors stress the importance of identifying where policy acceleration or breakthroughs are needed through an assessment of current trajectories. On the domestic side, they consider how all layers of govern-ment, business, universities, communities, and civil society can pursue individual and collaborative strategies that allow all Canadians to achieve all the SDGs. Cru-cially, they argue that the engagement and leadership of indigenous people and substantial improvements in outcomes for indigenous people will be a sine qua non for Canada's SDG progress. Internationally, the authors present a series of guiding questions to identify where an advanced economy like Canada can make the greatest contributions to both collective and external global challenges.

The SDG ambition to "leave no one behind" will be tested at the agenda's inter-face with civil society. In chapter 13 Dhananjayan Sriskandarajah describes the need for a multidimensional accountability revolution, guided by citizen partici-pation. To frame the challenge, Sriskandarajah asks what it would take for a public official ever to lose her job if an SDG target is not met. For such a thought exper-iment to be tractable, he argues that civil society's own approaches need to evolve too. Amid increasing concerns of repression in many countries, the implicit norms of SDG governance require civil society to engage in both advocacy and implemen-tation at all scales, while also promoting accountability. This will require revamped funding models that empower community-level action, but only 1 percent of offi-cial aid has gone directly to civil society in developing countries. Community foun-dations offer potentially important vehicles in this regard. Civil society will also need to develop increasingly sophisticated approaches to managing collaboration boundaries with private sector actors. And it will need citizens at the heart of the data revolution. After having played such an important role in contributing to the SDG agreements, civil society must keep innovating at the nexus of these issues to ensure the goals deliver meaningful results in citizens' lives.

Official development institutions tend to be oriented toward doing projects, and their governance systems reflect this proclivity. Projects are an efficient way of delivering specific activities, but they have limitations when multiple players and multiple issues need to be connected. In chapter 14 Naoko Ishii highlights four complex systems that are stressing planetary resources because of the scale of human activity and the difficulties encountered when trying to address these systems through traditional development institutions. She argues that a new approach is needed to manage food, energy, cities, and circular economy issues as systems that have a clear purpose, orient a range of actors, provide the right incentives, have feedback loops, and recognize nonlinearities and tipping points. Developing such systems, and the governance that drives them forward, needs urgent attention. She describes examples of multistakeholder coalitions that provide a sound building block for such systems' governance and advocates extending their use in the four critical areas identified.

Sound global governance systems must also adapt to new constraints and threats. Global health initiatives have proliferated since 2000, many of them created to coordinate an expanding number of key actors. As Ikuo Takizawa explains in chapter 15, many of these initiatives are not yet equipped to address twenty-first-century transnational health issues affecting a cross section of citizens across countries. The spread of some recent epidemics and the inadequacy of existing governance structures to prevent them are illustrative. Takizawa notes that the existing global health initiatives are hampered by resource constraints, fragmentation, and proliferation. One obvious solution would be to consolidate the global health architecture by removing duplication and overlap. In addition to consolidation, Takizawa proposes greater reliance on specific health issue "regimes," or systems of rules that establish incentives and set expectations for a defined group of players. After examining some instances in which global health regimes hold potential for expanded responsibility, Takizawa concludes that these regimes are likely to be more agile in addressing cross-border health issues than existing health initiatives.

Ultimately, successful implementation of the SDGs rests on providing adequate finance in an appropriate policy and institutional context. In developing countries, multilateral development banks (MDBs) can help with both—they provide financing, directly and indirectly, along with significant knowledge products to guide their clients. But multilateral development banks have traditionally been oriented exclusively towards the public sector. As market-oriented development takes root and as business becomes an ever more crucial prime vehicle for scaling up finance, especially in middle-income countries, the MDBs must adapt to complement and catalyze private finance. Mahmoud Mohieldin and Jos Verbeek in chapter 16 consider bringing together a "cascade and a portfolio" approach: a cascade of logical decision making to determine when and under what conditions to bring in private finance and a portfolio of projects that private institutional investors can invest in. Such an approach brings with it a new perspective on risk, something that is hard to change under current governance arrangements in MDBs.

Conclusion

When the SDGs were adopted, there was hope that implementation would take off rapidly, based on successful planning and institutional experiences established under the MDGs. While some sectors and geographic areas have moved faster than others, much more effort is needed to shift the world from a business-as-usual regimen. It is becoming increasingly clear that new approaches are needed, globally, nationally, and locally, to accelerate implementation in many areas. These new approaches are untested and will require a period of innovation and experimentation.

The chapters that follow offer a collection of views on some aspects of innovation that could lead to breakthroughs. The magnitude of the challenge is daunting, but we are excited by the broad-ranging discussions now taking place in business boardrooms, in multilateral institution management offices, within national governments around the world, among local officials, among activists, and in science and academia. This volume offers just a sampling of the dialogue. We hope it inspires our readers to reflect on how they too might join the conversation and stimulate breakthrough movements to help achieve the SDGs by 2030.

References

Business and Sustainable Development Commission. 2017. *Better Business, Better World.* London.

Desai, Raj M., and Homi Kharas. 2017. "Is a Growing Middle Class Good for the Poor? Social Policy in a Time of Globalization." Brookings Global Economy and Development Working Paper 105. July.

Gertz, Geoffrey, and Homi Kharas. 2018. "Leave no county behind: Ending poverty in the toughest places." Brookings Global Economy and Development Working Paper 110. February.

Gertz, Geoffrey, Homi Kharas, John W. McArthur, and Lorenz Noe. 2017. "When Will Things Change? Looking for Signs of Progress on Ending Rural Hunger." Brookings Institution.

Hearn, Sarah. 2017. "What Does the Populist Wave Mean for Global Aid and Development?" *World Politics Review*, February 21.

Jensen, Nathan, and Leonard Wantchekon. 2004. "Resource Wealth and Political Regimes in Africa." *Comparative Political Studies* 37 (7): 816–41.

Kharas, Homi. 2017. "The Unprecedented Expansion of the Global Middle Class." Brookings Global Economy and Development Working Paper 100. February.

McArthur, John W., and Krista Rasmussen. 2016. "How Close to Zero? Assessing the World's Extreme Poverty-Related Trajectories for 2030." Brookings Global Views No. 6. November. Brookings Institution.

———. 2017. "Who and What Is Getting Left Behind? Canada's Domestic Status on the Sustainable Development Goals." Brookings Global Economy and Development Working Paper 108. October.

———. 2018. "Change of Pace: Accelerations and Advances during the Millennium Development Goal Era." *World Development* 105 (May): 132–43

McArthur, John W., Krista Rasmussen, and Gavin Yamey. 2018. "How Many Lives Are at Stake? Assessing 2030 Sustainable Development Goal Trajectories for Maternal and Child Health." *The BMJ* 360:k373 (https://doi.org/10.1136/bmj.k373).

Meernik, James, Eric L. Krueger, and Steven C. Poe. 1998. "Testing Models of US Foreign Policy: Foreign Aid during and after the Cold War." *Journal of Politics* 60 (1): 63–85.

Nnadi, Chimeremma, Andrew Etsano, Belinda Uba, Chima Ohuabunwo, Musa Melton, Gatei wa Nganda, Lisa Esapa, Omotayo Bolu, Frank Mahoney, John Vertefeuille, Eric Wiesen, and Elias Durry. 2017. "Approaches to Vaccination among Populations in Areas of Conflict." *Journal of Infectious Diseases* 216 (Suppl. 1): 368–72. doi: 10.1093/infdis/jix175.

Saravelos, George, and Robin Winkler. 2016. "Deglobalization Is Here to Stay: What It Means for Global Macro." *Deutsche Bank Special Report* 16. November 16.

Schmidt-Traub, Guido. 2018. "The Role of the Technical Review Panel of the Global Fund to Fight HIV/AIDS, Tuberculosis and Malaria: An Analysis of Grant Recommendations." *Health Policy and Planning* 33(1): 335–44.

Steffen, Will, Katherine Richardson, Johan Rockstrom, Sarah E. Cornell, Ingo Fetzer, and others. 2015. "Planetary Boundaries: Guiding Human Development on a Changing Planet." *Science* 347 (6223): 1259855.

United Nations. 2015. "Transforming Our World: The 2030 Agenda for Sustainable Development." Resolution adopted by the General Assembly A/RES/70/1. September 25. Published October 21. (www.un.org/ga/search/view_doc.asp?symbol=A/RES/70/1&Lang=E).

United Nations Environment Program (UNEP). 2017. *The Emissions Gap Report 2017*. Nairobi: UNEP.

United States Environmental Protection Agency (EPA). 2018. *Inventory of U.S. Greenhouse Gas Emissions and Sinks: 1990–2016*. EPA.

World Bank. 2018. World Development Indicators database (http://databank.worldbank.org/data/reports.aspx?source=world-development-indicators).

World Data Lab. 2018. "World Poverty Clock" (http://worldpoverty.io/).

PART I

Capturing Value

CHAPTER TWO

Expanding Women's Economic Opportunities

Jeni Klugman and Laura Tyson

G ender equality and women's economic empowerment are central to the realization of inclusive and sustainable growth, the overarching goal of the 2030 Agenda adopted by the United Nations in 2015. But economic, social, and political gender gaps around the world remain large, pervasive, and persistent. This chapter focuses on innovative actions to reduce gender gaps on two key fronts that are major determinants of economic opportunities and outcomes for women—the distribution of unpaid care and financial inclusion. The need to address unpaid care is explicitly recognized in the UN's Sustainable Development Goals (target 5.3), and financial inclusion is essential to achieving progress on many of these goals.

Given the multiplicity, strength, and entrenchment of the constraints on women's economic opportunities, there is no single or simple solution to eliminating gender gaps and empowering women. While addressing unpaid care and financial inclusion can move the needle, simultaneous interventions on a number of fronts by businesses, governments, and civil society are necessary. The chapter concludes with a discussion of innovative interventions in employment and procurement that businesses and government can and should take to accelerate progress on closing gender gaps in the world of work.

Where Do We Stand? Gender Gaps in the World of Work: Large, Pervasive, and Persistent

To frame the discussion of innovative solutions, we need to understand the challenges. This section reviews the key patterns, trends, and prospects for women in the world of work.

We begin by summarizing some of the persistent gender gaps in the world of work based on the availability of relevant data and evidence (key terms and sources are defined in appendix table 2-1). For each gap, we show both regional differences and the range of country differences within each region. We use the standard UN Women's regional classifications (as listed in appendix table 2-2) and present population-weighted regional and world averages. The data show that economic gender gaps vary significantly across regions and are larger in developing economies than in developed economies.[1] But even within regions there are significant differences among countries, indicating that there is considerable scope for progress in all regions and at all development levels.

Persistent Gaps in Labor Force Participation

About 700 million fewer women than men of working age were in paid employment in 2016—1.27 billion women compared to 2 billion men. Female rates of labor force participation remain lower than male rates in all regions, most markedly in South Asia and the Middle East and North Africa, which have the lowest female participation rates (figure 2-1).[2]

Aggregate male and female rates have both declined in recent decades. Globally, the rate of labor force participation for women more than 15 years old fell from about 53 percent in 1990 to 50 percent in 2015. Female youth (15–24 years old) participation rates dropped from 52 to 37 percent over the period, which is a major concern, because while more young women are staying in school, in most countries larger shares of female than male youth are "not in employment, education or training" (or NEET). In the 108 countries for which data are available, about one in three young women are counted as NEET, compared with one in ten

1. The main databases used in this chapter: Barro and Lee, EUROSTAT, Food and Agriculture Organization of the United Nations, Global Financial Inclusion Database (Global Findex), GSMA, International Labour Organization Key Indicators of the Labour Market (ILO–KILM), ILOSTAT database, IFC Enterprise Finance Gap Data, Laborstat database (IBRD), Posadas, OECD Gender, Institutions, and Development Database, National Bureau of Statistics of China, OECD Stats, United Nations World Population Prospects, Women, Business, and the Law database, World Development Indicators, and World Values Survey.

The authors are grateful for the assistance of Arjun Krishnan.

2. The female labor force participation rate—the most widely cited measure of women's engagement in work—is flawed, however. It does not count what women do in developing countries to grow food for their families' consumption, for example, or what women in all countries do to provide similar unpaid household and care services. Despite such shortcomings, it is the broadest available measure on women in paid work, whether formal or informal. The female labor participation rate (age 15+) exceeded the male rate in six countries in 2015, specifically Burundi (2 percentage points higher), Lao People's Democratic Republic (0.7), Malawi (0.4), Mozambique (7.1), Rwanda (3.2), and Togo (0.5).

Figure 2-1. Female Labor Force Participation Rates, Age 15+,
Across Regions, 2015

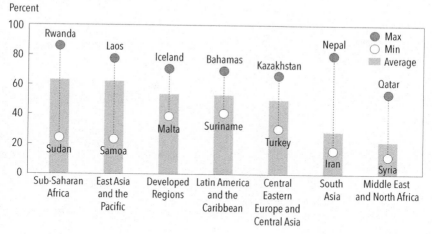

Source: International Labour Organization, Key Indicators of the Labour Market, 2015, Table R3.
Note: Weighted regional average of 180 included countries.

young men. In South Asia, the youth gender gap in NEET is huge: 54 percent for women and 5 percent for men.[3]

Persistent and Pervasive Gender Gaps in Unpaid Work and Care

Globally, women take on upwards of three times more unpaid work and care than men.[4] The value of unpaid care work done by women is at least $10 trillion, which constitutes 13 percent of global GDP.[5] Of course, some unpaid work and care reflect individual preferences. As incomes rise, some women may decide to allocate more time both to unpaid work and care for their families and to volunteering. But because many women (like many men) follow gender norms and

3. NEET rates are by region weighted by population 15 to 24 years of age in 2015. Number of youth female not in employment, education, and training is data from 108 countries, latest year available (2008–14, except Nicaragua, which is 2005). Female youth are 15 to 24 years of age except in ten countries with slightly different age ranges. Population data are from UN Population and NEET data from ILO-KILM. All data accessed August 2016.
4. McKinsey Global Institute (2015).
5. Estimate based on McKinsey Global Institute (2015).

Figure 2-2. Unpaid Care Work by Males and Females, by Region, 2014

Male-female ratio

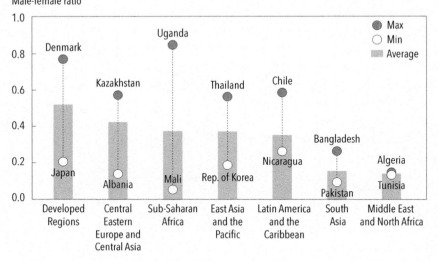

Source: OECD, General, Institutions, and Development Database, 2014.
Note: Unweighted regional average of sixty-nine countries included.

stereotypes, it may be difficult to distinguish norms from preferences in how men and women share unpaid work and care responsibilities.

There are large variations in the gender gap in unpaid care across countries, with men doing up to about 80 percent of the unpaid care work done by women in Denmark down to 10 percent in Tunisia (figure 2-2).

Mixed Picture of Trends in Gender Gaps in Paid Work: Good News and Bad

There is evidence of positive changes alongside persistent gender gaps and seg- regation in paid work. Wage and salary employment is a rising share of women's paid work, and worldwide, women are as likely to have wage jobs as men. Still, in low-income countries, the share in wage and salary work averages 25 percent for men but 17 percent for women, whereas the average shares for women and men in wage and salary work in developed countries are both high and tilt in favor of women, at 88 and 83 percent, respectively (figure 2-3).[6]

Across all regions, men are twice as likely as women to be employers, though employers account for a very small share of total employment in all regions. We look at women-owned enterprises below.

6. Statistics for low-income countries are from ILO–KILM, Table R3.

Figure 2-3. Men and Women by Employment Status, Selected Regions, 2015

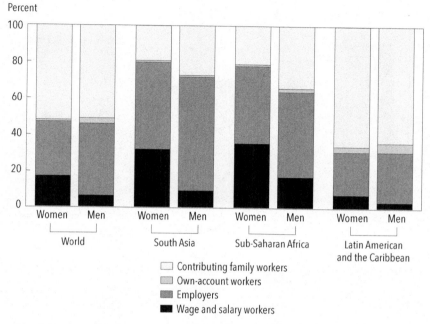

Percent

Legend:
- ☐ Contributing family workers
- ▨ Own-account workers
- ▦ Employers
- ■ Wage and salary workers

Source: International Labour Organization, Key Indicators of the Labour Market, 2015, Table R3.
Note: South Asia is equivalent to Southern Asia in ILO KILM's regional groups.

Paid Work in Developing Countries Is Largely Informal, Especially in South Asia and Sub-Saharan Africa

More than four in five employed women in the nonagricultural sector in South Asia and about three quarters in sub-Saharan Africa are informally employed, as shown in figure 2-4.[7] Informal employment is largely self-employment in sub-Saharan Africa, whereas informal work in Central and Eastern Europe and Central Asia is mainly wage employment in formal and informal businesses.[8]

7. The ILO regards an employment relationship as informal if it is not, in law or in practice, subject to national labor legislation, income taxation, social protection, or entitlement to certain employment benefits (advance notice of dismissal, severance pay, paid annual or sick leave, and so on): 17th International Conference of Labour Statisticians (ICLS) in 2003. For details of the progress made on statistics on informal employment, see WIEGO (2016).

8. Data on informal work generally are not collected for agriculture, and data on informal employment are not consistently available for developed countries.

Figure 2-4. Informal Employment as Share of Nonagricultural Employment, Across Regions, 2004–10

Percent of informal employment

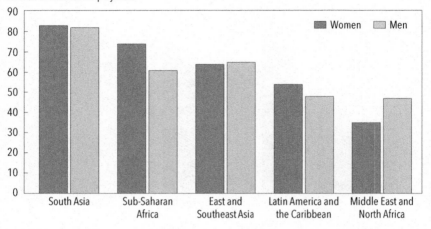

Source: Vanek and others (2014).
Note: East and Southeast Asia excludes China; regional estimates are based on forth countries with direct measures and eighty countries with indirect measures.

Occupational Segregation Persists

Women tend to be overrepresented in lower-paying sectors and lower-paying occupations (figure 2-5). Women are overrepresented—especially in developed countries—in the low-paying sectors of health, domestic work, social work, education, wholesale-retail trade, and communication services, with very little change over time. For example, women account for almost two-thirds of service workers in developed countries, where their average pay is about 70 percent of the national average. Men dominate the senior official and management category, with mean earnings more than double the national average, in both developing and developed countries.

Gender Pay Gaps Remain Prevalent

Globally, the gender pay gap has been narrowing, in part due to gains in female education, which have enabled women to enter more skilled occupations. It is notable, however, that progress in closing gender pay gaps has stalled in most developed countries over the past two to three decades. The continuing gap can be traced to several interrelated factors—including gender gaps in part-time work,

Figure 2-5. Participation of Women in Various Occupations, 2008–15

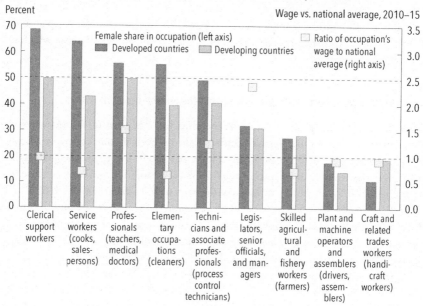

Sources: International Labour Organization, ILOSTAT database, ILO Key indicators of the Labour Market database, and EUROSTAT, Structure of Earning Survey 2010.

Note: Data available for forty-three countries, data are the most recent available. The figures are not weighted by population. Developing countries include Brazil, Ecuador, Egypt, Macedonia, Mongolia, Pakistan, Panama, Peru, Philippines, Sri Lanka, and Turkey. Developed countries include Austria, Belgium, Bulgaria, Croatia, Cyprus, Czech Republic, Denmark, Estonia, Finland, France, Germany, Greece, Hungary, Iceland, Ireland, Israel, Italy, Latvia, Lithuania, Luxembourg, Malta, Netherlands, Norway, Poland, Portugal, Romania, Slovakia, Slovenia, Spain, Sweden, Switzerland, and the United Kingdom. Only data based on Internatonal Standard Classification of Occupations (ISCO)-08 and ISCO-88 classifications are included.

unpaid work and care responsibilities, occupational segregation, social norms, implicit biases, discrimination, and weak labor market institutions.

The best available earnings data, adjusted for hours worked, suggest that the global gender wage gap presently averages around 16 percent.[9] The much larger gender wage gaps in South Asia and sub-Saharan Africa—relative to other regions—are broadly associated with several factors, including the continuing importance of agriculture to women's work, the time women spend on unpaid household work and care, high fertility rates, and discriminatory social norms.[10]

9. Belser and Vazquez-Alvarez (2016), figure 23.
10. Jayachandran (2014).

The gender pay gap is larger among the highest-paid occupational categories and at the top end of the wage distribution. Women are much less likely than men to become CEOs, and when they do, their pay is lower: the gender pay gap among CEOs is about 40 percent—twice as high as the overall gender pay gap, which is about 20 percent.[11]

Women Are a Minority of Enterprise Owners in the Formal Economy

There are large gender gaps in entrepreneurship. Stylized facts on women-owned enterprises (WOEs) in the formal sector are clear—even if comprehensive global data are lacking—starting with the overall gender gap in enterprise ownership. In 134 countries, women are a minority of employers, ranging from lows of close to 0 in Qatar and Saudi Arabia to highs of 66 percent in Namibia (figure 2-6).

Firms that women own are more likely to be micro or small in size and informal in nature. The best data available suggest that women own about one-third of micro firms (fewer than 10 employees), one-third of all small firms (10–49 employees), and one fifth of medium-sized firms in developing countries (50–250 employees).[12]

Consistent with patterns of occupational segregation, WOEs tend to be concentrated in sectors where profits and growth opportunities are lower—retail, beauty, food service, and other services—and rarely in mining, construction, electronics, or software.[13] In Africa and Asia, around 75 percent of female entrepreneurs are in consumer-oriented sectors (against 45 percent of male entrepreneurs).[14] Because WOEs typically concentrate in less profitable activities, they often perform less well than male-owned formal firms. In sub-Saharan Africa, women's businesses tend to fail at a higher rate than men's, which has been traced to differences in firm size and access to capital and to the concentration of WOEs in sectors characterized by fewer barriers to entry, lower profit margins, and lower returns on capital.[15]

One of the major recurring constraints limiting WOEs is access to finance. An estimated 63–69 percent of women-owned SMEs in developing economies are unserved or underserved by financial institutions, which equates to a credit gap of $260 to $320 billion.[16] Actions to reduce gender gaps in access to finance are explored below.

11. Belser and Vazquez-Alvarez (2016), p. 81.
12. IFC Enterprise Finance Gap Data 2010 (www.smefinanceforum.org/data-sites/ifc-enterprise-finance-gap).
13. Bardasi, Sabarwal, and Terrell (2011); Hallward-Driemeier (2013); De Mel, McKenzie, and Woodruff (2014).
14. Kelley and others (2015).
15. Klapper and Parker (2010).
16. Stein, Ardic, and Hommes (2013), p. 19, box 2.

Figure 2-6. Women Who Are Employers, by Region, 2000–15

Percent as employers

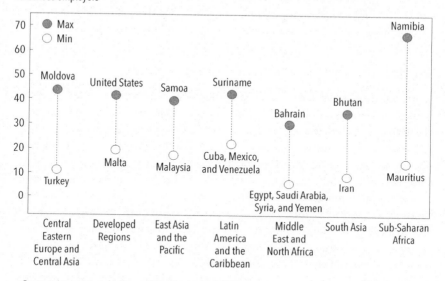

Source: International Labour Organization, ILOSTAT.
Note: Data from 119 countries are included from 2010 to 2015, the latest year available.

Why: The Constraints Behind Gender Gaps in Work

Several overarching constraints face many women in all types of work, in all regions, and at all development levels, namely, adverse social norms; restrictive and discriminatory laws and lack of legal protections; unpaid household work and care; and a lack of access to financial, digital, and property assets.

Adverse Social Norms

Gender norms shape women's economic opportunities in many ways. Society may expect that women do care work "for free" and may assess paid work such as teaching young children and offering personal care as low-skill and low-value work. Some of the most restrictive norms are those that require a woman to spend most of her life within her home. In many communities in South Asia and West Asia, a woman seen in public brings "shame" to the family. Adverse norms limit women's pay and prospects in two ways: by affecting their expectations about whether they should work outside the home and by limiting their aspirations about which occupations they should pursue. Discriminatory norms can also constrain prospects for women's leadership and restrict their business activity to less profitable sectors.

Adverse gender norms interact with laws and regulations in ways that constrain women's economic independence. For example, norms are reflected in requirements that husbands cosign banking applications for their wives in some countries, limiting women's access to financial services and property ownership.

Restrictive and Discriminatory Laws and Gaps in Legal Protection

Laws and regulations affect the economic opportunities for many women. According to the World Bank, 90 percent of economies have at least one law that discriminates against women, and there are 943 legal gender differences among 170 economies, as shown in figure 2-7.[17] Discriminatory laws have a range of effects—for example, making it more difficult for women to own property, open bank accounts, start businesses, and take jobs and enter professions restricted to men. Legal discrimination is also associated with financial exclusion. Where husbands legally control marital property, women are less likely to have an account at a financial institution,[18] and thus even less likely to start a business due to lack of collateral and finance. When men and women have *equal* inheritance rights, women are more likely to have official bank accounts and credit.[19] Recent IMF analysis shows that lower gender equality in the law is associated with fewer girls attending secondary school relative to boys, fewer women working or running businesses, and a wider gender wage gap.[20]

Alongside the gender-based discrimination that characterizes property, family, and even contract law in many countries, both informal workers, many of whom are women, and informal businesses and activities, are also regulated by a complex range of laws, rules, and enforcement practices—often in the realm of public law—that are restrictive and often punitive. Due to licensing ceilings in Mumbai, for example, about 236,000 street vendors operate without a license and are subject to treatment as criminals under the Indian Penal Code and to payment of bribes in order to get licenses.[21]

Even in countries where women have equal legal protection and rights, weak implementation by the authorities, low awareness among rights-holders and those

---

17. Only UN member states are included. World Bank (2016a) includes 173 economies but three countries are not UN member states (Kosovo, Puerto Rico, and Taiwan, China).

18. World Bank analysis shows that 18 percent of females have an account at a financial institution in full/partial regimes with husband's property control versus 57 percent in full/partial regimes with joint property control. See World Bank (2015a).

19. Demirgüc-Kunt, Klapper, and Singer (2013).

20. World Bank (2015a).

21. As cited in Chen, Madhav, and Sankaran (2014).

Figure 2-7. Gender Legal Differences, by Region, 2015

Number of differences

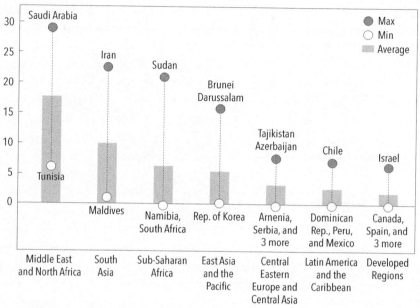

Source: Women, Business, and the Law database, 2016 (wbl.worldbank.org).
Note: Unweighted sample average of a total of forty-seven legal restrictions from 170 countries. In developed regions, Malta, the Netherlands, and New Zealand also have the least legal difference scores. In Central and Eastern Europe and Central Asia, Estonia, Hungary, and Slovakia also have the least legal difference scores.

responsible for implementing the law, and constraints on women's access to legal resources—all limit enforcement of existing laws and undermine effective legal protection for women.[22]

Figure 2-8 brings together the foregoing analysis and summarizes how economic gender gaps—in terms of labor force participation, pay, and occupational segregation—are linked to several systemic and overarching constraints on women's economic opportunities. We now turn to the two areas of unpaid care and access to finance, which are among the constraints that affect women around the world and are especially severe for poor women in developing economies.

22. Klugman and Twigg (2015).

Figure 2-8. Major Systemic Constraints and Persistent Gaps
in Women's Economic Opportunities

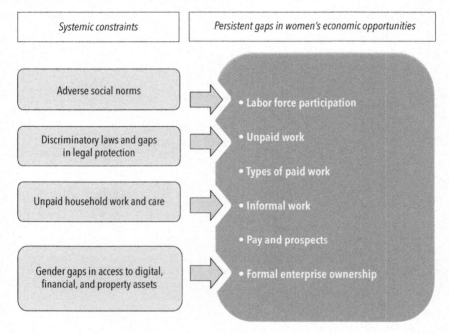

What Can Be Done? Investing in Care—SDG 5.3

In countries at all development levels and to varying degrees, women face challenges and limited choices in balancing their time across unpaid care work, paid economic opportunities, education, leisure, and rest.[23] In a recent business poll, the three most commonly cited barriers preventing women from advancing in the workplace were all related to balancing domestic and professional responsibilities.[24] Unpaid care constraints are especially severe for women from poor households who cannot afford market substitutes for their unpaid labor. More than half of women aged 20 to 24 in a recent Latin American study said that their unpaid responsibilities at home were the main reason they could not look for paid work.[25]

Looking ahead, changing demographics flag that elderly care will loom larger as societies age and fertility rates decline in many developed and developing countries

23. McKinsey Global Institute (2015).
24. Business Fights Poverty/CARE (2016).
25. Antonopoulos (2008).

Figure 2-9. Old Age and Child Dependency, Selected Countries, Groups, 2015–65

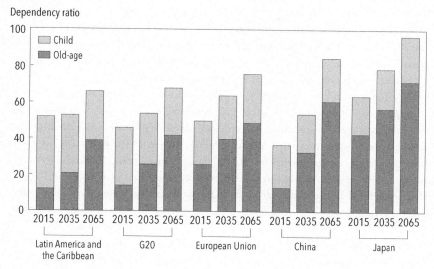

Dependency ratio

Sources: United Nations, Department of Economic and Social Affairs, Population Division (2015); World Population Prospects: The 2015 Revision (DVD ed.).

Note: Weighted regional average; old-age dependence ratio is the ratio of population 65+ per 100 population aged 15–64, and child dependence ratio is the ratio of population 0–14 per population aged 15–64.

alike, as shown in figure 2-9.[26] Most countries do not provide any long-term support for elderly care, partly because of the failure to recognize the value of unpaid elderly care provided primarily by female family members.[27] Estimates from the United States, for example, indicate that daughters spend more than twice the number of hours than sons do caring for elderly parents.[28] A survey in China found that 95 percent of women have responsibilities for elderly relatives, and "daughterly guilt" affected an extraordinary 88 percent of Chinese women surveyed.[29]

Progress on the agenda to expand women's economic empowerment depends, to a large extent, on closing the major and persistent gender gaps in unpaid work and investing in care. Legislative, policy, and private sector innovations can all play roles on this front, although much depends on what happens at the household

26. WHO (2016); World Bank (2016).
27. Scheil-Adlung (2015).
28. Levtov (2016).
29. Hewlett (2011).

level. Appropriate and effective solutions vary with development level and within the local context. The challenges are linked to women's remuneration for paid work—low-paying jobs and high marginal tax rates on secondary family earners in developed countries reduce the opportunity costs of women's time. The Organization for Economic Cooperation and Development (OECD) has estimated that Japan's low female labor force participation rate would rise significantly (almost 13 percent) with favorable changes to its secondary-earner tax.[30]

Key barriers on both the supply and the demand side drive gender disparities in unpaid care, pointing to possible interventions. For example, investments in key infrastructure—water supply, sanitation, electricity, clean energy, roads, and safe transport—are important and can reduce the time spent on unpaid care, help ensure safe environments for unpaid work, and increase the productivity of women who produce goods and provide services from their own homes.[31] Recent IMF analysis of household-level survey data across Indian states shows that poor infrastructure dampens female labor force participation: women living in Indian states with greater access to roads are more likely to be in the labor force.[32]

Public investment in care services can reduce the time that women spend on unpaid work and care. Such investments boost women's labor force participation, create paid jobs in the care sector, generate long-term social benefits for the development of children and for the educational attainment and skill levels of future workers and citizens, and, in developing countries, free time for older children in the family (typically girls), as evaluations in Guatemala and Colombia have confirmed.[33] Currently 134 countries provide some form of public or subsidized child care services for children under the age of primary education. According to World Bank research, in economies with publicly provided or subsidized child care, 30 percent of women reported receiving wages, against only 13 percent in economies without it.[34]

The cost of child care affects women's economic opportunities in paid work. Many studies find that lowering the price of child care is associated with an increase in women's paid work, and vice versa, although the estimated magnitude

30. Ferrant, Pesando, and Nowacka (2014).
31. Jacobson, Mohun, and Sajjad (2016).
32. Das and others (2015).
33. Evaluations of community day care Hogares Comunitarios programs in Guatemala City and rural Colombia found positive effects on the nutrition and development of young children, in addition to increases in the probability of female labor force participation as a result of availability of good-quality child care services. The Colombia study also found better academic performance of older children. Discussed in Buvinic and others (n.d.).
34. World Bank (2015a).

varies.[35] IMF research covering ten OECD developed countries found that halving the cost of child care increased the labor supply of young mothers by 6.5–10 percent.[36] In Chile, which historically had among the lowest rates of female labor force participation in Latin America, the government introduced free child care for families with children between four months and four years; the evidence indicates that women who accessed these centers were 16 percentage points more likely to work and that the program successfully targeted marginalized groups of women such as those with high school diplomas or less.[37]

Opening and changing the dialogue on gender roles can change social norms about unpaid care and facilitate the redistribution of care responsibilities at home.[38] Successful innovations include engaging men and community organizations about the distribution of unpaid care; promoting role models; supporting peer groups for women; and encouraging national awareness efforts through mass and social media.[39] But while change in social norms about unpaid work has been slow (and varied across countries), many men say they want to perform more unpaid care work and, in particular, be more involved in the lives of their children.[40] IMAGES data from eight countries show that most fathers (from 43 percent in Mali and Bosnia Herzegovina to 77 percent in Chile) report that they would work less if it meant that they could spend more time with their children.[41] In the United States, one survey found that 46 percent of fathers said they were not spending enough time with their children, compared with 23 percent of mothers.[42]

Starting young to change norms and household practices about the distribution of unpaid care is important. Roots of Empathy—a program in primary schools in Canada, Germany, Ireland, New Zealand, Switzerland, the United Kingdom, and the United States—has been shown to familiarize both boys *and* girls with the basic underpinnings of caring for young children.[43]

Almost every country in the world now offers some paid leave for mothers, with the United States a notable developed-country exception. Research on OECD countries found that female labor force participation rose when paid parental/family leave became available, increasing the rates at which mothers returned

---

35. For example, the U.S. elasticity estimates range from –0.20 to –0.92 in studies by Connelly (1992) and Kimmel (1998), respectively, while Jenkins and Symons (2001) estimate elasticity of –0.09 for single mothers in the United Kingdom. See also Viitanen (2005).

36. Elborgh-Woytek and others (2013).

37. Betancor (2011).

38. Levtov (2016).

39. Institute for Reproductive Health (2011).

40. Heilman and others (2017).

41. Levtov (2016).

42. Levtov (2016).

43. See www.rootsofempathy.org.

to work after childbirth.[44] But leave benefits and their enforcement vary greatly across countries, and in most countries informal workers are not covered.

It is increasingly well recognized that going beyond maternity benefits is critical. In particular, *paternity* leave and benefits—especially if nontransferable—increase fathers' involvement with young children and combat gender stereotyping. Over half of OECD countries offer fathers paid paternity leave when a baby arrives.[45] Paternity leave can affect norms and behavior around care at home. In the United Kingdom, fathers who took leave after their child's birth were 19 percent more likely to participate in feedings and to get up with the baby during the night a year later, relative to fathers who did not take leave.[46] And fathers who engage more with their children generally report greater life satisfaction and better physical and mental health than those who interact less.[47] By supporting early engagement in care, policymakers send a message to employers and parents alike that both parents are expected to be actively involved in the care of their children and may sometimes be absent from work for that reason.[48]

Nontransferable leave entitlements increase fathers' participation in child care. A growing number of countries have introduced statutory leave entitlements for fathers, increasing from around forty countries in 1994 to at least ninety-four countries out of 170 using ILO data.[49] But paid paternity leave averages only seven days, against 106 days for mothers.[50]

Leave benefit levels should be adequate to ensure higher participation rates. In 2007 Germany switched from a low-paid, income-tested, two-year flat-rate payment to a higher-paid, earnings-related benefit (two-thirds of prior earnings) payable for ten months, plus two additional months if a partner, typically a father, used at least two months. This led to a strong uptick in fathers' parental leave, especially among highly educated fathers and those working in the public sector.[51]

Long-term support for the elderly is a growing challenge, especially in many European and East Asian economies facing rapid population aging. Among the potential care reform options in the formal sector are ensuring that unpaid caregivers have the right to request flexible work arrangements, that employers are obliged to reasonably accommodate their leave requests, and that care work is better recognized in pension systems. To extend long-term care coverage to those

44. Adema, Clarke, and Frey (2015).
45. OECD (2016). Backgrounder to this Policy Brief was prepared by ELS/SPD in the context of Grant Agreement VS/2013/0449–SI2.662151 (DI130461).
46. Levtov (2016).
47. OECD (2016).
48. Erikkson (2015).
49. Addati and others (2016).
50. World Bank (2015b).
51. OECD (2016); Geisler and Kreyenfeld (2012).

in the informal economy, mixed financing mechanisms, through contributions and tax subsidies, need to be developed.[52]

What Can Be Done? Financial Inclusion and Women's Access to Credit

Financial inclusion plays a prominent role in global development efforts. Many of the SDGs refer to the significance of financial services as a catalyst for development, and the World Bank aims for universal financial access by the year 2020.

The myriad benefits of financial inclusion for inclusive economic development are well documented.[53] Access to financial services allows individuals and families to smooth consumption, to manage risk and increase resilience, to save for investments in education and health, and to start, sustain, and expand small businesses. A recent study even found a happiness effect: people who have bank accounts tend to be happier regardless of income, age, gender, or education—and the effect is larger for women.[54] These microeconomic benefits are mirrored in macroeconomic gains. Financial inclusion increases aggregate savings, increases the availability and reduces the price of credit for investment and entrepreneurship, and leads to a more efficient allocation of labor and capital, fostering faster economic growth in the long run.[55]

Financial inclusion begins with a deposit or transaction account at a bank or other financial institution or through a mobile money provider to make and receive payments and to store or save money. Despite progress in recent years, in emerging market economies 2 billion people—about 45 percent of all adults—remain unbanked, that is, without a formal account at a bank, a financial institution, or with a mobile money provider.[56] The unbanked rate is even higher for the poor, for people living in rural areas, and for women.

Globally, almost six out of ten women (58 percent) have a formal account that can be used for payments and savings, up from less than half (47 percent) in 2011. Although women's account ownership has significantly increased in all developing regions except the Middle East, the gender gap in account ownership has not narrowed. Worldwide, men are 7 percentage points more likely than women to have an account—9 percentage points in developing countries—and these numbers have not changed since 2011. The gender gap in financial access varies by country and by region, with the largest gaps in the Middle East and South Asia. Overall,

---

52. Scheil-Adlung (2015).
53. McKinsey Global Institute (2016).
54. Esipova, Klapper, and Kellison (2016).
55. Sahay and others (2015).
56. Demirgüc-Kunt and others (2015).

Figure 2-10. Figure Adults (Aged 15+) with Financial Accounts, 2014

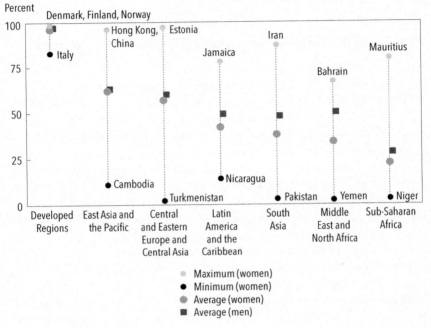

Source: Global Findex (Global Financial Inclusion Database) 2014.
Note: Unweighted regional average of 140 countries included.

half of the women in developing countries—about 1.1 billion women—are still unbanked.[57]

The gender gap in account ownership extends to a gender gap in account usage. Gender gaps in the quality of financial products and services have also been documented (figure 2-10).[58] Even among adults with accounts, in many developing countries and regions, women are less likely than men to use their accounts for deposits, withdrawals, and payments. Only 22 percent of adults in developing countries save money at a formal financial institution; nontraditional forms of saving—such as buying jewelry and livestock or hiding money at home—are used by about 46 percent of savers. Men are more likely to save in formal channels: in South Asia, for example, not only are men 8 percentage points more likely than women to save, they are almost twice as likely to use formal saving vehicles.

57. Data in preceding paragraph and in the next two paragraphs, unless otherwise noted, are from Klapper and Hess (2016).
58. Klugman and Tyson (2016), p. 50

The use of credit in developing countries remains low for both men and women. In East Asia and the Pacific, in Central Asia, and in Latin America and the Caribbean—developing regions where borrowing from formal channels is most common—about 10 percent of women borrow from financial institutions compared to an estimated 14 percent of men. The biggest gender gaps in access to formal credit are found in advanced industrial countries.[59]

During the last two decades, most of the attention on increasing the access of poor women to financial services in developing countries has focused on microfinance. Microfinance programs have often been the first credit financing option available to these women. In 2013 microfinance programs covered an estimated 211 million people, about three-fourths of whom were women, many living on less than $2.00 a day.[60] The introduction of microcredit brought the hope that such credit would dramatically increase entrepreneurship and help women and their families out of poverty, but the results have been mixed and modest at best.[61] Overall, researchers have found that access to microcredit does not lead to significant reductions in poverty or to sustained increases in income or consumption.[62] A recent rigorous summary of seven randomized evaluations from around the world found that microcredit did not have a significant impact on average household incomes for borrowers. Expanded credit access did lead some entrepreneurs to invest more in their businesses, but this rarely resulted in profit increases. Overall, access to microcredit did afford households with more freedom of choice in how they made money, consumed, invested, and managed risk, but it did not have a substantial effect on women's economic empowerment, nor did it result in more spending on health or education.[63]

Self-help groups (SHGs), also known as mutual aid or support groups, are small voluntary groups formed by women, often with the support of governments or nonprofit organizations, for a specific purpose. They are created on the assumption that women working together can take action toward overcoming obstacles and attaining social changes that result in individual or collective empowerment. SHGs often play a role in microfinance programs with group members collectively responsible for the loans made to individual members. A recent review found that they can have positive effects on women's economic, social, and political empowerment through many channels, including enhancing members' familiarity with handling money, encouraging independence in financial decision making, and

---

59. Global Findex (Global Finance Inclusion Database) 2014 (http://datatopics.worldbank.org/financialinclusion/).
60. Microcredit Summit Campaign (2015).
61. Banerjee and others (2015); Demirgüc-Kunt, Klapper, and Singer (2017).
62. Field, Holland, and Pande (2016).
63. Loiseau and Walsh (2015).

improving social networks.[64] The review finds that women may need training to gain the skills necessary to handle money before they can realize the economic empowerment effects of access to credit through a microfinance program or a link to a formal financial institution or a mobile money provider. Another finding is that the poorest women are less likely to participate in SHGs or the microfinance programs with which they are linked. Overall, the evidence indicates that SHGs like microfinance programs have modest effects on women's economic empowerment and inclusive economic development. As a result, policymakers and international organizations are focusing more of their interventions on ways to increase women's access to formal financial institutions and mobile money accounts.

Barriers to Women's Financial Inclusion

In developing countries, about six out of ten unbanked adults, both men and women, cite poverty as the single most important barrier to having a formal financial account.[65] The poor are caught in a vicious circle—poverty is a major impediment to access to financial services, and the lack of such services is a major impediment to poverty reduction. Poor women are particularly disadvantaged. The gender gap in financial access is largest for the poor: poor women are 28 percent less likely than poor men to have a formal account.[66]

For women, lack of identification documents and sexist laws and norms are also significant barriers. In developing countries, one in five people lack official identification, compared to only one in ten in advanced economies.[67] Women often lack birth registration certificates and are significantly less likely than men to have national ID cards. Nearly one-fifth of unbanked women in developing countries do not have the documentation necessary to open a bank account.[68] Moreover, as noted above, legal discrimination against women remains extensive; research shows that women's financial account ownership is lower in places where their legal rights to work or own property are restricted.[69]

Social norms that undermine women's independence also result in lower account ownership—for example, when women are unable to travel to bank branches, use mobile phones, or log on to the internet, they cannot access financial services. Finally, reflecting adverse social norms and stereotypes, banks are

---

64. Brody and others (2016).
65. Demirgüc-Kunt, Klapper, Singer, and Oudheusden (2015).
66. Klugman and Tyson (2016), p. 50.
67. McKinsey Global Institute (2016).
68. Tyson and Lund (2016).
69. Demirgüc-Kunt, Klapper, and Singer (2013).

often unaware of women's specific financial needs and offer products that have little relevance for women or are difficult for them to use.[70]

Boosting Women's Financial Inclusion

Governments and the private sector can increase women's financial inclusion in numerous ways. A first step for governments is eliminating discriminatory laws limiting women's rights in inheritance, property ownership, and choice of work.

The procedures to obtain official personal identification should also be simplified. This has become a major focus in many developing countries, and new technologies that allow digital/biometric systems to establish identity for individuals who lack traditional paper documents can speed the process. A nationwide digital financial identification system recently launched by the Indian government has simplified the identification requirements for opening a bank account. Over the last three years, more than 280 million accounts have been opened, with 60 percent in poor rural areas.[71] In Nigeria, UN Women and Mastercard are partnering to provide women with personal identification cards that have electronic payment functionality.

Without personal identification cards, women often lack the necessary documentation to meet traditional "know-your-customer" (KYC) regulations for opening bank accounts. Tiered KYC regulations can help banks reduce the transactions costs and risks of establishing them.[72] Since poor people make small transactions and maintain low balances, they should face lower regulatory barriers to establish simple accounts. For example, accounts capped by balance or cumulative value of transactions can enable banks to ease KYC requirements for low-income, low-usage individuals. This approach has increased deposit accounts in Mexico.[73]

Reducing the cost of opening and maintaining a savings account has also been shown to increase their adoption. When researchers offered unbanked women in Kenya and Nepal free savings accounts, more than 80 percent accepted.[74]

Agent banking—providing financial services at retail shops and post offices—is an effective way to reach women who lack access to traditional bank branches. In partnership with Women's World Banking, for example, Malawi's NMB bank offers savings accounts to women through a network of agents. Customers make deposits or withdrawals at local shops using a mobile phone, and NMB employees visit customer homes to help them set up digital accounts. Nigeria's Diamond

70. Zollmann and Sanford (2016).
71. Pradhan Mantri Jan Dhan Yojana, Ministry of Finance, India (www.pmjdy.gov.in/account).
72. Klapper and Hess (2016).
73. Faz (2013).
74. Klapper and Hess (2016).

Bank uses agents to offer women mobile savings accounts with no fees or minimum balance requirements.

Digital finance is growing rapidly and has the potential to change the landscape of financial inclusion dramatically. Mobile phones and the internet can reduce the need for cash and bypass traditional brick-and-mortar channels. This reduces the costs of financial service providers and makes their services more convenient and accessible for users, especially those living in remote rural locations. McKinsey Global Institute estimates that it costs providers 80–90 percent less to offer customers digital bank accounts than accounts through traditional bank branches.[75] The cost reduction makes it feasible for providers to meet the needs of low-income customers even when their account balances and volume of transactions are small.

Mobile money allows monetary value to be stored on mobile phones and transferred to other users via text messaging. Mobile money transforms mobile phones into mobile wallets, allowing individuals to store, send, and transact money. The system depends not on scarce physical bank branches and expensive fixed-line telecommunications networks but on cheap and widely available mobile phones.

Digital finance is still in its infancy—only about 2 percent of adults worldwide report having a mobile money account and about 1 percent have only a mobile money account, compared to nearly 60 percent who have only an account at a financial institution.[76] But that translates into an estimated 411 million mobile money accounts around the world. Mobile money is now available in ninety-three countries, including in 85 percent of countries where the majority of the population lacks access to a formal financial institution.[77] In nineteen countries, there are now more mobile money accounts than bank accounts, and thirty-seven countries have at least ten times as many mobile money agents as bank branches. In developing countries, only about 55 percent of adults have a bank or financial services account, but nearly 80 percent have a mobile phone. The 25-percentage-point gap is a measure of the potential progress in financial inclusion that can be achieved through the expansion of mobile banking.[78] As figure 2-11 shows, there is a strong correlation between women's mobile phone ownership and average financial inclusion rates around the world, with a lot of variation around the fitted line, especially at lower levels of financial inclusion. Figure 2-12 underlines that significant gender gaps remain in internet and mobile access in developing countries, and these gaps limit women's access to digital finance.

75. McKinsey Global Institute (2016).
76. Demirgüc-Kunt, Klapper, and Singer (2017).
77. GSMA (2016a).
78. McKinsey Global Institute (2016).

Figure 2-11. Women's Mobile Phone Use and Financial Inclusion

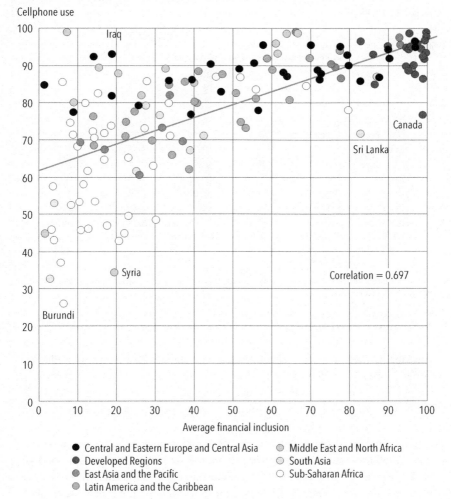

Source: Authors' calculations using Gallup data.

The potential of mobile money and digital finance is most apparent in sub-Saharan Africa, where only one in three adults has access to banking services and financial services penetration rates are the lowest in the world for both men and women. But in this region, almost a third of account holders—or 12 percent of all adults—have a mobile money account, with half having only a mobile money account.[79]

79. Demirgüç-Kunt, Klapper, and Singer (2017).

Figure 2-12. Internet Access and Mobile Phone Ownership, by Region, 2015

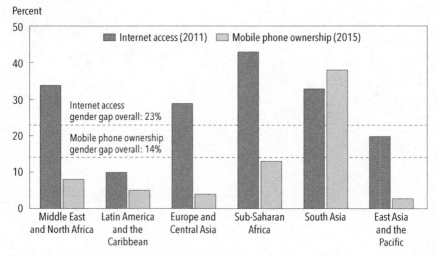

Sources: Internet access data from Dahlberg (2012); mobile phone ownership use data from Gallup Organization (2016).
Note: Regional gender gaps are weighted for internet access and unweighted for mobile phone ownership. Gender gap average includes 144 low- and middle-income countries for internet access and 139 low- and middle-income countries for mobile phone ownership.

Globally, there are thirteen countries where at least 10 percent of adults use mobile money, all in sub-Saharan Africa. Outside of sub-Saharan Africa, mobile money account ownership in emerging markets remains low. The share of mobile money accounts is only 3 percent in South Asia, 2 percent in Latin America, and less than 1 percent in other developing regions.[80]

The rapid spread and widespread use of mobile money in Kenya demonstrates its potential for financial inclusion and economic development. Through M-Pesa, the Kenyan mobile money system, mobile money is ubiquitous in Kenya—at least one individual in nearly all (96 percent) Kenyan households now uses mobile money, and there are 110,000 agents who provide deposit and withdrawal services in 81,000 small agent outlets, compared to only 2,700 automatic teller machines.[81] Traditional financial services accounts tend to grow at the pace of

80. Figures from 2014 Global Findex Report, cited in GMSA (2016a).
81. Figures are from June 2016. In June 2015 the number of ATMs was 2,698, in June 2014, 2,618, and in June 2010, 1,943. Central Bank of Kenya website: www.centralbank.go.ke/national-payments-system/payment-cards/number-of-atms-atm-cards-pos-machines/.

national income, but M-Pesa's adoption rate has been dramatically faster, demonstrating that digital finance can achieve significant market penetration rapidly in even poor countries.

A recent study of M-Pesa published in *Science* shows the beneficial effects of mobile money on financial inclusion and economic welfare. Using detailed household panel surveys, researchers found that access to mobile money increased per capita consumption levels and savings, lifting 2 percent of Kenyan households out of poverty and improving the lives of poor women and members of female-headed households.[82]

The success of mobile money depends on a number of factors. Mobile phones with affordable usage plans must be widely available. More than 1.7 billion women and about 1.5 billion men in low- and middle-income countries do not own mobile phones, with by far the largest gender gap in mobile phone ownership in South Asia. Even when women own mobile phones, the gender gap in mobile phone usage remains, especially for more sophisticated services such as the mobile internet. And even when women have personal identification documents, they must be amenable to digital authentication. Tiered KYC approaches represent a strong opportunity to increase the adoption of mobile money services among women.

Cost remains the greatest barrier to owning and using a mobile phone, particularly for women.[83] Governments have an important role to play in addressing costs by working with private providers and nonprofit organizations to extend mobile networks to poor populations and remote areas. Governments must also ensure that networks between banks and telecommunications companies are interoperable; otherwise, the widespread use of mobile phones for financial services and payments is impossible. And governments must provide a regulatory framework that allows businesses without full banking licenses to provide basic financial products. M-Pesa is not a bank—it is a service offered by Safaricom, a telecommunications provider that now runs the largest mobile money operation in the world. In contrast to Kenya, India has stymied the growth of mobile money through regulations that restrict the ability of nonbanks to provide mobile financial services and limit the interoperability of bank networks.

Governments can also promote the shift to digital finance by shifting from cash to digital payments of social benefits. Of the adults in developing countries who receive government transfers digitally, 36 percent opened their first bank account specifically for that purpose. About 80 million unbanked women in developing

---

82. Suri and Jack (2016).
83. GSMA (2016b); Alliance for Affordable Internet (2016).

economies receive government transfers in cash.[84] Shifting these payments into digital form could help women join the formal financial system while reducing the scope for theft and corruption. Governments can also encourage women's use of formal financial services by accepting digital payments for routine services such as utility fees and school fees. Women in rural areas in developing countries frequently need to spend time, pay transportation costs, miss work, and risk their physical security to travel long distances to pay their bills. Innovations allowing for digital payment of fees would have the additional benefit of eliminating these costs.

Finally, digital finance can also ease credit constraints on female entrepreneurs who are more likely to be unbanked than their male counterparts and therefore lack credit histories to qualify for loans. In Kenya and the few other countries in which mobile money is widespread, a borrower can now file a request for a loan using a mobile phone.[85] An automated set of algorithms can then review the applicant's financial history—such as mobile money transactions and the use of mobile airtime—assess her creditworthiness, and decide on the loan request quickly.

Looking ahead, mobile money and other forms of digital finance are likely to be major channels to accelerate progress on financial inclusion to help meet the SDGs.[86]

What Can Be Done by Businesses and Governments as Employers and as Buyers of Goods and Services

As major employers and as major buyers of goods and services in the global economy, businesses and governments have significant impact on economic gender gaps. In this section, we identify proven and possible actions that businesses and governments can take in employment and procurement practices to advance women's economic opportunities and close gender gaps.

Changing Business Culture and Practices

Most women in paid employment are wage and salary employees, the majority of whom work for private sector businesses that take a variety of forms, from small

84. Klapper and Hess (2016).
85. Klapper and Hess (2016).
86. The McKinsey Growth Institute estimates that digital finance, if widely adopted, could add $3.7 trillion to the GDP of emerging market economies by 2025. That amounts to a 6 percent increase above business as usual, and as much as 12 percent in low-income countries. The boost comes through increased productivity, as businesses, households, and governments operate more efficiently, and from increased investment as personal and business savings shift to the formal financial system and are mobilized to expand credit.

informal firms to large global corporations. The cultures and practices of these businesses have major effects on economic opportunities for women and on the prospects for meeting the associated SDGs.

The incentives for businesses to support gender equality are strong. A growing body of research from around the world documents and measures the many ways that women contribute value to each link of the business value chain—as suppliers, leaders, employees, suppliers, customers, brand creators, and community members.

Companies with greater gender equality in their workforce and top management can reap a whole range of benefits.[87] Such companies are better able to attract and retain female talent, to motivate their female workers, to understand and respond to the needs of female customers, and to better address complex problems by incorporating more diverse views. Gender-diverse teams are correlated with higher financial returns[88] and higher innovation potential and outcomes.[89] And businesses with more women in top leadership and board positions enjoy stronger financial performance. For example, a 2016 Credit Suisse Research Institute study of more than 3,000 companies across all industries and regions found that companies with at least one female board director generated a compound excess return per annum of 3.5 percent since 2005 as compared to companies with all-male boards.[90]

Despite differences in size, type of work, composition of stakeholders, and place of operations, all businesses can take actions to promote gender equality at work, in their own organizations and in their relationships with customers, suppliers, investors, and governments, although the specific actions will vary by company.

Organizational Innovations

Based on recent research and experience, box 2-1 summarizes the promising and proven actions businesses can take.

As a first step, businesses should identify and address adverse stereotypes and implicit biases in their organizations. New research on implicit biases can help all types of businesses to design practices that combat gender biases in hiring, promotion, and pay practices.[91] Many large global companies now have mandatory training for managers to recognize and counter these biases in human resource practices, and new digital platforms are being developed to help organizations do so. Many businesses committed to gender equality in the workplace are setting

---

87. Noland, Moran, and Kotschwar (2016); Morgan Stanley (2016).
88. Hunt, Layton, and Prince (2015).
89. Gratton and others (2007).
90. Dawson, Kersley, and Natella (2016).
91. Bohnet (2016).

Box 2-1. What Companies Can Do to Eliminate Gender Gaps and Accelerate Women's Economic Empowerment

Commit business leaders to gender equality and women's economic empowerment.

Improve pay, conditions, and prospects for female employees:

- Change human resources policies and processes to eliminate implicit biases in recruitment, hiring, promotion, and pay.
- Establish measures of impact and targets to monitor progress on reducing gender gaps and increasing gender diversity—and hold managers accountable for the realization of targets.
- Conduct regular reviews of pay equity with avenues of recourse.
- Offer internal training and mentorship for women to develop hard and soft skills and sponsorship for advancement opportunities.
- Offer flexible work options.
- Offer family friendly policies including paid maternity and paternity leave and support for child care and elderly care.

Ensure equity and enhance opportunities for women's economic empowerment in the supply chain:

- Ensure that workers in company supply chains have safe and healthy working conditions, are not subject to exploitative conditions and human rights violations, are paid decent wages, and have basic labor rights.
- Increase the share of women-owned enterprises (WOEs) and female cooperatives in trade and procurement.

Design and offer products that meet women's needs and that can reduce the unpaid work and care burden women face.

Support campaigns and initiatives that promote gender equality and women's economic empowerment in the workplace, in value chains, and in communities more broadly.

Organize and fund socially responsible activities that empower women economically—for example, company-financed programs for STEM education for women.

Source: Tyson, Klugman, and Smith (2016).

targets or other impact measures to monitor progress on reducing gender gaps in recruitment, retention, and promotion and are linking managerial compensation to progress. Regular pay equity reviews and innovative pay equity processes—for example, setting explicit objective criteria for initial pay and promotion—have been shown to reduce gender pay gaps. Remediation processes to eliminate existing gaps are also effective tools.

Training and mentorship programs help female employees to develop their hard and soft skills, as do sponsorship programs to strengthen their advancement opportunities. Sponsorship programs in particular have been shown to be important in the promotion of women and the development of a strong pipeline of female talent in companies and among their suppliers.[92]

To attract and retain female workers and to reduce gender pay gaps, companies should offer flexible work options and other family friendly policies, including paid maternity and paternity leave benefits. The pervasiveness of motherhood wage penalties, with adverse effects on women's lifetime earnings, and fatherhood wage premiums attest to the importance of corporate policies and practices on this front. Creating more flexible work options reduces gender inequality in both paid and unpaid work.[93] The need or the preference for "temporal flexibility" in work shapes women's choices of occupations, jobs, and places of work and is a significant cause of the gender pay gap.[94] Yet many jobs in businesses, large and small, remain structured to meet the schedules of a stereotypical male who is expected to work long hours on a set schedule, leaving most if not all unpaid work and care in the home to a family partner or paid caregiver.

Supply Chain Innovations

Alongside changes in their workplace culture and practices, businesses can take actions to promote gender equality in their relationships with suppliers. A first step is assessing and addressing the risks of possible exploitation of women in business supply chains. Under the UN Guiding Principles on Business and Human Rights, all businesses are advised to exercise due diligence on issues of gender discrimination. These principles acknowledge that "businesses with large numbers of entities in their value chains" may find it difficult to conduct due diligence of adverse human rights impacts in all of them. If so, businesses should "identify general areas where risk of adverse human rights impacts is most significant."[95]

Some companies are partnering with the public sector or with civil society organizations to protect and empower female workers in their global supply chains. The Better Work program, sponsored by the International Financial Corporation and the International Labour Organization, brings together global companies, factories in their supply chains, governments, and worker organizations

92. Catalyst (2011); Hewlett (2013).
93. European Trade Union Confederation (2010).
94. Freakonomics (2016).
95. United Nations Human Rights Office of the High Commissioner (2011).

to improve factory conditions and safeguard the rights of workers in the garment industry. She Works, a public-private partnership organized by the International Finance Corporation, is working with private companies to improve gender equality and enhance employment opportunities for 300,000 women in company supply chains through mentorship programs, flexible working arrangements, and leadership training to increase diversity in management.[96] To encourage global companies to address problems of poverty, gender inequality, and poor working conditions in their supply chains, Oxfam runs the Behind the Brands campaign calling for stronger laws to support women workers.[97]

To promote gender equality, businesses can increase the share of women-owned companies and collectives in their supply chains. Comprehensive data are lacking, but anecdotal evidence suggests that most large corporations spend less than 2 percent of their procurement budgets with women-owned enterprises (WOEs), despite evidence that increasing gender diversity in supply chains generates economic returns.[98]

A growing number of global companies are committed to progress on this front. Some of these companies are members of WeConnect International, a non-profit organization that identifies, certifies, and provides training to WOEs and connects them to qualified local and multinational companies. To join, companies commit to having a global supplier diversity program.

Another example of procurement is the Empowering Peruvian Women Business Enterprises project, supported by the International Trade Centre, which connects WOEs producing alpaca garments to the U.S. market through promotional activities and trains women in market requirements.[99] Companies can also do more to source from women's collective enterprises in their supply chains. For example, when SABMiller's Nile Breweries in Uganda created a new beer designed to give small-scale subsistence farmers opportunities to participate in the value chain, it worked with farmer associations led by women, and these associations came to account for five of their top ten suppliers.[100]

Companies can aim to include women in their supply chains as distributors and retailers. Unilever's Shakti program in India, launched in 2000, relies on women and their family members to distribute Unilever products in hard-to-reach rural villages. At last count, some 70,000 women and their 48,000 husbands and brothers were working as "Shakti entrepreneurs," reaching more than

---

96. World Bank (2014).
97. For more information on Behind the Brands, see www.behindthebrands.org/en-us.
98. Ramaswami and Mackiewicz (2009).
99. International Trade Centre (2015).
100. Business Fights Poverty/CARE (2016).

4 million households in 162,000 villages.[101] These women generate an income of U.S. $41–$59 per month—double or triple the typical village income they would likely have earned without Shakti.[102] The program accounts for about 5 percent of Unilever's total revenues in India.[103]

Finally, companies can make a visible commitment to gender equality and women's economic empowerment at the global level by becoming signatories to the Women's Empowerment Principles, a joint initiative of UN Women and UN Global Compact. More than 1,280 companies have signed the principles since they were launched in 2011.

Changing Public Sector Employment and Procurement Practices

As major employers and procurers of goods and services, governments can accelerate progress toward women's economic empowerment in a variety of ways. Based on data for seventy-three countries, about 16 percent of women who work are employed in the public sector, ranging from almost half in Norway to only 2 percent in Uganda. Government procurement averages 10–15 percent of GDP and represents major purchasing power in all countries around the world. Under the SDGs, all governments have committed to the goals of gender parity and women's economic empowerment. As major actors in the economy in terms of employment and procurement, they have a spectrum of realizable actions to honor their commitments.

Employment Practices

Like private companies, governments can modify their recruitment, training, promotion, pay, and child care practices to eliminate implicit biases and stereotypes that disadvantage women and to promote gender equity. Gender pay gaps tend to be smaller in the public sector than in the private sector for several reasons, including collective bargaining, minimum wages, and greater pay transparency.[104] But gender pay gaps in public sector employment persist, and governments can do more to eliminate them.

Some governments, including many in the OECD, have set overall hiring targets for women in general or for those in top public service and political positions. Many governments have adopted measures to empower women in public service employment, including practices designed to enhance their recruitment,

---

101. Hindustan Unilever Limited (2015).
102. Coffey, Narsalay, and Sen (2012).
103. Porter and Kramer (2011).
104. Wild (2015).

promotion, and career advancement; regularly assess gender balance in employment at all levels; enforce legal provisions guaranteeing pay equality and pay equity; ensure leadership development and mentoring programs for women; impose accountability mechanisms for measuring and promoting gender balance; and monitor antidiscrimination laws. A 2014 study assessing the different approaches found interventions that establish organizational responsibility and accountability—including affirmative action plans, diversity committees, and diversity staff positions—to be very effective, while mentoring and networking programs were less effective. Diversity training alone had no measured impact.[105]

Procurement Practices

Public procurement accounts for 10–15 percent of GDP in developed countries and more than 30 percent in developing countries. Yet globally only an estimated 1 percent of public procurement contracts are awarded to women-owned businesses. There are many things governments can and are doing to create economic opportunities for women by increasing this share.

A critical first step is the establishment of criteria for the certification, registration, and participation of women-owned businesses in the government procurement processes. The regulatory and procedural constraints in these processes can be reduced to facilitate the participation of small and medium-sized companies. Women-owned businesses face numerous challenges that make it difficult for them to participate in these processes—including large contract sizes, complex and burdensome bidding procedures that advantage large firms, and delays in government payments for services or products delivered by contractors.

Some governments are using innovative, targeted assistance and goal-setting programs to encourage participation by WOEs in public procurement. Setting mandatory procurement targets or goals for WOEs is one approach. The United States, as one example, has a statutory target of not less than 5 percent of the total value of all federal contracts to be awarded to small businesses "owned, operated, and controlled" by one or more women. To achieve this target, individual government agencies have programs to identify and build the capacity of WOEs in sectors in which the agencies procure goods and services. Establishing subcontracting goals is another form of targeting. This approach requires that businesses that win government procurement contracts over a certain size submit plans with targets for participation by WOEs in their supply chains.

Preferences and reservations are more direct—and often controversial—forms of targeted assistance for designated groups in public procurement processes, which

---

105. Baird, Evesson, and Oxenbridge (2014).

can be justified given the implicit biases and entrenched discrimination against disadvantaged groups. Some examples: South Africa has a public procurement preference program for firms, including those owned by women, certified by their status as contributing to black economic empowerment. Kenya has a system requiring that 30 percent of government contracts be awarded to women, youth, and persons with disabilities. Other developing countries, including the Dominican Republic, Tanzania, and Zambia, have recently mandated that a portion of procurement contracts have some form of preferential access for women-owned businesses.

Another recent innovation is a government requirement that firms bidding for public procurement contracts disclose information about their gender pay equity. The Swiss government has been a leader, mandating that all firms competing for such contracts conduct pay audits using a standard tool supplied by the government. Firms must justify any gender wage variance that exceeds 5 percent, and when they cannot justify the variance, they must take measures to ensure that it is within the legal limits. Firms that fail to comply are excluded from bidding for future government contracts.

Collectives of women working in the informal economy should also be allowed to bid on government procurement contracts. India's Self Employed Women's Association (SEWA) has built, strengthened, and supported more than 100 cooperatives of informal women workers, including those providing services (child care, health care, and waste recycling) and producing goods. SEWA has negotiated procurement contracts for some of these cooperatives to provide goods (such as uniforms as well as fresh fruit and vegetables) and to provide services (such as cleaning) to public institutions like hospitals and schools.

Cooperatives of waste pickers in Colombia and India have bid for and secured municipal contracts to collect, sort, transport, and dispose of waste. Kagad Kach Patra Kashtakari Panchayat, a union of waste pickers in Pune, India, formed a cooperative that bid and secured a contract from the Pune Municipal Corporation. And the Asociación Cooperativa de Recicladores de Bogotá formed a pact with other recycling cooperatives in Bogotá and successfully bid for a solid waste management contract from the municipal government.

The Case for Gender Equality and Women's Economic Empowerment

There are many interrelated systemic constraints behind large, pervasive, and persistent gaps in the world of work, and there is no single solution or big idea to eliminate them. Instead, there are numerous proven and promising interventions that can be taken by individuals, businesses, governments, and civil society organizations to address them. In this chapter we focused on actions to tackle two major constraints on women's economic empowerment and opportunities—unpaid care and access to finance. We also identified actions that both businesses and government can take in their employment and procurement practices to accelerate progress toward gender parity at work and to improve women's economic opportunities and outcomes. It is noteworthy that most of the interventions we discuss do not require large additional commitments of resources but rather require changes in policies and practices and the social norms that underlie them.

Our review was not comprehensive. For example, we did not review the ways in which collective action, including among informal workers, can help to advance workers' rights. The UN High-Level Panel highlighted the ways in which SEWA successfully advocated in 2014 for the adoption of the first national legislation that supports and regulates street vending in India and successfully lobbied the Gujarat state government to issue identification cards for informal workers, so they could secure access to free health insurance and a range of other social services.[106] The use and enforcement of human and labor rights conventions is also key, such as the Convention for the Elimination of All Forms of Discrimination Against Women (CEDAW), an international "bill of rights" for women that was adopted by the United Nations General Assembly in 1979 and has been ratified by 189 states.[107]

Empowering women in the economy is the right thing to do to honor the world's commitment to human rights. As a growing body of research confirms, it is also the smart thing to do for economic development and business. And it is critical to achieving the goal of inclusive growth adopted by the global community.

106. Adapted from Chen (2016); Harvey and others (2016); IUF (2016).
107. See the website www.un.org/womenwatch/daw/cedaw/states.htm.

Appendix Table 2-1. Summary of Key Definitions Used

Term and definition	Source
Labor force: Sum of the number of persons employed and the number of persons unemployed, as a share of the population aged 15+ or 15–64. This chapter uses 15+.	Labor force surveys collected by national governments and curated by the ILO
Employees (wage and salaried workers): Workers who hold "paid employment jobs" where an explicit (written or oral) or implicit employment contract gives them a basic remuneration that is not directly dependent on the revenue of the unit for which they work. Employers: Workers who, on their own account or with one or a few partners, hold "self-employment jobs" (where the remuneration is directly dependent on the profits derived from the goods and services produced), and, in this capacity, have engaged on a continuous basis one or more persons to work for them as employee(s). Own-account workers: Workers who, on their own account or with one or a few partners, hold "self-employment jobs" (where the remuneration is directly dependent on the profits derived from the goods and services produced), and have not engaged on a continuous basis any employees to work for them. Contributing family workers: Those who hold "self-employment jobs" (where the remuneration is directly dependent on the profits derived from the goods and services produced) in a market-oriented establishment operated by a related person living in the same household, who cannot be regarded as partners, because their degree of commitment to the operation of the establishment in terms of working time or other factors to be determined by national circumstances, is not at a level comparable to the head of the establishment.	Resolution on the International Classification of Status in Employment (ICSE): 15th International Conference of Labor Statisticians (ICLS) (1993)
Informal employment: All employment arrangements that leave individuals without social protection through their work, whether or not the economic units they operate or work for are formal enterprises, informal enterprises, or households. So defined, informal employment includes the self-employed in informal sector enterprises (that is, unincorporated enterprises that may also be unregistered or small) and wage employed in informal jobs (that is, without employer contributions to social protection) for informal firms, formal firms, or households.	Statistical definition of informal sector, 15th ICLS (1993); Statistical definition of informal employment, 17th ICLS (2003)
Women-owned enterprise/business (WOE): Enterprise owned by at least one women, such as a female sole proprietor, or a business owned by at least one woman with key management or decision-making responsibilities.	IFC MSME Finance Gap Database

Appendix Table 2-2. UN Women Regional Groupings, 195 Countries

Sub-Saharan Africa (49)	Latin America and the Caribbean (33)
Angola, Benin, Botswana, Burkina Faso, Burundi, Cabo Verde, Cameroon, Central African Republic, Chad, Comoros, Congo, Côte d'Ivoire, Democratic Republic of the Congo, Djibouti, Equatorial Guinea, Eritrea, Ethiopia, Gabon, Gambia, Ghana, Guinea, Guinea-Bissau, Kenya, Lesotho, Liberia, Madagascar, Malawi, Mali, Mauritania, Mauritius, Mozambique, Namibia, Niger, Nigeria, Rwanda, São Tomé e Príncipe, Senegal, Seychelles, Sierra Leone, Somalia, South Africa, South Sudan, Sudan, Swaziland, Togo, Uganda, United Republic of Tanzania, Zambia, Zimbabwe	Antigua and Barbuda, Argentina, Bahamas, Barbados, Belize, Bolivia (Plurinational State of), Brazil, Chile, Colombia, Costa Rica, Cuba, Dominica, Dominican Republic, Ecuador, El Salvador, Grenada, Guatemala, Guyana, Haiti, Honduras, Jamaica, Mexico, Nicaragua, Panama, Paraguay, Peru, Saint Kitts and Nevis, Saint Lucia, Saint Vincent and the Grenadines, Suriname, Trinidad and Tobago, Uruguay, Venezuela (Bolivarian Republic of)

Central and Eastern Europe and Central Asia (30)	Developed Regions (29)
Albania, Armenia, Azerbaijan, Belarus, Bosnia and Herzegovina, Bulgaria, Croatia, Cyprus, Czech Republic, Estonia, Georgia, Hungary, Kazakhstan, Kyrgyzstan, Latvia, Lithuania, Montenegro, Poland, Republic of Moldova, Romania, Russian Federation, Serbia, Slovakia, Slovenia, Tajikistan, the former Yugoslav Republic of Macedonia, Turkey, Turkmenistan, Ukraine, Uzbekistan	Andorra, Australia, Austria, Belgium, Canada, Denmark, Finland, France, Germany, Greece, Iceland, Ireland, Israel, Italy, Japan, Liechtenstein, Luxembourg, Malta, Monaco, Netherlands, New Zealand, Norway, Portugal, San Marino, Spain, Sweden, Switzerland, United Kingdom, United States

East Asia and the Pacific (28)	Middle East and North Africa (17)
Brunei Darussalam, Cambodia, China, Democratic People's Republic of Korea, Fiji, Hong Kong, China (SAR), Indonesia, Kiribati, Lao People's Democratic Republic, Malaysia, Marshall Islands, Micronesia (Federated States of), Mongolia, Myanmar, Nauru, Palau, Papua New Guinea, Philippines, Republic of Korea, Samoa, Singapore, Solomon Islands, Thailand, Timor-Leste, Tonga, Tuvalu, Vanuatu, Viet Nam	Algeria, Bahrain, Egypt, Iraq, Jordan, Kuwait, Lebanon, Libya, Morocco, Oman, Qatar, Saudi Arabia, State of Palestine, Syrian Arab Republic, Tunisia, United Arab Emirates, Yemen

South Asia (9)	
Afghanistan, Bangladesh, Bhutan, India, Iran (Islamic Republic of), Maldives, Nepal, Pakistan, Sri Lanka	

Source: Regional classification from *Progress of the World's Women 2015–2016: Transforming Economies, Realizing Rights,* Annex 7, p. 303 (http://progress.unwomen.org/en/2015/pdf/ UNW_progressreport.pdf).

References

Addati, L., and others. 2016. "Women as Work: Trends 2016." Geneva: International Labor Organization (www.ilo.org/wcmsp5/groups/public/---dgreports/---dcomm/---publ/documents/publication/wcms_457317.pdf).

Adema, W., C. Clarke, and V. Frey. 2015. "Paid Parental Leave: Lessons from OECD Countries and Selected US States." November. Paris: OECD Publishing.

Alliance for Affordable Internet (A4AI). 2016. "Affordability Report 2015/2016." Washington (http://1e8q3q16vyc81g8l3h3md6q5f5e.wpengine.netdna-cdn.com/wp-content/uploads/2016/04/A4AI-2015-16-Affordability-Report.pdf).

Antonopoulos, R. 2008. "The Unpaid Care Work—Paid Work Connection." Working Paper 541. Annandale-on-Hudson, N.Y.: Levy Economics Institute.

Baird, M., J. Evesson, and S. Oxenbridge. 2014. "Advancing Women: Increasing the Participation of Women in Senior Roles in the NSW Public Sector." Sydney: NSW Public Service Commission.

Banerjee, A., and others. 2015. "Six Randomized Evaluations of Microcredit: Introduction and Further Steps." *American Economic Journal: Applied Economics* 7, no. 1: 1-21.

Bardasi, E., S. Sabarwal, and K. Terrell. 2011. "How Do Female Entrepreneurs Perform? Evidence from Three Developing Regions." *Small Business Economics* 37, no. 4: 417–41.

Belser, P., and R. Vazquez-Alvarez. 2016. "Global Wage Report 2016/17: Wage Inequality in the Workplace." Geneva: International Labor Organization (www.ilo.org/wcmsp5/groups/public/---dgreports/---dcomm/---publ/documents/publication/wcms_537846.pdf).

Betancor, A. 2011. "The Impact of Accessing Childcare Centres on Chilean Mothers' Probability of Employment." Manuscript. Santiago, Chile: Comunidad Mujer.

Bohnet, Iris. 2016. *Gender by Design.* Harvard University Press.

Brody, C., and others. 2016. "Economic Self-Help Group Programs for Improving Women's Economic Empowerment: A Systematic Review." January. International Initiative for Impact Evaluation. Oslo: Campbell Systematic Reviews.

Business Fights Poverty/CARE. 2016. Business Support for Women's Economic Empowerment: Results of the Business Survey Carried out for the Department of International Development. London, U.K. (http://community.businessfightspoverty.org/profiles/blogs/empowering-women-through-work-early-findings-from-business-survey).

Buvinic, M., R. Furst-Nichols, and E. Courey Pryor. (n.d.). "A Roadmap for Promoting Women's Economic Empowerment." Washington: United Nations Foundation (www.womeneconroadmap.org/sites/default/files/WEE_Roadmap_Report_Final_1.pdf).

Catalyst. 2011. "Sponsoring Women to Success" (www.catalyst.org/system/files/sponsoring_women_to_success.pdf).

Center for Global Development. 2016. "Financial Regulations for Improving Financial Inclusion." Washington (www.cgdev.org/publication/financial-regulations-improving-financial-inclusion).

Chen, M. 2016. "Expanding the Economic Potential of Women Informal Workers." WIEGO Background Paper. New York: United Nations.

Chen, M., R. Madhav, and K. Sankaran. 2014. "Legal Reforms for the Self-Employed: Three Urban Cases." *Indian Journal of Industrial Relations* 50, no. 1: 133–50.

Coffey, R., R. Narsalay, and A. Sen. 2012. "Hindustan Unilever: Scaling a Cost-Efficient Distribution and Sales Network to Remote Markets." *Accenture* (www.accenture. com/_acnmedia/Accenture/Conversion-Assets/DotCom/Documents/Global/PDF/ Dualpub_23/Accenture-Unilever-Case-Study.pdf).

Connelly, R. 1992. "The Effect of Child Care Costs on Married Women's Labor Force Participation." *Review of Economics and Statistics* 74, no. 1: 83–90.

Dahlberg. 2012. "Women and the Web" (https://www.intel.com/content/dam/www/pub lic/us/en/documents/pdf/women-and-the-web.pdf).

Das, M. S., S. Jain-Chandra, M. K. Kochhar, and N. Kumar. 2015. "Women Workers in India: Why So Few Among So Many?" International Monetary Fund Working Paper 15/55.

Dawson, J., R. Kersley, and S. Natella. 2016. "The CS Gender 3000: The Reward for Change." September. Zurich: Credit Suisse AG Research Institute.

De Mel, S., D. McKenzie, and C. Woodruff. 2014. "Business Training and Female Enterprise Start-up, Growth, and Dynamics: Experimental Evidence from Sri Lanka." *Journal of Development Economics* 106: 199–210.

Demirgüç-Kunt, A., L. Klapper, and D. Singer. 2013. "Financial Inclusion and Legal Dis- crimination against Women: Evidence from Developing Countries." Policy Research Working Paper 6416. Washington: World Bank (http://documents.worldbank.org/ curated/en/801311468330257772/pdf/wps6416.pdf).

———. 2017. "Financial Inclusion and Inclusive Growth: A Review of Recent Empirical Evidence." Policy Research Working Paper 8040. Washington: World Bank, April.

Demirgüç-Kunt, A., L. F. Klapper, D. Singer, and P. van Oudheusden. 2015. "The Global Findex Database 2014: Measuring Financial Inclusion around the World." Policy Research Working Paper 7255. Washington: World Bank.

Elborgh-Woytek, K., and others. 2013. "Women, Work, and the Economy: Macroeco- nomic Gains from Gender Equity." September 2013. SDN/13/10. IMF Staff Discus- sion Note. Washington: International Monetary Fund.

Erikkson, L. 2015. "Social Norms Theory and Development Economics." Policy Research Working Paper 7450. Washington: World Bank (http://documents.worldbank.org/ curated/en/999971468189875243/Social-norms-theory-and-development-economics; jsessionid=KslYxFMMhkwesIKIb6fAFX7F).

Esipova, N., L. Klapper, and L. Kellison, 2016. "Are Bank Accounts a Key to Happiness?" *Impatient Optimists* (blog), January 25. Seattle: Bill and Melinda Gates Foundation (www.impatientoptimists.org/Posts/2016/01/Are-Bank-Accounts-a-Key-to-Happiness).

European Trade Union Confederation. 2010. "Working Time, Gender Equality, and Reconciling Work and Family Life." Brussels: European Trade Union Confederation.

Faz, X. 2013. "Mexico's Tiered KYC: An Update on Market Response." June 25. Washington: Consultative Group to Assist the Poor (www.cgap.org/blog/ mexicos-tiered-kyc-update-market-response).

Ferrant, G., L. M. Pesando, and K. Nowacka. 2014. "Unpaid Care Work: The Missing Link in the Analysis of Gender Gaps in Labour Outcomes." December 2014. OECD Devel- opment Centre (www.oecd.org/dev/development-gender/Unpaid_care_work.pdf).

Field, E., A. Holland, and R. Pande. 2016. "Microfinance: Points of Promise." In J. Kimmel, ed., *Contemporary and Emerging Issues*. Kalamazoo, Mich.: W. E. Upjohn Institute for Employment Research.

Freakonomics. 2016. "The True Story of the Gender Pay Gap" (http://freakonomics.com/podcast/the-true-story-of-the-gender-pay-gap-a-new-freakonomics-radio-podcast/).

Gallup Organization. 2016. Gallup World Poll (http://www.gallup.com/analytics/213704/world-poll.aspx).

Geisler, Esther, and Michaela Kreyenfeld. 2012. How Policy Matters: Germany's Parental Leave Benefit Reform and Fathers' Behavior 1999–2009. MPIDR Working Paper WP 2012-021. Rostock, Germany: Max Planck Institute for Demographic Research. July (www.demogr.mpg.de/papers/working/wp-2012-021.pdf).

Gratton, Lynda, and others. 2007. "Innovative Potential: Men and Women in Teams." London Business School (www.lnds.net/blog/images/2013/09/grattonreportinnovative_potential_nov_2007.pdf).

GSMA (Group Speciale Mobile Association). 2016a. "2015 State of the Industry Report Mobile Money." London (www.gsma.com/mobilefordevelopment/wp-content/uploads/2016/04/SOTIR_2015.pdf).

GSMA. 2016b. "Connected Women 2015, Bridging the Gender Gap: Mobile Access and Usage in Low-and Middle-Income Countries." London.

Hallward-Driemeier, M. 2013. "Enterprising Women: Expanding Economic Opportunities in Africa." Washington: World Bank.

Harvey, J., R. Jhabvala, and S. Kumar. 2016. "Summary of SEWA and WIEGO Approach and Case Studies." High Level Panel Case Studies. New York: United Nations.

Heilman, B., R. Levtov, N. van der Gaag, A. Hassink, and G. Barker. 2017. *State of the World's Fathers: Time for Action*. Washington, D.C.: Promundo, Sonke Gender Justice, Save the Children, and MenEngage Alliance (https://sowf.men-care.org/wp-content/uploads/sites/4/2017/06/State-of-the-Worlds-Fathers-2017_EXECUTIVE_SUMMARY-Post-print_June8_WEB.pdf).

Hewlett, S. 2011. "Elderly Care, Child Care, and the Struggle of Chinese Women." *Harvard Business Review* (https://hbr.org/2011/04/eldercare-childcare-and-the-st).

Hewlett, S. 2013. *Forget a Mentor, Find a Sponsor: The New Way to Fast-Track Your Career*. Boston: Harvard Business School Publishing Corporation.

Hindustan Unilever Limited. 2015. "Enhancing Livelihoods through Project Shakti" (www.hul.co.in/sustainable-living/case-studies/enhancing-livelihoods-through-project-shakti.html).

Hunt, V., D. Layton, and S. Prince. 2015. "Diversity Matters." February. London: McKinsey and Company.

Institute for Reproductive Health. 2011. "Utilizing Participatory Data Collection Methods to Evaluate Programs for Very Young Adolescents: An Evaluation of Save the Children's Choices Curriculum in Siraha, Nepal." Washington: Institute for Reproductive Health, Georgetown University for the U.S. Agency for International Development (http://resourcecentre.savethechildren.se/sites/default/files/documents/5520.pdf).

International Trade Centre. 2015. "Unlocking Markets for Women to Trade." Geneva (www.intracen.org/uploadedFiles/intracenorg/Content/Publications/women_in_trade_web.pdf).

IUF (International Union of Food, Agricultural, Hotel, Restaurant, Catering, Tobacco, and Allied Workers' Association). 2016. "Informal Sector Workers in Gujarat Win Healthcare, Social Security with First Identity Card." March 21. Petit-Lancy, Switzerland (www.iuf.org/w/?q=node/4868).

Jacobson, J., R. Mohun, and F. Sajjad. 2016. "Infrastructure: A Game-Changer for Women's Economic Empowerment." Infrastructure and Cities for Economic Development Facility, UNHLP Background Brief. New York: UN High-Level Panel.

Jayachandran, S. 2014. "The Roots of Gender Inequality in Developing Countries." Working Paper No. 20380. Cambridge, Mass.: National Bureau of Economic Research.

Jenkins S., and E. Symons. 2001. "Child Care Costs and Lone Mothers' Employment Rates: UK Evidence." *Manchester School* 69, no. 2: 121–47.

Kelley, Donna, Candida Brush, Patricia Greene, Mike Herrington, Abdul Ali, and Penny Kew. 2015. *GEM Special Report: Women's Entrepreneurship.* Global Entrepreneurship Monitor (GEM). Babson Park, Mass.: Babson College.

Kimmel, J. 1998. "Child Care Costs as a Barrier to Employment for Single and Married Mothers." *The Review of Economics and Statistics* 80, no. 2: 287-299.

Klapper, L., and S. Parker. 2010. "Gender and the Business Environment for New Firm Creation." *World Bank Research Observer* 26, no. 2: 237–57.

Klapper, L., and J. Hess. 2016. "Financial Inclusion and Women's Economic Empowerment." Briefing for the UN Secretary-General's High-Level Panel on Women's Economic Empowerment, November. Washington: World Bank.

Klugman, J., and S. Twigg. 2015. "Gender at Work in Africa: Legal Constraints and Opportunities to Reform." Working Paper 3. Oxford Human Rights Hub. January (http://ohrh.law.ox.ac.uk/wordpress/wp-content/uploads/2014/04/OxHRH-Working-Paper-No-3-Klugman.pdf).

Klugman, J., and L. Tyson. 2016. "Report of the UN Secretary General High Level Panel (UNHLP) on Women's Economic Empowerment: A Call to Action for Gender Equality and Women's Economic Empowerment." New York: United Nations.

Levtov, R. 2016. "Men, Gender, and Inequality in Unpaid Care." Promundo/UN High-Level Panel Background Brief. New York: United Nations.

Loiseau, J., and C. Walsh. 2015. "Where Credit Is Due." Abdul Latif Jameel Poverty Action Lab and Innovations for Policy Action Policy Bulletin. February (www.poverty actionlab.org/sites/default/files/publications/where-credit-is-due.pdf).

McKinsey Global Institute. 2015. "The Power of Parity: How Advancing Women's Equality Can Add $12 Trillion to Global Growth." September. Washington: McKinsey and Company (www.mckinsey.com/global-themes/employment-and-growth/how-advancing-womens-equality-can-add-12-trillion-to-global-growth).

———. 2016. "Digital Finance for All: Powering Inclusive Growth in Emerging Economies." Washington: McKinsey and Company (www.mckinsey.com/global-themes/employment-and-growth/how-digital-finance-could-boost-growth-in-emerging-economies).

Microcredit Summit Campaign. 2015. "Mapping Pathways out of Poverty: The State of the Microcredit Summit Campaign Report, 2015." Washington.

Morgan Stanley. 2016. "Why It Pays to Invest in Gender Diversity." New York.

Noland, M., T. Moran, and B. Kotschwar. 2016. "Is Gender Diversity Profitable? Evidence from a Global Survey." Working Paper 6-3. Washington: Peterson Institute for International Economics (https://piie.com/publications/wp/wp16-3.pdf).

OECD. 2016. "Parental Leave—Where Are the Fathers." OECD Policy Brief (www.oecd.org/gender/parental-leave-where-are-the-fathers.pdf).

Porter, Michael, and Mark Kramer. 2011. "Creating Shared Value," *Harvard Business Review* 89, no. 1-2 (January–February): 62–77.

Ramaswami, R., and A. Mackiewicz. 2009. "Scaling Up: Why Women-Owned Businesses Can Recharge the Global Economy." London: Ernst and Young (www.ey.com/Publication/vwLUAssets/Scaling_up_-_Why_women-owned_businesses_can_recharge_the_global_economy_-_new/$FILE/Scaling_up_why_women_owned_businesses_can_recharge_the_global_economy.pdf).

Sahay, R., and others. 2015. "Financial Inclusion: Can It Meet Multiple Macroeconomic Goals." Staff Discussion Note SDN/15/17. September. Washington: IMF (www.imf.org/external/pubs/ft/sdn/2015/sdn1517.pdf).

Scheil-Adlung, X. 2015. "Long-Term Care Protection for Older Persons: A Review of Coverage Deficits in 46 Countries." Extension of Social Security Working Paper No. 50. Geneva: International Labor Organization (www.ilo.org/wcmsp5/groups/public/---ed_protect/---soc_sec/documents/publication/wcms_407620.pdf).

Stein, Peer, Oya Pinar Ardic, and Martin Hommes. 2013. *Closing the Credit Gap for Formal and Informal Micro, Small, and Medium Enterprises.* Washington: IFC (www.ifc.org/wps/wcm/connect/4d6e6400416896c09494b79e78015671/Closing+the+Credit+Gap+Report-FinalLatest.pdf?MOD=AJPERES).

Suri, Tavneet, and William Jack. 2016. "The Long-Run Poverty and Gender Impacts of Mobile Money." *Science* 354, no. 6317 (December): 1288–92.

Tyson, L., J. Klugman, and G. Smith. 2016. "Business Culture and Practice as a Driver for Gender Equality and Women's Economic Empowerment: A Summary of the Findings and Recommendations of the UN Secretary General's High-Level Panel on Women's Economic Empowerment." Policy Brief. November (http://hlp-wee.unwomen.org/-/media/hlp%20wee/attachments/other-materials/briefing-papers/business%20policy%20brief_v2.pdf?la=en).

Tyson, L., and S. Lund. 2016. "The Promise of Digital Finance." Project Syndicate, December 14 (www.project-syndicate.org/commentary/mobile-phones-digital-finance-by-laura-tyson-and-susan-lund-2016-12).

United Nations Human Rights Office of the High Commissioner. 2011. "Guiding Principles on Business and Human Rights" (www.ohchr.org/Documents/Publications/GuidingPrinciplesBusinessHR_EN.pdf).

Unilever. 2015. "Unilever Sustainable Living Plan—India Progress 2015" (www.hul.co.in/Images/unilever-sustainable-living-plan-india-2015-progress-report_tcm1255-483536_en.pdf).

Vanek, J., and others. 2014. "Statistics on the Informal Economy: Definitions, Regional Estimates and Challenges." WIEGO Working Paper (Statistics) 2. April. Cambridge, Mass.: WIEGO.

Viitanen, T. 2005. "Cost of Childcare and Female Employment in the UK." *Labour* 19: 149–70.

WHO. 2016. "Older People and Primary Health Care (PHC)" (www.who.int/ageing/primary_health_care/en/).

WIEGO (Women in Informal Employment: Globalizing and Organizing). 2016. "The Development of Statistics on the Informal Economy" Website Article. (http://wiego.org/informal-economy/development-statistics-informal-economy).

Wild, S. 2015. "The Growing Gender Pay Gap in the Public Sector Is a Problem for Us All." *The Guardian.* November 9.

World Bank. 2014. "IFC Launches She Works Partnership to Advance Women's Employment in the Private Sector" (www.worldbank.org/en/news/press-release/2014/09/22/
   ifc-launches-she-works-partnership-to-advance-womens-employment-in-the-private-
   sector).

————. 2015a. "Women, Business, and the Law 2016: Getting to Equal." Washington: World Bank (http://wbl.worldbank.org/~/media/WBG/WBL/Documents/
   Reports/2016/Women-Business-and-the-Law-2016.pdf?la=en)

————. 2015b. "Women Business and the Law 2016: Getting to Equal." Fact Sheet.
   Washington: World Bank (http://wbl.worldbank.org/~/media/WBG/WBL/Docu-
   ments/FactSheets/WBL2016-Getting-a-job.pdf).

————. 2016. "Development Goals in an Era of Demographic Change." Washington:
   World Bank and International Monetary Fund (https://openknowledge.
   worldbank.org/handle/10986/22547;jsessionid=3E2E44278FE100AA58B1BCD-
   F7AA2DDDA).

Zollmann, J., and C. Sanford. 2016. "A Buck Short: What Financial Diaries Tell Us
   about Building Financial Services That Matter to Low-Income Women." London:
   Bankable Frontier Associates/Omidyar Network (www.omidyar.com/insights/what-
   financial-diaries-tell-us-about-building-financial-services-matter-low-income-women).

CHAPTER THREE

From Green Bonds to Sustainable Development
The Case of Nigeria

Amina Mohammed with Simon Zadek

This chapter follows a unique narrative form in the book: it is told from the personal perspective of Amina Mohammed, who served as Nigeria's minister of the environment from November 2015 to February 2017. In that role, she collaborated with Simon Zadek, then codirector of UN Environment's Inquiry into the Design of a Sustainable Financial System, and other colleagues to launch Nigeria's first sovereign green bond. Here they describe many of the frontier issues tackled in that effort.

In late 2015 I arrived back in Nigeria from the United States as the newly appointed minister of the environment. My foremost task was to shift the narrative from the green-only language of environment and climate to a multihued vision of sustainable national development. To do so, the Ministry of the Environment still had to address many classic environmental challenges such as waste and sanitation, air and water pollution, and land degradation. But for issues of environmental stewardship and climate to move from a sidebar to the main policy agenda, they had to be at the heart of Nigeria's broader development strategy and practice.

Such a shift in the policy frame was not just a matter of rewriting the ministry's strategy or declaring new goals, although that would be needed. After all, Nigeria, like most developing countries, is overflowing with discarded visions, goals, and plans, some produced locally and others shaped by often well-meaning but disconnected international technocrats. Nevertheless, commitments and goals do count, as do plans, especially important and universally adopted ones such as the Sustainable Development Goals and the Paris Agreement on climate. But we had to find a way for such ambitions to be not only articulated by and between governments, but to be shared between individuals, families, and communities on the ground.

Making such ambitious goals and commitments count and lead to change hinges on linking them to peoples' struggles to take control of their own lives. They need to inspire, guide, and catalyze action in improving the lived experience of the many. Only through the real lives of people can the goals for climate and environmental mitigation and social and economic betterment be achieved, irrespective of the many reports and agreements created through endless committees in the international community. Our job, my job, was to help in making that vital connection between the documents, the aspiration, and how people, with our support, could turn those visions into reality.

My view, and hope, was that by engaging with people in their daily lives, we could overcome the outmoded boundaries of the Environment Ministry's mandate and approach. We needed "green" to be something that people embraced and incorporated as a matter of course in their workplace, family, and community. We sometimes see such integration in a few, often richer communities that are reliant on a stable natural environment for survival. But such integration is largely absent from most aspects of the development processes, particularly in urban environments around the world.

This disconnect does not arise because people do not see the problem. Rather, it is because they cannot make sense of the mixed signals they are getting. On the one hand, if to survive means more consumption, then to succeed is to consume as much as possible, with stewardship having no place in the intensity of urban life and our classical understanding of development. On the other hand, people know through real experience—often those in poverty, more than those who can protect themselves with wealth—that any kind of reasonable future depends on collectively getting a handle on reducing pollution and improving public health.

To make progress, it was clear that any such disconnects have to be addressed.

A core challenge was how to pay for the things that we know are required. Being the environment minister is an extraordinary privilege. Yet anyone who has had the honor of holding this role, in practically any country, has learned that it gives no mandate, let alone authority, across the domains of my fellow ministers who dealt with economy, industry, and infrastructure, let alone finance. Notably, influence over the domestic budget is very restrictive for most environment ministers because fiscal priorities tend not to reflect the fact that investment in the environment is often critical in helping us to boost sustainable productivity and livelihoods.

Engaging on issues of finance brings in many other dimensions of development. For Nigeria, there is an intimate link to security. Boko Haram is an existential challenge, as is Niger Delta militancy and the growing conflict in the north between nomads and farmers. So just for starters, the cost of security took a lot of the oxygen out of the public budget. Finance is also linked with governance challenges, with corruption and illicit financial flows further limiting the availability of public finance. One challenge, then, was how to mobilize and use resources in ways that did not fall foul of the same problem. And underlying these challenges was the simple fact of the profound need for much, much more infrastructure development.

Last but not least is perhaps Nigeria's greatest paradox, in that it is a nation presenting both a challenge and an opportunity. That we are a profoundly carbon-dependent economy is self-evident to anyone reviewing Nigeria's headline economic data. That this is not a viable basis for inclusive prosperity, today or tomorrow, is a view rejected for many decades but an idea whose time has, I believe, finally arrived.

My challenge, and Nigeria's problem, was that few people beyond the president could see any connection between the environment and the importance of delivering effective development through measures to address security, corruption, and infrastructure. Frankly, many of my colleagues at the time did not see or value the work of the Ministry of the Environment, except perhaps negatively as an institution that added time and costs to their burdens. We had to help people connect the dots in demonstrating the links between the solutions to fundamental development challenges and the environment. We had to point out convincingly the connection between Boko Haram and the climate, because of the desiccation, the drying up of Lake Chad. Similarly, we had to make the connection between pollution and the environment down in the Niger Delta and how long-term solutions need to address the militarization of the region.

We had to convince people of the basic argument that jobs and security, for example, were part of a policy ecosystem that included the environment. Broadly implanting this view would then open the way to securing support for action on the environment and climate, forging policy linkages with other parts of the national development agenda, and unlocking access to finance.

We needed funding, and lots of it, soon. We needed to pay for the things we had to do to fulfill our national aspiration and international climate commitments. More important, we needed to pay for the investments that would deliver positive environmental outcomes alongside other domestic cobenefits. Without this, we could not manage the international part.

Sometimes this would involve large numbers when it came to big infrastructural projects. But actually often those large numbers amounted to the financing of many smaller things, such as finding ways to support climate-friendly small businesses. We knew that there was an incredible opportunity to leverage the virtuous circle between economic development and environmental remediation and conservation. With a little help, small businesses could develop better practices that would be green in any number of ways and could also improve productivity and reduce costs. We knew that, but that did not mean that the banks knew it or wanted to do something about it even if they knew. Such financing seemed unnecessarily costly and risky to them, even more so than normal small- and medium-enterprise financing, when compared to lending for consumption or housing or to larger businesses.

So we needed to break out of a vicious circle, unable to get either public or private funds to invest in demonstrating that both governments and private capital had got it wrong, that they were missing the point—and moreover missing profitable lending and investment opportunities. My task was to break this destructive cycle.

The Global Surge in Green Finance

As we considered our options, and still today, everyone in the international development scene promoted "financial innovation." But Nigeria showed scant evidence of such innovation on the ground then. Knowing that there was a lot going on outside of the country, I undertook the task of figuring out which bits might be relevant to Nigeria.

Internationally, the conversation about financing the SDGs and Paris commitments on climate was evolving beyond the obvious importance of official development assistance and the commitment made by developed countries to deliver at least U.S. $100 billion per annum by 2020 to address climate-related financing needs. The Addis Ababa Action Agenda on Financing for Development agreed to in July 2015 had reinforced the importance of broadening the lens in recognition of the need to tap private capital in pursuit of sustainable development. Everyone knew this made sense, although it presented challenges that many of us, including most financial institutions, domestically and internationally, were not ready to deal with. Even in China, with a strong public balance sheet, the People's Bank of China concluded that no more than 15 percent of the U.S. $600 billion per annum of green finance needed domestically could be met from public sources.

But the most interesting development was the next step in the move toward embracing the need for private finance. Many people view private finance with distrust in Nigeria and elsewhere—including many in other developing countries and also now in developed countries. This is perhaps not surprising, since private, commercial, and especially international finance has for years been associated as part of the problem of misdirected development and underdevelopment.

History aside, private finance going forward will be critical to development. So the challenge for many is to work out how to tap its enabling strengths while keeping its problematic aspects at bay. As renowned economist Joseph Stiglitz, speaking at the Addis conference, reminded the audience, it is not just a matter of needing private finance; it is a question of what kind of private finance.

The idea that the financial system itself could be allied with the 2030 Agenda is not new. Many people have written about the social purpose of finance, but with little impact—until now, that is. Perhaps the right time for this agenda had finally arrived. The factors making this a historic moment for aligning the financial system with the 2030 Agenda are not that hard to discern. The financial crisis of 2008 plunged the global economy into disarray, resulting in profound distrust in the crisis's source, financial and capital markets represented by some of the world's leading and, until then, most profitable companies. The resulting legitimacy and resurgent role for financial policies and regulations provided one basis for action, alongside the need for the market to regain its license to operate. Central banks in particular came into their own, and not surprisingly have played a key if unexpected role in advancing green and sustainable finance.

The financial crisis also accelerated the ongoing shift in the balance of influence and power towards emerging nations, notably China. For the first time in modern history, financial market and policy leadership came from outside of the major financial centers such as London and New York. China, in particular, took two bold steps in the field. In 2014 the People's Bank of China began working with UN Environment (UNEP) in setting out an ambitious agenda to green China's financial system. Building on this in late 2015, China announced it was taking the topic to the G-20, placing it squarely in the finance track to signal the need for finance ministers and central bank governors to take note.

Last but not least, the development of the SDGs, and even more so the rising profile of the climate challenge, advanced a shift in narrative that improved alignment of finance with this global agenda. It was Mark Carney, governor of the Bank of England and chair of the Financial Stability Board, who most spectacularly broke the mold in stepping out as a leading central bank governor with a pronouncement on climate change. As well as initiating the world's first review of the impact of climate change on financial stability, he spoke of the need to "reset" the financial system in order to effectively address international climate goals.

While China and the United Kingdom offered exemplary leadership, there were many other like-minded developments, ably documented and catalyzed by the United Nations through UN Environment Program's Inquiry into how the financial system might be better aligned with sustainable development. Initiated in early 2014, the inquiry worked across more than twenty countries, highlighting the leadership being taken by developing countries as diverse as Bangladesh, Brazil, Colombia, Indonesia, Kenya, and Peru, as well as by a growing number of developed countries such as France, the Netherlands, Singapore, and Switzerland.

Today, these leadership countries have been joined by dozens more, ranging from Canada to Kazakhstan, Luxembourg, Morocco, and Vietnam.

What has been astonishing, however, has been not only the number of countries showing interest in advancing green and sustainable finance but also the depth of ambition in advancing national road maps to align their domestic financial and capital markets to be better able and willing to lend, invest, and insure in ways consistent with and supportive of sustainable development and climate goals. Certainly, improved measurement and disclosure of related risks have offered low-hanging "efficiency" moves. Beyond that, however, has been a growing willingness to experiment more broadly, deploying financial policies and regulations, financial standards, judicial and fiscal measures, and even the use of the public procurement of financial services as a driver of change.

Financial market actors have increasingly responded to these national and international developments, as well as more immediate market-facing opportunities and threats. Green bonds (see box 3-1) have emerged as a simple market innovation that encourages capital-raising in the fixed income market for defined and guaranteed green uses. Many of the world's largest asset managers, increasingly pressured by clients like pension funds and high-net-worth individuals, are offering low-carbon or even fossil fuel–free funds and investment strategies. Over sixty stock exchanges have committed to requesting or requiring improved disclosure of listed companies of their environmental, social, and economic-related financial risks. Credit rating agencies, accounting bodies, and in-market providers of tracker indexes and other guides to lending and investing are increasingly making aspects of sustainable development more visible as both independent objectives of, or risks to, the owners of capital.

Finance is the lifeblood of the global economy, and the financial system its cornerstone. So in light of all these evolutions, it became clearer that we needed to embrace the moment in Nigeria to draw on some of the innovative spirit we were seeing emerging elsewhere.

Nigeria's Sovereign Green Bond

In 2016 serious discussions began with the leadership of the Nigerian Stock Exchange, which had been engaging in international discussions about sustainable finance through the United Nations Conference on Trade and Development–hosted Sustainable Stock Exchange Initiative, the International Finance Corporation–hosted Sustainable Banking Network, and UN Environment. Because of these engagements, these bodies were actively exploring whether there was something that could be done, and we had little need to persuade them that the environment and finance related to each other.

Box 3-1. Green Bonds: Momentum in Financial Products and Capital Mobilization

The rapid growth of green bonds illustrates how public enterprise and market innovation can combine to mobilize capital for sustainable development. The year 2017 marked the green bond market's ten-year anniversary since it was launched by leading development finance organizations such as the European Investment Bank, the International Finance Corporation, and the World Bank. Total issuance of bonds with proceeds marked for green investment was about U.S. $115 billion in 2017 alone, bringing the total market outstanding to over U.S. $300 billion. The growth is impressive, but it still represents less than 1 percent of the total stock of global debt capital markets.

In that context, some key recent developments in green bond markets include:

- Rise of emerging economy issuance: China became the largest green bond issuer as of 2016, with over U.S. $30 billion of green bonds issued that year. This was underpinned by the development of green bond regulation from the People's Bank of China at the end of 2015. India's securities regulator also issued its own draft guidelines in January 2016, followed by the Moroccan Capital Markets Authority. Among other countries, Argentina, Colombia, Costa Rica, Malaysia, Morocco, and the Philippines have also issued their first green bonds.

- Sovereign green bond programs established: Green bonds are increasingly seen as a tool for governments to support financing climate targets pledged in Paris through the so-called Nationally Determined Contributions (NDC), essentially a country's climate-related commitments. Poland won the race to become the first sovereign green bond issuer with a 750 million euro issuance in December 2016. France followed shortly after with an impressive 7 billion euro green bond, with Fiji amplifying its role in chairing the Conference of the Parties (COP) and launching its own sovereign green bond in mid-2017.

- Growing use of market principles and standards: A liquid green bond market relies on the use of common approaches to ensuring trust and accountability. In 2016, 77 percent of issuance received reviews or certifications from external parties representing good practice in accordance with the voluntary Green Bond Principles. In some markets, Climate Bonds certification is the norm, as is the case in Australia.

- Innovative policy tools: the People's Bank of China is considering whether to provide preferential lending rates to banks that invest in green projects. In Singapore, the central bank has committed to a grant scheme to cover the costs of external reviews for green bonds. In Europe, the French Banking Association has proposed the implementation of preferential risk weightings for green investments.

- New market infrastructure: Bond funds, exchange-traded funds, indexes, and exchanges are making it easy to identify and invest in green bonds. The first green bond indexes and green bond funds were first launched in 2014—now more than five indexes and numerous funds are on the market. The first green bond ETFs were announced in early 2017, and more are expected in the future.

Source: Climate Bonds Initiative, adapted from "The Financial System We Need: Momentum to Transformation," UN Environment, 2016.

It was through these conversations that the potential of issuing a green bond began to crystallize in our minds. Green bonds were of interest in offering a possible vehicle for raising funds from private capital markets for environmentally attractive projects. But issuing a green bond was not just the way to mobilize funds for the environment, and actually would never happen if they were treated exclusively with this in mind.

Advancing a green bond was a way to engage a set of actors who did not in the main see any reason to talk to us, let alone focus on the environmental agenda. This included investors, of course, but centrally it included other ministries and ministers and other public bodies. It was an important opportunity to develop a process that would engender trust and integrity in the system.

Building on an agreement with UNEP's then executive director, Achim Steiner, at the UN Environmental Assembly in Nairobi in June 2016, the UNEP Inquiry mobilized a team to support the issuance of a sovereign green bond. Together with the UN Environment team and the Climate Bonds Initiative, we began the process of engaging different parts of the Nigerian government, players in the Nigerian capital market, local private sector actors, and international actors, the latter including key development finance institutions (see box 3-2). This was just as we had hoped: the socialization by trusted outside parties on the broader agenda of links between economy, environment, and climate through the practical lens of issuing a sovereign green bond. While it was clear that the team operated under a mandate from us, it was equally clear that their legitimacy in addressing these other actors played a very useful role that we could not achieve alone.

After nearly two years of hard work (see box 3-3), fast forward to December 22, 2017, when Nigeria became the first country to issue a Climate Bonds Certified Sovereign Green Bond. We were the first African country to issue any form of sovereign green bond and only the fourth in the world to do so, after Poland, France, and Fiji. The issuance of 10.69 billion naira (roughly U.S. $30 million) has been described by the Ministry of the Environment as a "pilot sovereign" of a foreshadowed 150 billion naira green bond program and will fund a range of renewable energy, afforestation, and environmental projects. Ibrahim Usman Jibril, minister of state for environment, said in announcing the issuance: "Climate change is real, and business, government and the capital market need to work together to slow its effects. This pilot green bond, which we expect to be the first of many more, has developed the platform to address the nation's target of reducing its emissions by 20 percent unconditionally and 45 percent conditionally by 2030."

The issuance of Nigeria's bond will provide funds for important projects geared toward protecting the environment and reversing the harmful effects of climate change. However, the issuance also signals the government's commitment to protecting the environment and taking climate change seriously. In that respect, it

Box 3-2. Green Bonds Capital Markets and Investors Conference, Lagos, February 2017

The delivery of Nigeria's Nationally Determined Contribution (NDC) to the Paris Agreement will require a fundamental re-orientation of financial flows within the country's economy. Capital will need to flow toward low-carbon, climate-resilient opportunities and away from carbon-intensive, polluting activities or those that exacerbate climate change.

While speaking at the February 23 conference, acting Nigerian president Yemi Osinbajo told participants that green bonds have considerable potential to help achieve the goals set out in Nigeria's NDC. The conference was attended by representatives from the public sector and private finance sector and civil society and was organized by the federal Ministry of the Environment and the Debt Management Office (DMO) at the Nigerian Stock Exchange (NSE) office in Lagos.

At the same event, Amina J. Mohammed, minister of the environment, outlined the wider context for green bonds: "Nigeria is committed to sustainable economic development. The Lagos Event is a concrete step in the process of developing our 2017 sovereign green bonds program. In Lagos, we are bringing together the institutional investors, banking, finance, and young social entrepreneurs' groups that will ensure this initial bond launch is a success; [we are] enabling the development of a green bond market while building our national climate finance capabilities."

International experience has shown that momentum is generated by the interplay between pub-lic enterprise and private sector innovation. The private sector has been integral to the sovereign green bond process from the outset and vocal in its support. Nigerian Stock Exchange CEO Oscar N. Onyema predicted that a first sovereign bond issuance would lay the foundations that other public and private sector issuers could leverage: "A sovereign green bond represents a new stage in the development of Nigerian capital markets and opens the way for further corporate issuance and international investment."

For Chapel Hill Denham CEO and Green Bond Advisory Group member Bolaji Balogun, the planned debut green bond issuance "demonstrates Nigeria's seriousness about its climate change commitments and is evidence of its willingness to subject itself to the discipline and transparency that capital markets require." The recently announced national Economic Growth and Recovery Plan has created confidence in these commitments. The plan will help "deliver long-term sustainable growth and reduce reliance on oil and gas revenues," according to the Kemi Adeosun, minister of finance.

While the focus of the conference was on green bonds, it was clear that a pivot away from a high-carbon economy is creating substantial opportunities for broader sustainable finance in Nigeria. These opportunities lie in sectors such as infrastructure and agriculture and could be mirrored across much of the African continent. A new economic model will require new types of financial instruments, new capabilities, and new sources of sustainable finance.

Nigeria's sovereign green bond process has started to lay the foundations for a new sustainable finance ecosystem that stretches well beyond bonds. However, the process has also required the development of new definitions, criteria, and guidelines. These can provide clarity and confidence to the market to develop a range of new instruments, institutions, and capabilities to meet the demands of the low-carbon economy of tomorrow.

Box 3-3. A Timeline for Nigeria's Sovereign Green Bond

May 2016: CEO of the Nigerian Stock Exchange (NSE) presents a sovereign green bond proposal to the minister of the environment

May 2016: Minister of the environment holds discussions on a Nigerian sovereign green bond on the margins of United Nations Environment Assembly in Nairobi, Kenya

June 2016: Minister of the environment agrees to develop national green bond guidelines with the Nigerian Stock Exchange, the Climate Bonds Initiative, and UN Environment

September 2016: Ministry of the Environment and Ministry of Finance co-convene a public-private sector stakeholder meeting in Abuja to launch Nigeria's green bond guidelines and propose plans to issue a sovereign green bond in 2017

September 2016: President Buhari announces during the UN General Assembly in New York that Nigeria will launch a sovereign green bond in 2017

November 2016: Green Bond Guidelines issued

January 2017: Launch of the Green Bond Advisory Council

January 2017: Projects for the portfolio identified

February 2017: Green Bond Project Advisory Team appointed

February 2017: Green Bonds Capital Markets and Investors Conference held in Lagos, bringing together public and private sector stakeholders—including Vice President Yemi Osinbajo—to promote the opportunity of green bonds for Nigeria

May 2017: DNV-GL appointed as third-party verifier to verify the green credentials of the sovereign green bond

May 2017: Nigeria's sovereign green bond receives green bonds certification under the International Climate Bonds Standard

December 2017: Domestic investor roadshow launched

December 2017: Moody's assigns a green bond assessment of GB1 (excellent) to the offering

December 2017: Sovereign green bond issued

creates a benchmark for subsequent issuances of green bonds by state-level governments and corporates for financing environmental projects. It further provides an opportunity for investors interested in preserving the environment to contribute to the country's efforts at environmental preservation, while earning income from a low-risk sovereign instrument. In so doing, this further diversifies the government's funding sources and deepens the domestic capital market by providing a wider variety of products for investors.

There have been some important broader positive spillovers from the process, even before launching the sovereign green bond. The deeper story is that the conversation between the Environment Ministry and the financial community has begun to change, and quite dramatically. International interest in the sovereign green bond has triggered engagement by domestic capital market actors, interested in how Nigerian debt can be made more attractive to international actors, as well as in buying the debt itself. With the financial community talking more about the nexus between environment, climate, and finance, the Finance Ministry has also become more interested, as has the central bank, parliament, and other key institutions. Green bonds, it turns out, are not just a way to raise money but a means of unlocking the very conversation that was needed—about the role of environmental stewardship and of climate in national economic development. Engaging with and about finance is a key step in shifting the broader political economy of sustainable development.

Imagining the Future

Looking forward, the successful financing of sustainable development will involve many moving parts, ranging from more effective policy and regulation to more truly productive market innovations. We need to take steps that we can manage, but change still needs to be systemic rather than ad hoc. Sustainable development has opened us to understanding change in both of these ways—step-by-step and systemic—without contradiction. For example, land use transformation is done acre by acre, tree by tree, and farm by farm. But we also know that systemic shifts in agriculture and forestry are essential to ensure food security, address climate challenges, provide sustainable livelihoods, and deliver improved public health. Similarly, we understand energy systems not just in terms of kilowatt hours, but in terms of the impact of sustainable energy on everyone's health and young peoples' education.

So too must it be with finance.

The financial system that channels our savings into productive and profitable investments needs to do this in a way that delivers an inclusive, environmentally sustainable, prosperous future. As a system, it has a purpose, and that purpose needs to be embedded in the mandates of its governing institutions, reflected in their guiding measures as the core of any performance assessment, and observed in the end-effects of financial flows. Finance offers private actors the opportunity for profitable rewards, but these need to be secured in return for ensuring that the system's underlying purpose is realized.

Resetting the purpose of the financial system requires the role of government, and governance, to be strengthened to ensure that finance flows in support of sustainable development. We all talk about improved governance, and money often lies at the heart of what prevents that talk becoming common practice. We need to reverse this line of cause and effect. Promoting sustainable finance can improve governance, not just vice versa. Green bonds are a small but illuminating case in point. Market discipline combined with agreed standards can deliver a certified use of proceeds and third-party reporting against not only the contracted use but also the investment's outcomes. As sustainable finance extends across financial and capital markets in Nigeria and around the world, so too can its promised underlying integrity expand through the relevant processes and outcomes.

Inverting traditional logic in this way helps to explain the unexpected phenomenon of how developing countries, often with relatively underdeveloped domestic financial systems, can play a leadership role in advancing sustainable finance. Atiur Rahman, at the time he was governor of Bangladesh's central bank, explained, "Central banking and development banking are not separate activities in developing countries; they are one and the same thing." Similarly, Madam Zhang, director of the Finance Institute of China's prestigious Development Research Centre of the State Council, was once asked if it would be better to advance green finance once China's financial system was fully developed. She argued that "green finance can improve the efficiency and effectiveness of the financial system," highlighting its links to good governance.

For Nigeria, although at an early stage, the initiative to advance a sovereign green bond has caught the attention of lawmakers as well as market actors, policymakers, and regulators. Parliament members for the first time came to us at the Ministry of the Environment saying that they wanted to play a role as lawmakers in advancing the implementation of the country's climate commitments. The key point is that parliament, ultimately Nigeria's means of representing the will of the people, wants now to be part of the solution, particularly as members sense how climate is connected to their other areas of concern, such as job creation and security.

The advance of sustainable finance should, of course, have significant, tangible impacts on Nigeria's progress toward sustainable development, including fulfillment of our climate commitments as articulated in our Nationally Determined Contribution, essentially Nigeria's climate-related commitments under the Paris Agreement. Some of these outcomes will be achieved directly through the impact of funded projects. But over time, this will be the smallest part of our overall impact. The big impacts will come through that broader shift we must make happen in Nigeria's political economy. It is inevitable and smart to move toward a low-carbon, climate-resilient, and inclusive green economy. Most of these changes will not happen simply because of anyone's consciousness of green issues—they will happen because smart businesses, investors, and politicians would not dream of doing anything else.

This is not as ambitious as it may sound to people who cannot imagine a green and inclusive Nigeria. In most parts of the world, for example, ever fewer governments or investors are using coal to build out their energy systems—green energy is simply the smart way to go given the options and likely future scenarios. Certainly, Nigeria might face more of a challenge in the short to medium term, because it still is so economically dependent on fossil fuel exports. Yet even Saudi Arabia is now set on deep-pocketed investments in a low-carbon future, beyond the country's current dependency on huge oil reserves.

One rather small green sovereign bond, or even a whole fleet of them, will of course not alone trigger the transformation needed. Yet such emblematic steps do matter. Internationally, green finance has become part of the mainstream narrative, design, and practice of financial and capital markets. Again, the numbers are still modest, but many forces are turning a side discussion into a major driver of market and nonmarket innovations. Just as Nigeria is leveraging these broader international developments, so are they being further advanced by a number of countries, regions, and financial institutions.

Such a virtuous cycle is of course what we all strive to stimulate in our work. Often such attempts flounder for many reasons, like short-term distractions, incumbent interests, failed experiments, weak leadership, and just plain bad luck. In the Nigerian case, however, the chances of success are high. Among politicians and citizens, awareness has never been greater about the imperative to protect our environment and address climate challenges. Ongoing advances in technology add favor to at least a greener outcome, if not yet one that is socially inclusive. We can see the potential of sustainable finance as a change agent. Our actions in Nigeria are amplified by, and can equally serve to amplify, the world's ongoing breakthroughs in sustainable finance.

CHAPTER FOUR

Collective Action on Business Standards, Goals, and Metrics to Achieve Scale and Impact for the SDGs

Jane Nelson

Private sector investment, innovation, and implementation capabilities will be essential to achieve the Sustainable Development Goals (SDGs). It will not be possible to reach the scale of corporate and investor engagement needed without establishing common standards, goals, and metrics for leveraging resources and comparing each market actor's contributions to sustainable development. Over the past two decades, a vanguard of pioneering companies and alliances has demonstrated the value of these joint actions. The challenge now is to make them a mainstream element of business and investment activities.

Existing efforts to implement common sustainability standards, goals, and metrics must be enhanced and spread more widely across different industry sectors and countries. They will need to become more rigorous and transparent, as well as industry relevant and broadly accepted. New models of collaboration will also be required to establish shared norms and protocols for rapidly emerging and converging science and technologies, which have enormous potential to deliver solutions to the SDGs, but these models also create ethical and social challenges.

The benefits are increasingly clear. Collective action to develop and spread common standards, goals, and metrics will enable companies, investors, regulators, customers, and other stakeholders to more effectively benchmark business performance on sustainability. Collaboration will make it easier for decision-makers to understand and compare sustainability-related risks and opportunities. In turn, this will help to shift policies, market incentives, and the allocation of capital and other resources in the direction of more inclusive and sustainable business outcomes. At the same time, greater transparency and accountability for results will help to build trust between business and other actors.

How can this be achieved in practice?

Two types of collective action will be essential for driving industrywide, issue-specific, or geographically focused sustainability standards, goals, and metrics:

—*Business coalitions and multistakeholder platforms:* Companies must work together on a noncompetitive basis to identify and overcome systemic obstacles or harness industrywide opportunities to support the SDGs. Collective action is required to achieve large-scale change, as no company can address these complex challenges alone. Companies can work together either through traditional business associations or by setting up more targeted corporate responsibility and sustainability coalitions. In many cases, these joint, business-led efforts will be more effective at driving change if they are undertaken in partnership with civil society and governments or intergovernmental agencies.

—*Collective action among financial sector institutions:* Financial institutions and intermediaries will also need to collaborate in order to drive the integration of sustainability standards, goals, and metrics into financial decision-making, asset allocation, and capital markets on a more consistent and comparable basis. Major commercial and investment banks, asset owners and managers, international finance institutions, rating agencies, and stock exchanges have a particularly important leadership role to play.

Moving from Business Pioneers to the Mainstream

Business engagement in the sustainable development agenda is not new. It has grown steadily since the 1992 UN Conference on Environment and Development, which catalyzed early leadership with a vanguard of about 100 business leaders working through the International Chamber of Commerce (ICC), the World Business Council for Sustainable Development (WBCSD), and the International Finance Corporation (IFC). These entities remain at the forefront today in mobilizing private investment and engagement in the SDGs.[1]

A growing number of business associations, corporate responsibility coalitions, and individual companies and investors are making public commitments to meet

1. The ICC's World Industry Council for the Environment and the Business Council for Sustainable Development merged in 1994 to form the World Business Council for Sustainable Development (WBCSD). WBCSD has grown in size from an original fifty business leaders at the time of the Rio Earth Summit to a CEO-led network of more than 200 of the world's major corporations, with combined revenues of U.S. $8.5 trillion in 2016 and some 19 million employees. WBCSD also has seventy national and regional business-led partner coalitions and a number of industry-specific working groups. The ICC has also increased its engagement in sustainable development and the SDGs. In December 2016, 193 members of the UN General Assembly (UNGA) granted Observer Status to the ICC. This is the first time in the UN's history that a business-led and -funded organization has been granted an official role and direct voice in the deliberations of the UNGA.

environmental, social, and governance standards and goals. Many have started to report publicly on their performance against these. About 250 to 300 companies have played a particularly important catalytic role in promoting sustainable development over the past two decades, both within their own business operations and value chains as well as through establishing dedicated business-led sustainability coalitions such as the WBCSD, among others.[2] There are now at least 300 business-led coalitions at global, regional, national, and industry sector levels (Grayson and Nelson, 2013).

Many other individual companies are starting to take action. KPMG and the Global Reporting Initiative (and others) estimate that some 7,500 companies produce annual sustainability or corporate responsibility reports in accordance with Global Reporting Initiative and other guidelines. More than 80 percent of the S&P 500 produced such reports in 2015 compared to less than 20 percent in 2011. The Dow Jones Sustainability Index (DJSI) undertakes an independent Corporate Sustainability Assessment of more than 3,400 companies every year to produce its family of sustainability-related indexes. Similar ranking and benchmarking efforts by others cover comparable numbers of companies, and several have started to harness Big Data analytics to improve their coverage and analysis of business performance. The institutional investor membership of the Principles for Responsible Investment (PRI) has reached 1,500 signatories, and corporate membership in the UN Global Compact now tops 9,000 companies, some two-thirds of them from emerging markets.

Yet, despite the progress made, the underlying challenges represented by the SDGs persist. Engagement by business to date has been too slow, superficial, and narrow to achieve the level of systemic change that is needed to transform business practices and drive markets toward more inclusive and sustainable growth. Many examples demonstrate how the individual efforts of progressive companies are undermined by their trade associations' lobbying against policies and regulations to improve environmental and social performance or by their competitors' preventing effective industrywide collaboration. In addition, the number of companies actively engaged in finding solutions represent a fraction of the more than 45,000 companies that were publicly listed on the member stock exchanges of the World Federation of Exchanges in 2016, let alone the millions of privately owned companies and small, medium, and microenterprises around the world (WFE, 2016).

2. A core group of about 250 to 300 companies has played an active role in advancing the sustainable development agenda over the past two decades, both as individual leaders (recognized by awards and ranking systems such as the Dow Jones Sustainability Index, Corporate Knights, FTSE4Good, the World Environment Center's Gold Medal Award, Fortune Magazine's "Change the World" rankings, Access to Medicines Index, Access to Nutrition Index, Behind the Brands, various UN and IFC award programs, and the ACCA Awards for sustainability reporting) and as key members of the major corporate responsibility coalitions during this period.

Likewise, investments, loans, and other products from financial institutions that explicitly measure their impact on sustainable development or that specifically target SDG-related funds or projects are still a small percentage of the estimated U.S. $135 trillion aggregate balance sheet of the banking sector globally and the approximately U.S. $100 trillion investment assets under management (BSDC, 2017b). While the signatories of the PRI collectively manage almost $50 trillion in assets, for example, at present it is estimated that less than 20 percent of these assets are explicitly managed according to environmental, social, and governance criteria or through a sustainability lens (PRI and PwC, 2017; Mace, 2017).

The core leadership challenge now is to move from the pioneers to the mainstream. This requires building on lessons learned during recent decades to markedly increase the quantity, quality, and accountability of business and investor engagement in the SDGs in order to transform markets and achieve systemic change. One of the single most important drivers of change in this direction will be the establishment of common sustainability standards, goals, and metrics.

Reforms in public policies and regulations are ultimately needed to mainstream common standards, goals, and metrics for the private sector, but companies and investors can also make substantial progress by acting on a voluntary basis. They can be particularly effective by working collectively. As co-chair of the Business and Sustainable Development Commission and CEO of Unilever, Paul Polman (2015), has commented: "Ultimately, we need system change. . . . And to achieve this change we must work in coalition."

Three interrelated areas of collective action are needed: common industry standards; shared industry goals, road maps, and financing mechanisms; and comparable and credible metrics and reporting.

Common Industry Standards

Common standards establish an agreed level of quality or attainment on key sustainability issues. They are essential for establishing consistent norms, models, and measures to facilitate comparative evaluations between different companies and industry sectors and to drive performance.[3] They include standards for business integrity and anticorruption measures, corporate respect for human rights, and environmental, social, and governance (ESG) management systems.

Implementation of common sustainability standards can range from statutory requirements to voluntary initiatives. They include legally binding operational

---

3. Definitions adapted from Oxford Dictionary (https://en.oxforddictionaries.com/definition/standard).

and reporting requirements, for example, in the areas of occupational health and safety and prevention of toxic emissions in many countries and industry sectors; consensus-based standards developed by international organizations such as the International Organization for Standardization (ISO) and various UN bodies, which may or may not become legally binding at the country level; and self-regulatory, voluntary standards and frameworks led by industry itself through trade associations and professional bodies or through multistakeholder initiatives.

Standards do not just support compliance. They support innovation. The ISO, which develops and publishes international standards, including in the area of corporate responsibility and sustainability, states, "Voluntary, consensus-based, market-relevant International Standards support innovation and provide solutions to global challenges. . . . [S]tandards underpin the technology that we rely on and ensure the quality we expect."[4]

Likewise, spreading responsible business standards is not only a case of improving risk management, "doing no harm," or mitigating the negative externalities of corporate activities. Such standards make a substantial positive contribution to the SDGs and to empowering people. As John Ruggie (2016), the former UN secretary-general's special representative for business and human rights, comments: "For business to maximize its contribution to the SDGs, it must put efforts to advance respect for human rights at the heart of the people part of sustainable development. . . . When companies drive respect for human rights across their own operations and their global value chains, they generate an unprecedented large-scale positive impact on the lives of people who may be most in need of the benefits of sustainable development."

Substantial ongoing efforts are needed to increase the uptake and spread of existing corporate responsibility and sustainability standards. Attention must also be focused on establishing additional standards as new technologies and scientific evidence, as well as growing stakeholder expectations, continue to disrupt existing business models.

Shared Industry Goals, Road Maps, and Financing Mechanisms

Setting shared goals is a second way to expand the business contribution to the SDGs. If common standards help to drive an agreed level of quality or attainment for corporate performance, ambitious industry goals or road maps for sustainable

4. The ISO is as independent, nongovernmental international organization. Standards are developed in response to market need and are based on consensus through consideration of global expert opinion and developed through a multistakeholder process, bringing together more than 160 national standard-setting bodies and more than 45,000 technical experts. To date, it has published some 21,912 international standards (www.iso.org/standards.html).

development can help to raise the bar for increasing investment, innovation, and competition that is targeted at delivering solutions for the SDGs. Goals establish a desired result or outcome that a company, sector, or system is committed to achieve. They make it easier to promote a common vision and to put targets, business plans, and incentives in place to get there, often within a defined timeframe. And they enable more rigorous benchmarking and accountability for results.

All companies and investors set individual goals for their economic and financial performance. In many cases, these are publicly disclosed. The pioneers in corporate sustainability have also started to set and publish goals for their social and environmental performance. The big opportunity now is to create incentives for many more companies to do so. One pathway is for business associations or multistakeholder initiatives to establish shared sustainability goals or road maps at the level of an entire industry or within a specific country or for a specific set of SDGs. Even if these goals or road maps are established on a collective basis, it is still possible for companies to compete with each other individually in terms of how they deliver on them in practice.

Shared goals can encourage a competitive "race to the top" by companies. They make it easier for investors, customers, employees, and other stakeholders to evaluate companies against each other. They also make it easier for public and private funders to decide where and how to allocate capital. In addition, they are important for establishing blended financial solutions that combine different sources of funding with different risk appetites in order to deliver market-based solutions for the SDGs that may not be commercially viable at the outset.

Setting industrywide goals or road maps and establishing blended financing mechanisms for the SDGs are ambitious and challenging tasks, but as the examples later in this chapter illustrate, they can be achieved. Anecdotal evidence in a number of industry sectors suggests that a relatively small group of ten to twenty leading and influential chief executive officers and companies can often catalyze broader change within an industry. Examples include public sustainability commitments made by the Consumer Goods Forum, the International Council on Mining and Metals, the New Vision for Agriculture, and the International Tourism Partnership, all of which were initially spearheaded by a small group of companies and their CEOs.

Comparable and Credible Metrics and Reporting

Companies and their stakeholders need to have a way to measure and evaluate business performance in implementing publicly committed sustainability standards and goals. Improving the quality and rigor as well as the comparability and consistency of companies' sustainability data, metrics, and reporting is essential to

—Improve corporate decision making and capital allocation;

—Strengthen the ability of investors, regulators, and other stakeholders to assess and compare the sustainability performance of companies in order to reward good practice and challenge laggards;

—Generate additional competition and innovation; and

—Increase transparency, accountability, and trust.

Over the past two decades a plethora of new initiatives have established corporate reporting standards and frameworks and researched, analyzed, and benchmarked corporate sustainability performance. In the case of research and ranking, for example, it is estimated that "at present, more than 100 sustainability raters administer questionnaires to thousands of companies worldwide, comprising a mix of investor and consumer-facing instruments ranging from issue-specific (for example, climate change) to multi-issue (integrated environmental, social, and corporate governance factors) ratings, rankings, and indices" (GISR, 2017). The number of ESG or sustainability themed indexes around the world rose from less than ten in 1993 to almost 500 in 2016 and continues to grow as more retail and institutional investors look to integrate ESG criteria into their investments.

The current diversity and inconsistency of data requests and analytical approaches are creating challenges for both companies and their investors. Individual companies, for example, can receive upward of twenty detailed questionnaires a year from different research and rating organizations, regulators, and NGOs, which vary in terms of their focus and methodology and are time consuming and costly to complete. Even when a company is clear about the ESG risks and opportunities that are most material for its own business success and most salient for the people affected by its business activities, different stakeholders often demand different types of information provided in various formats.

Investors are equally frustrated by the lack of comparability and rigor. One survey of investors found that 82 percent are not satisfied with the quality and comparability of existing corporate sustainability data (BSDC, 2017b). They argue that ESG data providers are not transparent enough about their methodologies or sources of data and are often inconsistent in terms of quality and robustness. Many investors are looking for quantitative data that they can model and compare across companies in the same way they model financial performance data. And they are looking for data that demonstrate a clear link between a company's sustainability initiatives and its ability to effectively manage risk or create value. Other stakeholders, from consumers to employees and certain investors, want to engage companies around a more qualitative set of questions and outcomes, exploring the broader systemic context and impact of a business as well as specific, measureable outcomes. They are looking for compelling stories and narrative, not only statistics and data.

The need is clear—the ecosystem of sustainability metrics, reporting, and benchmarking must become more effective and useful for all its participants. As Bloomberg (2017) summarized the challenge in its 2016 corporate sustainable impact report, there is an imperative to

align the myriad of reporting frameworks and help to address three core challenges:

—*Issuer perspective: What can be done to streamline reporting and relieve some reporting fatigue?*

—*Investor perspective: How can we move towards generating information that is investment-decision useful?*

—*Market perspective: How can we minimize "market confusion" around different reporting frameworks?*

Examples and lessons learned from existing collective action to establish common standards, goals, and metrics are outlined later in the chapter.

The Business and Investor Case for Collective Action

What is the business case for taking voluntary action on establishing common standards, goals, and metrics? Given intense competition in almost every industry sector, the impact of disruptive technologies, and pressure from most shareholders for short-term results, why should companies take action? Especially on a collective basis, which often entails high transaction costs, commitment to long-term horizons, and the need to act in a precompetitive manner.

The overarching argument is that the key megatrends driving business risks and opportunities have changed substantially over the past two decades. During this period, nonfinancial and intangible factors have become much more material to determining business reputation, costs, growth, and success. Among these, ESG or sustainability-related issues are increasingly important. They include climate-related impacts and shocks, natural resource scarcity and food insecurity, human rights abuses and grievances, unequal access to essential goods and services, political uncertainty, rising antiglobalization sentiment, demographic shifts, urbanization, changing consumer expectations and regulatory demands, and technological disruptions across a wide range of technologies and industry sectors.

Many of these issues are explicitly addressed by the seventeen SDGs. They provide, for the first time ever, a globally agreed, universally relevant, and comprehensive set of goals and targets that are as relevant for companies and investors as they are for governments, civil society organizations, and citizens. Yet they are not always written in business friendly language. More work is needed to align them to business interests and capabilities. Current public policies, market incentives, and business models often underestimate or undervalue sustainability risks to people, the environment, and business. They also underestimate or undervalue the business opportunities associated with developing new products, services, technologies, and commercially viable approaches for contributing to the SDGs.

The governance gaps and market failures are wide-ranging. They include the lack of a price on carbon and scarce water resources, weak labor rights and safety regulations in many countries, and obstacles to financing sustainable infrastructure and more inclusive business models and value chains. In many cases, companies are not legally required or incentivized to improve their sustainability performance. Although the situation is improving, there are usually inadequate market rewards, fiscal incentives, or recognition for the sustainability pioneers in business, insufficient penalties for bad performers, and weak remedies when people and the environment are negatively affected.

Companies and investors can play a vital role in overcoming some of these constraints and obstacles by working collectively, with a focus on improving risk management and business resilience, creating clearer incentives for investment and innovation, and enhancing stakeholder relationships and trust (Nelson and Prescott, 2008; BSDC, 2017a).

Improving Risk Management and Resilience

Environmental, social, and governance risks should be viewed as shared risks, both to a company and its affected stakeholders.

First, poor business performance on ESG issues or unintended consequences of new technologies create risks to people and the environment. Affected people may include those who are directly part of a company's operations as well as those along its value chain or surrounding communities, where the company may not have direct control but can still have measurable impact and influence.

Second, poor ESG performance can create risks and additional costs to the company. These can be operational, financial, reputational, and/or legal in nature. They can manifest in the immediate term, for example, in the case of an avoidable worker fatality, human rights abuse, or environmental disaster caused directly by a company's activities. Or they can evolve over the longer term, for example, as a result of climate change, water scarcity, public distrust in business, and stranded corporate assets caused by a complex and systemic combination of different companies and sectors where no one actor alone is fully responsible.

While the risks are most obvious to companies on an individual basis, there is anecdotal evidence that a sustainability-related crisis caused by an individual company can also affect the reputation and costs of other companies operating in the same industry sector or location. Working collaboratively to establish common industry standards for responsible business can help to address some of these risks. Industrywide standards can also provide stakeholders with a framework for holding companies to account, both challenging the laggards and rewarding the leaders.

Driving Incentives and Resources Toward Innovative Solutions

Collective action to set industrywide or issue- and location-specific standards and goals for sustainability can also help to drive incentives and more resources toward delivering the SDGs in ways that increase both business profits and development impact.

There are untapped opportunities for companies to create new business models, products, services, technologies, and financial instruments that can support the SDGs. This includes private sector solutions to address unmet human needs, build human capital, increase economic opportunity, improve resource efficiency, and/or strengthen environmental and social resilience—and do so in a manner that drives business productivity, cost efficiencies, new market opportunities, and ultimately brand equity and competitiveness. Examples range from circular, closed-loop production processes and industrial design to more inclusive business models that engage low-income producers, distributors, and entrepreneurs or deliver affordable products and services that meet the needs of low-income consumers.[5]

The Business and Sustainable Development Commission (BSDC) has made a compelling case for the business opportunities associated with delivering solutions to the SDGs. In its 2017 flagship report (BSDC, 2017a), the commission identified "60 sustainable and inclusive market 'hotspots' in just four key economic areas—food and agriculture, cities, energy and materials, and health and well-being—that could create at least U.S. $12 trillion by 2030 in business savings and revenue and create some 380 million jobs."

A vanguard of companies is proactively moving ahead on an individual basis to harness these business opportunities and to use sustainability as a driver of competitive advantage. Yet insufficient market incentives still prevent most companies from taking action at scale. One way to address this is for leadership companies in each industry sector or location to collaborate on setting ambitious shared goals for supporting the SDGs, but still continue to compete with each other in terms of how they develop specific business solutions to deliver these goals.

---

5. For more examples, see Nelson (2010).

Improving Stakeholder Relationships and Trust

As the Edelman Trust Barometer has shown for a number of years, trust in government and business, especially large companies, remains at a disturbingly low level in most countries and industry sectors.[6] Business leaders can start to address this challenge by increasing the level and transparency of their stakeholder engagement activities and by improving public disclosure on their sustainability performance and contributions to supporting the SDGs. Collective action to establish and then report performance against industrywide standards, goals, and metrics for respecting human rights, meeting basic needs, and creating jobs is one way to improve stakeholder relationships with business. In turn, better stakeholder relationships are essential for building trust and strengthening the social contract between business, government, and civil society.

Not surprisingly, the case for investors to take collective action on establishing common standards, goals, and metrics is similar to that of companies. This can be summarized in terms of more effective risk management, opportunities for achieving alpha, and better information to create blended finance and other innovative financing mechanisms. A report by Principles for Responsible Investment and the professional services firm PwC identified five overarching arguments in making an investment case for the SDGs. These range from their role as a definitive list of the material ESG factors that should be taken into account as part of investors' fiduciary responsibility to their growing relevance in improving the way that investors manage both macro- and micro-risks and opportunities (PRI and PwC, 2017).

In order to better understand SDG-related investment risks and opportunities, there is a strong case for investors to go beyond developing their own internal and proprietary models. They can gain valuable insights and data by also working collectively with other financial institutions and intermediaries to develop common standards, goals, and metrics for assessing company performance on a more comparable basis.

Building Effective Coalitions to Drive Scale and Impact

Given the increasingly strong business and investor case for working not only individually but also collectively to develop common sustainability standards, goals, and metrics that support the SDGs, what can we learn from existing joint efforts? The overarching message is one of untapped potential for business and financial leaders to redouble their efforts in working with their industry peers as

6. See Edelman's 2017 Annual Global Survey.

well as other stakeholders to move the agenda forward on a voluntary, consensus-based, and market-driven basis.

Coalitions to Spread Common Industry Standards

Over the past two decades, three key streams of coalition building have taken shape in developing and spreading common standards for sustainability performance by companies. All three of them continue to have a role to play in the drive toward achieving the SDGs.

First have been *cross-industry aspirational principles and frameworks*, of which the UN Global Compact is a well-known example. Other examples have included the Sullivan Principles (developed in 1977), the Caux Principles (1994), the Principles for Responsible Investment (2005), and more recently, the B Team's ten-point framework, Plan B (2013).[7] Such aspirational approaches play a valuable role in raising awareness, sharing knowledge and best practices, and creating a sense of shared understanding among companies from different industry sectors, geographies, and ownership structures.

Second has been *rigorous cross-industry performance standards and guidance*, based on extensive multistakeholder consultations and evidence-based learning. Examples include the development of the ISO 26000 international standard published in 2010, which provides guidance on how businesses and organizations can operate in a socially responsible way, as well as the earlier ISO 14001 focused on improving environmental management systems.

The IFC Performance Standards, created in 2006 and revised in 2012, are another example. Although intended specifically for banks providing project finance in developing countries, they have been incorporated into many projects and investments around the world by a variety of companies and sectors. Their model has also been adapted for other purposes. Between 2006 and 2016, they have influenced an aggregate of U.S. $4.5 trillion in financing (IFC, 2016).

A more recent example, also based on extensive multistakeholder consultation and research, is the UN Guiding Principles on Business and Human Rights endorsed by the UN Human Rights Council in 2011. In addition to providing detailed guidance to individual governments and companies on the State Duty to Protect Human Rights, the Corporate Responsibility to Respect Human Rights, and the provision of Access to Remedy, the UNGPs have spread as a result of

---

7. The ten aspirational challenges outlined in Plan B are as follows: Drive Full Transparency; Restore Nature; Create Thriving Communities; Ensure Dignity and Fairness; Value Diversity; Foster Collaboration; Scale True Accounting; Reinvent Market Incentives; Redefine Reward Systems; and Lead for the Long Run (www.bteam.org/planb).

their incorporation into the standards or guidelines of a variety of international and regional institutions and professional bodies. These include the Organization for Economic Cooperation and Development, the European Union, the Association of Southeast Asian Nations, the African Union, the G-20, the International Finance Corporation, the International Bar Association, and the Fédération Internationale de Football Association, or FIFA.

Third has been the emergence of sector-, issue-, commodity-, and/or location-specific business standards and certification frameworks. These are focused on spreading responsible business practices that are more targeted and easier to audit and benchmark. They have been particularly important in sectors with complex ESG risks and challenges such as oil, gas and mining, apparel and electronics manufacturing, food and agriculture, and travel and tourism.[8]

The results of these collective efforts at standard setting have been mixed in terms of both uptake and impact, but they offer useful guidance for the way forward. Four key lessons are relevant for increasing the scale and impact of existing initiatives and building new platforms.

First, auditing has a role to play but is not sufficient to drive sustained change at scale. Many of these initiatives have evolved from an audit-only approach to a more holistic strategy that includes audits and oversight but also focuses strongly on building the capacity of participating companies, suppliers, workers, farmers, communities, NGOs, and labor organizations, especially at the local or operational level.

Second, environmental, social, and economic issues are often interrelated and need to be addressed holistically. Many of these initiatives started with a strong focus on environmental standards and are now expanding their mandate to also incorporate human rights and social standards. This is likely to make them more comprehensive and better aligned with the SDGs.

Third, broad stakeholder engagement and local inclusion are essential. Efforts are under way to ensure these initiatives become more inclusive in terms of engaging affected people as core participants, not simply looking at them as passive beneficiaries. Some of these initiatives also engage governments in their core

8. Examples of these approaches include the Extractive Industries Transparency Initiative, the International Council on Mining and Metals, and the Voluntary Principles on Security and Human Rights in the extractive sector; the Electronic Industry Citizenship Coalition (now the Responsible Business Alliance), the Fair Labor Association, the ACCORD and Alliance initiatives in Bangladesh, the International Labor Organization's and IFC's Better Factories program, and AIM Progress in the apparel and textile sectors; and a variety of certification schemes in agriculture, forestry, and marine products. These range from sectorwide initiatives such as those supported by the Consumer Goods Forum, the Forestry and Marine Stewardship Councils, and the Sustainable Agriculture Initiative Platform to commodity-specific alliances that bring together key companies and other actors in specific commodity value chains, such as BonSucro, the World Cocoa Initiative, the Better Cotton Initiative, and the Roundtables on Sustainable Palm Oil, Beef and Soya.

governance and implementation structures, while others aim to influence government and public policy through advocacy.

Fourth, action-based goals and commitments are needed in addition to broad principles or standards. Participating companies, financial institutions, and other stakeholders must be able to demonstrate their progress, both individually and collectively, toward a shared vision for change. Accountability must move beyond "box-ticking" exercises to more interactive dialogue, shared learning, and improvement.

There is a growing trend toward more sector-, issue-, or location-specific standards, which makes sense given both the sector specificity and complexity of many sustainability issues. In all cases, however, it will be important to learn from and build on the lessons outlined above. One area of increasing importance is the establishment of common protocols and standards in the area of rapidly emerging and converging technologies, and box 4-1 outlines some evolving good practice.

Coalitions to Establish Shared Goals, Road Maps, and Financing Mechanisms

Coalitions have taken shape around specific industry sectors, development issues, and locations aimed at establishing shared goals and leveraging resources to drive business engagement in sustainable development.

Sector-Specific Collective Action. Joint efforts are under way in a number of industry sectors to use the SDGs as a framework for creating common goals and road maps as well as innovative financing mechanisms for achieving transformational sectorwide change. The Business and Sustainable Development Commission (BSDC, 2017a) has argued that

> "Business as usual" will not achieve market transformation. Nor will disruptive innovation by a few sustainable pioneers be enough to drive the shift: the whole sector has to move. Forward-looking business leaders are working with sector peers and stakeholders to map their collective route to a sustainable competitive playing field, identifying tipping points, prioritizing key technology and policy levers, developing the new skill profiles and jobs, quantifying the new financing requirements, and laying out the elements of a just transition."

Aiming to achieve systemic change of this nature is not easy. A critical mass of leaders is needed in each sector to catalyze industrywide action. As mentioned earlier, ten to twenty corporate leaders can be enough to galvanize action. Strong facilitation or backbone support is usually required to coordinate the process of identifying the biggest opportunities and barriers to change, agreeing on common solutions, goals, and metrics for progress, and then holding each other to account

Box 4-1. Collective Action to Develop Protocols and Standards for Emerging Technologies

The development and spread of new technologies offer one of the greatest opportunities for achieving the SDGs. From greater connectivity, satellite imagery, and robotics to biotechnology, blockchain, and the shared economy, there are numerous ways that science and technology can deliver solutions to the SDGs. This includes enhancing food, energy, and water security; ensuring better access to health care, education, and financial inclusion; tackling climate change; delivering greater industrial productivity and consumer choice; and creating platforms for better governance by strengthening the political voice of citizens and the accountability of policymakers and business. Yet there are also enormous challenges.

As has always been the case, new technologies have potentially negative ethical, social, and environmental impacts, which are either uncertain, unknown, or not given sufficient attention at the outset. Today, these challenges are exacerbated by the sheer speed, complexity, and scale of emerging technologies and the convergence between them. Governments must take the lead in creating enabling environments for innovation and ensuring oversight of new science and technology, but the R&D, financing, and scaling of these advances are being led mostly by the private sector. As such, companies must play an active role, both individually and collectively, in building trust in new technologies and demonstrating corporate responsibility in terms of how they are being implemented.

Some trade and industry associations are developing science and technology road maps and making public commitments to support the SDGs, while also aiming to build public trust in scientific and technological innovations. Examples include GSMA, the association for mobile operators; ESOA, the Satellite Operators Association for Europe, Middle East, and Africa; ICCA, the International Council of Chemical Associations; and IFPMA, the International Federation of Pharmaceutical Manufacturers and Associations. In 2016, Amazon, Apple, DeepMind, Facebook, Google, IBM, and Microsoft jointly established the Partnership for Artificial Intelligence, aimed at developing and sharing good practices and common principles for the responsible development and deployment of AI and advancing dialogue and public understanding.

These are a few examples of collective action by companies that are leaders in science and technology research and development. Yet obvious challenges of gaining stakeholder trust remain when only the companies that stand to benefit from commercial applications of new technologies are engaged. As such, a number of initiatives are establishing independent expert groups, civil society advisory councils, and other stakeholder engagement mechanisms to enhance transparency and accountability. One example is the Center for the Fourth Industrial Revolution. This was established in 2017 by the World Economic Forum as a hub for "global, multi-stakeholder cooperation to develop policy frameworks and advance collaborations that accelerate the benefits of science and technology."[a] Initiatives are under way to develop norms and principles in areas such as artificial intelligence and machine learning, autonomous vehicles, digital trade and cross-border data flows, and precision medicine, among others.

While still early days, platforms like this will be essential to develop the common standards, goals, and metrics that are needed to mitigate the risks and share the benefits of rapidly emerging, and often disruptive, advances in science and technology. Their success will be an important factor in determining whether or not we achieve the SDGs.

a. World Economic Forum, Center for the Fourth Industrial Revolution (www.weforum.org/center-for-the-fourth-industrial-revolution/about).

for performance against these.[9] Initial examples of using the SDGs as a framework to drive sectorwide change illustrate what is possible. They include the following:

—Food and agriculture—A number of collective initiatives are under way to establish shared goals and road maps. The challenge is to ensure that they reinforce each other rather than compete. Examples include public commitments with specific time-bound targets that have been made by the Consumer Goods Forum—a CEO-led business association with over 600 manufacturing and retail member companies—to address deforestation, the use of HFC refrigerants, food waste, forced labor, and health and wellness. Other examples are the New Vision for Agriculture, the Global Agribusiness Alliance, the Sustainable Agriculture Initiative Platform, and the Food and Land Use Coalition, which among them are mobilizing hundreds of companies alongside other development partners and commitments of billions of dollars in investment to support more inclusive, sustainable, and healthy food systems.

—Mobile technology—GSMA, which represents some 800 mobile operators, was the first industry association to produce a public report to explicitly outline the sector's contribution to the Sustainable Development Goals. It aims to "establish a benchmark through which the industry will assess its success in contributing to the SDGs and serve as a blueprint for other industries as they commit to achieving the SDGs" (GSMA, 2016). The organization's Mobile for Development initiative supports a variety of scalable mobile technology solutions aimed at improving health, agriculture, financial and digital inclusion, and disaster response.

—Textile and apparel—In 2017 more than 500 textile and apparel leaders joined forces to develop a 2030 road map for the industry at the Textile Exchange under the framework of "United by Action: Catalysing the Sustainable Development Goals in Textiles." Among other activities, the coalition has launched the Textile Exchange's Preferred Fibre Benchmark, which will track the use of sustainable materials by participating companies.

—Tourism—the International Tourism Partnership, whose members operate about 26,000 hotels around the world, made a public commitment to four industrywide sustainability goals in 2017. These have specific, time-bound targets and are explicitly aimed to contribute to the SDGs and Paris climate agreement. They are focused on youth employment, water stewardship, science-based carbon reductions, and respect for human rights.

These examples illustrate only a few sector-specific efforts under way to collectively set shared goals and develop industrywide road maps and financing

9. See the model of system leadership ("Cultivate a shared vision for change; Empower widespread innovation and action; and Enable mutual accountability for progress") presented in the report by Nelson and Jenkins (2016).

mechanisms to support the SDGs. Every industry sector and business association could undertake similar approaches.

Issue-Specific Collective Action. A number of cross-industry alliances have also emerged in recent years to pursue joint business solutions and policy objectives around specific sustainable development challenges. Some of the most successful have been in the area of tackling climate change, and they offer useful models for addressing other complex global challenges.

The We Mean Business coalition, for example, was established to provide a collective and consistent voice for business in the lead-up to the Paris climate negotiations. It consists of other business and investor coalitions, as well as almost 500 individual companies and 180 major institutional investors. Its participants make public commitments to undertake business actions and investment decisions aimed at accelerating and scaling the transition to a low-carbon economy, while also jointly advocating for specific public policies to support this transition.

We Mean Business is also active at national levels. Of particular note, the coalition has worked closely with other business and investor groups in the United States, as well as city mayors and state governors to provide a robust counteraction to the Trump administration's decision to exit the Paris Agreement. This has included the creation of multistakeholder initiatives such as the We Are Still In Coalition and America's Pledge. A report, released at the COP23 meeting in Bonn in 2017, estimated that the We Are Still In Coalition represents "more than half the U.S. economy. If it were its own country, the coalition would therefore be the world's third-largest economy" (America's Pledge, 2017).

Other cross-industry initiatives are emerging to tackle a variety of complex systemic challenges linked to the SDGs. They range from collective global initiatives to build the "circular economy," tackle deforestation, and reverse plastic pollution in oceans to improving youth employment and gender diversity.

Location-Specific Collective Action. Collective action at the country- or city-level offers enormous untapped potential to establish shared SDG goals, road maps, and financing mechanisms. Some of the examples outlined above have a strong focus on supporting country ownership and leadership, but more could be achieved in this area.

National or local chambers of commerce as well as country-level trade associations in key industry sectors could take a much stronger lead on implementing common standards and establishing shared goals and financing mechanisms for the SDGs. The World Business Council for Sustainable Development, for example, has some seventy national and regional affiliates around the world, a growing number of which are starting to mobilize the collective action of their members to more explicitly support the SDGs.

Likewise, there is untapped potential at the level of cities. The 100 Resilient Cities initiative and C40 are two notable examples where the private sector is joining forces with municipal governments and civic organizations to establish shared goals and financing mechanisms to achieve the SDGs and urban resilience.

Coalitions to Develop Comparable and Credible Metrics and Reporting

Improving the quality and rigor as well as the comparability and consistency of business sustainability data, metrics, and reporting is necessary for improving corporate and investor decisionmaking as well as other stakeholder evaluations of business. In turn, these are key to allocating more capital toward the SDGs and to increasing transparency, accountability, and trust.

Over the past two decades, there has been an evolution toward more sector- and issue-specific reporting on corporate sustainability, in line with the same trends seen in the area of standards and goals. Broad and largely aspirational cross-industry reporting frameworks led the way in the late 1990s, including updates of the OECD Guidelines on Multinational Enterprises, the creation of the UN Global Compact, the first generation of the Global Reporting Initiative (GRI), and other process-oriented accountability frameworks such as AA1000 and SA8000.

More prescriptive reporting criteria and rigorous analysis of corporate data followed, with a growing emphasis on sector-specific approaches and a strong focus on the concept of materiality, which can be defined as identifying the ESG risks and opportunities most relevant or material to a particular industry sector. These efforts have included the publication of sector-specific GRI guidance and the creation of the Sustainability Accounting Standards Board (SASB) in 2011. SASB aims to bring the same rigor to corporate sustainability reporting as the Financial Accounting Standards Board has done for corporate financial reporting since it was established in 1973. To date, SASB has developed sustainability accounting standards to cover seventy-nine industries. Both GRI and SASB have multistakeholder governance bodies and undertake extensive consultation processes with both the providers and the users of corporate sustainability reporting.

The past decade has also seen the emergence of reporting frameworks and benchmarks focused on improving corporate disclosure and accountability around specific sustainability issues. These have included CDP (formerly the Carbon Disclosure Project),[10] the Greenhouse Gas (GHG) Protocol, the Science-Based Targets

---

10. CDP tracks and analyzes carbon, water, and forest metrics from some 5,600 companies, more than 500 cities, and 100 states and regions. It has "built the most comprehensive collection of self-reported environmental data in the world, [with a] network of investors and purchasers, representing over $100 trillion in investments and a supply chain network with a combined U.S. $2.7 trillion in purchasing power" using its data (CDP, 2017a).

initiative, the UN Business and Human Rights Guiding Principles Reporting Framework, the Natural Capital Coalition, and the Natural Capital and Social Capital Protocols. These more-targeted reporting frameworks have enabled companies, investors, and other stakeholders to obtain greater depth of comparable data on a company's performance, albeit only in the specific issues covered.

The emergence of commercially driven ESG research and rating services has been another driver of sustainability reporting over the past few decades. These have become key providers of ESG data and analysis for institutional investors. Some of them are asset managers themselves, while others are independent research agencies.[11] Several provide the data that underpin well-known ESG or sustainability benchmarks and indexes, such as the Dow Jones Sustainability Index, FTSE4Good Index, MSCI ESG Indexes, STOXX Sustainability Indexes, and the more recent Solactive "Sustainable Development Goals World Index." The fact that companies have to meet certain performance criteria to be listed on these sustainability indexes provides a mechanism for investors and other stakeholders to compare companies within and across industry sectors, although there are challenges of methodology in some cases.

There have also been several NGO- and foundation-led initiatives that benchmark company sustainability performance. They include the Access to Medicines Index, the Access to Nutrition Index, and Oxfam's Behind the Brands ranking, focused on the supply chains of leading food and beverage brands.

In addition, stock exchanges around the world are establishing sustainability indexes and integrating ESG reporting criteria into their listing requirements. The Sustainable Stock Exchanges initiative was launched by five exchanges in 2009, with support from the UN. Today it includes sixty-six exchanges that have made public commitments to work with policymakers, issuers, and investors to make ESG reporting mainstream among publicly listed companies.

The growth in corporate sustainability reporting has also been driven by a number of national, state, and city governments that are implementing public disclosure requirements to increase corporate transparency and accountability on social and environmental performance. These range from an EU Directive mandating nonfinancial reporting from about 6,000 companies to mandatory disclosure requirements on specific issues. The latter range from long-standing requirements on the disclosure of the use of toxic chemicals by companies to more

11. Leading examples of rating and ranking agencies that track a universe of between 3,000 and 11,000 companies include MSCI; RobecoSAM; Trucost; Vigeo EIRIS (formerly Ethical Research Investment Services); Sustainalytics; Morningstar; Thompson Reuters Eikon; RepRisk; Solactive; Arabesque Partners; and Bloomberg's ESG <GO>, which is available on more than 320,000 Bloomberg terminals.

recent mandates aimed at tackling human rights abuses, such as the UK's Modern Slavery Act and California's Transparency in Supply Chains Act.

All of these developments represent progress from an era when companies were neither required nor motivated to publicly disclose their ESG performance—and when regulators, investors, and other stakeholders had little interest in tracking such performance. The crucial challenge now is to achieve greater standardization of business sustainability metrics and reporting frameworks. No one group can do this alone. The following four areas of collaboration among leading metrics and reporting intermediaries offer potential for progress.

Cooperation between Financial and Sustainability Reporting Standards. A relatively small group of organizations act as intermediaries for setting global standards and frameworks for both financial and sustainability reporting. There is untapped opportunity for greater coordination and, where relevant, mutual recognition between them.

One initiative with potential is the Corporate Reporting Dialogue, established in 2015 to address the challenge of standardizing sustainability reporting. It is currently an informal coalition of eight of the principal organizations charted with establishing reporting standards and guidelines, including financial reporting standards. Several are themselves multistakeholder coalitions. They are IFRS (the International Financial Reporting Standards committee of the International Accounting Standards Board [IASB]); ISO (the International Organization for Standardization); GRI (the Global Reporting Initiative); SASB (the Sustainability Accounting Standards Board); the Integrated Reporting Initiative; CDP (formerly the Climate Disclosure Project); and CDSB (the Climate Disclosure Standards Board).

Between them, these platforms already influence the reporting quality of many of the world's largest companies. Additional partners that could further strengthen the reach and influence of the group include the Financial Accounting Foundation (the home of the Financial Accounting Standards Board, FASB, and the generally accepted accounting principles, GAAP); the Financial Stability Board; the Reporting Framework for the UN Guiding Principles on Business and Human Rights; and the Global Initiative for Sustainability Ratings.

These twelve influential organizations could play a valuable role by working more closely together to establish more harmonized sustainability accounting and reporting standards and guidelines, including sector-specific materiality criteria.

Convergence on Reporting the Financial Implications of Climate Change. According to research by CDP, more than 1,400 companies are using or plan to use an internal price on carbon for their business planning and investment decision making, a number that has increased eightfold since 2014 (CDP, 2017b). Yet, corporate disclosure on climate-related business risks and opportunities is still deemed to be insufficient, especially by investors.

Research commissioned by HSBC Holdings plc. (HSBC, 2017), for example, surveyed a thousand companies and institutional investors. It found that more than 68 percent of investors intend to increase their low-carbon-related investments to accelerate the energy transition, but that 56 percent consider companies' transparency efforts in this area to be highly inadequate. Likewise, the KPMG Survey of Corporate Responsibility Reporting in 2017 found that 72 percent of large companies globally do not acknowledge the financial risks of climate change in their annual financial reports, and of those that do disclose climate-related risk, only 4 percent provide investors with an analysis of the potential financial or business impact of this risk based on scenario modeling or quantification (KPMG, 2017).

The Task Force on Climate-Related Financial Disclosures (TCFD) has the potential to facilitate a fundamental shift toward more rigorous and comparable corporate disclosure on climate risk. TCFD was established in 2015 by the Financial Stability Board to develop a disclosure framework on climate-related financial risks. The initiative was supported by a group of central bankers, leading financial institutions, responsible for managing assets worth a combined $20 trillion, and companies from diverse industry sectors, with a combined market capitalization of some $1.5 trillion. It undertook extensive research and multistakeholder consultations to develop a set of recommendations, released in June 2017, and focused on disclosures related to organizational governance, strategy, risk management, and metrics and targets (TCFD, 2017).

The goal now is to integrate the TCFD recommendations into stock exchange listing requirements, credit rating agencies, corporate governance standards, relevant government policies, and individual company and investor practices. Already coalitions of private sector leaders are making voluntary commitments based on the recommendations. For example:

—In October 2017, working through the UNEP Finance Initiative (2017), sixteen major banks committed to work together in developing industry relevant analytical tools and indicators to strengthen their assessment and disclosure of climate-related risks and opportunities.

—In September 2017, ten major European-based companies from different industry sectors jointly announced their commitment to use the recommendations to report on the implications of climate to their business model within the next three years (Harvard Law School, 2017).

—CDP disclosure requirements will be fully aligned with the recommendations by 2018 and the Climate Disclosure Standards Board (2017), a network of companies and environmental NGOs, has established a platform to help companies implement the recommendations by 2020, to provide information on a "common and comparable basis to their investors."

These initial examples of collective action, within a few months of the publication of the TCFD recommendations, illustrate the momentum that can be achieved if companies and investors work collectively toward common standards, goals, and metrics.

A Common Framework for Reporting on Business and Human Rights. Since the UN Human Rights Council unanimously endorsed the UN Guiding Principles on Business and Human Rights (UNGPs), hundreds of companies have published human rights policies, implemented due-diligence processes, established grievance mechanisms, and exercised leverage on their business partners. At the same time, the UNGPs have influenced public and private financial institutions, from export credit agencies to commercial banks and investors, as well as legal bar associations and numerous ESG rating and ranking initiatives. In 2013, for example, UBS convened a group of banks, called the Thun Group, to share good practices with each other on embedding the UNGPs into their investment and credit risk frameworks. In 2017 the Interfaith Center on Corporate Responsibility (ICCR) drew on the UNGPs to establish the Investor Alliance for Human Rights, "a collective action platform to facilitate investor advocacy on a full spectrum of human rights and labor rights issues" (ICCR, 2017). More than forty governments have also established or committed to establish National Action Plans for business and human rights.

In 2016 the UNGPs Reporting Framework was created as a reporting standard for companies to use in publicly disclosing their human rights performance and for investors, governments, and other stakeholders to use in assessing and comparing company performance. One of the key findings of the KPMG Survey of Corporate Responsibility Reporting in 2017 was that human rights are now recognized as a global business issue by 73 percent of the 4,900 companies in the sample, representing the top 100 companies by revenue in each of forty-nine countries, and by 90 percent of the world's largest 250 companies by revenue (KPMG, 2017). Although many of the respondents have yet to publish human rights policies or align their reporting to the UNGPs, this trend is likely to grow. The UNGPs Reporting Framework offers a common standard for all companies, investors, and other stakeholders to follow.

Developing Common Reporting Frameworks on Business Contributions to the SDGs. A fourth area where there is growing momentum to develop common metrics and reporting frameworks is in reporting company contributions to the SDGs. KPMG found that up to 43 percent of the companies surveyed for its 2017 report had either started to align their activities and reporting to the SDGs or were planning to do so in the future. From the investor perspective, a 2017 study by S&P Global found that 95 percent of institutional investors said they plan to engage with the companies in their portfolios about issues related to the SDGs but find the lack of a standard ESG framework continues to be a major obstacle (S&P Global, 2017).

As with climate change and human rights, several collective action platforms have been launched to develop common reporting standards and metrics to help companies publicly report their contributions to the SDGs and for investors to directly assess company performance in this area. For example, Aviva has part-nered with the Index Initiative, the UN Foundation, and the Business and Sus-tainable Development Commission, among others, with support from the Dutch, Danish, and U.K. governments, to launch the World Benchmarking Alliance. The WBA has consulted widely with companies and investors to develop a shared methodology for ranking companies within and across industry sectors on their sustainability performance and contributions to the SDGs. GRI has also worked with the UN Global Compact and PwC, among others, to produce a detailed analysis aimed at aligning existing corporate sustainability reporting frameworks with the seventeen Goals and 169 Targets of the SDGs.

These and other collective initiatives, including new indexes that are focused specifically on tracking business performance on supporting the SDGs, are still at an early stage. They are likely to grow in importance, alongside the efforts to develop common approaches to reporting on the financial impacts of climate change and the corporate responsibility to respect human rights.

Conclusion and Recommendations

This chapter has argued that the world will not be able to achieve the SDGs with-out increasing the quantity, quality, and accountability of business and investor engagement. The development and spread of common sustainability standards, goals, and metrics will be essential to accelerating and scaling this private sector engagement.

There is an urgent challenge to move beyond the pioneers to ensure that sus-tainability criteria are embedded into the core business strategies and practices of all companies, alongside financial and operational goals. While a vanguard of leaders is active in almost every industry sector, there are few industries where business leadership on the SDGs is widespread. The development of common standards, goals, and metrics can help to overcome some of the market failures, governance gaps, and trust deficits that impede the progress of individual com-panies toward more inclusive and sustainable growth. Collective action and new models of partnership among companies and between business, government, and civil society will be needed to make these common standards, goals, and metrics a reality.

Leadership will be especially important in the following three areas.

Personal Leadership Is Essential

Individual business leaders must continue to focus on improving and disclosing sustainability performance within their own companies and in requiring and supporting their suppliers and business partners along their global value chains to do likewise. In addition, they can be champions for collective action and strong advocates for policy reforms and market transitions in the industry sectors and countries where they operate. This requires sustained commitment. Building nontraditional partnerships to tackle complex challenges and achieve systemic change is difficult, time consuming, and often costly. Senior executives must balance demands they face for short-term performance with a long-term commitment to making such coalitions work.

Sector or Issue-Specific Business Coalitions Offer Great Potential

Business coalitions are most likely to be effective within specific industry sectors or targeted at addressing specific sets of sustainability challenges. There are untapped opportunities for representative trade and industry associations as well as corporate responsibility coalitions to set common standards, goals, and metrics to support the SDGs that are most material and salient to their sector, while recognizing and managing the linkages between all the SDGs. And there are enough existing examples to demonstrate that these joint efforts can work in practice.

Collective action is needed in all industry sectors, but financial institutions and capital market intermediaries have a vital leadership role to play. Ultimately, progress will be insufficient unless the financial institutions that lend to, invest in, and insure companies integrate ESG criteria into all their due-diligence, decision-making, and evaluation processes. The intermediaries that provide the architecture for well-functioning markets must do likewise, ranging from standard-setting bodies, rating agencies, and stock exchanges to business associations and the business media.

Country-Level and City Platforms Are Key for Implementation

To achieve scale, governments at both national and local levels must implement policies, regulations, and incentives to drive the integration of ESG criteria into business and financial market activities. There is untapped potential for policymakers to work collectively with domestic and foreign companies and investors, local business associations, and civil society organizations to agree on common standards, goals, and metrics for achieving the SDGs and then to establish mechanisms to hold each other to account for their delivery. It is only through this collective action at the operational level, focused on implementation on the ground, that the ambitious commitments made at global summits will be translated into national and local solutions. Giving the private sector a seat at the table, alongside civil society, will be essential to achieving results.

References

America's Pledge. 2017. "America's Pledge Phase 1 Report: States, Cities, and Business in the United States Are Stepping Up on Climate Action." November.

Bloomberg. 2017. "Our Bottom Line Is Impact: 2016 Impact Report." New York.

BSDC (Business and Sustainable Development Commission). 2017a. "Better Business Better World: The Report of the Business and Sustainable Development Commission." London.

———. 2017b. "Ideas for Action for a Long-Term and Sustainable Financial System." London.

CDP (Climate Disclosure Project). 2017a. About Us (www.cdp.net/en/info/about-us).

———. 2017b. "Putting a Price on Carbon: Integrating Climate Risk into Business Planning."

Climate Disclosure Standards Board. 2017. Commit to Implement the Recommendations of the Task Force on Climate-Related Financial Disclosures (www.cdsb.net/commit-implement-recommendations-task-force-climate-related-financial-disclosures).

GISR (Global Initiative for Sustainability Ratings). 2017. *Why GISR* (http://ratesustainability.org/about/why-gisr/).

Grayson, David, and Jane Nelson. 2013. *Corporate Responsibility Coalitions: The past, present and future of alliances for sustainable capitalism.* Greenleaf Publishing and Stanford University Press.

GSMA. 2016. "2016 Mobile Industry Impact Report: Sustainable Development Goals." London.

Harvard Law School. 2017. "FSB TCFD Guidance on Climate-Related Financial Disclosures: Regulatory and Market Responses." Forum on Corporate Governance and Financial Regulation. Cambridge, Mass. (https://corpgov.law.harvard.edu/2017/10/30/fsb-guidance-on-climate-related-financial-disclosures-regulatory-and-market-responses/).

HSBC Holdings plc. 2017. Growing Investor Appetite for Green Assets Puts Pressure on Companies to Explain Their Climate Strategies. News release. September 12. London.

ICCR (Interfaith Center on Corporate Responsibility). 2017. ICCR Launches New Alliance to Amplify Global Investor Influence on Human Rights (www.iccr.org/iccr-launches-new-alliance-amplify-global-investor-influence-human-rights).

IFC (International Finance Corporation). 2016. "Sustainability Is Opportunity: How IFC Changed Finance." November (www.ifc.org/wps/wcm/connect/news_ext_content/ifc_external_corporate_site/news+and+events/news/impact-stories/how-ifc-has-changed-finance).

KPMG. 2017. The Road Ahead: The KPMG Survey of Corporate Responsibility Reporting 2017.

Mace, Matt. 2017. Investors urged to engage with Sustainable Development Goals. *Edie Newsroom*. October 26 (www.edie.net/news/7/Investors-urged-to-engage-with-Sustainable-Development-Goals/).

Nelson, Jane, and Beth Jenkins. 2016. "Tackling Global Challenges: Lessons in System Leadership from the World Economic Forum's New Vision for Agriculture Initiative." Corporate Responsibility Initiative, Harvard Kennedy School. Cambridge, Mass.

Nelson, Jane, and Dave Prescott. 2008. *Business and the Millennium Development Goals: A Framework for Action*. UNDP and International Business Leaders Forum. New York and London.

Nelson, Jane. 2010. "Expanding Opportunity and Access: Approaches That Harness Markets and the Private Sector to Create Business Value and Development Impact." Corporate Responsibility Initiative, Harvard Kennedy School. Cambridge, Mass.

———. 2017. "Partnerships for Sustainable Development: Collective Action by Business, Governments and Civil Society to Achieve Scale and Transform Markets." Report commissioned by the Business and Sustainable Development Commission. Corporate Responsibility Initiative, Harvard Kennedy School. Cambridge, Mass.

Polman, Paul. 2015. Speech to the UN Global Compact Summit, UN General Assembly, New York. June 25.

PRI (Principles for Responsible Investment) and PwC. 2017. The SDG Investment Case. New York.

Ruggie, John G. 2016. Keynote address at the United Nations Forum on Business and Human Rights. Geneva. November 14 (www.ohchr.org/Documents/Issues/Business/ForumSession5/Statements/JohnRuggie.pdf).

S&P Global. 2017. A Standard ESG Framework Is Key to Unleashing Markets' Responsible Growth. New York.

TCFD (Task Force on Climate-Related Financial Disclosures). 2017. "Final Report: Recommendations of the Task Force on Climate-Related Finance Disclosures" (www.fsb-tcfd.org/publications/final-recommendations-report/).

UNEP Finance Initiative. 2017. "Updated: 16 UNEP FI Member Banks Representing Many Trillions of Dollars Are First in Industry to Jointly Pilot the TCFD Recommendations (www.unepfi.org/news/industries/banking/eleven-unep-fi-member-banks-representing-over-7-trillion-are-first-in-industry-to-jointly-pilot-the-tcfd-recommendations/).

WFE (World Federation of Exchanges). 2016. Annual Statistics Guide (www.world-exchanges.org/home/index.php/statistics/annual-statistics).

CHAPTER FIVE

Professionalizing Cross-Sector Collaboration to Implement the SDGs

Ann Florini

Partnership across business, government, and civil society, as SDG 17 tells us, is key to implementing all of the goals—so it is time to start teaching people how to partner.

Although cross-sector collaborations have a substantial history, they have yet to live up to the promise or the expectations for large-scale problem solving. They fall short not merely due to inadequate financial resources but even more because of the paucity of professionals with the skills to organize, manage, lead, and scale these collaborations. The necessary skills are not generally acquired in traditional graduate or professional education. Thus efforts to improve such professional training through university programs and in other settings are critical to the success of the SDGs. As this chapter shows, a number of universities, NGOs (nongovernmental organizations), and consultancies are already experimenting with such programs. Now many more such groups should step forward. Countries will need innovative approaches to train leaders so that they have the requisite skills to make SDG-focused cross-sector collaborations succeed.

SDG 17 calls on the world to "strengthen the means of implementation and revitalize the global partnership for sustainable development." There are two specific targets under the subhead of "multistakeholder partnerships":

17.16: Enhance the global partnership for sustainable development, complemented by multistakeholder partnerships that mobilize and share knowledge, expertise, technology, and financial resources, to support the achievement of the sustainable development goals in all countries, in particular developing countries

17.17: Encourage and promote effective public, public-private, and civil society partnerships, building on the experience and resourcing strategies of partnerships.

The author is grateful to Jenny Costelloe for excellent assistance with this article.

This call for collaboration builds on a decades-old trend toward involving diverse sectors in large-scale initiatives to solve large-scale social problems, variously called multistakeholder initiatives (MSIs), trisector collaboration, and a host of other terms.[1] The trend reflects a norm evolution in the international system, as reflected in the language of Agenda 21 of the 1992 UN Conference on Environment and Development, the emphasis on partnerships in the 2002 World Summit on Sustainable Development, and on through the SDGs themselves. It also reflects a much broader set of changes in how global governance is conceived and practiced, involving nonstate actors working with governments or sometimes governing without the involvement of governments (Florini, 2005, 2014).

MSIs are deemed better able to deal with complex, "wicked" issues than the slow formal negotiations of the interstate system. At their best, it is argued, cross-sector collaborations can be flexible, open, innovative, and can combine the legitimacy and coercive power of government with the resources and managerial acumen of the private sector and the expertise and local access of civil society to solve problems that no sector can manage on its own. Already, collaborations play key governance roles that are clearly essential to SDG achievement: providing transnational business regulation in the absence of a coherent intergovernmental process able to do so (Abbott, Green, and Keohane, 2016); bolstering more effective, accountable, and inclusive national public governance (Brockmyer and Fox, 2015); and delivering basic services (Beisheim and others, 2014).

But evidence to date suggests that expectations have outpaced performance by a considerable margin. It is much easier to declare partnership than to get anything done. As one recent study shows, even on the lowest of standards—producing any relevant output at all—many of the collaborations officially registered with the United Nations have little to show for themselves (Pattberg and Widerberg, 2016, p. 44):

> First, on analyzing the sample of 340 partnerships after more than five years since inception, approximately 38 percent show low levels or no measurable output. Moreover, roughly 42 percent (86) of the partnerships with measurable output engage in activities without direct relation to their publicly

---

1. These include the "type 2 partnerships" that emerged at the UN's World Summit on Sustainable Development in Johannesburg in 2002, which were explicitly intended to complement "Type 1" intergovernmental outcomes and agreements in pursuit of the Johannesburg agenda (LaViña, Hoff, and DeRose, 2003). But the phenomenon goes far beyond the few hundred partnerships that emerged from the WSSD to include a vast array of what are variously termed polygovernance models (World Economic Forum, 2016), multistakeholder governance (Stanley Foundation, 2016a), cooperative multistakeholder action (Stanley Foundation, 2016b), global action networks (Waddell, 2011), global public policy networks (Reinicke, 1999–2000), public-private partnerships (Brinkerhoff and Brinkerhoff, 2011), collaborative governance (Zadek, 2006), and more.

stated goals and ambitions. . . . Summing up, of these numbers, 211 partnerships are inactive, lack any outputs, or fail to match their stated ambition with their observed activities.

Other assessments have reported similar results, with some collaborations
undertaking activities that lead to achieving significant outcomes but others failing to do much of anything (Beisheim and Leise, 2014; Beisheim and others,
2014). A few MSIs succeed in moving the world ahead significantly—GAVI's
success in vaccinating millions of children is a frequently cited case that reveals
the potential of the approach. Overall, however, despite what now amounts to
extensive experience, cross-sector collaborations continue to struggle, with many
failing outright and most falling short of their potential.

The abundant literature now provides scores of recommendations to improve
the performance of cross-sector collaborations (Pattberg and Widerburg, 2016;
Beisheim and others, 2014; Brockmyer and Fox, 2015). But these recommendations are strikingly impersonal, focused on structures rather than specific agents
and their capabilities. Glasbergen (2010, p. 131), for example, refers to the need
for "specific management capabilities, which we relate to emotional and transactional aspects of networking and the capacity to create an enabling environment."
He notes that effective action networks require initial "brokers" to create shared
vision and "entrepreneurs" to build the requisite organizational capacity (pp. 139–
40). But there is no mention of what kinds of knowledge and skills the individuals
in these roles need to have. Similarly, Pattberg and Widerburg's (2016, p. 47) list
of nine conditions required for partnership success include "leadership," but they
confine themselves to a vague call:

> While good leadership is recognized as an important feature of successful
> partnerships, it remains difficult to operationalize. Most observers simply
> note that leadership is essential yet provide little information on the condi-
> tions for effective leadership and means to foster it. Nevertheless, it remains
> critical to identify and manage the different types of leadership needed for
> the partnership to succeed.

It is past time to answer that urgent need to understand what is required of
MSI leadership and to foster the capacities of those leaders. As has been repeatedly
recognized, reaching the SDG targets truly does require contributions from all
sectors, working together. The traditional providers of public goods and collective action—governments and the intergovernmental organizations they create—
are under extreme stress and lack resources. The world needs a broader fount of
diverse, innovative solutions, with concomitant diversity of skill sets and resources.

All organizations and institutions ultimately depend in significant part on the competence and intentions of key people. This is more true of MSIs than of more formalized single-sector organizations, as MSIs have few routinized processes or deep institutional ecosystems to draw on. Nonetheless, cross-sector collaboration to achieve societal goals continues to be treated as something anyone can do just by convening stakeholders.

In reality, partnering is a challenging undertaking, requiring deep knowledge and concrete skills that differ from what is usually taught in business and public policy schools. It requires specific kinds of informed leadership and specific approaches to facilitation and management. To make good use of the call in SDG 17 for "multi-stakeholder partnerships that mobilize and share knowledge, expertise, technology, and financial resources" to implement the SDGs, it is imperative to professionalize the practice of cross-sector partnership.

Lessons from Experience: Three Stories

Just as the variety of governance failures and market failures need different types of responses, so too do a variety of collaboration failures, which can be addressed by people knowledgeable and skilled in cross-sector collaboration.

Education and Health

Perhaps the most common cause of partnership breakdown is simple incomprehension across the sectors, given their very different training, incentives, legal structures, and mind-sets. One partnership in India between a multinational snack food company and an international NGO provides a small-scale but telling example. The intended collaboration should have contributed to the education and health SDGs, but fell into conflict and faded away without accomplishing much.

The two organizations had informally agreed to collaborate to achieve education and health goals by delivering an awareness-raising campaign in schools via an interactive exhibition in a converted bus. The company was to provide financial support and the NGO would design and implement the awareness-raising campaign. No written Memorandum of Understanding or other clarification of roles and responsibilities was in place.

Once activities got under way, however, it became clear that each party had unspoken expectations that reflected deep misunderstandings about the other's operations and motivations. The company, it turned out, primarily wanted publicity for its brand and opportunities for employee volunteering aligned with the firm's corporate social responsibility (CSR) strategy (a philanthropic strategy not well connected to the company's core business). It expected the NGO to provide the equivalent of PR services, such as by displaying the company logo on the bus. The NGO, for its part, was focused on the education and health campaign to raise issue awareness in the schools. It had neither interest in nor capacity for brand-building publicity, and it was uncomfortable with displaying the logo of a large snack-food business whose products were not compatible with the goals of the campaign. The NGO was happy to receive the funding but had not thought that anyone would need to know who funded the project.

Furthermore, the company asked the NGO to organize volunteering opportunities for its employees. This is a common request in partnerships from private firms wanting to foster "employee engagement" and one that NGOs and other partners often dread. Managing unneeded volunteers with no relevant skills constitutes a significant drain on NGO management resources.

Matters came to a head when the company wanted the NGO to organize a ribbon-cutting event for senior leaders and the media to attend, which the NGO was unwilling to do. The partnership had reached the point of breakdown.

Eventually an external mediator was engaged to help (paid for by the company). In separate conversations with the company and the NGO, the mediator uncovered the fundamental misconceptions in both partners of what role the other partner could—and "should"—be playing. The mediator challenged these assumptions and educated the partners on the other sector's role, guiding the partners toward a renewed understanding and a refreshed commitment to the project. After mediation, the bus project was successfully completed but not repeated. The two organizations had lost trust in one another—but not in the idea of partnership, as each went on to partner with different companies and NGOs.

Of course, some companies—or individuals within companies—attempt more sophisticated types of partnerships with a broader conception of the firm's role in contributing to the provision of public goods. But they find it hard. Firms exist to optimize, to set up systems to do a small number of things very efficiently. That organizational mind-set struggles when confronted with the much more complex problems involved in achieving significant social change. Another small but telling example follows.

Women's Empowerment

In 2012 the global beverage alcohol company Diageo launched a strategy to deliver women's empowerment in seventeen countries in the Asia-Pacific region. The company, regarded as a leader in employee diversity, believed that gender equity was both aligned to its corporate culture and necessary for economic prosperity in the countries where the firm operated. However, as Diageo began looking at how it might empower women, company staff began to see that the reasons for inequality are far more complex than they had understood and that the company could not possibly address all the relevant issues: cultural norms, religious beliefs, legal frameworks, political freedom, access to education, mobility, traditional roles in the home, access to finance, health care, and so on. Nor was it easy for the company to develop a strategy that could account for wide variations across countries and localities (in Sri Lanka, for example, it is not customary for women to handle money, which inhibits them from working in roles that require them to handle cash, while in parts of Indonesia, women often manage the money at a household level, but may not qualify for a bank account or credit). How could one company address this complex, systemic problem of discrimination of women across all seventeen countries?

The answer was to develop localized activities to address specific dimensions, through partnerships with NGOs and trusted local organizations. All of these were under the rubric of the Plan W strategy and built on four key focus areas in which the company has greatest influence: within the company, in the hospitality industry, in the communities where they operate, and among consumers. Notably, the implementation of Plan W was driven by a company employee who was one of the first participants in the Master's of Tri-Sector Collaboration at Singapore Management University (described below).

To address both the industrywide and community angles, Diageo collaborated with CARE International in a global strategic partnership that CARE was able to customize to address specific barriers in specific places. In Sri Lanka, the partnership led to a "Skills for Youth" training program for the rapidly growing hospitality industry, with a focus on young women. In addition to hospitality-sector skills training leading to a recognized certificate, participants also went through a Life Skills Program that covered everything from time and financial management to gender sensitivity. Diageo thus combined its self-interest in an expanded hospitality industry with a contribution toward gender equity (SDG 5) and decent work (SDG 8). As of the end of 2016, the program had trained over 600 youth, most of whom found relevant jobs.

A Plan W community project, also done with CARE, initially looked like a fairly standard development project, an initiative to teach Dalit women in India how to develop small enterprises to sell their farm produce. Unusually, however, the company stuck with the project over several years, and the project focus expanded over time. The women first received training to improve their self-esteem and address the apprehension that they felt about going to market with their produce, then to manage a business out of growing vegetables. As the success of the project became evident, CARE International and the community leaders began a dialogue with local government officials. Eventually, legislation prohibiting Dalit people from owning land in the area of the project was revised, affording this marginalized community the right to own the land on which they had worked for generations. Thus what started as a small bit of philanthropy turned into a cross-sector collaboration involving the local community and local government as well as the multinational company and the international NGO. This range of collaborations has now evolved into a five-year global strategic partnership between Diageo and CARE focusing on research, programs, and advocacy projects intended to deliver a sustainable and holistic impact on gender equality.

Food and Agriculture

Our third story picks up what has become a common theme for larger-scale collaborations: reliance on a professional "platform" or secretariat to coordinate and often guide the collaborators. The World Economic Forum's Shaping the Future of Food Security and Agriculture System initiative includes an action platform known as the New Vision for Agriculture (NVA). The NVA was established in 2009 to improve food security, environmental sustainability of food production, and economic opportunity, each by 20 percent by 2030. To achieve this goal, a transformation of the agriculture sector was deemed essential and would be obtained through multistakeholder partnerships. A core staff of World Economic Forum (WEF) employees dedicated to the initiative created and built a global network of stakeholders from almost 600 organizations engaged in activities that support the NVA goals. These stakeholders hail from the private sector (not just WEF member companies), civil society, and governments from twenty-one countries.

Within the NVA family are two spinoff platforms: Grow Africa and Grow Asia. We focus here on Grow Asia as a regional entity, and on the Indonesia network within the Grow Asia family.

At the regional level, the Grow Asia platform is a partnership with the ASEAN Secretariat, affording it an unusual degree of immediate legitimacy with governments.[2] Its overarching goals are to reduce greenhouse gas emissions by 20 percent, reduce poverty among smallholder farmers by 20 percent, and increase farm yields by 20 percent, all by incorporating smallholder farmers into agribusiness value chains. Its founding staff, although small, included practitioners with deep experience in business and in development, including donor agencies. That depth of cross-sector experience helps to explain the well-thought-out governing structure, which includes separate councils for business and civil society, tied together under a steering committee with representation from both councils, the ASEAN Secretariat, donors, farmer associations, and the WEF. And even so, those

2. Note that information in this section refers to the original staff of Grow Asia, as significant staff changes occurred in 2017.

founding staff speak of an intense learning curve as each learned to understand more deeply—not least from one another—the vernacular, habits, and practices of the sectors in which they had not previously worked.

Most of the work within the Grow Asia umbrella is carried out at the national level in the five Southeast Asian countries where Grow Asia operates: Cambodia, Indonesia, Myanmar, the Philippines, and Vietnam. To take perhaps the most institutionalized case, the Partnership for Indonesia's Sustainable Agriculture, or PISAgro,[3] was set up in 2010 (before the Grow Asia platform but since incorporated) to simultaneously achieve sustainable development goals and business goals in the Indonesian agriculture sector. At the outset, there was clear leadership from several local and multinational businesses and strong support from four government ministries. However, the founding committee had the foresight to recognize that such momentum would be difficult to maintain, and it created a transparent governance model that allows for changes in personnel and encourages rotation of members. PISAgro's governance has been tested over the years, with changes in the leadership of businesses and government agencies, an influx of new members, and given the usual personality issues in MSIs. Like the regional body and most Grow Asia–affiliated national groups, PISAgro has a small professional secretariat with three staff and is funded by membership fees.

What such cases demonstrate clearly— and hundreds more are documented in the academic literature—is that among many other factors, successful collaborations to achieve societal goals need people with partnership expertise. These people may be external mediators, internal staff "intrapreneurs," or platforms/ secretariats staffed by experienced professionals.

As collaboration moves from "flavor of the month" to a more widely accepted means for businesses, governments, and social groups to solve their problems, and as people discover that collaboration does not just happen, some employers are starting to seek people with extensive partnership expertise and cross-sector experience. Many larger cross-sector collaborations are driven from the top down, by leaders from one or more sectors who come together to agree that they should work together in a given issue area. In the best of such collaborations, the leaders understand the enlightened self-interest that, for example, spurs soft drink companies to help protect watersheds or agribusinesses to bolster smallholder farmer incomes in their supply chains. That enlightenment, however, often fails to trickle down to the operational levels charged with implementing projects on the ground. Employees at that level focus primarily on shorter-term business incentives, not longer-term sustainability of the business model, in part because

---

3. See more about PISAgro at www.pisagro.org/. Its launch was announced at the World Economic Forum in East Asia, 2011.

they do not understand the broader issues and in part because they are strongly incentivized to concentrate on conventional business metrics.

The executive director of a trade association in Asia, for example, noted that in hiring people to work on partnerships, he needed to prioritize experience in more than one sector over technical ability. He found that the capacity to understand and "speak the language of more than one sector" was crucial, and that technical knowledge could be learned later. But when candidates were "die-hard private sector" and "immovable NGO-types," they "just can't put themselves in each other's shoes."

But there are not enough such people currently available to foster the emergence of cross-sector collaborations at the scale needed to implement the SDGs in the years remaining to 2030. Without training and education programs at scale to shortcut the years of cross-sector experience that successful collaborative governance practitioners to date have needed, it is hard to see how the cross-sector approach to governance can begin to live up to its potential.

What Partnership Professionals Need to Know: The "Tradecraft of Shared Discretion"

Most efforts to date to train people to develop and manage MSIs focus on partnership nuts-and-bolts: how to identify and engage stakeholders, what the memorandum of understanding among participating organizations should look like, what steps should be taken to keep moving along the "partnering cycle." All of this, what Donahue and Zeckhauser (2011, p. 5) call the "tradecraft of shared discretion" in collaborative governance, is indeed necessary. But it is not enough.

Even practitioners who have been successful in a given collaboration may not have the broader knowledge needed to ensure that the SDGs are implemented as a holistic package. Successful implementation of Agenda 2030 requires that efforts to achieve any one of the goals not undermine efforts toward the others. Even experience with an abundance of ad hoc experiments with cross-sector collaborations does not provide the systemic overview and understanding of complex systems needed in the new profession of partnership to implement the SDGs.

In addition to the lessons learned from the extensive academic literature, the following draws on hundreds of conversations with practitioners over the past decade, especially in the context of designing what appears to be the world's only master's degree program dedicated to professionalizing the practice of partnership: the Master's of Tri-Sector Collaboration (MTSC) at Singapore Management University. These conversations with leaders in all sectors, primarily in Asia, Europe, and North America, were designed to elucidate what skills and knowledge are most needed in such education programs.

From all this, I suggest that the knowledge and skills that can and should be taught should ensure that partnership professionals can do the following:

1. Understand the very different mind-sets, incentives, and operating practices of each sector in its specific political economy given the varied roles played by different sectors in different countries and regions;

2. Have a broad overview of the state of the world, including a holistic framework for understanding the SDGs and the interactions among the various targets, to ensure that efforts focused on a specific SDG target or goal are not harmful to the achievement of other targets or goals;

3. Understand complex systems and the unpredictability and nonlinearity with which global trends are unfolding;

4. Know how to measure and report on the achievements—or failures—of a given collaboration in ways that are meaning to all stakeholders, including those concerned with the ultimate impact on, for example, achievement of the SDGs;

5. Possess specific skills, beyond standard facilitation, on how to bring together extremely diverse and often mutually distrustful groups to align their efforts. Such skills include knowledge of useful institutional mechanisms for governance and longevity of partnerships, techniques for encouraging the development of a shared vision and a partnership mind-set, and so on.

Understanding Each Sector

Most people spend their careers primarily in one sector: in for-profit, nonprofit, or government settings. In some cultures, such as the United States, cross-sector experience is a bit more common, although even there it is rare to find people with deep understanding of all three. Not only are business, government, and civil society usually ignorant about each other, they often have a history of hostility and distrust between the sectors. That distrust is based in part on what may be fundamental differences in objectives and goals, and in part on deeply institutionalized modes of thinking that can be sharply at odds and create significant misunderstandings. Government officials, for example, often see "partnership" as meaning "delegation," with government remaining in charge, rather than a collaborative co-creation. Even the basic vocabulary is specialized to each sector, so that people literally do not understand one another across the sectoral divide. A development agency (donor or NGO) may want to collaborate around a "theory of change," while the business participants come in talking about "value propositions" and "customer funnels."

Professional training for these different career paths reflects, and fosters, these fundamental differences and misunderstandings. Business schools teach little about governments or nonprofits, and public policy schools focus almost exclusively on government. Both are constrained by accreditation processes that require that they continue to do what they have done before, and an academic culture in which faculty are rewarded primarily for publishing in journals that also have a heavy bias in favor of existing academic siloes.

This siloed approach to study and career paths creates a pipeline of people who can be very good at working in one sector, while having almost no understanding of the vernacular, constraints, legal frameworks, and metrics that drive the behavior of the others. The predictable results unfold time after time, as the case of the Indian partnership demonstrated. Hundreds of conversations with leaders from each sector, primarily in Asia, Europe, and North America, have revealed similar patterns of intersectoral incomprehension.

This is a solvable problem. The basic concepts, vocabulary, mind-sets, and incentive structures in each sector can be fairly readily explained, whether in a short training, an intensive week-long module, or a university semester course. This is the most basic element for improving the success rate of cross-sector collaborations, akin to providing interpreters for international negotiations. But, as the Indian example demonstrated, cross-sector "interpreters" also need to be able to explain the underlying incentive structures and frameworks of each sector to the others. Such explanation makes it possible for all participants to comprehend from the beginning what can reasonably be expected from the other participants.

The Political Economy of Partnerships

Beyond the basics, practitioners need to understand more deeply the political economy of the region in which they are working. States and markets operate very differently in different parts of the world. Academic literature on "varieties of capitalism" has explored some of these differences, but not in a way readily available to practitioners. So another part of deep training in collaborative governance needs to include a focus on regional and national political economy.

Such training would dig more deeply into the specific nature of each sector in each country or region. Governments that are democratic and representative face somewhat different incentives and may have different time frames (tied to electoral cycles) than those that are more authoritarian. The private sector varies even more dramatically and may have different forms of power (Ruggie, 2017). Most research on partnerships assumes the standard Western (and especially Anglo-American) model of publicly traded corporations with a heavy focus on relatively short-term fluctuations in share prices—not useful when working in Southeast Asia with its enormous family-held conglomerates or in China with its many state-owned enterprises. Civil society organizations abound in India and the Philippines but are severely constrained in China and Russia.

Here academia can readily be of help. Political economy is taught in most political science and/or economics programs. With such training, a partnership professional would be equipped to navigate the specifics of a given country. Such training can shortcut the extensive in-country experience and detailed personal knowledge that most successful national-level cross-sector collaborations have depended on to date, enabling many more collaborations to address the scale of the SDG challenge.

The View from 30,000 Feet: Understanding the Whole of the SDGs

A partnership professional's education needs to address a broad range of trends. Power is flowing away from traditional governors, but not necessarily toward any well-structured institutions that can reliably set rules for the changing global order. Hurricanes, typhoons, floods, and droughts provide regular and deadly reminders of shifting climate patterns that exacerbate looming resource shortages in food and water. Social unrest is rising as inequality soars, and no one is sure where the jobs of the future will come from. Technology is upending the nature of human interaction and quite possibly the nature of human beings. New technologies sometimes bring us closer together, collapsing the tyrannies of distance, time, and cost: people are able to collaborate remotely, instantaneously, and, often, for free; policymaking is more responsive and timely, addressing events as they happen; and, as "the next billion" citizens are brought online, financial and social inclusion make the alleviation of poverty and disease ever more feasible. But at the same time, social and economic gaps are increasing. In countries where technology gains are the most prevalent, social mobility is often *decreasing*. Moreover, new technologies challenge a society's ability to reap the benefits they offer because of their disruptive impact; policymakers all too often are challenged by the speed of change, struggling to keep up with trends, let alone being able to create forward-looking frameworks that would enable a society and economy to benefit and grow.[4]

All of this can be taught, and elements exist in a number of sustainability-focused programs. But those elements are rarely part of the professional training of the people who find themselves leading MSIs. Those who wish to help implement the SDGs need to understand them as they were designed: a holistic approach to global transformation, not a set of unconnected targets. To have that holistic mind-set requires an understanding of the broader global trends underlying the problems that the SDGs are intended to correct. Without such an understanding, partnership professionals can too easily fall into the trap of creating a

---

4. This description of relevant technology trends is adapted with permission from Peter Lovelock.

collaboration that contributes to one target but undermines others and can be blindsided by unexpected developments.

A key mind-set shift required for successful collaborations that aim at significant societal change is to move from traditional, linear policy thinking to a deeper understanding of complexity and its associated phenomena: nonlinear change, tipping points, and the propensity of diverse systems to be more resilient than "efficient" but fragile systems (Colander and Kupers, 2014). Formal policy analysis and design assumes that the best way to solve a problem is to know as much as possible about it and then design a solution based on what seems to be a reasonable forecast for the future. The massive amount of work in the past few decades on complex adaptive systems demonstrates convincingly that the types of transformations the SDGs seek do not lend themselves to such approaches but instead require a much more experimental approach, involving a much wider range of actors. Indeed, part of the rationale for cross-sector collaboration as a key mechanism for SDG implementation is the need for such massive experimentation.

Once again, academia can be of help, drawing on the growing literature on the application of complexity theory to policy (Colander and Kupers, 2014) to design courses that introduce the complex adaptive systems mind-set for partnership practitioners. Specifically, practitioners benefit from understanding how and under what conditions to apply experimental approaches to problem solving.

Metrics

Metrics and measurement are currently the Achilles heel of cross-sector collaboration. The metrics to assess sustainability and partnerships are still at best in development. As organizations in all three sectors experience a major push for enhancing social and environmental sustainability, often by means of cross-sector partnerships, a plethora of often-competing standards, metrics, and reporting requirements are emerging that purport to enable appropriate measurement and accountability of such factors as social and natural capital. There is even less agreement on how to measure the contribution of cross-sector collaborations (World Vision International, 2015).

Partnership professionals need to be aware of the frameworks in use and the debates among them and need to be able to keep up with the rapidly changing formats for accountability in and of collaborative governance. Such accountability is becoming an increasing part of collaborative governance, although the metrics for assessing partnership performance are still in development and very much contested. Nonetheless, practitioners need to be able to draw on the best available practice and ensure that participants in a collaboration agree on how to assess success and if necessary make changes during the course of the collaboration.

The Skills and Tools of Partnership

Specific tools and step-by-step of partnership creation and management is the most widespread and well-developed element of partnership professionalization. A number of major agencies already offer their staff a few days of such training. For example, within the U.S. Agency for International Development, the Global Development Lab (the agency's innovation hub) includes a focus on Global Development Alliances, which since 2001 have been the agency's primary mechanism for collaborating with the private sector. In support of those alliances, the Global Development Lab provides internal training to USAID staff on how and why USAID engages in cross-sector partnerships in courses that range from two to five days. Over the past several years the lab has conducted on the order of four to six trainings per year, reaching a total of roughly 1,000 USAID staff.

World Vision International similarly has trained roughly a thousand of its staff on partnership processes, using materials available from The Partnering Initiative (see below). The World Bank's Collaborative Leadership for Development program has developed a plethora of tools to help bank staff understand and utilize partnership approaches in its development programs.

In addition, an array of executive education and certificate programs exist that offer intensive (two-five day) courses on the mechanics of partnering. The Promoting Effective Partnering facility, initiated by the Dutch government in connection with its co-chairmanship of the Global Partnership for Effective Development Co-operation, brings together five of the major organizations involved in promoting collaborative approaches to development and problem solving. It aims to "unleash the partnering potential for the SDGs." It does not offer training itself, but has a useful report that briefly surveys some of the training that is available elsewhere.[5]

The Partnering Initiative (TPI), based in Oxford, United Kingdom, was launched in 2003 as a global nonprofit organization that aims to "unleash the power of partnership for a prosperous and sustainable future."[6] It has developed a range of tools and guidance for effective partnering and delivers both customized and open training courses with over 3,500 alumni to date. Its current open courses include a three-day interactive training called "Building Effective Public-Private Partnerships for Development" (BEPD). Participants who opt to submit a supervised essay after the course can be awarded a "Certificate in Partnering

---

5. See "About" at the Promoting Effective Partnering website. The report, "Collaboration for the SDGs," is available at www.effectivepartnering.org/wp-content/uploads/2016/11/Support-system-final-draft-version.pdf.

6. See more at the organization's website, https://thepartneringinitiative.org/.

Practice." The course, which is run half a dozen times annually in locations around the world, includes sessions on creating value through collaboration; the partnering cycle; transactional versus transformational collaboration; enhancing skills for partnering; building trust and managing power; initiating and developing partnerships; the building blocks of effective partnerships; effective partnership agreements; managing and reviewing partnership; and so on.

The London-based Partnership Brokers Association, previously housed within The Partnering Initiative and independent since 2012, offers a four-day foundational course (it now boasts some 2,500 alumni) and a five-day Advanced Skills in Partnership Brokering course.[7] The foundational course primarily covers processes of building, managing, maintaining, reviewing, and revising partnerships. Alumni of the foundational course are eligible for a three-to-four-month online program leading to accreditation as a Partnership Broker. Some PBA courses are offered in partnership with the World Economic Forum, which in 2015 registered with the Swiss government as the "International Organization for Public-Private Partnership."

In 2018 Pepperdine University is launching its version of the U.S.-focused Cross-Sector Leadership Fellows program previously housed at the Presidio Institute in San Francisco, which ran a similar program in 2014–17. It includes four-day sessions in San Francisco, Washington D.C., and New York City spread out over a year.[8]

The Partnership Resource Center (PrC) is a specialist research center at Rotterdam School of Management, Erasmus University. It offers executive training programs on partnerships for sustainable development.

Other efforts to professionalize cross-sector collaboration are now defunct. For example, Cambridge University was a pioneer in providing training for cross-sector collaboration. Its Post-graduate Certificate in Cross-Sector Partnership, intended for people in full-time employment, included two residential weeks and nine months of online discussions. It ran for about a decade starting in 2001.

All of these efforts are variations on a crucial theme: what to do, step by step, to inspire, create, and manage collaborations across wildly diverse actors whose incentives and mind-sets have little in common, other than concern with a shared problem. The specific skills required range from what to include in a formal Memorandum of Understanding for the partnership to how to deal with a change in leadership of a key collaborating organization. Such practical skills are essential to the practice of cross-sector collaboration at any scale.

7. See more about the training program at http://partnershipbrokers.org/w/training/.
8. See more at https://publicpolicy.pepperdine.edu/cross-sector-leadership-fellows/.

Getting to Scale in Partnership Leadership

As we saw in the example from India, even simple transactional relationships between donors (such as corporate philanthropies) and implementers (such as NGOs) often fall victim to misunderstandings. Such problems could readily be avoided by partnership brokers with knowledge of the mind-sets of multiple sectors and the convening and facilitation skills to build a shared vision. So the in-house training and short courses on partnering skills do matter. But much more is needed.

Fostering and managing partnerships capable of achieving the SDGs requires much deeper knowledge and skills. MSIs are evolving into a new institutional form, with unique capacities, legitimacy bases, accountability mechanisms, and resource requirements (Abbott, Green, and Keohane, 2016). And that institutional form needs to be managed in a way that supports the entirety of the SDG package, without allowing progress in one area to undermine another.

Few partnership training and education programs have yet progressed beyond the relatively narrow focus on partnership practices to develop the rich array of courses and experiences found in other professional training, such as MBA and MPA programs. To get to scale, three approaches are needed. One is to build issue-specific training for collaborations in specific arenas, as we are already seeing in such fields as infrastructure. The second is to develop programs at the national level. And finally, to ensure the existence of a sizable number of people trained to develop and lead the wide array of cross-sector collaborations required for SDG implementation, universities should create full postgraduate degree programs, on a par with business and public policy degrees. Examples of all three exist and can be more widely replicated and expanded.

Issue-Specific Programs: Infrastructure Example

Public private partnerships (PPPs) abound in infrastructure projects. These are different from most of the MSIs described elsewhere in this paper, because they are structured, contractual relationships between governments and firms, rarely involving civil society organizations, and are closer to procurement than collaboration. The World Bank's Public Private Partnerships in Infrastructure Resource Center (PPPIRC), an online portal of resources and webinars, defines this subcategory of cross-sector collaboration as "a mechanism for government to procure and implement public infrastructure and/or services using the resources and expertise of the private sector" that "combine(s) the skills and resources of both the public and private sectors through sharing of risks and responsibilities."[9] In

9. See https://ppp.worldbank.org/public-private-partnership/about-public-private-partnerships.

many countries, they are what people think is meant by PPP, and many governments have PPP centers dedicated solely to facilitating private sector involvement in infrastructure projects.

Several institutions offer training on infrastructure PPPs. For example:

—The World Bank's PPPIRC portal hosts an archive of webinars on PPPs, which address the financing of PPPs, PPP proposal evaluation, PPP legal frameworks, and so on, with a wide range of countries used as case studies.

—For nearly a decade, Harvard's Kennedy School, under contract with the IFC, has offered a case-based "Senior Training Program on Public-Private Partnerships and Project Finance" for government representatives, donors, and staff from the World Bank, MIGA, and the IFC.

—In Singapore the Asia Leaders Programme in Infrastructure Excellence is offered annually at Singapore Management University, bringing together public and private sectors. Unlike most PPP programs, the SMU training explicitly addresses broader contexts (including the SDGs) and problems of cross-sector engagement.

National Programs: Indonesia Example

One program in Indonesia brings together a new cohort of thirty business, government, and civil society leaders each year for three one-week intensive sessions on how to collectively make progress on the big challenges facing Indonesia and the world. United in Diversity (UID), an Indonesian nonprofit organization that began in 2003 as the United in Diversity Forum, was founded by Gajah Tunggal Group (with connections to the Singapore-headquartered Giti Group company), MIT Sloan School of Management, and University of Indonesia. This forum was a high-level gathering of business, government, and civil society leaders focused on "Building Trust for our Common Future." This aspiration was created at a time when many feared Indonesia was headed for disintegration during the 1997–2003 period. Through a decade of the learning journey, UID evolved into a nonprofit organization with a focus on an education platform and on acting as a catalyst for cross-sector collaboration and sustainable development in Indonesia and for the world. UID is actively engaged with a global organization, the UN SDSN (Sustainable Development Solutions Network), which champions the Sustainable Development Goals Agenda. UID is mandated as chair of UN SDSN–South East Asia and co-chair of UN SDSN–Indonesia with the University of Indonesia.

One of the flagship learning programs, offered with the MIT Sloan School of Management, is IDEAS: Innovative, Dynamic Education and Action for Sustainability. IDEAS–Indonesia, a joint professional leadership education program by United in Diversity and MIT Sloan School of Management, brings together thirty leaders from the three pillars of culture (business, government, and civil society) to develop the key leadership capacity for addressing challenges in the twenty-first century and employs them to collectively explore and prototype transformational Sustainability-Oriented Solutions (SOS). Through six workshops and ten months of self-guided action learning and research, IDEAS–Indonesia participants explore the key variables and driving forces of Indonesia's societal system from new perspectives, investigate the meaning and purpose of their leadership, and based on their new insights, collectively develop prototypes and take steps toward a different future.

The philosophical-methodological foundation of IDEAS–Indonesia is built on two schools of thought: the Fifth Discipline by Professor Peter Senge and Theory U by Professor C. Otto Scharmer, which introduced to Professor Senge's work the critical importance of awareness quality in successful actualization of leadership capacity. Starting with the sixth cohort, recruited in 2017, IDEAS is using the SDGs as its main topic to encourage innovation and creativity in creating profound transformations at all levels of society.

Professional Master's Degrees: Singapore Master's of Tri-Sector Collaboration

To date, the Master's of Tri-Sector Collaboration at Singapore Management University is the most developed and comprehensive training available for partnership professionals. Like Indonesia's IDEAS program, it predates the SDGs but has since adopted them as a framing mechanism.

Intended for midcareer professionals from all sectors, its areas of focus are personal leadership development, organizational management skills, understanding policy issues, and broad problem-solving skills. Program elements include complex systems thinking; political economy; leadership; global trends; futures and forecasting methodologies; partnership mind-set; partnership skills and practices; understanding the three sectors; and applications via individual and group projects

The program is designed in a format like that of an executive MBA, although the curriculum is quite different. The midcareer participants come together from across Asia for seven required intensive core courses (introduction to collaboration, leadership, political economy, global trends, partnership mind-set, public policy for the private sector, and complex systems and public policy) and also choose three electives, most offered in Singapore.

Conclusion and Recommendations

In most areas of human endeavor, it is taken for granted that training and education are keys to success of any large-scale undertaking. People have to know what to do and how to do it. So it is striking how little has been invested in training and education to achieve large-scale social goals, such as the SDGs, through the mechanism in which such hopes have been invested: cross-sector collaboration.

To date, academia has generally lagged, with little available in MBA or public policy degree programs and surprisingly little in the way of more specialized programs, even as certificate or executive education programs. The steps to change this are fairly obvious, and academic entrepreneurialism is badly needed:

—Revamp business and public policy programs to include cross-sector understanding, recognizing the degree to which graduates of these mainstream programs are likely to find themselves working with other sectors.

—Replicate national and transnational programs like IDEAS–Indonesia and the MTSC in Singapore to other parts of the world. Both are needed to ensure the development of cohorts able to work within and across borders.

—Offer specialized programs in specific issue areas aligned around SDG targets or in broader realms (sustainability and finance, agriculture, fisheries, and so forth).

In addition to these formal studies, governments, business, and NGOs can contribute. All can build up what are currently small-scale and ad hoc personnel development programs that give exposure to other sectors via "implants" and secondments. They can also seek out training and education from the programs listed above and others like them and make clear to academic institutions that they want more such programs.

As the popularity of cross-sector models outpaces the performance, it has clearly become imperative to professionalize the practice of partnerships.

References

Abbott, Kenneth W., Jessica F. Green, and Robert O. Keohane. 2016. "Organizational Ecology and Institutional Change in Global Governance." *International Organization* 70 (Spring): 247–77.

Beisheim, Marianne, and Andrea Liese, eds. 2014. *Transnational Partnerships: Effectively Providing for Sustainable Development?* Basingstoke: Palgrave MacMillan.

Beisheim, Marianne, Andrea Liese, Hannah Janetscheck, and Johanna Sarre. 2014. "Transnational Partnerships: Conditions for Successful Service Provision in Areas of Limited Statehood." *Governance,* 27, no. 4: 655–673.

Brinkerhoff, D., and Jennifer Brinkerhoff. 2011. "Public–Private Partnerships: Perspectives on Purposes, Publicness and Good Governance." *Public Administration and Development* 3, no. 1: 2–14.

Brockmyer, Brandon, and Jonathan Fox, 2015. "Assessing the Evidence: The Effectiveness and Impact of Public Governance-Oriented Multi-Stakeholder Initiatives." Open Society Foundation Transparency and Accountability Initiative. September.

Colander, David, and Roland Kupers. 2014. *Complexity and the Art of Public Policy.* Princeton University Press.

Donahue, John D., and Richard Zeckhauser. 2011. *Collaborative Governance: Private Roles for Public Goals in Turbulent Times.* Princeton University Press.

Florini, Ann. 2005. *The Coming Democracy: New Rules for Running a New World.* Brookings Institution Press.

———. 2014. "The Public Roles of the Private Sector in Asia: The Emerging Research Agenda," *Asia and the Pacific Policy Studies,* January. doi: 10.1002/app5.1.

Glasbergen, Pieter. 2010. "Global Action Networks: Agents for Collective Action." *Global Environmental Change* 20: 130–41.

LaViña, Antonio, Gretchen Hoff, and Anne Marie deRose. 2002. "The Successes and Failures of Johannesburg: A Story of Many Summits." World Resources Institute Issue Brief. September 23.

Pattberg, Phillip, and Oscar Widerberg. 2016. "Transnational Multistakeholder Partnerships for Sustainable Development: Conditions for Success." *Ambio* 45: 42–51.

Reinecke, Wolfgang. 1999–2000. "The Other World Wide Web: Global Public Policy Networks." *Foreign Policy* 117 (Winter): 44–57.

Ruggie, John Gerard. 2017. "Multinationals as Global Institutions: Power, Authority, and Relative Autonomy." *Regulation and Governance.* doi: 10.111/rego.12154.

Stanley Foundation. 2016a. Policy Dialogue Brief, "A Multi-Stakeholder Governance Agenda: What Are the Opportunities?" October.

———. 2016b. "Synthesis Report from the e-Consultation on Cooperative Multi-Stakeholder Action: Constructive or Confusing Global Governance?" August.

Waddell, Steve. 2011. *Global Action Networks.* New York: Palgrave MacMillan.

World Economic Forum. 2016. "Poly-Governance Model to Address Global Challenges." White paper. Global Agenda Council on Global Governance and the Future of Regional Organisations. October.

World Vision International. 2015. "Advancing the Debate: Cross-Sector Partnerships, Business, and the Post-2015 Development Agenda" (www.wvi.org/united-nations-and-global-engagement/publication/advancing-debate-cross-sector-partnerships-business).

Zadek, Simon. 2006. "The Logic of Collaborative Governance." Working Paper 17. Cambridge, Mass.: Harvard Corporate Social Responsibility Initiative.

CHAPTER SIX

Building Sustainable Financing Architecture to Achieve the SDGs

The Case of Brazil

Rogério Studart

Despite many social gains in the past two decades, including declines in poverty and inequality, Brazil has an infrastructure and logistics (I&L) sector that falls short of the demand for basic services, is a drag on national productivity and competitiveness, and is inconsistent with the transition to a low-carbon economy. The country, like many other middle-income economies, is finding that its path to sustainable development goes through scaled-up investments in sustainable I&L. If Brazil can generate a sufficient volume and quality of such projects, it could be transformational. If it cannot, it may not be able to achieve many of the other goals of Agenda 2030.

The challenge of boosting I&L investment seems, however, enormous. It will require substantially increasing public investment at a moment of severe fiscal and political challenges, promoting private investments in a very uncertain environment, addressing deficits in project development capabilities, and, particularly, dealing with the long-standing shortfall of long-term financing and the high cost of capital available in the private sector.

Brazil has presented a review of its areas of focus in implementing Agenda 2030 at the 2017 High-Level Political Forum.[1] The report identifies infrastructure as a priority for Brazil while underlining the practical issues in finding solutions at subnational levels that are fiscally responsible, environmentally sustainable, and socially inclusive.

This chapter argues for the need for innovative thinking, policies, and instruments to develop a platform for sustainable infrastructure investment and suggests

---

1. Voluntary National Review of the Sustainable Development Goals (https://sustainabledevelopment.un.org/content/documents/15806Brazil_English.pdf).

that Brazil's national development bank (BNDES) could, and should, play a critical role in doing this. It argues that because the sustainable development goals (SDGs) are transformative, transformational solutions are needed. In this case, a new architecture of long-term capital market development, project pipeline development through building capacity in government and private business to develop sustainable infrastructure, and familiarization and standardization of risk management tools and instruments must move together. Orchestrating change over so many dimensions, and socializing it among many players including subnational governments, requires a strong focal point and sustained engagement. A national development bank like BNDES can play this role.

The chapter is organized as follows. The first part assesses the I&L gaps and their consequences for Brazil's growth and discusses why raising I&L investment presents an opportunity to help overcome the current crisis, setting a new and promising path of sustainable development. The next reviews the role that BNDES has had in promoting such an investment, and what role it could have in the future. Last, I summarize the findings and offer some key conclusions.

Trapped by I&L Gaps

Brazil's growth in the past three decades has been characterized as a case of "middle-income trap" (Kharas and Kohli, 2011). Indeed, its per capita GDP trajectory, which had been quite robust in the 1970s, was almost nil during the whole 1980s and extremely low in the 1990s: in 1980 Brazil per capita GDP was R$ (reais) 4,411, and in 2003 it was R$4,594 in constant price terms. In the 2000s this performance improved, but the country has lost 10 percent of its income between 2013 and 2017. Political turmoil and economic recession continue to dim future prospects.

A Brief History of Brazil's I&L Gaps

Brazil's industrialization started between the First and Second World Wars, as a market-driven result of the closure of international trade (Furtado, 1959), and deepened as a result of a government-sponsored import substitution policy. This process was accompanied by rapid urbanization and emergence of an incipient middle-class, particularly in industrial cities such as Sao Paulo. These changes had social, political, and economic consequences, as the pace of demand growth generated constant mismatches of aggregate supply and demand of goods and services.[2]

2. In many ways a dramatic version of the "unbalanced growth" situation described by Albert O. Hirschman (1969), this period was not surprisingly accompanied by macroeconomic imbalances, inflation or balance of payments difficulties, and increased social and political tensions.

In the 1960s the nation suffered its first economic cyclical downturn as a partially industrialized economy, followed by a significant fall in economic activity, unemployment, and inflation. Politically, a period of economic turmoil and social unrest ended with a military coup in 1964 and twenty-five years of military dictatorship. Following several years of structural adjustment, reforms, and stagnation, in 1974 the military regime resumed import substitution industrialization, anchored in the development of intermediary goods—including the chemical complexes.

Despite the high levels of investment, long-term financing remained an "Achilles' heel" of Brazil's development in the 1970s (Studart, 1995). Indeed, despite the attempts to reform the national financial sector, and particularly the incentives created for the deepening of a domestic long-term securities market, long-term financing in local currency remained very scarce. The high cost of capital in the domestic market, together with the excessive liquidity in international markets in the early 1970s, created strong incentives for national public and private investors to finance their undertakings with debt in foreign currency. The economy became highly vulnerable to external shocks, and, not surprisingly, the 1979 international interest rate increases transformed a relatively small external debt situation into a full-fledged debt crisis.[3]

It was the beginning of a "lost decade" characterized by structural adjustment, economic stagnation, and rampant price increases that ended with hyperinflation. This period was also marked by processes that had a direct impact on flagging infrastructure investments in Brazil (figure 6-1). The legacy has been a rapid decline of private and public investments, particularly in I&L, and deterioration of the state capacity to develop, implement, and monitor massive investment undertakings.

Brazil began a new critical phase at the end of the twentieth century. Politically it was the return of democracy, which came with a new "citizen" constitution approved in 1988—coined that way because of its emphasis on inclusiveness. On the macroeconomic front, in 1994 a very successful stabilization program managed to conquer hyperinflation, a massive achievement after multiple failures.

The Size of the Problem

Two enormous deficits were carried forward from the lost decade. Poverty and inequality remained critical issues, even though the achievement of macroeconomic

---

3. The years of "economic miracle" left shortcomings that would haunt Brazil's development in the subsequent decades. One of them was obviously the appalling levels of poverty and inequality—which reached a peak in the late 1980s (see figure 6-2 below)—low levels and quality of education, and poor governance standards. Another one was a dysfunctional bank-based financial sector.

Figure 6-1. Infrastructure Investment

Percent of GDP

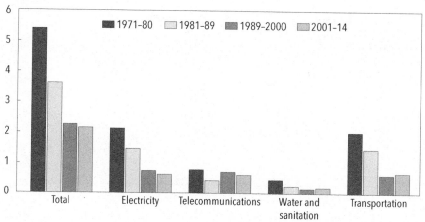

Source: CNI (2016).

stability opened the possibility of addressing the social debt, and an enormous I&L gap emerged.[4]

Regarding poverty and inclusion, metrics such as the unemployment rate and the Gini index improved substantially in the 2000s (figure 6-2). But the results were less impressive on infrastructure, and both private and public investment in I&L as a percentage of GDP declined even further, reaching only slightly more than 2 percent of GDP since 2000. This has created profound shortcomings to Brazil's inclusive development path, because I&L gaps have remained enormous throughout the 2000s (for example, Castelar Pinheiro and Frischtak, 2014), whatever measure used.

For instance, despite the large infrastructure projects in the 2000s (discussed later), in the 2014 World Economic Forum report the overall economic inequality in Brazil ranked 120, out of 144 countries surveyed. Brazil has a better ranking than some competitors only in electricity and telecommunication, areas in which it has invested comparably more in recent years—with greater interest and participation of the private sector. As another indicator of the infrastructure deficit, the 2010 World Bank Enterprise Survey pointed out that 28 percent of firms in

---

4. Poverty and inequality did fall as a one-off consequence of price stabilization. However, they remained at very high levels until the 2000s, when they began to fall with the introduction of successful conditional cash transfer programs and a progressive minimum-wage policy, accompanied by a decline in unemployment. More on this below.

Figure 6-2. Brazil: Poverty and Inequality

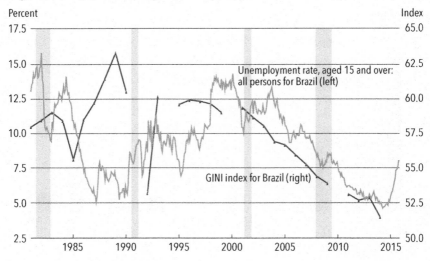

Source: Federal Reserve Bank of St. Louis.

Brazil considered transportation to be a major constraint, compared to an average 23 percent in other Latin American countries (Garcia-Escribing, Goes, and Karpowicz, 2015). These data are evidence that I&L gaps represented a drag on the national business environment and competitiveness throughout the 2000s.

In addition to being a drag on productivity and competitiveness, infrastructure gaps remained significant in other areas critical for the achievement of SDGs. For instance, in 2014 improved sanitation was still denied to 12 percent of the urban population, and almost 50 percent of the rural population (table 6-1). Less than 15 percent of Brazil's roads are paved (including municipal roads), and multi-lane roads are still relatively rare—although they have doubled over the past half-decade. In a country where the national fleet of cars and trucks has almost doubled, this makes traffic jams a major concern in any of its largest urban centers. Finally, in Brazil, most I&L projects are not climate smart, inadequately dealing with both mitigation and adaptation issues, even though the effects of climate change are already being felt.

More Recent Approaches to Dealing with Infrastructure Gaps

Before turning to the question of how to build an I&L program that could help put Brazil on a path of low-carbon, climate-resilient, and inclusive growth, it is useful to look at the attempts made in the past two decades.

Table 6-1. Social Infrastructure as Reflected by Access to Water, Electricity, and Sanitation

Percent, unless otherwise shown

Indicator	1990	2000	2008	2012	2014
Population with access to					
Improved water source	88.5	93.5	96.2	97.5	98.1
Improved sanitation facilities	66.6	74.7	79.4	81.6	82.7
Electric power consumption (kWh per capita)	1,447.3	1,886.6	2,198.5	2,463.0	2,577.8
Days before a business is launched	n.a.	n.a.	147.0	122.0	83.6
Access to electricity, urban (urban population)	98.8	99.1	99.9	100.0	100.0
Access to electricity (total population)	87.5	94.5	98.5	99.5	99.7
Access to electricity, rural (rural population)	55.4	74.3	91.4	97.0	97.8
Urban population (total)	73.9	81.2	83.7	84.9	85.4

Source: World Bank.
n.a. = not available

During the 1990s privatization and concessions opened key infrastructure sectors—such as telecommunications, energy, and transport to private investment. Overall this approach only meant the transfers of infrastructure and logistics assets from public to private investors, with no significant change in the levels of overall investment. Another important feature of the period was the continued loss of public project development capabilities, something that would have significant consequences in the future for the national and subnational authorities' ability to plan, build, and oversee complex infrastructure projects.[5]

In President Luis Inácio Lula da Silva's second mandate (2007–11), the approach changed significantly. The Lula da Silva government abandoned the privatization drive, and due to the intense pressure put on the government to overcome the infrastructure gap, a large I&L plan was launched.[6] PAC-1, or the

5. This loss of capacities, in turn, may have had a significant role in the problems future governments had in promoting private participation in infrastructure projects in an efficient and transparent way, which may explain some of the governance issues that led to the highly publicized corruption scandals that are currently under investigation in Brazil.

6. As indicated by Amman and others (2016), "A firm national consensus had developed around the necessity to tackle the infrastructural deficiencies and bottlenecks retarding growth and, by extension, the further alleviation of poverty. . . . Business groupings (such as the National Confederation of Industry), trade unions and civil society were in broad agreement over the need to tackle a severe structural issue, while the government proved more than willing to step forward with a pragmatic solution embracing elements of market liberalization and state-directed investment."

Table 6-2. I&L Investments as Share of GDP
Percent

Segment	PAC-1				PAC-2			
	2007	2008	2009	2010	2011	2012	2013	2014
Electric energy	0.56	0.61	0.63	0.69	0.72	0.7	0.7	0.66
Telecommunications	0.46	0.8	0.56	0.41	0.49	0.5	0.42	0.52
Sewage	0.14	0.22	0.24	0.21	0.17	0.19	0.2	0.19
Transportation	0.62	0.74	0.90	0.96	0.84	0.84	0.96	0.92
Roads	0.35	0.4	0.55	0.57	0.48	0.39	0.47	0.44
Railroads	0.11	0.16	0.11	0.14	0.14	0.13	0.14	0.16
Urban mobility	0.05	0.1	0.17	0.1	0.08	0.1	0.15	0.16
Airports	0.03	0.02	0.01	0.02	0.03	0.06	0.11	0.09
Ports	0.07	0.04	0.03	0.1	0.09	0.15	0.08	0.06
Hydroways	0.01	0.02	0.03	0.03	0.02	0.01	0.01	0.01
Total	1.78	2.37	2.33	2.27	2.22	2.23	2.28	2.29

Source: CNI (2016).

Growth Acceleration Program, had a budget of R$503.9 billion between 2007 and 2010 (around 2.2 percent of the GDP per year), and soon after the 2009 global financial crisis, it became one of Brazil's main countercyclical instruments.

The Dilma Rousseff administration (2010–15) continued the program under the name PAC-2, which expanded PAC-1 to encompass six key initiatives: housing; water, sanitation, and electricity; safety and social inclusion; urban infrastructure; railroads, highways, and airports; and energy (renewables, oil, and gas). A logistics investment program (PIL) was launched in 2012 to promote concessions of 7,500 kilometers of highways and 10,000 kilometers of railroads. The total planned investment over twenty-fve years was to reach R$133 billion (R$42 billion for roads and R$91 billion on railway systems), with R$79.5 billion planned for the first five years (table 6-2).

One of most outstanding features of PAC-1 and PAC-2, however, was the difficulty in raising the volume of finance. The number and the volume of investments made with private participation (figure 6-3), however, went up significantly. But this financing structure also added overwhelming problems.

The Role Played by the National Development Bank, BNDES

BNDES's history is profoundly connected with Brazil's postwar development (Studart and Ramos, 2016), and it became a critical player in major government

Figure 6-3. Greenfield Projects with Private Participation in Infrastructure

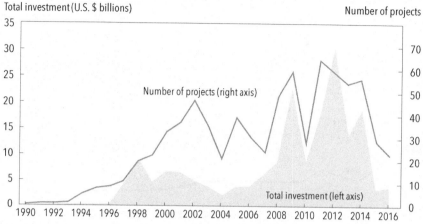

Source: World Bank PPI database (https://goo.gl/LZMQCt).

infrastructure investment programs in the 2000s.[7] Its business model and funding strategy were adapted to facilitate private participation (PPI) in I&L and other government programs, and its disbursements multiplied by more than four times. It became one of the largest financial institutions in Brazil—in addition to becoming one of the five top development banks in the world (De Luna-Martinez and Vicente, 2012). This growth was partly due to its role in supporting the two large I&L investment programs (Studart and Ramos, 2016).

This market position did not come without challenges. One was related to the financing strategy. For many years, the primary sources of financing for BNDES had been "quasi-public" funds,[8] returns of its outstanding loans and equity investments, bond issuance, or borrowing from multilateral institutions. This financing structure has changed since 2009, when BNDES stepped in to fill the crisis created by the retrenchment of private financing. Incapable of tapping the market at a pace compatible with the expansion of its loan portfolio, BNDES became highly dependent

7. Analyzing this recent experience can be illuminating on two fronts: (i) pointing to primary constraints on boosting I&L investment in Brazil; and (ii) revealing the role that a national development bank such as BNDES may have in building bridges to overcome I&L gaps.

8. Such as the Programa de Integração Social (PIS) and Programa de Formação do Patrimônio do Servidor Público (PASEP), which are funds comprising social contributions payable by private and public companies to finance insurance for unemployment, child benefit, and allowance for low-paid workers, and Fundo de Amparo ao Trabalhador (FAT), which is a fund associated with unemployment benefit.

Figure 6-4. TJLP and SELIC Deflated by General Price Index

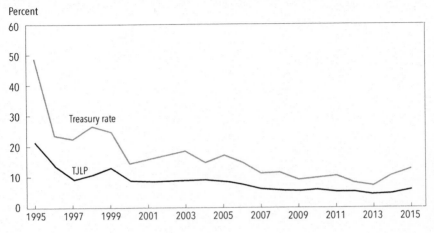

Source: Central Bank of Brazil database.

on transfers from the National Treasury, and the volume of resources coming from it increased substantially, growing to more than 50 percent of the total.

This extraordinary growth of transfers from the national Treasury revived an old and extremely divisive controversy on the societal costs of promoting industrial policies. The problem lies in the fact that Brazil does not have a developed term-structure interest rate curve; most private debt instruments have short maturities. For that reason, BNDES uses a long-term benchmark rate (TJLP) around which it sets its loan rates.

Albeit positive in real terms for most of the time since its creation, TJLP has been set systematically below the Treasury interest rates, even the SELIC, the rate on the short-term government bond—as can be seen below. As a result, the Treasury lost money on each BNDES loan, borrowing at SELIC rates and on-lending through BNDES essentially at TJLP rates. As the participation of Treasury loans to BNDES grew, the fiscal costs of such a financing scheme became quite significant, and a fierce debate took place about the cost and benefits of BNDES interventions.[9] (See figure 6-4.)

These shortcomings illustrate the long-standing problem of the shortfall in long-term financing in Brazil and the associated difficulty of expanding private

9. For many critics, the difference between TJLP and the Treasury rates represents "handouts" that are higher than the societal benefit coming from the projects financed. Besides, some claim that the BNDES strategy to lend to large companies or exporters should not have been part of its mandate as an instrument of public policy, as it supposedly created distortions in the macroeconomic supply of credit (see Lazzarini and others, 2011).

participation in the financing of infrastructure investment, at a reasonable cost of capital.

It is important to note that despite the heated debate around the implicit subsidy of BNDES loans, the TJLP remained quite high over the past fifteen years when compared to interest rates found in industrialized economies and in other emerging market economies (EMEs). It was only low compared to the very high real interest rates on short-term government debt in Brazil. The gap between Brazilian and other countries' long-term interest rates has become even more significant since 2008, because developed and other emerging market economies have maintained very low real, and sometimes negative, interest rates as countercyclical tools against the consequences of 2008 global crisis.

This "unsustainable" financing structure reflects the shortcomings of Brazil's failure to address what became a structural dysfunctionality in Brazil's economic landscape: the underdevelopment of long-term credit and securities markets, the excessive short-termism of the private sector, and the extraordinary cost of capital. Interestingly, some of the policies recently attempted by BNDES to overcome its funding difficulties may shed light on how to address these structural problems.

Leveraging and Crowding-in Private Capital: The Case of BNDES

As mentioned earlier, BNDES's role as a financier of I&L was enhanced further as it became a critical player in the government commitment to address I&L gaps though large programs such as PAC and PIL. In both programs, BNDES had a pivotal role in helping build a financing structure for the concessionaires that won the auctions for specific projects. That is why there is a significant correlation between overall infrastructure investments and BNDES disbursements to the sector. PAC and PIL aimed to expand access and improve infrastructure services for the emerging middle class. Therefore, in addition to guaranteeing the feasibility of higher risk and more complex projects, the explicit goal of BNDES intervention was to allow lower tariffs to be charged once the project became operational (see figure 6-5).

BNDES's financing model traditionally included fixed and variable income products with very favorable financing conditions—both in term of maturities and cost. BNDES, through its subsidiary BNDESPAR, has also bought stakes in companies that could prospect for new business in the sector. For that reason, BNDES ended up assisting federal and state governments to structure concessions for the industry and public-private partnerships (PPP).

In the 2000s BNDES's "coverage" of I&L sectors widened in scope and commitments as large volumes of its investments went to energy production, transmission, distribution, and efficiency. BNDES also financed large logistics projects, such as highways, railways, airports, navigation systems, and ports. Urban mobility

Figure 6-5. Infrastructure Investments and BNDES Disbursements

Billions of reais (R$)

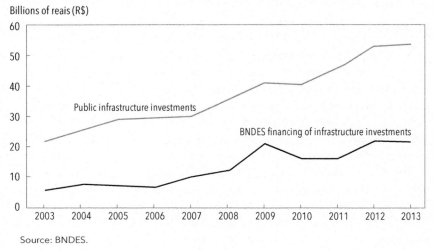

Source: BNDES.

projects grew in number and volume, amounting to R$92 billion in 2014. Investments in high- and medium-capacity transport systems financed by BNDES became part of a larger block of investment headed by the federal government PAC programs dedicated to mobility in the states.

The financial arrangements around the concessions issued by the federal government always involved BNDES directly as financier or cofinancier. This involvement had positive and negative consequences. First, BNDES support increased the share of I&L investment in Brazil's GDP and private participation in the concessions of the I&L investment programs (PAC and PIL). In fact, according to the World Bank, in 2014 Brazil was a leader among developing countries in private participation in I&L project, with 44 percent participation (Ministry of Finance of Brazil, 2015). This situation only reversed in 2015 as the federal government promoted a fiscal retrenchment, mainly through cuts in public expenditure in I&L projects.

Second, BNDES loan pricing was used as an "adjustment variable" to make infrastructure projects viable. That is, the federal government was determined to keep the tariffs charged by I&L concessionaires as low as possible, even though the private cost of capital remained extraordinarily high. To make the overall cost of capital for those projects low, BNDES had to provide loans at rates that were even lower than its benchmark rate plus its funding and operating expenses.

To compensate BNDES, the Treasury created an "equalization account" with BNDES and provided significant support from the National Treasury. This funding strategy increased BNDES dependency significantly on Treasury transfers and was already becoming a source of concern for the government and BNDES management. That is why initiatives were introduced to attract and crowd-in private sources to finance I&L, as was the case for its program to sponsor the infrastructure bonds markets.

Fostering the Market for Infrastructure Bonds

BNDES has a history of policies and instruments to leverage its resources. It includes lowering final loan costs through cofinancing projects; mitigating risk through tier-2 (indirect) lending operations; and risk sharing through its project finance platform and guarantee funds.[10]

Another example of risk sharing is the evolution of a very peculiar type of project finance operations carried out by BNDES since 2003. Typically, project finance is backed by the expected cash flows of the project rather than the balance sheets of its sponsors. But in the case of projects sponsored by BNDES, corporate or banking guarantees (based on balance sheets) were required from the companies participating in a concession consortium. Despite the limitations of this "sponsored" project finance, by introducing this innovation BNDES is able to share risks by inducing private players, both developers and their private bankers, to increase their participation in infrastructure financing. Indeed, in the past, private financial institutions increased their involvement in such projects— with equity, advisory services, collateral offers, guarantees, and insurance, and by leading loan consortia.

Risk sharing through guarantees became part of BNDES's attempt to leverage private financing. The increased funding constraints on BNDES resulted in the creation of guarantee funds to reduce the uncertainty of individual projects and to leverage private sector funding in areas previously only supported by public institutions. Two mechanisms were established to support small and micro-enterprises

---

10. Cofinancing and indirect lending have been part of BNDES's model for a long while. Indeed, indirect operations through a network of public and private banking agents constitute approximately half of its credit operations. The partner banks conduct project analyses and take on the credit risk behind loans. The returns of financial intermediaries come directly from project financing, but they also derive from their access to BNDES resources with longer maturities. This access allows them to increase the customer base with which they can intensify their business relationship—including managing cash flow, structuring of new operations, absorbing employees' salary accounts, and selling direct services. In a way, BNDES's indirect operations do more than just reduce loan costs: once private banks become more acquainted with particular types of clients, sectors, and investments, they can better analyze the credit risk and directly finance the best customers. On some occasions, this has led private banks to take the lead in consortia to fund long-term undertakings. This partnership also gives capillarity to BNDES financial products, since the network reaches commercial banks in most of the 5,570 Brazilian municipalities.

in securing credit with financial intermediaries: Investment Guarantor Fund (IGF) and Guarantee Fund of Free Investment Credit (FGI—free credit).

In 2011 the federal government launched an effort to build the market for infrastructure bonds, and BNDES became an important part of this initiative. For that, the government created several tax benefits for investments in market instruments to channel funds to finance I&L investment. These incentives included a tax exemption on incomes generated by bonds acquired by domestic and foreign investors. BNDES, in turn, expanded guarantees-sharing clauses in its financing contracts, equalizing the level of seniority of the bond holder to loans cofinanced by BNDES. Last, in some projects, BNDES relaxed financial requirements in its credit operations in case bonds were issued.[11]

The government intensified these efforts in 2015 for two reasons. First, under severe fiscal pressure, it could no longer commit to an increased volume of public investment, as it had done in the last twelve years. Second, again because of fiscal constraints, the government decided not to increase the funding to compensate BNDES with Treasury resources.[12] BNDES responded to this reduced Treasury support by enhancing its infrastructure bond issuance program, including additional de-risking engineering and pricing incentives.

The efforts paid off. From 2012 to 2016 total issuances reached R$11 billion in fifty-five issuances. While this may seem to be a significant amount, it is significantly smaller than the total investment needed. In 2013 alone, according to the Brazilian Association of Infrastructure and Basic Industry, the annual infrastructure investments, excluding the oil and gas sector, amounted to R$125 billion. Such results should not be seen as a failure of the government's attempt to foster the market for infrastructure bond for at least three reasons.

First, as pointed out by Wajnberg (2014), there is a learning curve needed for both potential issuers and potential bondholders to start operating with such instruments. Second, there are high costs involved in this learning process—such as hiring banks, lawyers, rating agencies, and auditors, as well as costs related to documentation and record keeping. So only issuances that exceed a certain critical value manage to reach the market. Third, and perhaps most important, the macroeconomic environment was not friendly, as the launch of the bond instrument

11. The first was to reduce coverage ratio of debt services, increasing the maximum leverage of the projects, which improved profitability and reduced the capital requirement of the project. The second was to change the amortization schedule for the issuance of bond infrastructure to allow redistribution of the cost of capital for later phases in the investment cycles.
12. As mentioned above, from 2009 to 2014, total Treasury funds to BNDES amounted to about U.S. $430 billion. The way to reconcile the growth of investments in infrastructure, which is one of the guidelines to move the Brazilian economy towards a new growth cycle, is to promote private participation, not only as an investor in concession projects but in long-term financing as well.

coincided with the years of greatest economic turmoil and a steep rise in Treasury interest rates.

No matter what incentives are created to promote the issuance of infrastructure-backed assets, developing an infrastructure bond market will depend on the capacity and interest of institutional investors to acquire them. In other words, it will require "building bridges" between potential demanders of long-term funds for I&L projects and those institutions that have a need to acquire such types of assets. In Brazil, the potential is there.

The pension fund segment in Brazil, for instance, is relatively large, and has been growing well. The total amount of its investments in September 2016 was R$750 billion (around 12 percent of national GDP). There is plenty of room for infrastructure bonds in this segment's portfolio—indeed, little more than 2 per-cent of Brazilian pension funds' assets are in infrastructure-backed assets.

However, difficulties remain in placing infrastructure bonds with pension funds. The first difficulty is more intrinsic to infrastructure projects: uncertainty about the funded project's ability to generate sufficient resources for the payment of interest, especially in the first years of operation. Second, infrastructure proj-ects have a high degree of indivisibility—that is, most of the investment occurs before cash generation. Thus it is not possible to adapt it over time, and if the desired degree of use is not achieved during the planned period, cash flows will be insufficient for the payment of financial obligations. Third, pension funds in Brazil are accustomed to allocating their resources to fixed-rate investments in government bonds and public companies that have low-risk profiles and relatively high returns. They lack the incentives and capabilities to diversify their portfolios toward long-term riskier assets, particularly in companies that are not listed.

Finally, the development of I&L bond markets depends on the existence of a pipeline of projects that in turn requires public and private project development capabilities. This is a critical issue that deserves a discussion of its own.

Project Development Capacity

One of the greatest challenges to boost sustainable infrastructure is to create a project pipeline that is simultaneously technically solid, environmentally smart, and financially sustainable. Infrastructure projects are not exactly "plain vanilla" investments, and their "risk" depends on how well they are developed.

Despite the sophistication of domestic players, the country faces project devel-opment constraints for reasons already mentioned. Indeed, from the 1980s until the 2000s, the state's capacity to plan, develop, implement, and monitor massive investment undertakings had deteriorated—particularly in the subnational levels. There were at least three consequences of this process.

The first one is straightforward: the government's capacity to plan and develop large-scale infrastructure projects shrank, which naturally later created problems in project development and implementation—particularly at subnational levels. The problem became more evident in the 2000s, due to the push from PAC and PIL programs, including PPPs and concessions as part of Brazil's federal government effort to boost infrastructure investments, which demanded resources far beyond the existing budgetary and other public funds. Not surprising, a strong effort was made in the 2000s to promote the recovery of such capabilities, some of which directly involved BNDES, such as the creation in 2008 of the Brazilian Project Development Company—Estruturadora Brasileira de Projetos S.A.

Second, project development was transferred to private actors, but the financing of such projects often involved governments' budgets or funding from public institutions. This transfer made it difficult for governments to evaluate and monitor projects independently and may partly explain excessive delays in their construction and governance problems that became evident in recent corruption investigations—as I will discuss later.

A third characteristic is indirectly related to the bankability of projects. Indeed, it is entirely possible that a significant number of the infrastructure concessions could be developed with the view of using private sources at the outset. That is, if the projects had been structured from the beginning with the view of mitigating the risks throughout their life cycle, many of them could have had access to private financing, at least from international capital markets. However, if the public entities possess limited project development capabilities, their capacity to propose alternative financial modeling for the projects brought to them is constrained. It creates a "catch-22" situation, where the dependency on public financing is perpetuated.

Despite efforts to build capacity on the part of the public institutions, most project development capabilities remain concentrated in the hands of a few large private developers and consulting firms. Smaller companies have been thriving in new types of infrastructure projects—such as those in sustainable infrastructure—but are even less prepared to produce projects that are simultaneously technically sound, environmentally smart, and bankable from the outset. This concentration may create important challenges for attracting the interest of private investors, even in a friendlier macroeconomic environment of steady growth and low and stable interest rates.

BNDES may play a role in capability building, sponsoring the development of an investment financing architecture, just as it has done in the case of its support for sustainable infrastructure projects and particularly for renewable energy ones (Studart and Ramos, 2016). It is worth then describing, even if briefly, this experience.

BNDES and Sustainable Infrastructure: A Chapter on Its Own

Like other national development banks in the world (Studart and Gallagher, 2016), BNDES has not only implemented government directives toward "greening the economy," but it has had a role in drafting and improving them. Indeed, when assessing direct and indirect nonautomatic operations, it not only checks if they comply with its environmental standards but also assesses the environmental risks and promotes environmentally related improvements in investment and company management.

Additionally, BNDES has for a while offered products and instruments to other sectors, with financial conditions that depend on sustainability standards. It also manages three dedicated "green funds": Amazon Fund, BNDES's Atlantic Forest Initiative, and the Climate Fund. Indeed, BNDES disbursements increased almost six times from 2004 levels to 2014. Despite this growth, the proportion of green investments never exceeded 15 percent of total lending, still a small portion of loans outstanding (Studart and Ramos, 2016).

The potential role of BNDES as a promoter of sustainable I&L, although already substantial, is still far from being fully tapped. First, a significant part of the BNDES "green" pipeline still consists of hydroelectric power plants, but the case for diversification for other sources of renewable energy is there. For instance, in the past ten years, the Brazilian energy matrix has not been able to keep up with demand, forcing the more intensive use of costlier and environmentally damaging coal-generated energy. This mismatch of supply and demand are due to a rise in consumption and to the intense droughts, a probable consequence of climate change, and can only be mitigated through expansion in renewable energy. Because of Brazil's location and weather conditions, there is significant scope for cleaner sources of energy—such as solar power and wave power—and, definitely, for more energy efficiency.

Further, freight and transportation systems in Brazil are still highly geared toward automobiles and trucks—and this explains why oil and derivatives produce almost 40 percent of its energy. The roads are in a sorry state and unfit to address the current demand, which is the primary source of traffic congestion in urban areas and of an inefficient freight transportation system. Developing alternative, "green" transportation systems would not only reduce transportation costs for consumers and producers but also improve urban mobility.

Finally, BNDES can be a key player in financing, leveraging, and crowding-in private capital to I&L—a sine qua non condition for a sounder and more stable funding of the sector in the future. The Climate Bond Initiative (2016) indicated that despite the macroeconomic and political uncertainties, the outstanding volume of bonds in Brazil 2016 was U.S. $2.4 billion. Of those, 54 percent were transportation projects, and 23 percent were associated with clean energy. The potential expansion of this market is significant, particularly if it develops an appropriate architecture (of regulation, institutions, and risk management tools and instruments) that can build the bridge between final demanders and suppliers of such bonds.

BNDES efforts in boosting such investments show its comparative advantages as a central point in establishing this architecture—a role that has successfully been played by other national development banks (Studart and Gallagher, 2016). BNDES has been undermined by many external factors—notably the limited pipeline of technically sound and "financeable" projects and the constraining political and macroeconomic environments.

Summing Up and Concluding Remarks

For Brazil, the 1980s, or the "lost decade," was a period of macroeconomic disarray: hyperinflation; loss of public management capacity; rising unemployment, inequality, and poverty; and widening infrastructure gaps. Things began to change with the successful stabilization program in 1994, which also opened the possibility of addressing the social debt. Poverty and inequality fell, and GDP per capita started to advance in the 2000s. In this process a new middle class emerged and access to credit expanded significantly, which led to a boom in consumption.

Despite these achievements, different attempts to address I&L gaps have failed, and these failures may represent one of the most significant obstacles for Brazil in achieving the SDGs. The low level of public and private investment has generated a sizable overall infrastructure gap in many nations, but particularly in Brazil, and this has created strict "constraints" on potential socially inclusive and environmentally sustainable paths. Indeed, Brazil would appear to be an "extreme case" of such phenomena, where infrastructure gaps have become structural impediments in overcoming a middle-income trap. So, not surprising, despite the recent socioeconomic achievements and despite being one of the eight largest economies on the planet, Brazil now faces daunting new challenges related to its outdated, and to some extent dysfunctional and "climate-dumb," infrastructure. If it aims to continue advancing toward its SDGs, Brazil must find ways to fill its significant sustainable I&L gaps.

This will not be an easy task for many reasons. The capacity of governments, in different spheres (federal, state, and municipal), to expand their required investments in a very delicate (to say the least) fiscal situation is limited. But beyond fiscal constraints, one of the consequences of the decline of public investments, and the I&L strategies followed in the 1980s and 1990s, is a significant loss of government's capabilities in planning, building, and overseeing large infrastructure projects. This policy failure in turn may have had an important role in the problems subsequent governments had in promoting private participation in infrastructure projects in an efficient and transparent way. It is also apparent in the limited capacity of national and subnational authorities to thoroughly evaluate the complex technical issues presented by those bidding for large projects. The limited number of players with suitable capacity may have contributed to collusion and other corrupt practices that have become endemic in Brazil's construction sector and now are under investigation.

Another constraint is peculiar to the Brazilian national financial landscape. Despite significant transformations, sophistication, and openness to international markets, one feature has not changed in Brazil's financial markets: private capital continues to be allocated to short-term assets, and securities markets are relatively shallow. This has led to a "catch-22" situation, whereby the financing of long-term or riskier undertakings has been left mainly to public financial institutions, creating all kinds of ad hoc adaptations and significant political and economic vulnerability.

These findings lead us to three top conclusions. First, promoting transformational investments in sustainable infrastructure is a sine qua non condition for Brazil to overcome the trap of low productivity and competitiveness, required for guaranteeing an inclusive and environmentally sustainable path.

Second, an increase of such investments will require an effort to raise public investments, to expand the pipeline of technically solid and financially smart projects, and to leverage public finance and crowd-in private capital. A new I&L financing architecture will be needed to create the grounds for origination and funding of greenfield investments in I&L—with particular focus on the construction phase, where there is need to develop and finance sound sustainable projects with long-term maturities and highly uncertain returns.

Such an architecture requires coordinated macroeconomic, financial market–enhancing, industrial policies, with strong incentives in each area. It will also require specific incentives (embedded, for instance, in a carbon-pricing system), appropriate regulatory framework, new players, innovative instruments, and markets. It is also needed to expand the pipeline of projects, improve the efficiency of public money dedicated to them, and bridge the gaps between ultimate borrowers and large institutional investors. It will require "institutional leadership" to speed up a process that in many economies took decades to be built. It is where a national development bank, such as BNDES, is fundamental.

Third, due to its experience and history, BNDES is perhaps one of the few institutions in Brazil that can play that leadership role by investing more in project development, particularly in support of developers in building a pipeline of technically sound and bankable projects. For that, it should increase in-house capabilities and expertise in project development or develop an "origination" fund that can be used to outsource that expertise. And it should also foster the development of new instruments that can leverage additional resources from private banks and that can create a bridge between infrastructure developers and institutional investors.

While this chapter has focused on Brazil, its findings may be applicable to other upper-middle-income countries also struggling to fund the large infrastructure needs associated with Agenda 2030. The lessons from Brazil are clear. Public sector financing is important to raise investment volumes, but they are rarely sufficient, and fiscal constraints can quickly become binding. Building long-term capital markets is essential, and the pace of expansion of sustainable infrastructure needs to be modulated to match the speed with which such capital markets can be developed. Brazil's experience also shows the value of a dedicated agency with the technical expertise, in both finance and technology, to prepare and help implement a pipeline of sustainable projects.

References

Amman, Edmund, Werner Baer, Thomas Trebat, and Juan VillaLora. 2016. "Infrastructure and its role in Brazil's development process." *Quarterly Review of Economics and Finance* 62 (November): 66–73.

Castelar Pinheiro, A., and R. Frischtak. 2014. *Gargalos e Soluções na Infraestrutura de Transportes*. Rio de Janeiro: Editora FGV.

CNI (Confederação Nacional da Indústria). 2016.
O Financiamento Do Investimento Em Infraestrutura No Brasil: Uma Agenda Para Sua Expansão Sustentada. July.

Furtado, C. 1959. *Formação Econômica do Brasil*. São Paulo: Companhia Editora Nacional, 30 Ediçã, 2001.

Garcia-Escribing, Mercedes, Carlos Goes, and Izabela Karpowicz. 2015. "Filling the Gap: Infrastructure Investment in Brazil." Working Paper WP/15/180. Washington: World Bank.

Hirschman, Albert O. 1969. "The Strategy of Economic Development." In A. N. Agarwal and S. P. Singh, eds., *Accelerating Investment in Developing Economies*. Oxford University Press.

Kharas, H., and H. Kohli. 2011. "What Is the Middle-Income Trap, Why Do Countries Fall into It, and How Can It Be Avoided?" *Global Journal of Emerging Market Economies* 3, no. 3, 281–89.

Lazzarini, S., A. Musacchio, R. Bandeira-De-Mello, and R. Marcon. 2011. *What Do Development Banks Do? Evidence from BNDES, 2002–2009*. Brazil: Social Science Research Network.

De Luna-Martínez, J., and C. Vicente. 2012. *Global Survey of Development Banks*. Policy Research Working Paper 5969. Washington: World Bank (https://doi.org/10.1596/1813-9450-5969).

Ministry of Finance of Brazil. 2015. *Informativo Mensal de Infraestrutura*. Secretary of Economic Monitoring. June (https://Goo.Gl/Wfxqpz).

Studart, R. 1995. *Investment Finance in Economic Development*. London: Routledge.

Studart, R., and K. Gallagher. 2016. "Infrastructure for Sustainable Development: The Role of National Development Banks." GEGI Policy Brief 007-10/2016. Boston: Global Development Policy Center (https://goo.gl/bXt9e1).

Studart, R., and L. Ramos. 2016. "Financing Sustainable Infrastructure in the Americas." GEGI Working Paper 007-07/2016. Boston: Global Development Policy Center (https://Goo.Gl/Kf7cbg).

Wajnberg, D. 2014. Debêntures de infraestrutura: emissões realizadas e perspectivas. In *Revista do BNDES* 41 (http://goo.gl/U8W2BR).

World Economic Forum. 2014. *Brazil—The Global Competitiveness Report 2014–2015*.

PART II
Targeting Places

CHAPTER SEVEN

Making Rural Areas Places of Opportunity
Not Just a "Rural Agenda"

Bettina Prato

The future of agriculture and food systems depends on the energy, ideas, and commitment of hundreds of millions of people—including young women and men—who are willing and empowered to build dignified rural lives for themselves and for others. Though perhaps less obvious, so does the future of many societies where inclusive growth and sustainable development today have—and will continue to have at least in the near future—strong rural dimensions, due to the structure of the economy, demography, and other factors. For this to be possible, rural areas must be transformed to become more hospitable to the aspirations of rural people, and their relationship with urban areas needs to change. Rural-urban gaps in quality of life need to be bridged, taking advantage of new technology solutions in energy, infrastructure, and information and communication technologies (ICTs), and with more and better investment in quality services. A spatial rebalancing of value generation and value capture in agrifood systems is needed, bringing more of both to rural areas and to those actors who are on the lower segment of agrifood markets. All this amounts to a transformation of rural livelihoods that is not only about raising productivity and strengthening resilience—the standard "rural agenda"—but is also about changing the relationship between rural livelihoods, urban markets, and the broader economy—the "rural areas" spatial agenda. From this perspective, a new, forward-looking agenda for rural development is not just about implementing the second Sustainable Development Goal (SDG 2). It is an agenda that concerns all of these goals insofar as they have implications for rural livelihoods, for the ways in which urbanization occurs and is governed, and for the dynamics of social inclusion and exclusion—including on the basis of gender, age, and other factors beyond rural-urban.

Research assistance from Anna Pierobon is gratefully acknowledged.

One and a half years since the adoption of the 2030 Agenda, rural areas across the world often remain synonymous with a backwater environment, and rural life is often synonymous with poor services, poor infrastructure, and social marginalization. In many countries—including some where the "Green Revolution" has been most successful—agricultural livelihoods still entail heavy toil, low incomes, and high exposure and vulnerability to a range of risks and shocks, particularly for small-scale producers and poor farming households. Under such conditions, while many young people strive to remain and to transform, at times with great entrepreneurial spirit, their rural areas of origin, many millions of their peers see no alternative but to migrate—to urban areas, other parts of the country, or abroad.[1] Of course, urbanization and migration are normal features of the development process. However, in many parts of the world they are now occurring in ways unlikely to be sustainable. This is especially true in contexts characterized by stagnant urban economies, weak industrialization, and urbanization patterns centered on one or two overcongested megacities.

Transforming rural areas and livelihoods and their relationship with urban areas can require significant investments, particularly in locations less favored in geographic and agro-ecological terms. In general, and particularly in such areas, the public sector has a key role to play in laying out an agenda for change, ensuring that enabling policy and institutional conditions are in place, and directly deploying and leveraging the needed investments. However, competing priorities, resource constraints, and political economy issues often stand in the way.

How to move forward? The argument here is that ongoing developments in agrifood systems, driven particularly by changes in demand and by the restructuring of markets and supply chains linking rural and urban areas, offer new opportunities to foster value creation in rural areas, potentially including many that are currently considered "backwaters." In particular, such developments can help to change public cost-benefit considerations vis-à-vis investment in rural infrastructure and services—notably but not only those directly underpinning agrifood markets. There is evidence of such dynamics being at play in some initiatives involving coordinated public and private investments along agricultural "growth corridors" in parts of Africa or around "territories" with distinct agrifood "identities" in Europe or Latin America. Going forward, further progress can be facilitated by technology developments in energy and ICT that can reduce at least some of the costs of rural infrastructure and service coverage. However, both agrifood markets and technological developments need to be consciously steered

1. Numerous poignant examples of this were most recently in the spotlight at a conference on rural development organized by the government of Germany in the context of its presidency of the G-20 in April 2017, as this chapter was being written.

toward more inclusive rural and urban development. Although no panacea, inclusive spatial governance models can help in this regard.

Working on this agenda can bring both short- and long-term benefits—better rural livelihood opportunities, better functioning and more inclusive food systems, but also change in the political economy of decisionmaking around public investments in many domains, with more diffuse distribution of power.[2] In turn, such change is key to sustain a long-term agenda to transform rural areas, because a broad constituency of actors who see their future linked to rural transformation can better hold the public sector accountable for its role in making rural areas into places of opportunity.

Situating the Challenge with Respect to the 2030 Agenda

While the international community grappled with the design of a universal agenda for sustainable development, the statement that the "battle for sustainable development would be won or lost" in cities was so often heard that alternative perspectives seemed not to exist or to be out of touch with the reality of a rapidly urbanizing world. The first United Nations conference following the endorsement of the 2030 Agenda—the third United Nations Conference on Housing and Sustainable Urban Development, or Habitat III—centered indeed on a "New Urban Agenda" (NUA).[3]

With most of the global population living now in urban agglomerations of various sizes, the large environmental footprint of urban infrastructure and industry, and the advantages associated with high density of human settlements in terms of efficient delivery of public services and clustering of economic activities, the effort to translate the 2030 Agenda into an *urban* agenda was certainly of great importance.[4] As recognized both in the SDGs and in the NUA, however, towns and cities are nested in landscapes that include different forms of "rurality." There is, indeed, a reference to rural-urban linkages in a "means of implementation" target under the SDGs of "making cities and human settlements inclusive, safe, resilient and sustainable" (target 11.a), calling for national and regional development

2. For instance, decentralized patterns of urbanization have been shown to have a more positive impact on rural poverty than large city development, a classic reference being Christiaensen, De Weert, and Todo (2013). There is also evidence that diversification associated with greater value creation in rural areas in agrifood value chains can be a powerful driver of job-rich growth, as articulated for instance in IFAD and World Bank (2017).

3. The NUA can be accessed at www2.habitat3.org/bitcache/99d99fbd0824de50214e99f864459 d8081a9be00?vid=591155&disposition=inline&op=view.

4. See UNDESA (2015). Urban areas occupy 3-4 percent of the world's land surface but use 80 percent of its resources and release most of the planet's waste. See Roseland and Spiliotopoulou (2016).

planning that supports "positive" rural-urban linkages. The NUA also recognizes the importance of the latter.

The universality of the 2030 Agenda makes it, of course, relevant beyond urban areas. Its ambitions to end poverty and "leave no one behind," in particular, prompt attention to the geography of poverty and inequalities, including across the rural-urban divide. Several goals and targets are of most direct significance for rural areas and people—notably those related to sustainable agriculture and several of those related to ecosystems. That said, nowhere does the 2030 Agenda explicitly call to make rural areas "inclusive, safe, resilient and sustainable," as it does for urban areas.

The different treatment of rural and urban areas in the SDGs is material, given that goals and targets are meant to focus political and policy attention. In this regard, it is important to keep some key facts in mind. To start, around 80 percent of people with incomes below U.S. $1.90 a day live in rural areas, and an estimated 64 percent work in agriculture.[5] Despite rapid urbanization in all regions, as of 2030 the majority of the population will still be rural in sub-Saharan Africa—where extreme poverty is expected to be most prevalent.[6] Large urban-rural inequalities persist across regions on virtually all development indicators.

Demography is another key factor to consider, as some regions confront both the aging of rural populations and the entry of large and growing numbers of rural youth into the job market (see figure 7-1). In Africa, for instance, young entrants into the rural labor market are expected to number around 440 million by 2030.[7] While it is crucial to foster decent urban job and entrepreneurial opportunities for these youth, urban economies will not absorb most of them.[8] Seen from a different perspective, a large "youth dividend" could be delivered to Africa in the coming years, but only if opportunities for young people open up in rural areas.

Under current trends, many countries are facing a continued depopulation of rural areas and/or a continuous aging of the population employed in agriculture, trends that in many contexts are not driven by productivity growth in the sector and the consequent release of labor to more productive (nonfarm rural or urban) sectors, as in stylized structural transformation processes. Rather, they are driven by the erosion of rural livelihoods due to environmental, economic, and demographic reasons, operating as "push" factors even in the absence of vibrant industry or services sector that can provide a strong "pull." The aggregate impact

5. World Bank (2016).
6. Potts (2012).
7. IFAD and World Bank (2017).
8. Losch, Fréguin Gresh, and White (2012).

Figure 7-1. Youth Entering Labor Markets as a Proportion of the Existing Labor Force, by Region, 1950–2013

Percent of labor force

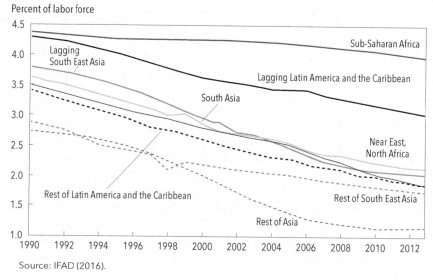

Source: IFAD (2016).

of such trends on the realization of the 2030 Agenda may range from mildly to severely negative, depending on country and local context. Climate change will further complicate the picture, undermining the viability of rural livelihoods in many parts of the tropics but also challenging urban settlements in some coastal areas in Asia and elsewhere.

All the above is of particular concern today, as new pressures from economic growth and urbanization on agriculture and the rural sector have emerged, which require effective responses that this sector is challenged to provide. These include increased demand for food (notably higher quality and protein-rich food), other agricultural products, and rural services, and growing competition over water, land, and other natural resources. Efforts to realize the SDGs will also—and rightly—intensify such pressures. Eradicating hunger and malnutrition, preserving and restoring ecosystems, and integrating agricultural practices to mitigate and adapt to climate change will all require profound changes in the sector. There will be a need to boost productivity, sustainability, and resilience in all rural activities that have a bearing on the natural resource base, as well as a need to make agrifood systems more inclusive, efficient, and nutrition sensitive.

Clearly, this presents a tall-order agenda, and one that can be exceptionally challenging, particularly when so many young people are emigrating from rural

areas and abandoning agriculture. It is an agenda that requires the active contribution of young women and men, including the hundreds of millions who today
live in various forms of poverty and deprivation.

The large number of National Voluntary Reviews presented at the High Level
Political Forum in its recent editions shows that many countries are making efforts
to develop strategies for sustainable development that "leave no one behind" and
that deliver opportunities to all—women and men of any age and in any location.
At least in principle, the development of such strategies provides critical opportunities to each country to identify and surmount obstacles in the way of balanced
rural and urban development, as part of the process of working toward inclusion
and ensuring that targets are met for all citizens in all parts of the country. However, each country's approach will also be affected by pre-existing political economy conditions, which often reflect rural-urban inequalities insofar as these affect
the capacity of rural and urban constituencies to influence public decisions and
public processes.[9] Comparative analysis presented in a 2016 report from the International Fund for Agricultural Development shows that without focused attention
on the social, economic, and also political empowerment and inclusion of rural
people—including rural women and youth—traditional patterns of structural
and rural transformation associated with the development process are unlikely to
deliver fast and widespread poverty reduction.[10] The success of strategies of social
and economic transformation inspired by the 2030 Agenda, particularly in countries that have yet to complete their rural and structural transformation processes,
will thus depend also on the empowerment of rural constituencies, which is both a
precondition and a consequence of inclusive and sustainable rural transformation.

Defining "Rural Areas" and "Rural Lives"

The challenge at hand is about making rural areas more hospitable to the aspirations of rural people, notably young rural women and men. But what is it about
the idea of *rural* that is so inhospitable? It is useful in this regard to note that different definitions of *rural* depend on context and purpose. According to the United
Nations Statistics Division, relevant factors defining *rural* generally include a low
density of settlements, a high share of economically active population employed
in agriculture, and a lower relative standard of living and quality of services and
infrastructure.[11] Consideration of these factors yields various definitions of *rural* in

---

9. Prato (2016).
10. IFAD (2016).
11. The following draws on UN Statistics Division recommended standards for housing and population censuses. See http://unstats.un.org/unsd/Demographic/sconcerns/densurb/densurbmethods.htm.

different countries, making it difficult if not impossible to draw rigorous comparisons. This lack of definitional precision and comparability is important to remember, both because it encourages thinking in nondichotomous terms (beyond rural versus urban), and because the variety of rural landscapes means that it is impossible to establish a global blueprint for rural futures.

The UN Statistics Division points to three dimensions of rurality that are of particular interest from the perspective of transforming rural livelihoods as well as how these communities engage with urban economies and urban areas. First, it highlights the key role that agriculture plays in rural economies. This is generally true even in countries where agriculture is no longer a main source of income for most rural people (as is true in most of Asia, Latin America, and generally in most Organization for Economic Cooperation and Development countries), but it has become an important driver of off-farm and nonfarm activities. Looking to the future, this suggests the need to ask how agricultural livelihoods and practices need to evolve, but also how value creation around agriculture can be fostered in new or better ways. Second, the definition of the UN Statistics Division suggests that poor access to infrastructure and services in rural areas is so frequent and pervasive that it is, de facto, a defining feature of the rural environment. Going forward, a key question is to what extent new technology and market dynamics can be leveraged for change in this regard. Third, the reference to density of settlement points to a continuum between rural and urban settlements. Looking to the future, the question is what patterns of density may be functional and sustainable in different contexts under new demographic, environmental, market, and technology conditions.

The answers to these questions—and the practical strategies and actions that they can inform—can have a transformative impact both on rural areas and on the very definition of *rural* in the coming years. This will not matter very much, however, if similar impact is not achieved on rural lives. At present, the majority of people living in extreme poverty are rural—most living in Asia and sub-Saharan Africa. Most of these women and men depend on agriculture for their livelihoods, but nonfarm incomes are already between one-third and one-half (or more) of rural incomes in many developing countries, particularly in Asia and Latin America. That said, rural lives are even more diverse than rural areas. The same density of settlement may mean different things for individuals and households with different access to urban jobs or markets, because of gender, education, or asset base. The same degree of reliance on agriculture may lead to widely different outcomes in income terms depending on asset base, skills, market linkages, and so forth. Access to infrastructure and services is also mediated by a range of socioeconomic or cultural factors.

Inequalities within rural societies can depend on a range of factors besides income—age, gender, ethnicity, disability, and other factors. Social inequalities can make rural life often particularly challenging for poor rural women compared to men, rural youth compared to older adults, and ethnic minorities compared to other groups. Sociocultural factors often interplay with challenges in accessing and securing control over productive assets, finance, and markets, resulting, for instance, in different outcomes in terms of productivity and incomes (best documented in the case of women working in agriculture). In recent times, several aspects of rural youth economic empowerment have been the subject of national, regional, and global forums. The economic empowerment of rural women has also been specifically discussed in some contexts—for instance, at the 2017 session of the Commission on the Status of Women. However, much remains unanswered to understand comprehensively how inequalities within rural societies are evolving and also how changes in agrifood systems (which span rural and urban societies) are also evolving in ways that bring about new patterns of inclusion but also of exclusion.

The three dimensions of *rural* proposed by the UN Statistics Division provide a useful grid for organizing some of the major opportunities and entry points for action on such inequalities, while not being a substitute for finer-brushed approaches in specific contexts. The first, and perhaps most obvious one, is to strengthen rural livelihoods and incomes, with a focus on generating and capturing more value in agriculture and in the agrifood sector in particular, and across gender and age groups. Second, and also quite obvious, is the need to bridge the gap in infrastructure and services in terms of supply, quality, and inclusive access. Third, and perhaps less clearly apparent, is the entry point of how public institutions in particular work around the spatial distribution of human settlements and the governance of these settlements and of their interlinkages, where there is often scope to promote better forms of integration across areas of different density (including various forms of rural and of urban).

While distinct, these issues lend themselves to being most effectively addressed in combination, taking advantage of ongoing patterns of change in agrifood systems in countries at all levels of development, as articulated below.

Redistributing Value Across *Rural* and *Urban* in Agrifood Systems and Supply Chains

Agrifood markets are undergoing major changes in every region of the world, generally becoming more complex and integrated in response to various supply and demand factors—such as growing and increasingly affluent urban populations, more sophisticated (and, in some cases, also more socially and environmentally "sensitive") consumers, environmental constraints, and technology developments. Such changes can entail new, often closer, but not necessarily more inclusive patterns of integration of rural and urban economies, in which agrifood supply chains are often a key connector.[12] These changes affect rural people as agricultural producers, but they also affect them as consumers, since most also purchase at least part of the food they consume. The impact is felt through prices and market opportunities, as well as through demand for and availability of different products in both rural and urban markets (and thereby impact on nutrition, among other things).[13] Moreover, depending on the shape these transformations take, nonfarm rural activities may also be affected both on the demand and on the supply side, for example, with new employment or entrepreneurial opportunities being generated both in agrifood supply chains and elsewhere in the rural economy.

The direction and nature of all these changes may vary with various patterns of evolution of both rural and urban markets and of the relationship between the two.[14] In general, however, for changes in agrifood systems to have a major positive impact on transforming rural areas and livelihoods, there needs to be an increase in the capacity of rural actors—women and men alike—to create value and also to retain value in agrifood systems. In this regard, for instance, the important role of value addition through agro-industry in employment generation in many low-income and emerging countries is well documented.[15] Evidence also exists of the multifold impact of improved post-harvest handling and storage of agrifood products, which is often associated with modern urban-oriented distribution systems, particularly if this is accompanied by investment in rural agro-processing and distribution systems. This impact covers not only reducing food losses in terms of volume, nutritional value, or monetary value but also creating new income opportunities.[16] More generally, there is evidence that when the capacity and opportunity to generate and add value in agrifood systems is enhanced among rural actors—including those in the lower segment of agrifood markets, such as small-scale producers and wage workers—positive impact can extend beyond individual incomes.

12. See, for instance, Reardon and Zilberman (2016).

13. The body of knowledge on the subject of the "nutrition-sensitive" food supply, or value chains, is growing, notably recently through research and publications of the UN Food and Agriculture Organization (FAO), International Fund for Agricultural Development (IFAD), and World Food Program (WFP), whose contributions were showcased at the Forty-Third Plenary Session of the Committee on World Food Security in October 2016. A related presentation can be found at www.fao.org/fileadmin/templates/cfs/Docs1516/cfs43/Pres/CFS43_RBA_Special_Event.pdf.

14. For instance, pattern diversity is documented in a number of Asian countries in Reardon and others (2014).

15. See, for instance, IFAD and World Bank (2017).

16. FAO (2014).

At present, urban-oriented chains are often characterized by much greater value being created or captured (or both) in the downstream urban segments, especially in markets for high-value products and processed foods, which are increasingly—though not everywhere—anchored in models led by relatively large local, regional, or international market retailers or agro-processors.[17] Where these segments are located in urban centers, the benefits primarily go to urban areas, both in terms of share of final product prices (with most value generation and capture in urban processing and distribution systems) and in terms of client orientation. There is, therefore, an overlap of spatial inequality and of supply chain value distribution skewed away from primary production and from rural areas. This interplays in complex ways with the gender-specific distribution of activities in these food supply chains and systems more broadly, which often reinforces existing gender-based inequalities affecting crop or livestock product specialization, access to paid versus unpaid or skilled versus unskilled opportunities, and access to productive assets, inputs, services, and markets.

This kind of spatial organization of many modern agrifood supply chains and systems is not an accidental reality. To the contrary, it typically results from weak capacity for value creation in the production segment, weak capacity particularly on the producers' side to engage effectively with other actors in supply chains, higher transaction costs and risks attached to locating value addition in rural areas (depending of course on location), and also weaker organization of rural producers and consumers. Change thus requires not only investing in rural areas but also in rural-urban and agrifood market linkages, lowering transaction costs and risks involved in generating and retaining value in rural areas, and strengthening the capacity of producers and other rural operators to create value and to engage on more equal terms with input providers, processors, and retailers. The role of the public sector—as regulator, facilitator, and investor in public goods—is critical on all these fronts.

Efforts have been made to build scenarios for the evolution of agrifood supply chains following the time horizon of the 2030 Agenda.[18] Several important unknowns exist, but many variables—such as demand for food items and

17. Note, however, the diversity of patterns analyzed in the study by Reardon and others (2014) and also the granular findings of research recently conducted by the International Institution for Environment and Development (IIED) Human Settlements Group concerning urbanization and its impacts on food systems in various countries, for instance, Marshall and Randhawa (2017).

18. For instance, the OECD and FAO jointly produce an Agriculture Outlook with projections for national, regional, and global commodity markets for a ten-year period; scenarios related to agriculture and natural resource management have been produced in recent years by AGRIMONDE; the CGIAR has a Global Futures and Strategic Foresight program using a variety of tools, including the IFPRI International Model for Policy Analysis of Agricultural Commodities and Trade (IMPACT), and the list may continue.

agricultural products linked to economic growth and evolving dietary preferences, or the impact of climate change on food supply capacity—are amenable to some policy influence to some extent. Other aspects are even more directly amenable to influence by policy or public investments—notably the institutional underpinnings of transparent, efficient, and competitive markets, land and water tenure systems, and inclusive supply chains.[19] All these therefore need to feature strongly in strategies led by the public sector to influence the future of agrifood systems in ways that may address demand, quality, and sustainability challenges, while also rebalancing value creation and value distribution in spatial terms as well as by age and gender.

Abstracting from context-specific circumstances, three main areas appear to deserve particular attention in this regard. The first area concerns the establishment of an "enabling environment" for agrifood and rural small to medium enterprises (SMEs), including market-oriented smallholder farms, to engage more competitively in modern agrifood systems. Without reviewing the full set of issues to be tackled in this area—well articulated in the recommendations on "Connecting Smallholders to Markets" of the Committee on World Food Security[20]—priority areas for public sector attention include land governance, rural finance and complementary services for rural SMEs, productive and market infrastructure, and related regulations. In that context, particularly worth flagging is the role of the public sector in regulating and facilitating supply chain relationships that deliver improved terms of engagement for smallholder producers, agricultural workers, and agrifood SMEs, with particular attention to gender inclusion.[21] The role of legislators and public administrators in establishing enabling conditions for capable and inclusive organizations of agricultural producers and rural and agrifood SMEs also deserves emphasis, as these can greatly help to generate economies of scale for value creation and for more effective market engagement. The role that public policies and investment in public goods can play in directing greater rural concentration of activities such as agro-processing and manufacturing is also of major importance (this is, indeed, an area of interest at present among several governments and also among development finance institutions, for example, the African Development Bank).

19. This was extensively documented, for instance, in the Regoverning Markets research program undertaken by a consortium of about twenty research institutions and development partners between 2005 and 2007 (see www.iied.org/regoverning-markets for a list of related publications).

20. See the report by the Committee on World Food Security at www.fao.org/3/a-bq853e.pdf.

21. In recent years, IFAD has developed a specific approach to brokering such relations and complementing the work of public and private investors involved, referred to as the Public-Private-Producer-Partnership (4P) approach, which hinges on the specific role that the public sector can play in brokering, facilitating, and regulating inclusive agrifood supply chain models.

A second area concerns the role that the public sector—again, as regulator, as facilitator, and as investor—can play in supporting value creation in the rural sector by adopting environmental sustainability practices and an agenda based on climate change adaptation and mitigation. There are numerous examples of progress in this area in different parts of the world today and many relevant regional and global initiatives.[22] However, many of these are in their early stages, on a small scale, or driven by opportunistic considerations. Future scenarios are alarming in terms of viability of agricultural or natural resource–based livelihoods in many parts of the tropics as well as in terms of projected climate change effects on agricultural production, rural employment, migration, and urbanization.[23] A widespread shift to more resilient and sustainable agriculture and natural resource management is partly about research and technology development, partly about better adoption of existing technologies, and partly about enabling factors in a range of other areas—from skills development to relevant institutional and governance frameworks, from better environmental information systems to improved risk assessments and risk management systems.

Globally, there are important windows of opportunity to advance progress in the coming years linked, for instance, to the integration of country plans for the SDGs with plans for climate adaptation and mitigation. It is important to note, however, that even the best strategies for environmentally sustainable and resilient agrifood systems will vary in terms of impact on rural lives, generating winners and losers—including by gender and age groups. Critical for positive and broad-based impact are the empowerment of rural individuals and stakeholders to take an active part in designing and rolling out these strategies, their grounding in local realities, and the alignment of policy incentives to tip agrifood markets toward staying the course in terms of both inclusion and sustainability.

Coming to the third area, the public sector also has an important role in supporting a diversification of value creation around agriculture via improved

22. For instance, the African Climate Smart Alliance works within the Comprehensive Africa Agriculture Development Program (CAADP) to develop scaling up plans for climate-smart agriculture practices in Ethiopia, Kenya, Malawi, Niger, Uganda, Tanzania, and Zambia (see http://africacsa.org/). On a global scale, the "4 per 1000" initiative encourages commitments from governments, the private sector, research institutions, NGOs, and others, to increase carbon sequestration in the soil via agro-ecological practices, agroforestry, landscape management, and conservation agriculture (see http://4p1000.org/). Some international institutions are advanced in their efforts to develop programs and tools to finance and support climate adaptation in agriculture—IFAD, for instance, hosts the largest global program financing smallholders' climate adaptation. The global business community is active on these issues via technology development, extension services, better integration of climate resilience and/or environmental sustainability considerations into supply chain management, and so forth. See, for instance, Root Capital (2015).

23. FAO (2016a).

valuation of goods and services typically associated with rural areas. This includes goods and services produced by agriculture (for example, food, fuels, fiber, but also carbon sequestration, re-use of wastewater, pollination regulation) and by rural-based natural resource management (for example, preservation of ecosystems and related services, clean water, micro-climate regulation, forest carbon sinks). In the past decades, initiatives in natural capital accounting have proliferated, also including natural resources predominantly associated with rural livelihoods.[24] Moreover, many examples of policies and schemes have rewarded the production of environmental services. Impacts on the environment and on rural livelihoods have been mixed, notably in terms of participation and benefits to poor households and to smallholders, but the potential for greater value creation and better rural-urban distribution of economic value associated with these services is there.[25]

Experience shows that policy and public schemes can provide incentives for production of environmental services that impact the market value of these services and the products underpinning them. For instance, they can affect the price of land, attract both local and nonlocal private investments, and contribute to the development of new markets, and possibly also foster a less "extractive" and more "regenerative" approach to agriculture.[26] Trade-offs may emerge in rolling out specific initiatives, and positive changes may be slow to materialize, especially as technical, policy, and institutional gaps in many areas are still large.[27] Yet the revaluation of environmental goods and services associated with rural livelihoods can both help align incentives for different stakeholders to shift toward more sustainable practices and direct more resources toward the rural sector. From a perspective of making rural life more attractive, the stakes could hardly be greater. What is at issue is not only the economic positioning of value produced in the rural sector but also a rebranding of rural livelihoods as producers of valuable goods and services beyond food, and the distribution and governance of entitlements over land and other types of natural capital, on which the production of

24. This proliferation has not, however, made significant impact on policy decisions, particularly in developing countries. See Jeantil, Recuerdo Virto, and Weber (2016).

25. Critical factors in this regard include, for instance, whether the documented provision of services requires evidence of ownership over specific assets, financial, technological, or know-how barriers, service and payment aggregation challenges, and also preferences for different types of rewards, with nonfinancial rewards appearing to be more appealing to communities in some contexts, according to Jourdain and others (2016).

26. This is particularly critical in relation to restoring soils, well articulated in Teague (2017).

27. This includes gaps in the process of valuation even in areas where practice is more advanced, such as in water ecosystem services. See Hackbart, de Lima, and dos Santos (2017). Valuation of ecosystem services provided at the local level and in remote areas is often especially challenging, as documented in Pandeya and others (2016), pp. 250–59.

such good and services depend. Again, the quality of governance of changes in this domain and the empowerment of rural women and men to help shape it are critical for positive impact to converge.

Harnessing Changes in ICT and Energy Technology to Reduce Infrastructure Gaps

Reducing risks and transaction costs associated with creating and retaining more value in rural areas and in agrifood systems depends on an enabling environment for investment. In turn, this involves many facets, from good governance to specific enabling policies, from infrastructure to good quality services, from a more skilled and better nourished rural population to conducive market conditions. The point here is that recent advances in models for ICT and energy generation can facilitate the job of the public sector in advancing progress on all these fronts, if explicitly harnessed to that effect. For instance, more pervasive coverage of ICTs and energy in rural areas can facilitate productive investments in activities that generate economic value in rural areas while also delivering on other socially valued objectives (for example, education, nutrition, climate resilience, and so on). Improving access to communication and energy sources can also empower producers and other entrepreneurs, including small-scale entrepreneurs and new entrants into the market, such as young people, to raise their productivity, better access a range of services, and strengthen their relationships with other actors in agrifood systems. In addition, improved access can facilitate collective action and the exercise of active citizenship for social groups who may confront challenges in terms of mobility or active presence in the formal public sphere (as is sometimes the case for rural women, for instance).

The World Bank dedicated the 2016 edition of the *World Development Report* to analyzing what was needed to ensure that the "dividends" of inclusive access to digital technologies paid off in terms of inclusive development.[28] The report documented substantial gaps in access to such technologies, with around 60 percent of the world population still "offline" and rural-urban gaps increasing in terms of access to the internet, but less so with regard to mobile telephony. On the positive side, the report documented the efforts of several developing and emerging countries to invest in digital infrastructure and technology in rural areas, at times with measurable positive impact, particularly on local economic activities.[29]

---

28. World Bank (2016a).

29. China is perhaps the best-known case in this regard, but there are also other examples in Latin America (for example, Peru) and elsewhere of sustained public investment in rural digitalization, via a combination of infrastructure and public services.

Although only offering tools dependent on supportive infrastructure, economic opportunities, quality of information and services delivered, and the skills of users, ICT has great potential to transform rural lives. The technology can be used in a range of applications, from internet-based educational services to mobile-based information services and payments (including social payments such as pensions or e-vouchers in lieu of cash transfers), to e-finance more broadly.[30] Even under the simple heading of mobile-based information services lies a broad range of applications, from weather-related data gathering and advisories to price information services, to agricultural extension and advisory services, and more.[31] If information is sound and users have the skills, assets, and opportunities to put it to constructive use, the speed and affordability of access that ICT enables can be transformative for rural livelihoods—for example, informing better decisions about investments, farm practices, and engagement with markets. Intuitively, young women and men often have an advantage over their older peers with their natural proclivity to ICT-based information and services, as well as the opportunities to become entrepreneurs in the ICT sector.

Particularly worthy of mention here is the potential impact of more widespread access to ICT in agriculture. As documented in a recent report to the G-20 prepared by the UN Food and Agriculture Organization (FAO), with input from the International Food Policy Research Institute (IFPRI), and the Organization for Economic Cooperation and Development (OECD),[32] there are a variety of applications for ICT in agriculture as well as upstream and downstream in agrifood chains. Examples include mobile-based collection and dissemination of information about weather-related phenomena, vegetation cover, state of crops, state of water points, and other relevant information (urban growth patterns, proxies of

30. One of the best-known examples in this area is the work of M-PESA in Kenya and other parts of Africa, as documented, for instance, in Rouse and Verhoef (2016). According to Vodafone's Safaricom operator, which launched M-PESA in 2007, in ten years the system has reached 30 million people in ten countries. Although rural-urban disaggregation of this figure is not readily available, there are several studies of the use of M-PESA (as well as studies of other digital financial inclusion platforms) in rural areas, some of which are summarized by Ndaye (2014). In more recent times, e-finance is also evolving further with the use of new platforms supported by blockchain technologies, digital identity programs and devices, and more.

31. As is the case for digital finance, while aggregate figures for rural access to ICT-based services in agricultural extension, for instance, may not be readily available, country-specific assessments of the development of different ICT-based platforms as well as their outreach exist in some cases. One case in point is Zhang, Wang, and Duan (2016), who map out a complex system of services based on SMS messaging, telephone, web portal, interactive videos, and self-support online platforms, among others, each characterized by a different mix of pluses and minuses for different users and uses, and an expected trend toward a growing role particularly of services based on smart phone technology in the coming years.

32. FAO (2016b). A report to the G-20 Agriculture Deputies by FAO with inputs from IFPRI and OECD.

growth such as electricity consumption maps, and so on) to internet-based market transactions, linking agribusinesses to suppliers or consumers with information about inputs, product quality, prices, and so forth. E-finance and mobile finance occupy a particularly important place, given the wide gaps in financial inclusion in this sector and the rapid pace of growth in technological solutions and service platforms in this domain in recent years.[33]

As for energy, it is important to recall that energy poverty is often a major factor of rural underdevelopment—particularly where communities are sparsely distributed and where geographical or other factors make grid-based infrastructure and services highly costly (see figure 7-2). According to the International Energy Agency's *World Economic Outlook* for 2016, 80 percent of people living without access to electricity today are in rural areas, notably in Asia and sub-Saharan Africa.[34] This is not only an issue of concern to some regions or for low-income countries, however—even in a continent such as Europe, rural populations often confront inefficient access to energy grids that prompt reliance on off-grid technologies and resources when available. Yet energy—particularly electricity—is a critical factor for investment and productivity growth, as well as quality of life in rural areas. For instance, improved access to electricity is essential to reduce food losses, for example, through the "cold chain" (including refrigeration infrastructure and refrigerated supply and transport food networks), as well as to sustain value addition and processing as well as rural manufacturing. Access to electricity and to sources of fuel alternatives to biomass is also important to decrease the toil associated with some tasks often carried out by rural women and girls, to reduce health hazards linked to use of coal and biomass for cooking, and to facilitate education and use of ICT.[35]

Based on analysis of sixteen rural regions in Europe and North America, a 2012 report, which predated increases in solar power investment in some large emerging economies, looked at whether boosting investment in renewable energy may have significant impact on rural economies both in these regions and in other parts of the world with similar characteristics.[36] The report found a range of direct and indirect benefits from substantial investment and innovations in renewable energy technologies, via creation of some new jobs and income sources, empowerment of communities and local institutions, and—most important—improved access to affordable energy. At the same time, the report pointed to trade-offs

33. IFAD and Ministero dell'Economia e delle Finanze (Italy) (2015).
34. The WEO 2016 database can be accessed at www.worldenergyoutlook.org/resources/energy development/energyaccessdatabase/.
35. Carr with Hartl (2010).
36. See OECD (2012); and "Mapping the Global Frontiers for Clean Energy Investment," Climatescope 2016 (http://global-climatescope.org/en/).

Figure 7-2. Access to Electricity by Rural Population, 2012

Percent

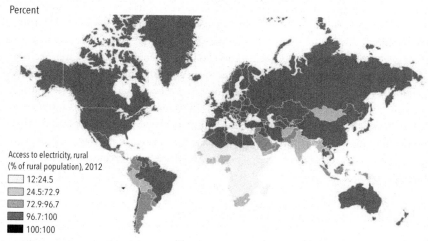

Access to electricity, rural
(% of rural population), 2012

☐ 12:24.5
▨ 24.5:72.9
▨ 72.9:96.7
▨ 96.7:100
■ 100:100

Source: World Bank, World Development Indicators (http://databank.worldbank.org/data/reports.aspx?source=world-development-indicators).

among several factors—local energy security, climate change mitigation, and job creation—and recommended that public plans for renewable energy investments be integrated into strategies for rural economic development to maximize positive impact. In addition, inclusive governance of any energy strategy for rural areas is critical for effective impact on rural transformation.[37]

As with the ICT sector, there has been a proliferation of technologies for energy production and access in recent years, as well as many initiatives to facilitate penetration of such technologies in rural areas in developed and developing countries, including through support to local energy or related technology SMEs.[38] Progress in bringing electricity to vast numbers of people has been significant (particularly in parts of Asia), both through conventional and through renewable energy.[39] The agenda ahead remains, however, huge. Much international attention has been spent on the "trillions" of dollars needed to finance implementation of the

37. Herington and others (2017).

38. The latter efforts have encountered mixed results but have also generated a number of interesting experiences and useful lessons for policymakers, financiers, and development partners. See, for instance, the analysis of the UNEP-supported African Rural Energy Enterprise Development (AREED) program in Haselip, Desgain, and MacKenzie (2015).

39. For instance, Bangladesh, China, Laos, Mongolia, and other Asian countries have had a numbers of successes and failures using solar systems, biogas plants, hydropower, and other approaches, as in Sovacool and Drupady (2012).

2030 Agenda goals for environmentally sustainable and climate-smart infrastructure and energy investments in developing countries. This opens up an important window of opportunity in many countries to also push for an agenda of "rural energy inclusion," which can at least in part be facilitated by or anchored in agrifood systems and rural-urban connectors. For any given strategy and approach to extending the coverage of energy services in specific rural areas, however, winners and losers may emerge, depending on choice and mix of technologies, the relative roles of public and private investors, local socioeconomic factors, and impact on the economic value of local assets (land, biomass, water, mineral resources). This points once again to the importance of inclusive governance of relevant strategies and investments also in the energy sector, in which rural people—women and men alike—have a recognized and active role.

Spatial Planning and Governance Implications

Strengthening value creation in rural areas has implications in terms of governance insofar as it can in itself empower rural women and men, including youth, to take part in relevant decisionmaking processes on a stronger footing. Moreover, it has implications in terms of spatial governance, because agrifood systems typically exist across different locations—including across rural and urban areas—thus strengthening value creation in agrifood systems (or other types of economic systems connecting rural and urban) and requiring managing spatial relationships in ways that can facilitate that process. In this regard, and no blueprint exists showing the appropriate shape of governance solutions to the challenges of specific areas, it is useful to consider territorial governance and territorial development approaches and what they may offer in the search for solutions. In practice, at issue is a variety of models and institutional mechanisms for the governance of social, economic, and environmental assets and processes whose inter-relations are particularly dense in a given space or "territory." Depending on context, these practices often include strongly inclusive and multistakeholder decisionmaking processes.[40]

For the agenda at hand, territorial governance or territorial development approaches are of particular interest because they all rest on an explicit appreciation of spatially situated webs of socioeconomic relations, typically including one or several "urban centers" of various sizes and different types of rural hinterlands,

---

40. For instance, Hussein and Suttie (2016, p. 4) argue that a "territorial approach to development" can be characterized by the development of a territory (including both areas that are "more rural" and those that are "more urban" in a defined region) by addressing the development of multiple sectors, implemented by a range of stakeholders and structured by multilevel governance—or governance that involves coordination and collaboration between local, regional and national level authorities and stakeholders."

which are functionally related to each other. As agrifood systems and supply chains are often key "functional" connectors across space, these governance approaches can help address a range of social, economic, and environmental issues related to the shape of specific systems and of specific markets or supply chains within these systems. This includes, for instance, the impact on employment, access to productive assets (for example, land and water), food security, and nutrition both in rural and urban areas, and so forth. Moreover, the history of territorial development approaches suggests that they have often—though not by default—taken the form of inclusive platforms, where different stakeholder groups, different levels of governance, and different interests are addressed and political economy issues are engaged.[41]

Territorial approaches often recognize and work around the importance of rural towns and intermediate urban centers for inclusive growth and poverty reduction—an appreciation that is beginning to percolate into some of the debates on sustainable urbanization linked to the implementation of the 2030 Agenda. The development of decentralized patterns of urbanization—including the growth of rural towns and the promotion of quality and affordable services around these towns—can transform the reality of rural lives in countless ways, as witnessed in many parts of Europe in past decades. From an economic standpoint, decentralized urbanization can bring growth by facilitating (local) rural access to urban demand for agricultural and other rural services and products, or by promoting employment opportunities that rural dwellers can access by commuting rather than migrating. Of particular interest for this chapter is that decentralized urbanization and the emergence of "rural towns" can support greater concentration of value-added activities such as agro-industry and manufacturing more conveniently and arguably more sustainably than the creation of more artificial agglomerations like agro-processing or manufacturing "zones."

It is unclear what prospects for integrated territorial or urban-rural governance approaches are emerging today. And the response is unlikely to be a general one. On the one hand, there is a well-established and perhaps growing interest and engagement in place-based and territorial approaches, including from a rural development perspective in many OECD countries. Several Latin American countries have a strong tradition in this area, as do parts of Africa (and within New Partnership for Africa's Development [NEPAD], at the continental level).[42] There are many efforts to "localize" the implementation of the 2030 Agenda, but

41. Whether or not this is always the case in practice is an empirical question, as recent reflections on the experience of Latin American countries with territorial development approaches show, indicating that genuinely inclusive institutional approaches to local and territorial development are often the most challenging part of "territorial development."

42. See, for instance, OECD (2015) and www.nepad.org/programme/rural-futures.

many of these efforts take a narrow urban focus, at least in part owing to unequally distributed institutional capacity and resources at the local and subregional levels. The next few years present a window of opportunity to take stock of different experiences, gaps, and successes with spatial governance, particularly as the development implications of changes in agrifood systems and in energy and ICT technology become progressively clearer at different levels and in different regions.

Conclusions

Transforming rural areas to make rural lives more "attractive" to young rural women and men is not about narrow sectoral interventions, nor is it about rural areas alone. To the contrary, it is about working on the connectors between rural and urban spaces and economies, and particularly so on agrifood system connectors, changing how value is produced and distributed along the rural-urban continuum.

There is no denying the urgency of a new approach to make rural areas into places of opportunity. The numbers of those living in rural areas, especially among those suffering from extreme poverty in all its dimensions, are simply too large to imagine any alternative solution that could be effective by 2030.

In the above analysis, I have proposed essentially three game changers:

1. Concentrate more value in rural areas by seizing trends in agrifood markets and innovative approaches to environmental service production and rewards to raise rural productivity, diversify rural economies, and improve the terms of engagement with urban markets and urban sectors for rural economic operators, with a systematic mind-set of rigorous learning from experience, sustainability, and scaling up.

2. Accelerate access to ICT and energy in rural areas. The benefits from such investments are well documented, but costs (especially initial costs) can be high. Determined national and provincial government efforts will be needed to reduce rural infrastructure gaps in a material way. Absent this, efforts to shift value added to rural areas will not be successful.

3. Develop inclusive spatial planning and territorial governance approaches that cut across the rural-urban dichotomy in an integrated manner and with clear provisions for the empowerment of rural communities, rural citizens (women and men of all ages), and rural producers and economic operators on a par with their urban counterparts.

These game changers can mean different things in different contexts and are likely to encounter different political economy obstacles, particularly in the short term, but the potential for transformation that lies in agrifood-sector development, energy, and ICT technology can be leveraged to facilitate broad-based coalitions of interests behind an agenda of inclusive and sustainable rural transformation. The key lies in effective and inclusive governance mechanisms that recognize and address diversity, complementarities, and also areas of conflict across the rural-urban interface and ensure that those most marginalized have an active role and say in shaping change. The prize lies in a future in which "rural" is no longer defined by its relative "lacks" but by what it contributes, in a positive manner, to sustainable and inclusive development to the benefit of all.

References

Carr, M., with M. Hartl. 2010. *Lightening the Load: Labour Saving Technologies and Practices for Rural Women*. Rome: IFAD and Practical Action Publishing.

Christiaensen, L., J. De Weert, and Y. Todo. 2013. "Urbanization and Poverty Reduction: The Role of Rural Diversification and Secondary Towns." Policy Research Working Paper 6422. Washington: World Bank.

FAO (UN Food and Agricultural Organization). 2014. *Food Losses and Waste in the Context of Sustainable Food Systems: A Report by the High Level Panel of Experts on Food Security and Nutrition*. HLPE Report 8 (www.fao.org/3/a-i3901e.pdf).

———. 2016a. *Climate Change and Food Security: Risks and Responses*. Rome.

———. 2016b. "Information and Communication Technology (ICT) in Agriculture." Report to the G-20 Agriculture Deputies. Unpublished final draft. November.

Hackbart, V. C. S., G. T. N. P. de Lima, and R. F. dos Santos. 2017. "Theory and Practice of Water Ecosystem Services Valuation: Where Are We Going?" *Ecosystem Services* 23: 218–27.

Haselip, J., D. Desgain, and G. MacKenzie. 2015. "Non-Financial Constraints to Scaling-Up Small and Medium-Sized Energy Enterprises: Findings from Field Research in Ghana, Senegal, Tanzania and Zambia." *Energy Research and Social Science* 5.

Herington, M. J., E. van de Fliert, S. Smart, C. Greig, and P. A. Lant. 2017. "Rural Energy Planning Remains Out-of-Step with Contemporary Paradigms of Energy Access and Development." *Renewable and Sustainable Energy Reviews* 67.

Hussein, K., and D. Suttie. 2016. *Territorial Approaches, Rural-Urban Linkages and Inclusive Rural Transformation*. Report from a Global Policy Engagement Forum and Technical Meeting held at IFAD on December 11, 2015. Rome: IFAD.

IFAD (International Fund for Agricultural Development). 2016. "IFAD Rural Development Report: Fostering Inclusive Rural Transformation." Rome.

IFAD and Ministero dell'Economia e delle Finanze (Italy). 2015. "Finance for Food: Investing in Agriculture for a Sustainable Future." Rome.

IFAD and World Bank. 2017. "Rural Youth Employment: A Synthesis Study." Unpublished draft, forthcoming under the German Presidency of G-20.

Jeantil, M., L. Recuerdo Virto, and J. L. Weber. 2016. "Natural Capital Accounts and Public Policy Decisions: Findings from a Survey." French Association of Environmental and Resource Economists (FAERE) Policy Paper, 2016-04.

Jourdain, D., E. Boere, M. Van den Berg, D. D. Quang, C. P. Thanh, and F. Affholder. 2016. "Cash-Based versus Water-Based Payment for Environmental Services in the Uplands of Northern Vietnam: Potential Farmers Participation Using Farm Modeling." In T. V. Mai Van, D. V. Tran, S. J. Leisz, and G. P. Shivakoti, eds., *Redefining Diversity and Dynamics of Natural Resources Management in Asia: Upland Natural Resources and Social Ecological Systems in Northern Vietnam*, vol. 2. Amsterdam: Elsevier.

Losch, B., S. Fréguin Gresh, and E. T. White. 2012. *Structural Transformation and Rural Change Revisited: Challenges for Late Developing Countries in a Globalizing World.* Washington: World Bank.

Marshall, F., and P. Randhawa. 2017. *India's Peri-Urban Frontier: Rural-Urban Transformations and Food Security* (http://pubs.iied.org/pdfs/10794IIED.pdf).

Ndaye, Oumy Khairy. 2014. "Is the Success of M-Pesa 'Empowering' Kenyan Rural Women?," March 31 (www.opendemocracy.net/5050/oumy-khairy-ndiaye/is-success-of-mpesa-%E2%80%98empowering%E2%80%99-kenyan-rural-women).

OECD. 2012. Linking Renewable Energy to Rural Development. Paris: OECD.

———. 2015. *A New Rural Development Paradigm for the 21st Century: A Toolkit for Developing Countries* (http://pac-files.oecd.org/acrobatebook/411605 1e.pdf).

Pandeya, B., W. Buytaert, Z. Zukafli, T. Karpouzoglou, F. Mao, and D. M. Hannah. 2016. "A Comparative Analysis of Ecosystem Services Valuation Approaches for Application at the Local Scale and in Data Scarce Regions." *Ecosystem Services* 22, 250–59.

Potts, D. 2012. "Whatever Happened to Africa's Rapid Urbanisation?" London: Africa Research Institute Counterpoint.

Prato, B. 2016. "Opportunities and Challenges for 'Rural Transformation' in the Emerging Post-2015 Agenda." *Development* 58, nos. 2 and 3.

Reardon, T., T. Tschirley, M. Dolislager, J. Snyder, C. Hu, and S. White. 2014. "Urbanization, Diet Change, and Transformation of Food Supply Chains in Asia" (www.fao.org/fileadmin/templates/ags/docs/MUFN/DOCUMENTS/MUS_Reardon_2014.pdf).

Reardon, T., and D. Zilberman. 2016. "Climate-Smart Food Supply Chains in Developing Countries in an Era of Rapid Dual Change in Agrifood Systems and the Climate," in D. Zilberman, N. McCarthy, L. Lipper, S. Asfaw, G. Branca, eds., *Climate Smart Agriculture: Building Resilience to Climate Change.* Rome: FAO.

Root Capital. 2015. *Investing in Resilience: A Shared Value Approach to Agricultural Extension.* Policy Brief 3 (www.rootcapital.org/our-approach/publication/investing-resilience-shared-value-approach-agricultural-extension).

Roseland, M., and M. Spiliotopoulou. 2016. "Converging Urban Agendas: Toward Healthy and Sustainable Communities." *Social Sciences* 5, 28.

Rouse, M., and G. Verhoef. 2016. "Mobile Banking in Africa: The Current State of Play." In B. Batiz-Lazo and L. Efthymiou, eds., *The Book of Payments. Historical and Contemporary Views on the Cashless Society.* UK: Palgrave MacMillan.

Sovacool, B. K., and I. M. Drupady. 2012. *Energy Access, Poverty and Development: The Governance of Small-Scale Renewable Energy in Developing Asia.* Farnham, Surrey, UK: Ashgate.

Teague, W. R. 2017. "Bridging the Research Management Gap to Restore Ecosystem Function and Social Resilience," in D. J. Field, C. L. S. Morgan, and A. B. McBratney, eds., *Global Soil Security.* Springer.

UNDESA (UN Department of Economic and Social Affairs). 2015. *World Urbanization Prospects: The 2015 Revision* (https://esa.un.org/unpd/wpp/publications/files/key_findings_wpp_2015.pdf).

World Bank. 2016a. *Digital Dividends. World Development Report 2016.* Washington: World Bank.

——. 2016b. *Poverty and Shared Prosperity 2016: Taking on Inequality.* Washington: World Bank.

Zhang, Yun, Lei Wang, and Yanqing Duan. 2016. "Agricultural Information Dissemination Using ICTs: A Review and Analysis of Information Dissemination Models in China." *Information Processing in Agriculture* 3.

CHAPTER EIGHT

Using Remote Sensing and Geospatial Information for Sustainable Development

Linda See, Steffen Fritz, Inian Moorthy, Olha Danylo,
Michiel van Dijk, and Barbara Ryan

The United Nations 2030 Agenda for Sustainable Development consists of seventeen overarching Sustainable Development Goals (SDGs), each with targets, which can be further quantified and monitored over time using around 230 indicators (see United Nations, 2015a).

At present the SDGs suffer from the same basic problem that plagued the MDGs—a lack of data needed for effective monitoring and implementation. Progress toward the MDGs had traditionally been measured using censuses and surveys, which can be expensive, not uniform, and unreliable. For the SDGs, new sources of information and technology should be exploited, including satellite imagery and products derived from remote sensing as well as other geospatial data, both open and commercially available, which are being generated through the current "data revolution." Such data could permit more effective spatial planning and more strategic investment in the SDGs.

This chapter provides an overview of the value of remote sensing and geospatial data, both of which could be used more effectively to monitor and implement many of the SDGs. At the same time, we recognize that there are challenges to using these data sources, which we outline below. Two examples are then provided that illustrate how SDG 1 can be monitored in Senegal, using mobile phone and satellite data, and in North Korea, using data derived from remote sensing in combination with census data. This is followed by some successful examples of the use of remote sensing from the Group on Earth Observations (GEO) as part of its Earth Observation for SDGs (EO4SDGs) Initiative. Finally, we consider what ongoing actions are helping to promote the data revolution for sustainable development, and what is still needed to make tangible progress on SDG implementation using these new data sources and technologies.

Harnessing the Data Revolution to Support the SDGs

An early report to discuss the shape of the post-2015 development agenda proposed a new global partnership to eradicate poverty and transform economies through sustainable development (United Nations, 2013). This report called for a "data revolution for sustainable development," recognizing the need to improve statistical data but also to harness new technologies and data sources including crowdsourcing. The Independent Expert Advisory Group on a Data Revolution for Sustainable Development then further defined the approach to include the integration of new data sources with more traditional data to provide more detailed and timely information for monitoring sustainable development. Another key requirement is greater openness and transparency of data, which will ultimately lead to better evidence-based governance and an empowered population (IEAG Secretariat, 2014).

There are at least two key players involved in fostering the data revolution for the SDGs. The first, referenced earlier, is GEO, which is promoting the use of remote sensing and in situ data for SDGs, which collectively are generalized as Earth Observations (EO), through the EO4SDG Initiative (http://eo4sdg.org/). GEO also provides access to EO data through the information infrastructure, coined a Global Earth Observation System of Systems (GEOSS) portal, as well as a Discovery and Access Broker (DAB) for finding relevant EO data and information. The second is the Global Working Group (GWG) on Big Data for Official Statistics, out of the United Nations, which recognizes the potential of all kinds of Big Data for the SDGs and is part of the UN's Global Geospatial Information Management (UN-GGIM) effort. Here we concentrate on two new data sources and technologies: remote sensing and geospatial data.

The Value of Remote Sensing

Remote sensing is defined as the acquisition of information about an object using a remotely located sensor, which can be mounted on satellites, aircraft, or even drones. However, in this chapter we will focus on satellite remote sensing since there are a number of advantages associated with satellites that are directly relevant to the SDGs and its Leave No One Behind philosophy when compared to more traditional sources of data such as household surveys. In particular, satellites have very frequent and comprehensive spatial coverage of the Earth. Unlike household surveys, which may take place every year or often less frequently, satellite data are received on a daily, weekly, or every few weeks basis, which means that indicators derived from remote sensing can be monitored more often than using household survey data alone. The spatial coverage, which can be global and readily disaggregated to local administrative levels, means that the indicators are directly comparable between and among countries, in contrast to traditional methods of data collection, which may not be standardized globally and which may not be representative at local scales. In addition, a long time series of data exist for some satellites, which means that it is possible to look at the historical trends of some SDG indicators; hence data from remote sensing can be both temporally and spatially richer than more traditional data sources.

To understand the value of different satellites and the types of derived information products relevant to the SDGs, we need to go back to 1972, when the Earth Resources Technology Satellite (ERTS-1) was launched, later renamed Landsat. This marked the start of a slow-burning revolution in optical satellite remote sensing. With Landsat it became possible to see images of the Earth at a resolution of around 30m so features such as forests, urban conurbations, and river catchments could be monitored from space for the first time. By the mid-eighties Landsat had become commercial and was selling data on a scene-by-scene basis, so it was not being used regularly for global or large-scale mapping. Moreover, the information technology (IT) infrastructure to support global mapping at a Landsat-scale did not become available until quite recently.

By the late nineties new optical satellite sensors were being launched, but they mapped the Earth at a coarser resolution than Landsat, for example, AVHRR (Advanced Very-High-Resolution Radiometer) at around 8 kilometers, which led to the production of the first global land cover map (De Fries and others, 1998). Land cover maps are representations of the biophysical cover of the land's surface and are useful inputs for at least seven of the SDGs (Romijn and others, 2017). This was followed by the launch of more sensors at higher resolutions from 1 kilometer to 300 meters, for example SPOT-VEGETATION, the AQUA and TERRA sensors on MODIS satellites and the MERIS sensor onboard Envisat, which led to the production of more global land cover maps at a higher resolution, for example the GLC-2000 (Fritz and others, 2003), the annual MODIS land cover maps (Friedl and others, 2010), and GlobCover for 2005 and 2009 (Defourny and others, 2006; Bontemps and others, 2011). This trend continued with the recent launch of the ESA-CCI (European Space Agency Climate Change Initiative) global land cover time series products at a 300 m resolution for 1992–2015, which was originally aimed specifically at the climate modelling community but can represent a potentially valuable resource for the SDGs (ESA, 2017a).

Another interesting source of satellite imagery is from DMSP-OLS (Defense Meteorological Satellite Program—Operational Linescan System), which provides nighttime lights imagery for the years 1992–2013 at a 1-kilometer resolution. This imagery can be used to show where there is access to electricity, which is an important indicator of development. For example, Elvidge and others (2009) developed a global poverty map at a resolution of 1 kilometer by combining nighttime lights imagery with population data while nighttime lights have been shown to be a useful proxy for GDP in countries or regions where the data are of poor quality or completely missing (Chen and Nordhaus, 2011; Henderson, Storeygard, and Weil, 2012).

The VIIRS (Visible Infrared Imaging Radiometer Suite) sensor on the Suomi-NPP satellite also provides nighttime lights imagery from November 2016 onward at a resolution of 750m, while higher resolution information can be obtained for individual cities from the Cities at Night initiative (http://citiesatnight.org/). To date, more than 17,000 volunteers have helped to georeference photographs of cities around the world that have been taken at night from the International Space Station (ISS). From these photographs, high-resolution information on nighttime lights can be extracted.

Two other major events have revolutionized the world of satellite remote sensing: (i) the opening up of the Landsat archive in 2008; and (ii) developments in very-high-resolution commercial satellite remote sensing, some of which have become accessible to the public through Google applications and Microsoft Bing. After 1972 seven Landsat satellites were launched (one failed upon launch), resulting in a rich, continuous picture of the Earth's surface for more than four decades. By opening up access to this vast data archive, many new global products have been developed. Matt Hansen's global characterization of deforestation from 2000 to 2012 represents the first big advance in global mapping with Landsat, and he required the computing power of Google to realize this achievement. Since then, other global products have appeared, such as land cover (Gong and others, 2013; Chen and others, 2015), water bodies (Pekel and others, 2016), built-up areas (Pesaresi and others, 2013; Esch and others, 2017), and cropland (Xiong and others, 2017). As a result of the open data policy of Landsat, the European Commission has followed suit and opened up access to the European Space Agency's (ESA's) optical satellite equivalent, called Sentinel-2. Fully operational as a pair of orbiting satellites since March 2017, these satellites revisit the Earth every five days collecting data at a resolution of 10m. In combination with the Landsat satellites, the Sentinel satellites represent an explosion of data about the Earth's surface and can compensate for the persistence of clouds in certain parts of the world.

In parallel with these developments, the commercial satellite sector has developed very-high-resolution optical sensors and are now capable of viewing the Earth at a resolution of 30 cm. While often used for military purposes, these satellites do not map the whole Earth continually but instead collect data over specific locations of the Earth based on customer need or, in the event of a disaster, through the International Charter on Space and Major Disasters. Access to the data is often costly, but in 2005 Google Earth began to provide visual access to this imagery, creating a mosaic of varying resolutions from Landsat to very-high-resolution commercial imagery, covering the entire world. Since then, the amount of very-high-resolution imagery has increased, and access is also now provided through Microsoft's Bing application. As an example of the potential of very-high-resolution satellite imagery for the SDGs, Jean and others (2016) have used household survey data, nighttime lights, and very-high-resolution satellite imagery obtained from Google to create fine-grained maps of consumption and asset wealth for five African countries. Using a deep-learning data mining method to relate features found in the very-high-resolution satellite imagery with the indicators of poverty, they were able to improve on both the use of either nighttime lights data or mobile phone data alone and show that the method performs well when trained in one country and applied to another, something that is particularly useful in countries where household survey data are limited or nonexistent. However, data-mining algorithms are technically not allowed to be applied to the very-high-resolution satellite imagery contained in Google applications, which limits the scaling-up of this method to other countries.

There are also other satellites and sensors available that have not been mentioned above but which can contribute to SDG monitoring, for example, Sentinel-1 and other radar-based sensors, or satellites that measure CO2, among other constituents. To help understand how remote sensing, and EO more generally, can be useful for the different SDGs, GEO has taken an active role through its EO4SDGs Initiative by determining those SDG targets and indicators that can currently be supported by EO, some of which are listed in table 8-1. With the exception of SDG 4, which is focused on education and lifelong learning, EO can make a contribution to all the remaining SDGs. However, in table 8-1 we have listed only those SDGs where the benefits from EO are direct. For example, in some cases, remote sensing can provide inputs to the actual indicator, for example, SDG indicator 11.3.1 (Ratio of land consumption rate to population growth rate) by providing remotely sensed measures of land consumption in combination with statistical data, while in other cases, it provides in situ support, for example, SDG indicator 1.4.2 on land tenure rights through new mobile-based initiatives such as LandMapp, which can help individuals and communities map and register their land. EO can also contribute indirectly to SDGs 8, 10, 12, 13, 16, and 17, which are not listed in the table but which are included in different aspects of GEO's work such as capacity building and institutional governance; more information can be found in GEO (2017).

Table 8-1. SDG Targets and Indicators Supported by Earth Observation

SDG	Target (contribute to progress on)	Indicator (direct measure or indirect support)
1 No poverty	1.4: Equal rights to basic services and resources 1.5: Build resilience of the poor to shocks and disasters	1.4.2: Proportion of total adult population with secure tenure rights to land, with legally recognized documentation and who perceive their rights to land as secure, by sex and by type of tenure
2 Zero hunger	2.3: Double agricultural productivity and income of small food producers 2.4: Ensure sustainable food production systems 2.c: Proper functioning of commodity markets, timely access to market information and limiting extreme price volatility	2.4.1: Proportion of agricultural area under productive and sustainable agriculture
3 Good health and well-being	3.3: End disease epidemics (AIDS, malaria, tuberculosis, among others) 3.4: Reduce premature mortality by one-third from non-communicable diseases 3.9: Reduce number of deaths/illnesses from hazardous chemicals and other sources of pollutants 3.d: Strengthen capacity for early warning and risk reduction	3.9.1: Mortality rate attributed to household and ambient air pollution
5 Gender equality	5.a: Equal rights for women to economic resources, land ownership, other property, inheritance, etc.	5.a.1: (a) Proportion of total agricultural population with ownership or secure rights over agricultural land, by sex; and (b) share of women among owners or rights-bearers of agricultural land, by type of tenure
6 Clean water and sanitation	6.1: Universal and equitable access to safe/affordable drinking water 6.3: Improve water quality by reducing pollution/other hazardous materials 6.4: Increase water-use efficiency across all sectors 6.5: Implement integrated water resource management at all levels 6.6: Protect and restore water-related ecosystems 6.a: Expand international cooperation and capacity building to developing countries in water- and sanitation-related activities 6.b: Support/strengthen participation of local communities in improving water and sanitation management	6.3.1: Proportion of wastewater safely treated 6.3.2: Proportion of bodies of water with good ambient water quality 6.4.2: Level of water stress: freshwater withdrawal as a proportion of available freshwater resources 6.5.1: Degree of integrated water resources management implementation (0–100) 6.6.1: Change in the extent of water-related ecosystems over time
7 Affordable and clean energy	7.2: Increase share of renewable energy in global energy mix 7.3: Double global rate of improvement in energy efficiency 7.a: Enhance international cooperation in clean energy research 7.b: Expand infrastructure/upgrade technology for supplying sustainable energy services in all developing countries	7.1.1: Proportion of population with access to electricity

(continued)

Table 8-1 *(continued)*

SDG	Target (contribute to progress on)	Indicator (direct measure or indirect support)
9 Industry, innovation and infrastructure	9.1: Develop sustainable/resilient infrastructure to support economic development and well-being 9.4: Upgrade infrastructure/retrofit industries to make them sustainable 9.5: Enhance scientific research and increase number of R&D workers 9.a: Facilitate sustainable/resilient infrastructure in developing countries	9.1.1: Proportion of the rural population who live within 2 km of an all-season road 9.4.1: CO_2 emission per unit of value added
11 Sustainable cities and communities	11.1: Ensure access to adequate, safe and affordable housing/services 11.3: Enhance inclusive and sustainable urbanization 11.4: Protect and safeguard cultural and natural heritage 11.5: Reduce deaths/financial losses due to disasters 11.6: Reduce adverse per capita environmental impact of cities 11.7: Provide universal access to safe/accessible green and public spaces 11.b: Increase cities adopting integrated policies across multiple areas 11.c: Support least developed countries in sustainable/resilient buildings	11.1.1: Proportion of urban population living in slums, informal settlements or inadequate housing 11.2.1: Proportion of population that has convenient access to public transport, by sex, age and persons with disabilities 11.3.1: Ratio of land consumption rate to population growth rate 11.6.2: Annual mean levels of fine particulate matter (e.g. PM2.5 and PM10) in cities (population weighted) 11.7.1: Average share of the built-up area of cities that is open space for public use for all, by sex, age and persons with disabilities
14 Life below water	14.1: Prevent/reduce marine pollution 14.2: Sustainably manage and protect marine and coastal ecosystems 14.3: Address impacts of ocean acidification by enhanced cooperation 14.4: Regulate harvesting, end overfishing and illegal fishing 14.6: Prohibit subsidies that contribute to overfishing 14.7: Increase economic benefits to lesser developed countries/island states from sustainable use of marine resources 14.a: Increase scientific knowledge/research capacity in marine technology	14.3.1: Average marine acidity (pH) measured at agreed suite of representative sampling stations 14.4.1: Proportion of fish stocks within biologically sustainable levels 14.5.1: Coverage of protected areas in relation to marine areas
15 Life on land	15.1: Conservation/restoration/sustainable use of terrestrial and freshwater ecosystems 15.2: Implementation of sustainable forest management, halt deforestation, restored degraded forests 15.3: Combat desertification and restore degraded land 15.4: Conserve mountain ecosystems and biodiversity 15.5: Reduce degradation of natural habitats and halt biodiversity loss 15.7: End poaching and trafficking of protected flora and fauna 15.8: Reduce impact of invasive alien species 15.9: Integrate ecosystem and biodiversity values into planning	15.1.1: Forest area as a proportion of total land area 15.2.1: Progress towards sustainable forest management 15.3.1: Proportion of land that is degraded over total land area 15.4.1: Coverage by protected areas of important sites for mountain biodiversity 15.4.2: Mountain Green Cover Index

Source: Adapted from GEO (2017). Note that targets are shortened for presentation purposes but the full text can be found in UN (2015).

ESA (2017b) has also mapped its programs, activities, and initiatives onto the SDGs to indicate how they are supporting the SDG process. Support is provided to all of the SDGs in many different aspects, from capacity building to provision of actual products for the indicators.

Opportunities in Exploiting Geospatial Data

Geospatial data, or data with explicit geographical locations, is one of eight sources of data identified by Espey and others (2015) as being vital for monitoring the progress of the SDGs. Spatially comprehensive and explicit geospatial data, that is, data that are available at a fine resolution such as 100–1,000 m, are needed, in particular for SDGs related to environmental monitoring but also for disaggregated analyses of socioeconomic SDG indicators. For example, more targeted interventions are possible if a spatially explicit map of extreme poverty can be compared more accurately to one using only national or subnational statistics. Although general progress can be monitored with aggregate statistics, these numbers can hide the variation across space (United Nations, 2015b), and there is much greater value in knowing exactly where to target finite resources in the future. Moreover, the combination of multiple layers of geospatial data from a spatial data infrastructure means that more complex analyses can be carried out; for example, various accessibility measures regarding health, recreational spaces, and other resources can be calculated using road and public transport networks, among many other possible analyses. Estimates of the annual cost of investing in geospatial data for seventy-seven countries that currently qualify for concessional borrowing through the International Development Association was U.S. $80 million (Espey and others, 2015), which is considerably lower than the annual estimates for surveys (U.S. $320 million) and administrative data (U.S. $300 million) in these countries.

A number of different sources of geospatial data could be used more effectively for SDG monitoring and implementation, in particular SDG 1, which would extend table 8-1 with additional targets and indicators; some examples are provided below. The first set of products are gridded population data sets, which have been developed by different institutions using census data as the basis since virtually every country carries out a population census; by 2014, for example, 99 percent of countries will have carried out at least one census during the period 2005 to 2014. One of the earliest products was the Gridded Population of the World (GPW), published in 1995 by CIESIN (Center for International Earth Science Information Network) at Columbia University. Now version 4 of the GPW gives gridded population estimates for 2000, 2005, 2010, 2015, and 2020 at a resolution of 1 kilometer. In the future, gridded products of age and gender for 2010 will become available. Only census data sets made up this product, and these were then spatially disaggregated using administrative boundaries and an area weighted method. GPW data were then combined with nighttime lights data from satellite imagery to create a population and urban-rural layer for 1990, 1995, and 2000—referred to as GRUMP (Global Rural-Urban Mapping Project)—at a 1-kilometer resolution.

Other gridded global population products are now available that incorporate other underlying data sets from remote sensing and inputs such as road networks. One such example is the LandScan product developed by the Oak Ridge National Laboratory at a 1-kilometer resolution, but this product is currently proprietary. WorldPop has produced gridded population data at a 100-meter resolution for all low- to middle-income countries for 2000–20, and the data are also available by demographics, for example, age and gender.[1] The Joint Research Centre (JRC) has produced population density from its Global Human Settlement Layer (GHSL) of built-up areas at a 250-meter resolution for 1990, 2000, 2010, and 2014.

Another potentially valuable source of geospatial data for SDG implementation is mobile phone data since the number of unique mobile phone subscribers is greater than 5 billion (as of February 2017), representing around 70 percent of the world's population. Within the developed world, mobile penetration has reached almost full saturation in the 16–64 age bracket, while in the developing world, 83 percent of the population in the same age bracket owns a mobile phone (GMSA, 2017). However, the numbers are still low in some countries: for example, mobile subscriptions in 2016 were less than 50 per 100 people in fourteen countries, ten of these in Africa (World Bank, 2016). By 2022 the numbers will continue to increase, particularly for smartphone usage, which is predicted to almost double from 2016, reaching 6.8 billion subscriptions, with the majority coming from Asia, the Middle East, and Africa (Ericsson, 2017).

Mobile phone data consists of call detail records (CDRs) for each interaction within the mobile phone network. CDRs contain information such as the phone numbers of the incoming and outgoing parties, date and time of the call, call duration, cell towers in which the calls entered and left, and type of call, that is, voice, SMS, or other. These data can then be analyzed—aggregated and turned into different variables, which can then be used in applications of mobility, social interaction, and economic activity, including SDG measurement, monitoring, and implementation (UN Global Pulse and GSMA, 2017). Many demonstration projects have employed mobile phone data: 200 of these have been reviewed by

1. See www/worldpop.org.uk/.

UN Global Pulse and GSMA (Groupe Spéciale Mobile Association) (2017) as part of their report "Mobile Data for Social Good," such as predicting dengue fever outbreaks in Pakistan in 2013 and tracking of human migration in Nepal after the 2015 earthquake. Soto and others (2011) used CDRs to predict the socioeconomic level of a large city in a Latin American country with greater than 80 percent accuracy, while the studies by Smith and others (2013) and Blumenstock and Eagle (2010) were focused on constructing high-resolution poverty maps using CDRs for Côte d'Ivoire and Rwanda, respectively, demonstrating their relevance to SDG 1.

In addition to mobile phones, which represent only one type of sensor, citizens themselves are increasingly being considered human sensors, who contribute vast amounts of volunteered geographic information (VGI) (Goodchild, 2007), that is, information that is geolocated and hence can be mapped. One of the most successful examples of VGI is the OpenStreetMap (OSM) initiative (Jokar Arsanjani and others, 2015): a global map of buildings, roads, and many other features that have been digitized or uploaded by motivated citizens. Begun in 2004 by Steve Coast, it represented a free alternative to more expensive topographic data held by the UK Ordnance Survey. It has since expanded globally. The Humanitarian OpenStreetMap Team (HOT) is devoted specifically to mapping areas after a natural disaster or other crisis to provide useful and up-to-date information for emergency and strategic response just after an event occurs. Missing Maps is another initiative focused on mapping areas in OSM that do not currently have any good information. OSM represents a very useful source of open information where it is available; for example, it can provide information on the location of slum areas (SDG target 11.1) and greenspaces (SDG target 11.7).

Finally, there is a considerable amount of geospatial data being produced by social media and community-driven websites such as Facebook, Twitter, Instagram, Snapchat, and Tumblr, among many others. Facebook and Twitter currently have 2 billion and 328 million monthly active users, respectively (Constine, 2017; Statista, 2017), while Instagram users upload on average 52 million photographs per day (Statistic Brain, 2017), so the amount of text and photographs being generated on these sites constitutes Big Data. When locational information is available, for example, through geotagged photographs or geographical references in text, the data can become a very powerful source of information that could be used in the context of the SDGs. Recognizing this potential, the United Nations Institute for Training and Research (UNITAR), in collaboration with the UN Food and Agriculture Organization and iMark, an e-learning initiative, has developed an e-learning course on how to use social media for development, while the UN's GWG on Big Data for Official Statistics has compiled a catalog of Big Data projects that are relevant for official statistics, SDGs, and other decision-making purposes.[2] For example, the National Institute of Statistics and Geography (INEGI) in Mexico is currently investigating the feasibility of using Twitter to produce statistical and geographical information, while UN Global Pulse has a project looking at Twitter data for now-casting food prices in Indonesia, among several other ongoing projects listed in the catalog.

Challenges in Using Remote Sensing and Geospatial Data

There are a number of challenges in using remote sensing and geospatial data, which apply to many applications, not just the SDGs. In terms of remote sensing, the imagery that comes from satellites must first be transformed from the raw sensor data to information products such as land cover, forest loss and gain, built-up areas, and so on. These information products are generally derived through the application of automated classification algorithms, which have limitations in their ability to make accurate separations between and among different classes. As a result, some classes are incorrectly classified, which is measured using overall accuracy. This is a measure of how well such an information product represents reality on the ground, and the measure ranges from 61 to 87 percent for the set of global land cover maps that have been produced since 2011 (Herold and others, 2016).

It should also be noted these information products have been developed with different users in mind. For example, the annual global land cover maps generated for 1992 to 2015 by ESA-CCI do not show the major land-use changes from cropland to abandoned land that occurred in the former Soviet Union countries during this time, which is in sharp contrast to what is reported in the official statistics. In this case, the development of the ESA-CCI land cover products has been more focused on capturing forest loss and gain rather than changes in cropland (Lesiv and others, 2018). Hence, a related challenge is about having sufficient trust in the data for countries to be willing to use these products in SDG measurement and monitoring. Many countries maintain their own mapping agencies and do not require global products for SDG reporting, but where such capacity is currently lacking, global information products from remote sensing can fill a much-needed gap. From a user perspective, the key is to choose products that fulfill the needs of the different SDGs and/or to generate new products based on remote sensing that are tailored to capturing different SDG indicators where possible. GEO is playing an active role through its EO4SDGs Initiative

2. See www.imarkgroup.org/ for more about iMark.

in capacity-building activities that can help address this challenge (Anderson and others, 2017).

In contrast to remote sensing, which tends to have frequent and comprehensive spatial coverage of the Earth, and household surveys, which are designed to be representative of the population, the data from mobile phones and social media are inherently biased. For example, there are gender, age, and urban/rural biases in mobile phone ownership in many countries (for example, Blumenstock and Eagle, 2010; Wesolowski and others, 2012), while the existence of a digital divide in many places means that social media are not used equally across the population or in space (Gallagher, 2017). There is ongoing research looking into methods for reducing the bias (for example, Culotta, 2014; Williams and others, 2015; Morstatter and Liu, 2017), but it remains a challenge in the use of these data for development purposes and the SDGs.

Another barrier to the use of Big Data sources more generally is the availability of the data and the infrastructure and human capital needed to process and analyze the data. In some cases, the data are freely available while others are only available at high cost, for example, very-high-resolution satellite imagery from commercial providers. In the case of mobile phone data, there is a lack of a global regulatory framework to enable use of mobile phone data for humanitarian and development purposes and a lack of investment at the level of the decision-maker (UN Global Pulse and GSMA, 2017). Investments are also needed in infrastructure and in human capital requiring technical skills such as processing of remote sensing imagery, application of data mining algorithms and other modelling approaches, use of visualization tools, and analytics. The demand for persons with these skills, referred to as "data scientists," is currently greater than the supply, and they are often expensive resources to employ (World Economic Forum, 2012).

Finally, there are data privacy risks associated with using mobile phone records, although this could also apply to social media data or any data with personal information and/or precise geolocations. Although many countries have data protection laws, they differ among countries, and not all countries have or enforce these laws. Even if the data are anonymized and aggregated, it may still be possible to identify individuals or communities, which could lead to malicious or harmful use of the data. To help with this challenge, UN Global Pulse has developed a Risks, Harms and Benefits Assessment Tool for use in projects that use Big Data for development and humanitarian purposes (UN Global Pulse, 2016).

Although these challenges exist, many good demonstrations show how remote sensing and geospatial data can be used to support the SDGs. The next two sections provide some positive examples that could be scaled up to different countries or are currently in the process of being piloted in various parts of the world.

Recent Examples: How Remote Sensing and Geospatial Data Can Support SDG 1

SDG 1 is focused on ending poverty in all of its forms by 2030, where targets include the eradication of extreme poverty (measured as people living on less than U.S. $1.90 in 2011 purchasing power parity terms) and halving the proportion of men, women, and children living in poverty across multiple dimensions (this goes beyond only income). In order to meet these targets, countries must first determine where those most in need are located, implement the appropriate policies, and then monitor progress on a regular basis. Household surveys are the traditional mechanism for gathering this information, although not all countries carry out these surveys (Serajuddin and others, 2015). Below are two contrasting examples of where remote sensing and geospatial data can be used to create spatially explicit maps of multidimensional poverty or provide proxies that can indicate where extreme poverty may exist, or both. The first example, Senegal, is a relatively data-rich country when compared to the second example, North Korea, where very little data are currently available, yet both can benefit from the injection of remote sensing and geospatial data sources.

Multidimensional Poverty Mapping in Senegal

Senegal is a low-income developing country, currently ranked 162 out of 188 countries, according to the Human Development Index (United Nations, 2016a). Statistics from the World Data Lab indicate that 32.4 percent of the population currently live in extreme poverty, and the country is likely not to meet SDG 1 targets (World Data Lab, 2017). The Multidimensional Poverty Index (MPI), which is a composite of ten indicators covering health, education, and living conditions, is available for fourteen regions in Senegal (Alkire and others, 2011), so this provides a coarse resolution map of poverty across the country, which can be considered as a first approximation. However, by using mobile phone data and remote sensing, it is possible to produce higher resolution maps of poverty. Recent statistics show that Senegal has incredibly high mobile phone penetration rates—98.7 mobile phone subscriptions per 100 people (World Bank, 2016)—indicating that this is a potentially rich source of information that can be used for applications such as poverty mapping.

As part of the 2015 Data for Development Senegal Challenge, data from the mobile phone company Orange were made available to participants for the year 2013. Using these data, Pokhriyal, Dong, and Govindaraju (2015) created poverty maps of Senegal at the subnational level by finding relationships between the MPI and two variables derived from the mobile phone data. The first was the page rank, which reflects the importance of nodes in the network, calculated from mobile traffic flows between regions using data from more than 1,600 antennae across the country, while the second was based on user behavior, in this case the percentage of calls and texts initiated by the users. Both indicators were found to be highly correlated with the MPI, leading to regression equations that could be used to downscale the MPI to the finer subnational level resolution of 124 arrondissements.

In the most recent 2017 Data for Climate Action Challenge, Fritz, van Dijk, and Moorthy (2017) used the same mobile phone data but extended the analysis to include remote sensing data as well as more traditional sources of information, that is, the Demographic and Health Survey (DHS) for 2012–13, to produce an even higher resolution map of the spatial distribution of poverty in Senegal. The information from the DHS was used to produce a wealth index for each of the 200 enumeration areas. This wealth index was then correlated with a range of remotely sensed indicators, including nighttime lights from VIIRS and various climatic, topographic, and demographic indicators. Added to this mix are different indicators from CDRs from mobile phone data, including the number and average duration of outgoing calls as well as the network entropy, which is a measure of the network variability of different towers contacted from a given tower. The results showed that the nighttime lights, and the number and average duration of calls, were positively correlated with the wealth index, while the entropy indicator was negatively associated with wealth. A Bayesian regression modeling approach was then used to produce a spatially explicit map of poverty, shown in figure 8-1, by conflating both remotely sensed and mobile phone explanatory variables with a map of mobile phone coverage, approximated using a Voronoi polygon technique. Although such an approach has limitations—for example, you can see the large Voronoi polygons in the center of the country where the coverage by mobile phone antennae is sparser—by using extra data sources, the map shows an even finer distribution of poverty than that produced by Pokhriyal, Dong, and Govindaraju (2015).

Mapping Proxies for Extreme Poverty in North Korea

North Korea (Democratic People's Republic of Korea, or DPRK) is an example of a country classed as having extreme data deprivation (Serajuddin and others, 2015), defined in the context of monitoring poverty as having no data on poverty during the last ten years. In fact, very few official data sources are available for this country. At an aggregate level, the World Data Lab (2017) estimates that 43.1 percent of people in North Korea are living in extreme poverty in a country with just under 25.5 million people. This number is generated using a simple model

Figure 8-1. Poverty Map of Senegal

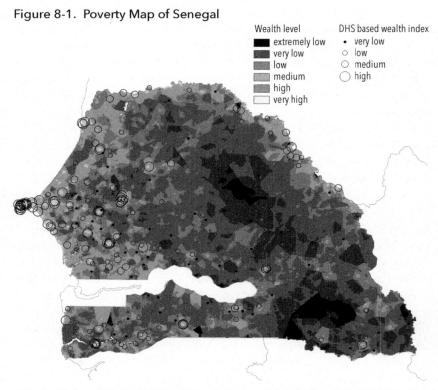

Source: Produced using DHS data, nighttime lights data, climate data, elevation data, WorldPop data, data on accessibility to populated places, and mobile phone data, courtesy of Orange Mobile from the 2017 Data for Climate Action Challenge.

Note: Map is shown at 1-km resolution on which the Demographic and Health Survey (DHS) data are superimposed with the radii proportional to wealth.

that takes the population and the country's GDP into account, but little is known about where this vulnerable group of people live within the country.

In the following example, we demonstrate how we can use remote sensing and geospatial data to highlight where the highest areas of poverty may be located in North Korea. Using nighttime lights from the DMSP-OLS satellite for the year 2013 and gridded population data from WorldPop for 2015, we can show the distribution of populated areas with electrification (figure 8-2). From this we can calculate the number of people who do not have electricity, which is around 17.8 million, or almost 70 percent of the people living in North Korea. If we assume that people who can afford electricity are not those living in conditions of extreme poverty, then such a map provides a first proxy for where those living in extreme poverty might be located.

Figure 8-2. Nighttime Light Intensity in Korea, Overlaid on Settlements, 2013

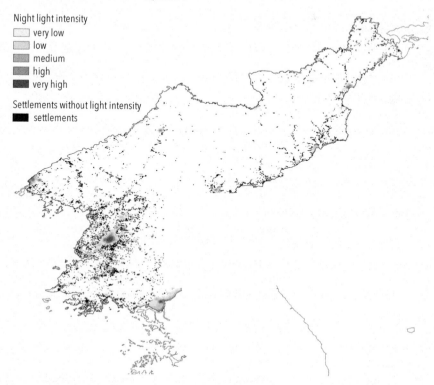

Night light intensity
- very low
- low
- medium
- high
- very high

Settlements without light intensity
- settlements

Source: Produced using nighttime lights data and the Global Urban Footprint (GUF+).
Note: The settlements without light intensity and lack of electrification correspond most likely to areas with extreme poverty.

We can further refine this analysis by creating a spatially explicit distribution of GDP across North Korea, using very little official data. The overall GDP for North Korea is estimated at U.S. $28 billion (CIA, 2017). The U.S. Central Intelligence Agency provides a further breakdown of GDP by sector: 21.6 percent from agriculture, 46.2 percent from industry, and 32.3 percent from services, and a labor force breakdown for 2008 of 37 percent in agriculture and the rest in industry and services. Census data for 2008 are available from the Central Bureau of Statistics in Pyongyang (2009), which provides aggregated data at the level of nine provinces. In the census, there are two tables that provide the working population by major industry group, which links to the sectors above, and by major occupation group, for example, senior officials, skilled workers, and other categories. The country and district level data can then be spatially distributed using a combination of a land cover map derived from remote sensing, that is, the ESA-CCI product for 2015 (available from www.esa-landcover-cci.org/) and the WorldPop data for 2015. The distribution process is as follows:

—The land cover map is used to extract those areas under agricultural production;

—The GDP from agriculture is distributed across the population living in these agricultural areas, using the WorldPop 2015 and district census totals from 2008 to guide the distribution process;

—The remaining population living in these areas is assumed to work in the service industry, and hence the GDP from services is distributed to these people in those locations;

—The rest of the land cover is assumed to be in the industrial sector, and the GDP for industry is distributed to the population living in these areas using WorldPop and district census data; and

—Any remaining population is assumed to be in the service sector, and the GDP is allocated accordingly.

The GDP is then divided by the number of people living in each 1-km^2 grid cell to produce a spatially explicit map of GDP. The final result is shown in figure 8-3, which highlights the higher GDP in the urban areas, decreasing in more rural areas.

Overall, both of these case studies show that it is possible to create a fine-resolution poverty map by conflating data from remote sensing with other geospatial data sets; these can be acquired at relatively low cost to add value to information collected from household surveys, such as in the case of Senegal, or to provide a first approximation of poverty when very little official data are available, such as in the case of North Korea.

Supporting Other SDGs with Remote Sensing and Geospatial Data

In addition to SDG 1, remote sensing and geospatial data can support other SDGs, either as a direct measure or indirect support to measuring indicators, or they can contribute to progress on the target as outlined previously in table 8-1. The four examples that follow illustrate the use of remote sensing, and to a lesser extent geospatial data, to support four of the 17 SDGs, which are taken from the recent report on GEO's activities to support the SDGs (GEO, 2017). Further examples can be found in Anderson and others (2017). Where possible, we have provided recommendations for where geospatial data could be further integrated into these case studies.

Figure 8-3. Distribution of GDP Across North Korea

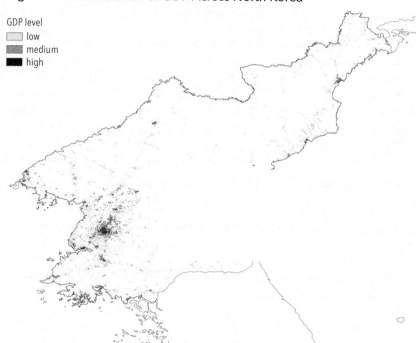

Source: Produced using North Korea census data, ESA-CCI land cover, WorldPop data, and census data.

SDG 2: Support via the GEOGLAM Initiative

The GEOGLAM (GEO Global Agricultural Monitoring) Initiative directly supports SDG 2, in particular target 2c: *Adopting measures to ensure the proper functioning of food commodity markets and their derivatives, and facilitate timely access to market information, including on food reserves, in order to help limit extreme food price volatility.* The aim of GEOGLAM, which was launched in 2011 at the G-20 Summit in Paris, is to make effective use of EO data to produce timely and accurate forecasts of agricultural production at multiple scales, from national to global. This includes baseline data sets such as the IIASA-IFPRI cropland mask (Fritz and others, 2015) that has been derived from remote sensing; cropland and drought monitoring through the use of multiple satellites; in situ data such as temperature and precipitation measurements, often used together with remotely sensed products; and other innovative data sources, including crowdsourcing. The latter category will likely be extended in the future to include mobile phone data, which might provide regular information on food prices, market accessibility, and conditions of pastureland, as well as social media, that might provide information on current conditions, food prices, or vulnerability. One of the key outputs of GEOGLAM is the Crop Monitor, that is, two bulletins aimed at agricultural monitoring and early warning, respectively, which directly addresses target 2c and indicator 2.4.1 (percentage of agricultural area under productive and sustainable agriculture). However, GEOGLAM also supports other targets in SDG 2 (2.1, 2.3, 2.4, and 2a), as well as other goals (SDGs 12 and 13).

SDG 6: Supporting the Sustainable Management of Water

Several examples show how remote sensing can support SDG 6, which is concerned with ensuring availability and sustainable management of water and sanitation for all. The Algal Early Warning System in Australia uses Landsat data to monitor turbidity, which is translated to algal bloom alert levels. This contributes directly to the monitoring of SDG indicator 6.3.2—*Proportion of bodies of water with good ambient water quality.*

The Global Satellite Mapping of Precipitation (GSMaP) data set uses remote sensing of precipitation with in situ data from rain gauges to produce hourly maps that are fed into a rainfall-runoff model to make flood predictions for early warning purposes. Flood prediction systems using this data set have been implemented in Bangladesh, the Philippines, Vietnam, and Pakistan, which contribute to SDG target 6.5 on the implementation of integrated water resource management. Potential sources of geospatial data to complement the remote sensing are amateur weather stations and low-cost rain gauges, which are becoming increasingly popular in programs such as Weather Underground. The Peta Jakarta Twitter app has used data from Twitter to map flood risk in Jakarta and could also provide validation data for hydrological models and early warning systems (Holderness and Turpin, 2015).

The global mapping of mangroves using radar data is being undertaken by the Global Mangrove Watch (GMW), which is a pilot project of the Ramsar Global Wetlands Observation System under the GEO-Wetlands Initiative. By 2018 the GMW will produce annual change maps of mangroves to complement the baseline map produced for 2010. This effort contributes directly to SDG indicator 6.6.1—Change in the extent of water-related ecosystems over time—where these ecosystems can then be better protected as part of SDG indicator 6.6. Wetlands are also being monitored for macrophytes, biomass, biodiversity, and the presence of invasive species using remote sensing, which is being investigated as part of a number of Horizon 2020 projects (for example, ECOPOTENTIAL and CYANOLAKE) for their potential contributions to SDG indicator 6.6.1.

SDG 11: Mapping Urban Extent and Air Pollution Monitoring

SDG 11 is concerned with making cities and human settlements inclusive, safe, resilient, and sustainable, where target 11.3 focuses on sustainable urbanization, particularly relevant in light of increasing urbanization. An estimated 54.5 percent of the world's population lives in cities, but this is set to rise to 60 percent by 2030 (United Nations, 2016b). Remote sensing is directly contributing to indicator 11.3.1 (*Ratio of land consumption rate to population growth rate*) through the development of remotely sensed global products on built-up areas. Using satellite data from multiple sensors, both optical and radar, the GHSL and GUF+ products represent high-resolution delineations of the urban footprint of all cities. Both will be operationalized to create products on an annual or biennial basis, allowing the progress of SDG target 11.3 to be measured, monitored, and plans implemented to promote sustainable urbanization.

Remote sensing, in combination with in situ data and numerical models, can be used to monitor air pollution, in particular fine (PM2.5) and coarse (PM10) particulate matter, which can cause health problems. This can contribute directly to target 11.6 on reducing adverse environmental impacts and indicator 11.6.2 on measurements of fine particulate matter in cities. Here there is a great additional potential for crowdsourcing and social media, for example, through mobilization of low-cost air pollution sensors by citizens and text analysis of social media, both of which may indicate hot spots of air pollution.

SDG 15: Sustainable Management of Forests and Halting Biodiversity Loss/Land Degradation

Remote sensing is being used to monitor forested areas through efforts at the University of Maryland, NASA, and the Global Forest Observations Initiative (GFOI). Using Landsat data, the University of Maryland and NASA are working with a number of countries to provide estimates of SDG indicator 15.1.1 (*Forest area as a proportion of total land area*) and to produce a range of indicators on forest change to support assessment of 15.2.1 (*Progress towards sustainable forest management*). Peru has already adopted the methods for official reporting, while other countries such as Costa Rica are currently experimenting with these methods.

Remote sensing can also be used for monitoring habitat change over time more generally, which can help monitor losses in biodiversity. A number of remotely sensed time series data sets can aid in this process, for example, the forest loss-and-gain maps of Matt Hansen referenced earlier, the water bodies layer developed by the JRC, and the ESA-CCI land cover time series. The accuracy of these findings is highly dependent on the training data, which still require improvement, and the ESA-CCI is only a first attempt at a land cover time series, which is not yet of sufficient quality to fully monitor habitat loss. However, more time series products will be developed in the future that can contribute to this goal. These could then be linked to the Biodiversity Intactness Index (Scholes and Biggs, 2005; Newbold and others, 2016), and the change in biodiversity could then be approximated. This could help toward monitoring the progress of SDG 15.5 on halting the loss of biodiversity.

The GFOI has developed methods and guidelines for estimating carbon stocks in forests and helps national governments establish measurement, reporting, and verification (MRV) systems that are consistent with other reporting frameworks such as IPCC (Intergovernmental Panel on Climate Change) and REDD+ (Reducing Emissions from Deforestation and forest Degradation). GFOI also monitors forest change using Landsat and Sentinel-2 data and complements this with a range of other commercial radar-based satellite data. Their efforts are simultaneously contributing to support SDG indicator 15.2.1. Modeling tools such as economic land-use change models are used to give policy advice on improving, for example, the global carbon sink in the land-use sector, and remote sensing can help to ensure that policy instruments for this sector are working and on track.

Remote sensing is also being used to support SDG indicator 15.3.1 (*Proportion of land that is degraded over total land area*) as part of SDG target 15.3 on combating desertification and restoring degraded land. Several international organizations (Commonwealth Scientific and Industrial Research Organization, European Space Agency, Joint Research Centre, and United Nations Convention to Combat Desertification) are working on a method to measure and monitor SDG indicator 15.3.1 using a combination of land cover and change over time from the ESA-CCI land cover products, trends in land productivity based on remotely sensed time series of vegetation status, and soil organic carbon.

All of these efforts could be supported by other sources of geospatial data, in particular crowdsourcing of land cover, land cover change, and degraded land. Global Forest Watch and the World Resources Institute– Indonesia have launched applications that involve crowdsourcing in monitoring deforestation and land degradation. The Geo-Wiki tool for improving global land cover has involved the crowd in visual interpretation of very-high-resolution satellite imagery from Google Earth and Bing, where the data have been used to create a hybrid forest cover map (Schepaschenko and others, 2015). Such data could be integrated into products of forest cover and degraded land, or these crowdsourcing methods could be used by national agencies to involve citizens in SDG monitoring in their territories.

Moving from Data to Action to Impact

On the one hand, we talk about lack of data for SDG implementation, particularly when we refer to traditional sources of data such as household surveys, while on the other hand, we are surrounded by an ever-growing multitude of different sources of Big Data. How can we mobilize this ongoing data revolution into positive action for sustainable development? There are movements happening on many fronts, but ultimately, large-scale investments by decisionmakers in unlocking commercial sources of data and investing in human capital needed to process and analyze the data require solid evidence that the outputs are valuable for the SDGs. The Radiant Earth project from the Bill and Melinda Gates Foundation and Omidyar Network will make a considerable amount of very-high-resolution satellite imagery free for humanitarian and environmental causes. This could result in the scaling up of poverty mapping applications such as the one demonstrated by Jean and others (2016), which is currently hindered by lack of open access to very-high-resolution satellite imagery.

In the background, GEO continues to be a key proponent in providing this much-needed evidence for decisionmakers by advancing the agenda on the use of remote sensing and geospatial data for SDG implementation. One of the key aims of GEO's EO4SDG Initiative is to build a set of pilot projects in different GEO member states that focus on integrating EO with national statistical accounts; these efforts will continue to provide many examples of good practices that can be adopted by other countries. However, much of the focus is on remote sensing, or in situ data to support remote sensing, rather than mobile phone data or other types of geospatial data.

Focusing on mobile phone data, UN Global Pulse and the GSMA, which represent the interest of almost 800 mobile operators worldwide, have recognized the considerable value of CDRs for social good (UN Global Pulse and GSMA, 2017). As part of their 2017 report, they reviewed over 200 projects demonstrating the successful integration of mobile phone data in different settings, including for development purposes. However, because most projects were focused on research or demonstrating feasibility, few applications can operate at scale to encourage the necessary evidence for investment. To move things forward, UN Global Pulse and GSMA have proposed a set of milestones for 2018 that focuses on building one large-scale, community-driven impact project to demonstrate the scaled and systematized use of mobile data for development. Recognizing that the donor community will need to provide initial funding to catalyze the activities, an important phase in the project will be to create a public-private partnership that will serve as an operational mechanism for sustaining the application. Only then will the evidence be strong enough to move this field forward.

Another ongoing initiative that encourages data sharing is Global Open Data for Agriculture and Nutrition (GODAN), which has relevance for SDG 2. Launched at the Open Government Partnership Conference in 2013, GODAN has almost 600 partners from national governments, NGOs, and international and private sector organizations. Driven by the urgent challenge of ensuring world food security, GODAN is opening up access to numerous data sets, including commercial data, by expanding its partnership and focusing on building support for open data at an institutional level. GODAN is already actively involved in working toward supporting SDG 2, for example, in the development of the SDG 2 Accountability Framework, which is a tool for tracking progress of national commitments and the gaps that must be filled to achieve SDG 2 in terms of data, policies, and financing. The tool is intended for use by a range of stakeholders, from decision-makers to interested citizens, and actively promotes the transparency of the information. In a similar vein, the Global Partnership for Sustainable Development Data (GPSDD) is promoting the more effective use of data, including Big Data, by filling key data gaps at the national level and increasing openness and data access. By recruiting "data champions," they are coordinating 100 different data-driven projects that will contribute to the SDG agenda. In addition, international entities such as the Sustainable Solutions Development Network (SDSN) plays a key role in showcasing examples of cross-sectoral collaborations to promote joint learning and deliver responsive policies and programs.

Finally, we need to be aware that there is the possibility of "indicator fatigue" when considering the comprehensive nature of the SDG framework, coupled with the reporting requirements of several other international agreements and conventions. Hence we need to think in more coordinated and integrated ways when helping countries gather and report on different indicators, mapping out commonalities in data sources, and developing advanced methods that can satisfy multiple reporting requirements at the same time. We also need to demonstrate clearly that using Big Data sources such as remote sensing and geospatial data for SDG implementation can have multiple and mutual benefits. By having fine-resolution maps of different SDG indicators, strategic planning from urban to national scales can be improved. By having a disaster alert system in place, which may help fulfill different SDGs, people can become more resilient as a consequence. These additional cobenefits, which may not seem apparent from a pure SDG measurement and implementation perspective, should also be highlighted to increase the evidence base for the added value of remote sensing and geospatial data.

References

Alkire, S., J. M. Roche, M. E. Santos, and S. Seth. 2011. "Brief Methodological Note." *Multidimensional Poverty Index 2011*. University of Oxford.

Anderson, K., B. Ryan, W. Sonntag, and others. 2017. Earth Observation in Service of the 2030 Agenda for Sustainable Development. *Geo-spatial Information Science* 20: 77–96. doi: 10.1080/10095020.2017.1333230

Blumenstock, J., and N. Eagle. 2010. "Mobile Divides: Gender, Socioeconomic Status, and Mobile Phone Use in Rwanda." In *ICTD '10: Proceedings of the 4th ACM/IEEE International Conference on Information and Communication Technologies and Development*. Article No. 6. New York: ACM Digital Library. doi: 10.1145/2369220.2369225

Bontemps, S., P. Defourny, E. van Bogaert, and others. 2011. "GLOBCOVER 2009: Products Description and Validation Report." Toulouse, France.

Central Bureau of Statistics. 2009. "2008 Population Census." National Report. Pyong-yang, DPRK (https://unstats.un.org/unsd/demographic/sources/census/wphc/North_Korea/Final%20national%20census%20report.pdf).

Chen, X., and W. D. Nordhaus. 2011. "Using Luminosity Data as a Proxy for Economic Statistics." *Proceedings of the National Academy of Science* 108: 8589–94. doi: 10.1073/pnas.1017031108

CIA. 2017. *The World Factbook: North Korea* (www.cia.gov/library/publications/the-world-factbook/geos/kn.html).

Constine, J. 2017. "Facebook Now Has 2 Billion Monthly Users . . . and Responsibility." TechCrunch (https://techcrunch.com/2017/06/27/facebook-2-billion-users/).

Culotta, A. 2014. "Reducing Sampling Bias in Social Media Data for County Health Inference." In *JSM Proceedings, Statistical Computing Section*. Alexandria, Va.: American Statistical Assocation.

De Fries, R., M. Hansen, J. Townshend, and R. Sohlberg. 1998. "Global Land Cover Classifications at 8 km Spatial Resolution: The Use of Training Data Derived from Landsat Imagery in Decision Tree Classifiers." *International Journal of Remote Sensing* 19: 3141–68.

Defourny, P., C. Vancustem, P. Bicheron, and others. 2006. "GLOBCOVER: A 300 M Global Land Cover Product for 2005 Using ENVISAT MERIS Time Series." In *Proceedings of the ISPRS Commission VII Mid-Term Symposium: Remote Sensing: From Pixels to Processes*. Netherlands: Enschede (http://citeseerx.ist.psu.edu/viewdoc/summary?doi=10.1.1.116.1909).

Elvidge, C. D., P. C. Sutton, T. Ghosh, and others. 2009. "A Global Poverty Map Derived from Satellite Data." *Computers & Geosciences* 35: 1652–60. doi: 10.1016/j.cageo.2009.01.009

Ericsson. 2017. "Ericsson Mobility Report." June (www.ericsson.com/assets/local/mobility-report/documents/2017/ericsson-mobility-report-june-2017.pdf).

ESA. 2017a. "300 m Annual Global Land Cover Time Series from 1992 to 2015." CCI Land Cover (www.esa-landcover-cci.org/?q=node/175).

———. 2017b. "ESA and the Sustainable Development Goals" (www.esa.int/Our_Activities/Preparing_for_the_Future/Space_for_Earth/ESA_and_the_Sustainable_Development_Goals).

Esch, T., W. Heldens, A. Hirner, and others. 2017. "Breaking New Ground in Mapping Human Settlements from Space—The Global Urban Footprint" (https://arxiv.org/pdf/1706.04862.pdf).

Espey, J., E. Swanson, S. Badiee, and others. 2015. "Data for Development: A Needs Assessment for SDG Monitoring and Statistical Capacity Development" (http://unsdsn.org/resources/publications/a-needs-assessment-for-sdg-monitoring-and-statistical-capacity-development/).

Friedl, M. A., D. Sulla-Menashe, B. Tan, and others. 2010. "MODIS Collection 5 Global Land Cover: Algorithm Refinements and Characterization of New Datasets." *Remote Sensing of Environment* 114:168–182. doi: 10.1016/j.rse.2009.08.016

Fritz, S., E. Bartholomé, A. Belward, and others. 2003. "Harmonisation, Mosaicking, and Production of the Global Land Cover 2000 Database (Beta Version)." Luxembourg: Office for Official Publications of the European Communities.

Fritz, S., L. See, I. McCallum, and others. 2015. "Mapping Global Cropland and Field Size." *Global Change Biology* 21: 1980–92. doi: 10.1111/gcb.12838

Fritz, S., M. van Dijk, and I. Moorthy. 2017. "Tracking Poverty Using Satellite Imagery and Big Data." Submitted to Data for Climate Action Challenge. Laxenburg, Austria: IIASA.

Gallagher, K. 2017. "The Social Media Demographics Report." New York: Business Insider (www.businessinsider.com/the-social-media-demographics-report-2017-8).

GEO. 2017. "Earth Observations 2030 Agenda for Sustainable Development, V1.1." Japan Aerospace Exploration Agency, on behalf of GEO under the EO4SDG Initiative (www.earthobservations.org/documents/publications/201703_geo_eo_for_2030_agenda.pdf).

GMSA. 2017. Unique Mobile Subscribers to Surpass 5 Billion This Year (www.gsma intelligence.com/research/2017/02/unique-mobile-subscribers-to-surpass-5-billion-this-year/613/).

Gong, P., J. Wang, L. Yu, and others. 2013. "Finer Resolution Observation and Monitoring of Global Land Cover: First Mapping Results with Landsat TM and ETM+ Data." *International Journal of Remote Sensing* 34: 2607–2654. doi: 10.1080/01431161.2012.748992

Goodchild, M. F. 2007. "Citizens as Sensors: The World of Volunteered Geography." *GeoJournal* 69: 211–21. doi: 10.1007/s10708-007-9111-y

Henderson, J. V., A. Storeygard, and D. N. Weil. 2012. "Measuring Economic Growth from Outer Space." *American Economic Review* 102: 994–1028. doi: 10.1257/aer.102.2.994

Herold, M., L. See, N.-E. Tsendbazar, and S. Fritz. 2016. "Towards an Integrated Global Land Cover Monitoring and Mapping System." *Remote Sensing* 8: 1036. doi: 10.3390/rs8121036

Holderness, T., and E. Turpin. 2015. "PetaJakarta.org: Assessing the Rrole of Social Media for Civic Co-Management during Monsoon Flooding in Jakarta, Indonesia." SMART Infrastructure Facility, University of Wollongong (https://petajakarta.org/banjir/in/research/index.html).

IEAG Secretariat. 2014. "A World That Counts. Mobilising the Data Revolution for Sustainable Development" (www.undatarevolution.org/wp-content/uploads/2014/11/A--World-That-Counts.pdf).

Jean, N., M. Burke, M. Xie, and others. 2016. Combining Satellite Imagery and Machine Learning to Predict Poverty." *Science* 353: 790–94. doi: 10.1126/science.aaf7894

Jokar Arsanjani, J., A. Zipf, P. Mooney, M. Helbich, eds. 2015. *OpenStreetMap in GIScience*. Cham, Switzerland: Springer.

Lesiv, M., D. Schepaschenko, E. Moltchanova, and others. 2018. "Spatial Distribution of Arable and Abandoned Land Across Former Soviet Union Countries." *Scientific Data* 5:180056. *Nature*. doi: 10.1038/sdata.2018.56.

Morstatter, F., and H. Liu. 2017. "Discovering, Assessing, and Mitigating Data Bias in Social Media." *Online Social Networks and Media* 1: 1–13. doi: 10.1016/j.osnem.2017.01.001

Newbold, T., L. N. Hudson, A. P. Arnell, and others. 2016. Has Land Use Pushed Terrestrial Biodiversity Beyond the Planetary Boundary? A Global Assessment." *Science* 353: 288–291. doi: 10.1126/science.aaf2201

Pekel, J.-F., A. Cottam, N. Gorelick, A. S. Belward. 2016. "High-Resolution Mapping of Global Surface Water and Its Long-Term Changes." *Nature* 540: 418–422. doi: 10.1038/nature20584

Pesaresi, M., G. Huadong, X. Blaes, and others. 2013. "A Global Human Settlement Layer from Optical HR/VHR RS Data: Concept and First Results." *IEEE Journal of Selected Topics in Applied Earth Observations and Remote Sensing* 6: 2102–31. doi: 10.1109/JSTARS.2013.2271445

Pokhriyal, N., W. Dong, and V. Govindaraju. 2015. "Virtual Networks and Poverty Analysis in Senegal" (https://arxiv.org/pdf/1506.03401.pdf).

Romijn, E., M. Herold, B. Mora, and others. 2017. "Monitoring Progress towards Sustainable Development Goals. The Role of Land Monitoring" (www.gofcgold.wur.nl/documents/newsletter/Sustainable_Development_Goals-infobrief.pdf).

Schepaschenko, D., L. See, M. Lesiv, and others. 2015. "Development of a Global Hybrid Forest Mask Through the Synergy of Remote Sensing, Crowdsourcing and FAO Statistics." *Remote Sensing of Environment* 162: 208–220. doi: 10.1016/j.rse.2015.02.011

Scholes, R. J., and R. Biggs. 2005. "A Biodiversity Intactness Index." *Nature* 434: 45–49. doi: 10.1038/nature03289

Serajuddin, U., H. Uematsu, C. Wieser, and others. 2015. "Data Deprivation. Another Deprivation to End." Policy Research Working Paper 7252. Washington: World Bank (https://elibrary.worldbank.org/doi/abs/10.1596/1813-9450-7252).

Soto, V., V. Frias-Martinez, J. Virseda, E. Frias-Martinez. 2011. "Prediction of Socioeconomic Levels Using Cell Phone Records." In J. A. Konstan, R. Conejo, J. L. Marzo, N. Oliver, eds., *User Modeling, Adaption and Personalization*. Berlin, Heidelberg: Springer. pp. 377–88.

Statista. 2017. Number of Monthly Active Twitter Users Worldwide from 1st Quarter 2010 to 2nd Quarter 2017 (in millions). The Statistics Portal (www.statista.com/statistics/282087/number-of-monthly-active-twitter-users/).

Statistic Brain. 2017. Instagram Company Statistics (www.statisticbrain.com/instagram-company-statistics/).

UN Global Pulse. 2016. Data Innovation Risk Assessment Tool (http://unglobalpulse.org/sites/default/files/Privacy%20Assessment%20Tool%20.pdf).

UN Global Pulse and GSMA. 2017. "The State of Mobile Data for Social Good Report" (www.gsma.com/mobilefordevelopment/wp-content/uploads/2017/06/Mobile-Data-for-Social-Good-Report_29June.pdf).

United Nations. 2013. *A New Global Partnership: Eradicate Poverty and Transform Economies through Sustainable Development.* "The Report of the High-Level Panel of Eminent Persons on the Post-2015 Development Agenda" (www.post2015hlp.org/wp-content/uploads/2013/05/UN-Report.pdf).

———. 2015a. Sustainable Development Goals (https://unstats.un.org/sdgs/).

———. 2015b. "Report of the Capacity Building Workshop and Expert Group Meeting on Integrated Approaches to Sustainable Development Planning and Implementation." May 27–29. New York (https://sustainabledevelopment.un.org/content/documents/8506IASD%20Workshop%20Report%2020150703.pdf).

———. 2016a. *Human Development for Everyone.* Human Development Report 2016. UNDP (http://hdr.undp.org/sites/default/files/2016_human_development_report.pdf).

———. 2016b. *The World's Cities in 2016* (www.un.org/en/development/desa/population/publications/pdf/urbanization/the_worlds_cities_in_2016_data_booklet.pdf).

Wesolowski, A., N. Eagle, A. M. Noor, and others. 2012. "Heterogeneous Mobile Phone Ownership and Usage Patterns in Kenya." *PLoS ONE* 7:e35319. doi: 10.1371/journal.pone.0035319

Williams, N. E., T. A. Thomas, M. Dunbar, and others. 2015. "Measures of Human Mobility Using Mobile Phone Records Enhanced with GIS Data." *PLoS ONE* 10: e0133630. doi: 10.1371/journal.pone.0133630

World Bank. 2016. Mobile Phone Subscriptions per 100 People (https://data.worldbank.org/indicator/IT.CEL.SETS.P2?name_desc=true).

World Data Lab. 2017. World Poverty Clock (worldpoverty.io/index.html).

World Economic Forum. 2012. "Big Data, Big Impact: New Possibilities for International Development" (www3.weforum.org/docs/WEF_TC_MFS_BigDataBig Impact_Briefing_2012.pdf).

Xiong, J., P. S. Thenkabail, J. C. Tilton, and others. 2017. " Nominal 30-m Cropland Extent Map of Continental Africa by Integrating Pixel-Based and Object-Based Algorithms Using Sentinel-2 and Landsat-8 Data on Google Earth Engine." *Remote Sensing* 9, no. 10: 1065. doi:10.3390/rs91010

CHAPTER NINE

Enhancing Statistical Capacity for Development

Ryuichi Tomizawa and Noriharu Masugi

The Sustainable Development Goals place significant burdens on developing countries to monitor their progress, requiring improvements to the production and dissemination of statistical data. Although efforts have been made—with some success—to enhance the capacity of developing countries to produce reliable statistics, and there have been remarkable achievements in some countries and areas, the challenges that lie ahead are substantial and daunting. This chapter argues that developing countries and their partners must continue to develop their statistical capacity in order to take advantage of technological and data modernization. Drawing on the experiences of the Japan International Cooperation Agency (JICA) in a developing country, this chapter evaluates the types of external support that have proven effective in enhancing core statistical capacity.

The Challenge of National Statistical Capacity Development

The statistical systems and capacity of developing countries have been constructed with the assistance of various development partners and initiatives. For example, since 1993 the International Monetary Fund (IMF) and the Asian Development Bank (ADB) have mainly supported statistical development for economic and financial statistics in Cambodia, while the United Nations Development Programme (UNDP) and the United Nations Population Fund (UNFPA) have supported sociodemographic statistics in that country.[1] With the launch of the Partnership in Statistics for Development in the 21st Century (PARIS21) in 1999, the international statistical community recognized the need for a more effective process to help strengthen the statistical capacity of developing countries. The Millennium Development Goals (MDGs) increased the demand for wide-ranging support for

1. Morrison and others (2005), p. 14.

statistics as data are needed to monitor the progress of each goal. This increasing need for statistical capacity development is also reflected in Targets 17.18 and 17.19 of the new Sustainable Development Goals (SDGs). Yet statistical systems in many countries remain underfunded and lack the capacity to respond to growing demands for data.[2] In sub-Saharan Africa, only South Africa and Uganda have complied with standards for national statistical capacity set by the IMF.[3] Recognizing this in its report *A World That Counts*, the UN called for a new funding stream for statistical finance and a new global partnership for statistics.[4]

We now have a far greater understanding of ways in which support for statistical capacity building can be managed. An article by the IMF states that there is room for both development partners and partner countries to make more of an effort in preparing statistical capacity development strategies; assuring high-level and unified leadership and ownership of statistical capacity-building activities; giving due consideration to donor coordination; undertaking user consultations; appropriate phasing of project inputs; providing hands-on technical assistance; and carefully choosing the experts and mode of delivery.[5]

However, while there is now a number of project-based details concerning external efforts and initiatives for building national statistical capacity, there is still a dearth of evaluatory lessons from the concrete experiences of developing countries. We turn to a description of JICA's experiences in Cambodia before evaluating their results.

Building Statistical Capacity: The Case of Cambodia

For over three decades, JICA, the technical and financial cooperation arm of the government of Japan, has provided advisory services for capacity development for the collation of official statistics in developing countries. Starting with support for Indonesia's population census in the early 1980s, JICA has gone on to provide support to countries including Mexico, Sri Lanka, Argentina, Tanzania,

2. Open Data Watch (2015), pp. 2–3.
3. Jerven (2013), p.100. The IMF has set six criteria for national statistical capacity: prerequisite of quality, assurance of integrity, methodological soundness, accuracy and reliability, serviceability, and accessibility.
4. United Nations (2014), pp. 25–26.
5. Morrison and others (2005, pp. 6–8). A thematic study by Strode and others (2009, pp. x–xiii) sets out the eight pillars necessary for supporting statistical development, namely: results-based management, accountability of statistical systems including legal frameworks, institutional arrangements, strategic planning, a secured budget, management capacity within the national statistical system, qualified staff, and appropriate tools and methods. A paper by Open Data Watch (2015, pp. 15-16) recommends that development partners provide support during project preparations, provide systemwide approaches and budget support, work effectively with international partners, and maintain flexibility in implementation.

Table 9-1. Project Outcomes, JICA Statistical Capacity Development in Cambodia

Phase	Timing	Objectives	Tangible outputs	Intangible outputs
1	August 2005–March 2007		Technical training for NIS staff and the statistical staff of the provincial department of the Ministry of Planning and related ministries	None
2	April 2007–September 2010	Preparation and implementation of the 2008 population census	Allocating census enumeration districts for implementing a population census Conducting data processing, data analysis, dissemination, and small-area statistics for population and economic censuses Creating a database using the results of the population census and preparing and using a list of business establishments for economic statistics surveys	Establishing a mechanism to maintain the skills and knowledge necessary for official statistics even though information sharing among NIS staff had some room for improvement Arranging coordination between the related organizations and donors for population and economic censuses and other statistical surveys
3	October 2010–September 2015	Preparation and implementation of the 2011 economic census (first of its kind in the country)	Conducting the planning and implementation of statistical surveys Tabulating and scrutinizing data by staff of the provincial planning departments	

Myanmar, Cambodia, and most recently, Egypt and Nepal (see appendix). JICA typically works in collaboration with the Statistics Bureau of the Japanese Ministry of Internal Affairs and Communications and other Japanese statistical organizations to provide technical expertise for these projects.

As part of its assistance for the reconstruction process in Cambodia, JICA supported the development of staff capacity at the National Institute of Statistics (NIS) in three phases; the first two phases were aimed at the preparation and implementation of the population census, while the last (third) phase concentrated on the implementation of the economic census. Details of the timing, activities, and outputs from the three phases of the project are in table 9-1.

The initial plan was to provide hands-on advice regarding the implementation of the 2008 Population Census; however, the original plan was hindered by a delay in the preparation of a detailed plan for the 2008 census and a lack of funds, which NIS had intended to obtain from its development partners. The Royal Government of Cambodia, which had officially decided to conduct the population census in March 2008 by order of a sub-decree issued in January 2006, made a request for Japanese technical cooperation to help prepare and implement the 2008 Population Census. The effort also received funding from the UNFPA.

Throughout the three phases of the capacity development project, JICA provided various input and successfully managed to enhance the capacity of the NIS staff. The project was supported by the Japanese government's partners, such as the Statistics Bureau, the Statistical Research and Training Institute (SRTI), the National Statistics Center (NSTAC), and private entities, including the Japan Statistical Association (JSTAT) and the Statistical Information Institute for Consulting and Analysis (Sinfonica). JICA dispatched a total of seventy-eight Japanese short-term experts, conducted nine training programs in Japan for twenty-six NIS staff members, and carried out nine study tours to third countries (Indonesia, Sri Lanka, Lao PDR, Myanmar, and Nepal) for twenty-five NIS staff members.

During each of the training programs within Phase 1, a series of comprehension tests were carried out on all participants. While the average score for the pretraining test was 43.5 percent, the post-training average was 71.4 percent, an increase of 27.9 percent points; this demonstrates a considerable improvement in the capacity of the NIS staff.[6] In Phases 2 and 3, the project introduced mechanisms for quantifying the degree of improvement in capacity through the use of comprehension tests. The results of these evaluations, shown in tables 9-2 and 9-3, illustrate the remarkable improvement in the capacity of staff.[7]

However, the achievements were not straightforward. The project faced a number of challenges arising from the problems prevalent at NIS, such as low salaries, short working hours, an insufficient number of staff, and the burden placed on staff to cater to the activities of other development partners.[8] As a result, it was customary for most NIS staff to supplement their low salaries with a side job in order to earn a living. While UNFPA paid a supplement of about U.S. $180 a month to each NIS staff member, in keeping with long-standing JICA policy, its

6. JICA (2007a), p. 3.
7. JICA (2010a), pp. 31–32; JICA (2014), pp. 34–35.
8. Personal communication from Fumihiko Nishi, professor with Statistical Research and Training Institute (SRTI), Ministry of Internal Affairs and Communications, December 24, 2016. Nishi is the former chief adviser of the Project on Improving Official Statistics in Cambodia and the current chief adviser of the Project on Capacity Development for the Implementation of an Economic Census in Nepal.

Table 9-2. NIS Staff: Evaluation of Statistical Capacity, as of April 2007 and February 2010

	April 2007		February 2010	
Area of evaluation	Number of staff	Average score	Number of staff	Average score
1. Population census				
Management	5	3.89	5	4.52
Planning monitoring	4	3.92	4	4.58
Assistant planning/data processing/ cartography	6	3.20	6	3.90
Support staff planning/data processing/ cartography	6	3.61	6	4.28
Data entry supervisor	1	3.70	1	4.40
Editing/coding and data entry	4	3.14	4	3.71
Computer editing, programming, tabulation	3	3.20	3	4.10
2. Establishment listing				
Management	1	4.33	1	4.90
Finance and logistics	2	3.73	2	4.10
Planning	4	3.27	4	4.25
Manual editing and coding	1	3.50	1	4.54
Data processing	4	3.27	4	4.29

Source: JICA (2010a), pp. 31–32.

Table 9-3. NIS Staff: Baseline and Endline in Competency Assessment on Economic Census, 2011

Competency	Number of personnel evaluated	Average score	
		December 2010	September 2014
Management	4	3.70	3.78
Economic statistics	4	3.53	3.75
Planning and implementation	2	3.72	3.85
Census mapping	2	3.21	3.27
Sampling	2	3.00	3.29
Analysis and publication	2	3.24	3.65
Tabulation and coding	2	3.24	3.72
Data entry and computer editing	5	3.26	3.63

Source: JICA (2014), p. 34.
Notes: Figures are average values competency assessment of the personnel involved in the 2011 economic census. The number shown in parentheses is the number of personnel who received the evaluations. Scores, on a scale of 1 to 5, measure: 5 = excellent, 4 = good, 3 = sufficient, 2 = insufficient, 1 = poor.

counterpart staff at NIS were not paid an additional stipend. As a result, some NIS staff prioritized side jobs over project activities. In order to motivate core counterpart staff, JICA provided training opportunities in Japan, study tours to third countries such as Indonesia, and equipment such as personal computers for project activities.

Short working hours and a limited number of staff at NIS may have hindered the smooth progress of activities. NIS staff worked only six hours a day, and no overtime allowance was paid. The number of staff in the NIS headquarters was only about 300, and these staff members covered all the activities related to official statistics in Cambodia.[9] Thus, JICA experts and NIS staff prioritized project activities and changed them according to the circumstances.

In addition to the support given by JICA, other development partners simultaneously supported NIS. UNFPA assisted NIS in conducting the Demographic and Health Survey in 2005 and 2010. The Swedish International Development Cooperation Agency worked with NIS to implement the annual Cambodia Socio-Economic Survey beginning in 2007. Many of JICA's counterparts were involved in these projects, which caused an overflow in each individual duty. This was another reason that JICA experts had to adjust the volume of their activities. The Agricultural Census supported by the Food and Agriculture Organization—originally set for 2014 but brought forward to 2013—also placed a burden on the counterpart staff, causing delays in data analysis and writing analysis reports for the 2011 Economic Census.[10] As a result, JICA's experts had to take the initiative of writing these reports and providing trainings on data analysis and report writing for its NIS counterparts.[11]

Perhaps the biggest challenge for NIS and the project was the lack of financial resources for the 2008 Population Census. This lack of funds led to the government of Cambodia having to request financial support from a number of its development partners. The total cost of the 2008 Population Census was about U.S. $6 million, of which Japan contributed U.S. $2 million.[12] UNFPA and the German government also contributed funds. The establishment of the New Statistics Center at NIS in January 2008, which provided facilities, including a data-processing room, a training room, a library, and a data user service center, resulted in the need for further financial assistance. The total cost of the construction of the center, amounting to U.S. $0.9 million, was fully covered by Japan.[13]

9. As a comparison, the Statistics Bureau of the Ministry of Internal Affairs and Communications has approximately 500 staff and shares official statistics activities with statistical staff in other ministries.
10. JICA (2014), p. 36.
11. Personal communication from F. Nishi, professor, SRTI, December 24, 2016.
12. NIS (2008), p. 11; JICA (2007b), p. 5.
13. JICA (2007b), p. 5.

Initial Results

The statistical outputs of the censuses were used in various planning and policy-making processes. The government of Cambodia took advantage of the output data from the 2008 Population Census and used it to formulate its population policy[14] and to monitor MDG achievement.[15] Cambodian officials also used the data to formulate subnational democratic development.[16]

Data outputs from the 2011 Economic Census were incorporated into the formulation of Cambodia's economic policy agenda, especially for labor market development planning.[17] The same data were also quoted in many publications issued by the Cambodian government and private institutions in Cambodia, as well as by international organizations such as the Council for the Development of Cambodia (CDC), the World Bank, and UNDP.[18] For the first time, the CDC analyzed the current situation of the Cambodian economy by using data from the 2011 Economic Census.[19]

In addition to acquisition of skills, three types of changes in the attitudes and behavior of NIS staff were observed.[20] First, as the NIS staff experienced detailed practical work through conducting statistical surveys, they often made anticipatory preparations for the next round of procedures themselves before the JICA experts provided instructions. This was particularly notable toward the end of the project. Second, the working environment within NIS's provincial planning departments improved with the provision of computers. Trained staff began to prepare small-area statistics by themselves at the request of the provincial government. Up until that point, provincial planning departments had relied on the NIS headquarters for preparation of such statistics. Finally, NIS staff learned how to organize "user-friendly" reports. NIS staff have effectively used appropriate data, figures, and tables and have provided detailed accounts of the results of the surveys.

Toward a Model of Statistical Capacity Development

One of the characteristics of JICA's technical cooperation with other organizations is that it provides step-by-step, hands-on technical approaches, including

14. Royal Government of Cambodia (2014a).
15. Royal Government of Cambodia (2014b).
16. Royal Government of Cambodia (2010).
17. Royal Government of Cambodia (2013).
18. JICA and CDC (2012); World Bank (2012); United Nations (2013).
19. JICA and CDC (2013). Personal communication from F. Nishi, professor, SRTI, December 24, 2016.
20. Personal communication from F. Nishi, professor, SRTI, November 18, 2016.

technical advice and on-the-job-training that is supported by Japanese experts. This includes the careful assessment and monitoring of the capacity of counterpart personnel. For NIS to sustain its capacity, and as part of knowledge sharing, JICA experts developed manuals and guidelines for population and economic censuses in each operation in cooperation with the NIS staff.

Additionally, there are limits to what a single development partner can do to support a large national project. UNFPA was the forerunner in providing support to NIS as early as the 1998 Population Census. Before JICA launched Phase 1 in 2005, UNFPA supported the 2008 Population Census by dispatching experts and preparing the implementation schedule. JICA carefully cooperated with UNFPA to demarcate areas of support (UNFPA conducted census planning and enumeration, while JICA supported data processing, data scrutiny, data analysis, and the dissemination of outputs), which turned out to be successful.[21]

Appropriate expertise is also necessary. Bearing in mind the fact that there are many technical areas that make up a national census, JICA organized a team of Japanese experts to support the 2008 Population Census. JICA recruited experts from the government of Japan and from the private sector because in Japan, government and private entities work jointly when organizing a population census.

Implementation of a national census, finally, requires a concerted effort from the relevant ministries and agencies. In Phase 2, JICA and NIS promoted internal coordination of statistical activities within the government of Cambodia. One of the outputs of Phase 3 clearly aimed to enhance the coordination mechanisms used by NIS and its provincial planning departments to prepare and implement censuses and surveys. As a result, Cambodia set in place efficient internal coordination mechanisms, which contributed to an effective publicity campaign around the census and the smooth implementation of the census itself. JICA regards the enhancement of coordination and management capabilities as a "core capacity" needed for implementing projects and operations.[22]

Some Remaining Challenges

Following a decade of technical cooperation, several challenges still remain. The statistical capacity development of NIS staff, for example, still has a long way to go. In the *Open Data Inventory 2016*, NIS in Cambodia was ranked 157 out of 173 countries and was the lowest among the ten countries of Southeast Asia.[23] In

21. JICA (2010b), p. 6.
22. JICA Research Institute (2008), p. 18.
23. Open Data Watch (2016).

order to identify the measures needed to close the gaps in an effective and efficient way, it is important that the NIS staff acknowledge what they are capable of and what still poses a challenge.

First, NIS should formulate a budget plan to secure adequate financial resources for conducting future censuses. The Cambodian government's share of the burden of costs for censuses has increased in recent years, but the financial resources are still insufficient to cover all necessary costs. The government plans to conduct the 2019 Population Census, which will require funding from external sources.

Second, NIS should do more to disseminate the outputs of statistical surveys. It has established procedures for disseminating statistical results through means such as ceremonies and seminars, both at the national and provincial levels, published reports, distribution of CDs, and data uploaded onto its website. Although it is the policy of NIS to post as much information as possible on its websites for use by the public, the number of published reports posted on the two websites is very limited compared to its physical publications.[24]

Third, NIS still needs considerable technical assistance from its development partners to analyze economic data. The level of analytical capacity for economic censuses and surveys substantially varies among the officers because many of them have little experience conducting economic censuses and surveys.

Fourth, as an institution, NIS should effectively manage documents, particularly electronic copies of manuals and instructions, and share them widely within the agency. This can be done by improving the current data sharing system and its procedures. During the project period, information such as various operation manuals tended to remain in the hands of certain individuals rather than being widely disseminated. Moreover, NIS still relies on its development partners to manage the soft copies of a number of important documents.

Finally, monitoring of the SDGs will be another challenge and requires that the capacity of NIS staff be further enhanced. Additionally, coordination with other ministries needs to be improved. NIS staff have enhanced their capacity to implement official statistics activities including population and economic censuses throughout JICA's ten years of cooperation. The Cambodian government has appropriately used these outputs in its strategic planning. NIS is also expected to provide any necessary data related to the indicators of the SDGs. However, since the SDGs are much broader in context than the MDGs and will require vast amounts of data for monitoring, the development of further capacity for NIS will be indispensable.

---

24. The two websites are at www.nis.gov.kh and https://nada.nis.gov.kh.

Closing the Gaps in Statistical Capacity Development

Globalization and diversification of the socioeconomy and lifestyles today have pushed the world toward a need for faster, easier, and yet larger and more detailed information data to measure the most updated situation or to provide predictive trends on how a situation will perform in a given amount of time. It is difficult even for developed countries to capture all the phenomena by way of traditional statistical surveys where statistical staff collect data on foot. Since it takes a certain amount of time to compile and analyze that data, by the time the statistics are made public, it may be too late to use them for policymaking purposes. Traditional statistical surveys require a considerable budget and human resources, which might not be sustainable for developing countries. In this era of digitalization, and in tandem with administrative reform efforts, it is worthwhile reviewing statistical tools and investigating what we can do to promptly collect and compile statistical data while at the same time improving their quality and accuracy.[25]

Administrative Data

National statistics organizations (NSOs) may be able to save on costs and time if administrative data collected by other ministries are provided to NSOs. There are cases where countries, both developing and developed, have made use of administrative data when organizing official statistics. Normally, civil, land, welfare, finance, and tax records are administered by the respective ministries, which NSOs do not usually have access to. Governments should therefore compile lists of the available data in each ministry, including their frequency of collection, geographical coverage, and target groups, so that NSOs can collate them with their own data wish lists.

For instance, civil and real estate registration data may provide NSOs with information about where people live; this could then be useful for conducting population censuses. In cases where corporate enterprises submit financial statements and registration of property assets to the authorities, the data collected may identify the coverage and size of businesses and other behavioral information. This may provide supporting evidence of economic structures, which is one of the outputs of economic censuses.

Economic indexes are of great use and are important for developing countries as a reference for navigating their economies through timely and appropriate

---

25. As the economy grows and various entities perform economic activities, the types and numbers of statistical indicators are likely to increase. For example, in 2012 the Cambodian NIS published 115 indicators in its Annual Report. See NIS (2013).

policy implementation. Many developed countries create a public diffusion index-composite index as a means of determining the expansion and direction of economic growth. These indexes consist of various economic indicators provided by the government and the private sector, such as corporate profits, housing starts,[26] bankruptcy, machinery orders, employment and unemployment, the consumer price index, wage increases, and number of passenger transport units, to name a few. NSOs in developing countries would be able to compile and announce economic data if they could obtain these data from the private sector and the ministries in charge. While indicators used for these indexes vary between countries, governments can choose what indicators they wish to use according to data availability and which indicators best suit their own economic circumstances.

It would be highly adaptable if civil registration or voting register data are maintained appropriately and in electrical format. Since these data are often updated, governments would be able to make use of them unless they were otherwise unavailable. It would be useful for NSOs to use this group of data as the base figures and attributes for population censuses, as was done in Singapore.[27]

On the other hand, the use of administrative data is limited due to confidentiality and the need to observe data collection regulations. Other barriers include data not being organized in order, lack of correctness and reliability, differences in definitions of data, and so on. NSOs should work with the relevant ministries and identify which specific data may be used for their own purposes. If concerned parties come to an agreement, they may be able to discuss the ways in which they could align the definitions of data and the means of collection.

Where data is collected in the field, it would also be necessary to build the capacity of the statistics officers collecting the data, who in most cases are local officials. In the process of administrative reform, the government should include components for strengthening the human and institutional capacity of the NSO and its affiliates.

Web-Based Data

Tablet computers and web-based portals may reduce the amount of staff, time, and cost involved when compared to traditional methods. Additionally, the e-census has been introduced in some developed countries (online responses are already used in Australia, Canada, and New Zealand) and even in some developing countries, on a trial basis.

26. *Trading Economics* (2017).
27. ANCSDAAP (2016), p. 4.

The use of tablets for enumeration has many advantages. By selecting an answer from pull-down options, enumerators are able to prevent errors in data entry. By sending data through the internet, the risk of data being retained in tablets is reduced. Other advantages include the ability to confirm the progress of the survey immediately with digitally processed data, improved data reliability, and ease of processing, tabulating, and comparing data.

The use of tablets and e-census may seem like a game changer for governments, making their lives easier, more efficient, and effective. However, the costs required for the initial introduction of equipment (tablets, servers, networks, and so on), the development of software for enumeration and tabulation, and the supporting services provided by vendors are enormous. Switching to e-census also requires modification of administrative procedures such as preparation of legal frameworks for electronic statistical surveys, the revision of survey procedures, training for enumerators and supervisors, and public awareness campaigns. It is of course also necessary to allocate sufficient budgets for the maintenance and renewal of information technology (IT) systems.

In Australia, at the outset of the 2016 Population Census, the online forms experienced an outage due to denial-of-service (DoS) attempts and a hardware failure.[28] Protection of personal information is especially important in online statistical surveys. Therefore, distribution of printed questionnaires would still be necessary. Moreover, since security concerns such as hacking, phishing, and spyware are growing threats to digital society, security measures must be in place to protect online responses. This could be an extra cost burden. After thorough consideration, the United States did not use online responses for its 2010 population census.[29]

It may seem that developing countries can leapfrog today's developed countries by using an e-census. The prevalence of online administrative services and commercial infrastructure such as e-government, e-tax, internet banking, and online shopping in a society would enhance the IT literacy of the population, thus contributing to the achievement of a high response rate.[30]

Use and Abuse of "Big Data"

Use of Big Data in developing countries tends to be limited to supplemental information to official statistics. Big Data might make it possible to rapidly prepare accurate and high-quality statistical data at a low cost, overcoming the lack of

28. See Australian Bureau of Statistics (2016).
29. See United States Census Bureau (2010). See also Brown and others (2016), pp. 288–90.
30. Brown and others (2016), p. 291.

human and financial resources. For instance, geographic data and telecommunication data may allow you to identify where people live. Big Data on merchandise sales, customer information, logistics, and passenger transport could form the basis of economic indicators. The obstacles in making use of Big Data are, for example, the verification of who collects Big Data, who owns it, how frequently it is collected, whether it can be anonymized, whether NSOs can obtain the data and have the necessary skills to apply or edit it, as well as whether there are applicable laws and regulations for clearing the issues mentioned above.

Many multilateral and bilateral development partners, including the United Nations, have carried out various initiatives and studies on data revolution with the aim of promoting the monitoring of the SDG indicators. Gap analyses and costing on data availability and government capacity in developing countries have been conducted. What is required of developing countries is that they understand where they stand now and decide what target levels certain indicators should achieve so that their development efforts are showcased. They will need to extract applicable data, consolidate baseline data, obtain and analyze data continuously, and align and compare data in a time sequence.

NSOs and related ministries and agencies must join together to construct a cooperative relationship on which to establish a favorable foundation for conducting official statistics and handling Big Data. As many developing countries do not have a well-established system for organizing official statistics, such as for Big Data, they may face many challenges, including difficulty obtaining physical data (satellite images and mobile phone data, for example) and a lack of capacity for data mining and data processing. Additionally, those who are involved in development should not be left out in order to gain access to data. Once data are processed, they should be made available to the public for further use as a public good. NSOs should build quality and reliable statistics as a basis for policies that will include everyone without economic, social, ethnical, religious, linguistic, or physical discrimination.

Currently, there are few examples of Big Data being used for policymaking purposes.[31] With efficient coordination, researchers and practitioners can close the gaps in the use of Big Data for monitoring the SDGs. For example, JICA's initiative "Science and Technology Research Partnership for Sustainable Development," or SATREPS, may be one solution for ensuring efficient coordination between researchers and practitioners. A SATREPS project in Kenya developed a mobile short-message-service-based disease outbreak alert system (mSOS) for

---

31. The World Bank, for instance, has started an initiative that uses Big Data to create climate-resilient economies. See the World Bank (2016).

the immediate reporting of notifiable diseases.[32] Encouraged by results of testing, the Kenyan Ministry of Health decided to disseminate the mSOS throughout the country.[33]

There are various forms of Big Data that could be highly useful in monitoring progress in achieving the developmental goals—satellite images, mobile phone data, social network service data, and financial transactions, to name a few.[34] In developing countries, in order to make use of this information, technical support would need to be targeted toward relevant statistical authorities, research institutions, and universities. Components of the support include human capacity development, improvement of analysis methods, and institution building.

Other Areas

Among those methods that may provide solutions for closing the gaps in official statistics and statistical capacity development, some promising ideas that promote better, more efficient official statistics are noted below.

National ID

Governments may benefit by relying on various forms of civic identification—such as national ID cards and biometric IDs—for use in population censuses. It would make the work of national statistics easier if each datum contained a unique marker such that statistical offices could link them to other informative attributes. Countries that have a long history of using national ID numbers and those that are trusted for having a good track record of privacy protection may be in a better position to realize this idea. However, it may be difficult for some countries, as applying IDs for different purposes may raise concerns about privacy. Similarly, corporate IDs may be useful during an economic census, if combined with other administrative statistics.

Telecommunications Data

The International Telecommunication Union reports that about 60 percent of the world's population uses mobile phones.[35] During census time, telecommunication

---

32. Toda and others (2016), p. 711.
33. See JICA (2016).
34. For example, one of the key areas of discussion on official statistics in Japan is the creation of indexes similar to CPI using data from point of sales (POS) systems, credit card transactions, e-money, reward cards, and other sources of big data. Ministry of Internal Affairs and Communications (2016), p. 4.
35. eMarketer (2016).

companies may relay questionnaires to people's mobile phones using simple applications, so that they can answer through their device rather than relying on paper-based questionnaires. At the same time, by using that data, NSOs will know where people reside and their vital information. But this too may spark concerns over data privacy.

Geographic Data

At times of population and economic censuses, another layer of data such as geographic maps and satellite images would help NSOs to identify locations where people reside and where businesses are established. In countries where people live in remote areas, local officials visit them for distribution of questionnaires and interviews. At the same time, they can collect geographic information to refine mapping data. While censuses normally take place every five to ten years, a combination of regularly updated data such as telecommunications and geographic information, together with administrative data, would enhance the efficiency of data collection and analysis by NSOs.

Administrative Data and Citizen-Generated Data

Distribution data from pensions, subsidies, and public services (education, welfare, and utilities), as well as data from taxation, the voting register, and other similar sources, may be regarded as viable data that can be converted for use in demographic forecasting. Since these data are often updated often, NSOs can use them as base figures in between population censuses. Additionally, citizen-generated data (CGD) may complement administrative and Big Data. It is worth considering establishing a common platform for accommodating all data (administrative, CGD, Big Data, other statistics, and other data) in an integrated manner, to which both the public and private sectors can have access, share, and complement the development of statistics. NSOs should take the initiative of creating incentives for the private sector to provide their data, apply intellectual property rights for Big Data providers, settle on appropriate compensation, and anonymize data so as to protect people's privacy.

Conclusion

The Millennium Development Goals, and now the inclusive Sustainable Development Goals, seek to level the playing field for millions—economically, socially, ethnically, religiously, linguistically, or physically. These objectives have put pressure on the need for fundamental and high-quality official statistics. Social and economic structural changes such as globalization, digitization, diversification, and an increasing awareness of privacy have seen the use of traditional statistical survey methods as a way of bringing about new methods for more efficient, timely, and quality statistics. Use of administrative data, the internet, and Big Data are among those methods that may provide solutions for closing the gaps in official statistics and statistical capacity development. Our ideas on actions to close the gaps are to establish an e-government platform that incorporates administrative and private sector data by consolidating IT infrastructure; to strengthen the institutional and staff capacity of NSOs and other related organizations; and to promote and synchronize e-government and IT literacy within the public and private sectors. NSOs should fully commit to undertaking these actions with political backing.

This chapter analyzed the current status of statistical capacity development in developing countries and examined the experience of a capacity development project in Cambodia. It also identified some gaps in official statistics in developing countries as well as some ideas to simplify the work of national statistical agencies. A lack of financial resources and technical capacity is a significant challenge for any public activities in developing countries, even as technological advancement has helped solve these gaps in many countries with respect to statistics.

Gathering and using official statistics is a long-term process. Activities such as preparing and carrying out pilot projects, training staff, finding and training enumerators, actual implementation, and follow-ups may span a period of five to ten years; a long-term commitment from both developing countries and their development partners is therefore indispensable. Developing core capacities is also a long-term process. Core capacity is needed to produce results through the use of technical capacity and institutional management. JICA has supported the efforts made by its partners to enhance their core capacities, such as the management capability of the NSO and the attitudes of NSO staff, using a step-by-step, hands-on approach, with peer-to-peer technical expertise.

Having worked for more than thirty years in developing countries to help them develop their statistical capacity, JICA continues to provide support to expand the area of official statistics. With the further development of these projects, we may come across new findings and additional innovations. However, it should be kept in mind that it is an enhanced core capacity that will make use of technical innovations (for example, in information, communication, and technology and Big Data) and be a driver for producing results. In other words, it is not merely information technology and Big Data that produce results, but rather it is through a hands-on approach, joint activities, and trial and error that we can accumulate specific achievements and contribute to the SDGs.

It will take a concerted effort by members of the public and private sector to establish a common approach to creating efficient and more consolidated official statistics. NSOs, other ministries, and the private sector should join forces, recognize the current situation, design a road map, and designate tasks. NSOs should be fully committed to taking the initiative here, with political backing. In order for NSOs to push through with this work, they need to strengthen their core capacities to deal with the abundance of new, unstructured data sources as well as the demands from new actors and data users.[36]

36. Keijzer and Klingebiel (2017), p. 8.

Appendix: JICA's Major Projects on Statistical Capacity Development

Country	Name of project	Project period	Counterpart organization	Main field of cooperation
Indonesia	Expert on Improving Data Processing of Population Census and Other Statistical Surveys Using Computers	August1980– August 1983	BPS	Population census (data processing)
	Experts on Improvement of the 2000 Population Census	November 1997– November 2000	BPS	Population census
	Project for Developing the Information System of Small Area Statistics	August 2006– August 2008	BPS	Statistical information system development
Mexico	Project for Promotion of Population Activities	July 1984– September 1988	National Population Council	Development of population database, population estimation
Sri Lanka	Project for Population Information	November 1987– November 1992	Ministry of Plan Implementation, Department of Census and Statistics	Development of population statistics data bank
Argentina	Population Statistics Project	September 1995– September 2000	INDEC	Population census, statistical information system development
Tanzania	Expert on Supporting National Bureau of Statistics for PRSP Monitoring	March 2002– June 2002	National Bureau of Statistics	PRSP monitoring
	Expert on Supporting National Bureau of Statistics for Statistical Database Development	March 2003– April 2003	National Bureau of Statistics	Database development
	Project for Strengthening of Capabilities of the National Bureau of Statistics in Data Providing Service	February 2004– February 2007	National Bureau of Statistics	Statistical data management
Cambodia	Project on Improving Official Statistics Phase 1	August 2005– March 2007	National Institute of Statistics	Population census (training)
	Project on Improving Official Statistics Phase 2	April 2007– September 2010	National Institute of Statistics	Population census
	Project on Improving Official Statistics Phase 3	October 2010– September 2015	National Institute of Statistics	Economic census
Myanmar	Project on Strengthening the Capacity of Central Statistical Organization	October 2005– October 2007	Central Statistical Organization	Economic surveys, database development
Egypt	Project on Developing System of Statistical Quality at CAPMAS	March 2016– March 2019	CAPMAS	Quality enhancement (population census)
Nepal	Project on Capacity Development for the Implementation of Economic Census 2018	March 2016– February 2021	Central Bureau of Statistics	Economic census

Notes: BPS = Badan Pusat Statistik, INDEC = Instituto Nacional de Estadistica y Censos, PRSP = Poverty Reduction Strategy Paper, CAPMAS = Central Agency for Public Mobilization and Statistics.

References

ANCSDAAP (Association of National Census and Statistics Directors of America, Asia, and the Pacific). 2016. "Unique Features of Singapore's Census." 28th Population Census Conference. September 7–9, Minneapolis (Session 5) (www.ancsdaap.org/YZboard/view.php?id=49&code=bbs_02&start=&s_que=&mode=&field=&page=1 [28th PCC] Presentations_S04_S06.zip).

Australian Bureau of Statistics. 2016. "2016 Census Online Form Update" (www.abs.gov.au/Ausstats/abs@.nsf/dd0ca10eed681f12ca2570ce0082655d/5239447c98b47fd-0ca25800b00191b1a!OpenDocument).

Brown, Lawrence D., Michael L. Cohen, Daniel L. Cork, and Constance F. Citro, eds. 2016. *Envisioning the 2020 Census, Panel on the Design of the 2010 Census Program of Evaluations and Experiments*. Washington: National Academy Press (www.nap.edu/read/12865/chapter/17#288).

eMarketer. 2016. "Mobile Phone, Smartphone Usage Varies Globally." November 23 (www.emarketer.com/Article/Mobile-Phone-Smartphone-Usage-Varies-Globally/1014738).

Jerven, Morten. 2013. *Poor Numbers*. Cornell University Press.

JICA (Japan International Cooperation Agency). 2007a. "The Project on Improving Official Statistics in Cambodia." Summary of Terminal Evaluation Result. June (http://gwweb.jica.go.jp/km/ProjDoc021.nsf/VIEWJCSearchX/04B0D1379CB-7F2A1492572FF002BDA55/$FILE/終了時評価表.pdf).

———. 2007b. "Project on Improving Official Statistics in Cambodia Phase II (Technical Cooperation Project)." August (www.stat.go.jp/info/meetings/cambodia/pdf/booklet2.pdf).

———. 2010a. "Terminal Evaluation Study Report of the Project on Improving Official Statistics in Cambodia, Phase 2." July.

———. 2010b. "Project Completion Report, the Project on Improving Official Statistics in Cambodia, Phase 2." September.

———. 2014. "Terminal Evaluation Study Report of the Project on Improving Official Statistics in Cambodia, Phase 3." September.

———. 2016. "Activities for Nationwide Dissemination of mSOS." April (www.jica.go.jp/project/kenya/006/news/20160401.html).

JICA and CDC (Council for the Development of Cambodia). Various years. *Cambodia Investment Guidebook*. Phnom Penh: JICA and CDC.

JICA Research Institute. 2008. *Capacity Assessment Handbook—Project Management for Realizing Capacity Development*. Tokyo.

Keijzer, Niel, and Stephan Klingebiel. 2017. *Realising the Data Revolution for Sustainable Development: Towards Capacity Development 4.0*, PARIS 21, Discussion Paper No. 9. March (www.paris21.org/sites/default/files/CapacityDevelopment4.0_FINAL_0.pdf).

Ministry of Internal Affairs and Communications. 2016. "For a Comprehensive Consumer-Related Indicator with Quick Reporting." Statistics Bureau. September (www.soumu.go.jp/main_content/000473103.pdf).

Morrison, Thomas K., and others, eds. 2005. *Statistical Capacity Building: Case Studies and Lessons Learned*. Washington: IMF (www.imf.org/external/pubs/ft/scb/manual/SCB.pdf).

NIS (National Institute of Statistics). 2008. "2008 General Population Census of Cambodia" (www.stat.go.jp/info/meetings/cambodia/pdf/cen_sum1.pdf).

————. 2013. "Annual Report 2012." Ministry of Planning. December (www.nis.gov.kh/doc/Annual%20Report%202012_English.pdf).

Open Data Watch. 2015. "Partnerships and Financing for Statistics: Lessons Learned from Recent Evaluations." Washington. June 24 (http://opendatawatch.com/wp-content/uploads/2015/12/Partnerships-and-Financing-for-Statistics-Lessons-Learned-1.pdf).

————. 2016. "Country Profile: Cambodia, Open Data Inventory 2016" (http://odin.opendatawatch.com/ReportCreator/ExportCountryReport?countryId=120&app ConfigId=3).

Royal Government of Cambodia. 2010. National Program for Sub-National Democratic Development (NR-SNDD) 2010–19. May (www.gafspfund.org/sites/gafspfund.org/files/Documents/Cambodia_9_of_16_SATRATEGY_National_Program_for_Sub-National_Democratic_Development_0.pdf).

————. 2013. "'Rectangular Strategy' for Growth, Employment, Equity and Efficiency Phase III." September (www.cambodiainvestment.gov.kh/content/uploads/2013/11/2013-Rectangular-Strategy-III-En8.pdf).

————. 2014a. National Strategic Development Plan 2014-2018.

————. 2014b. "Annual Progress Report 2013, Achieving Cambodia's Millennium Development Goals." Prepared by Ministry of Planning, Phnom Penh. April (www.un.org/millenniumgoals/2014%20MDG%20report/MDG%202014%20English%20web.pdf).

Strode, Mary, Ian MacAuslan, Christine Spanneut, Mathew Powell, Mathew Christopher Willoughby, Philippe Ngango Gafishi, and Thomas Thomasen. 2009. *OPM (2009) Evaluation of the Implementation of the Paris Declaration, Thematic Study—Support to Statistical Capacity Development, Synthesis Report.* Paris: OECD. May.

Toda, Mitsuru, and others. 2016. "Effectiveness of a Mobile Short-Message-Service–Based Disease Outbreak Alert System in Kenya." *Emerging Infectious Diseases* 22, no. 4: 711.

Trading Economics. 2017. "United States Housing Starts 1959–2017" (www.tradingeconomics.com/united-states/housing-starts).

United Nations. 2013. "Cambodia: MDG Acceleration Framework. Promoting Women's Economic Empowerment." Published with Royal Government of Cambodia. May (www.undp.org/content/dam/undp/library/MDG/MDG%20Acceleration%20Framework/MAF%20Reports/RBAP/Cambodia%20-%20may%209%20WEB.PDF).

————. 2014. *A World That Counts: Mobilizing the Data Revolution for Sustainable Development.* Report prepared at the request of the UN Secretary General by the Independent Expert Advisory Group on Data Revolution for Sustainable Development. New York (www.undatarevolution.org/wp-content/uploads/2014/11/A-World-That-Counts.pdf).

United States Census Bureau. 2010. "What is the Census?" (www.census.gov/2010census/about/).

World Bank. 2012. "World Bank East Asia and Pacific Economic Update 2012." *Capturing New Sources of Growth.* Vol. 1. May (www.worldbank.org/en/news/feature/2012/05/23/east-asia-and-pacific-economic-update-may-2012).

————. 2016. "World Bank Big Data Innovation Challenge for Climate Resilience" (www.worldbank.org/en/news/video/2016/09/21/world-bank-big-data-innovation-challenge-for-climate-resilience).

CHAPTER TEN

Rescaling Government for an Urban Future

Reuben Abraham and Pritika Hingorani

Most people across the world now live in cities. This dynamic puts pressure on delivering critical urban infrastructure and services—universal access to safe water, sanitation, reliable transport, education and housing, to name a few—while creating urban economic opportunities and systems for disaster resilience. The issues are especially crucial for developing countries in emerging Asia and Africa, where most of the increase in the global urban population will take place through to 2050. According to UN estimates, developing country cities will add approximately 2.6 billion new urban residents, compared to 170 million in developed ones. Core development challenges will be addressed in cities, which must absorb rural migration, create jobs, and provide pathways out of poverty. In many cases the challenge will be amplified by a need to make up for decades of underinvestment.

Against this backdrop, Sustainable Development Goal 11 calls for cities that are inclusive, safe, resilient, and sustainable.[1] Delivering on this will require addressing fundamental interdependencies. For instance, safety is as much a function of strong policing as of access to shelter and economic opportunity. Resilience, both environmental and economic, requires well-planned physical infrastructure as much as it requires investing in an educated and globally competitive workforce. Urban

---

1. SDG 11 focuses on several problems that cities need to address and a set of targets to meet. One set relates to providing basic services and public goods. Another relates to disaster and risk management, specifically reducing death and economic losses caused by disasters, and increasing the number of cities that adopt and implement integrated strategies for climate change resilience and disaster risk management. Two targets relate to planning for sustainable urbanization; these emphasize participatory planning and management strategies, and the creation of positive economic, social, and environmental links between urban, peri-urban, and rural areas, through regional and national planning. Last, a set of targets draws attention to local culture and environment, which includes protecting cultural and natural heritage and supporting the use of sustainable and resilient local materials for buildings.

problems are often characterized as "wicked" problems, owing to the complex inter-relationships that underlie them. Solutions require coordination not only across policy sectors but also across geographies, time scales, and levels of government.

With this in mind, we argue that a fundamental first step to delivering on SDG 11 is for countries to revisit the governance architecture within which urban growth and its concomitant challenges (and opportunities) are managed. Urban growth has altered the underlying spatial reality and configuration of people, jobs, and opportunities. Governance and institutional frameworks must adapt and rescale in response.

Why is urban governance so important? The core issues that SDG 11 seeks to resolve are not new. Several were articulated in the Millennium Development Goals (MDGs) and have been echoed in the Paris climate accord, the New Urban Agenda, and other international agreements. Catalyzing delivery, however, will require that we move beyond the usual tinkering and undertake systemic fixes to address an execution gap.

The institutional frameworks of city management are often rooted in an anti-quated spatial, political, and economic construct. This legacy of local government can constrain or enable municipal agency. Some countries have been proactive in reframing the balance of power, accountability, and responsibility between tiers of government, although the precipitating factor in each case has varied. The waves of decentralization that swept Latin America in the mid-1980s and 1990s, the granting of home rule to some American cities, and radical decentralization in South Africa and Indonesia are just some examples. Ultimately, however, the incentive for, and nature of, reform depends on the underlying political economy, as a rescaling of governance necessarily upends established networks and systems of rents and power. Here we advance three ideas to inform the design of city governance frameworks for implementation of SDG 11.

Three Ideas to Help Break the Mold of Petrified City Governance

The first idea is that because the boundaries of urban growth are fluid, governance structures should be flexible enough to recognize, respond, and rescale to a changing spatial reality. This is of particular importance in regions such as South Asia and Africa that are seeing greater migration, peri-urban growth, and formal and informal agglomeration around smaller cities and towns. It is tied to the question of how we define what is urban, what value national governments place on urban growth, and the role of local government within the overall governance framework.

The second idea relates to how we structure horizontal relationships between local governments to enable economies of scale and better coordination. This may include service delivery arrangements between neighboring municipalities,

Table 10-1. Cities as Systems Integrators,
across Sectors and Levels of Government

Enabling infrastructure	Social infrastructure	Physical infrastructure
Law and order	Health	Transport
Governance	Education	Energy
Planning and urban form	Employment	Roads
Soft infrastructure	Housing	Water and sanitation
Finance		Public land
Technology		Waste
Sustainability		
Land markets		

the creation of metropolitan regions, or coordination of planned and unplanned growth along transit corridors.

The third idea is that we must recognize that cities are systems integrators, both horizontal and vertical, shaping the interface between urban citizens and all layers of government (see table 10-1). How do we design to facilitate coordination in this context?

SDG 11 Deeply Linked to Implementation of the Other SDGs

It will be important to achieve connectivity between the SDGs; beyond SDG 11, goals relating to poverty, gender, and income inequality, education, health care, water, fostering innovation, generating productive employment, and others will to a large degree rely on, or locate within, cities. Policies on law and order or education are often formulated by a higher tier of government, but executed and experienced in a city. Similarly, while cities may have emerged as the new locus of growth, they depend on the state, provincial, or national governments for the economic and regulatory context in which they operate. In recent years, Italy, Germany, the United Kingdom, and France are some of the countries that have tried to build better mechanisms to coordinate across sectors and different levels of government. What lessons can we draw from these examples?

In particular, it will be important to achieve convergence between SDGs 8 and 11; the former focuses on promoting inclusive economic growth and productive employment for all. A target linking Goals 8 and 11 could help focus global efforts on improving the competitiveness of cities. More important, it can help illuminate the underlying nature of urbanization; at its core, we think of urbanization as a process—a move to new opportunities, a restructuring of the economy, and the continual evolution and rebuilding of complex ecosystems. The world's most dynamic cities, from Barcelona to New York, have rebuilt and reimagined themselves over decades. Doing so requires that we appreciate the underlying causes and drivers of urban growth and not confuse them with the worst symptoms of urbanization, for example, high property prices or overcrowding. Alain Bertaud makes the critical case for cities as "primarily labor markets."[2] This may be an unromantic view, but it serves to orient policy more clearly. For instance, policies on housing, land use, and transport should focus on reducing transaction costs to movement within a labor market, rather than on restricting the growth of a city through a green belt, for example. Well-functioning labor markets in turn can drive the growth, innovation, and prosperity that fuel national economies.

Indeed, cities have emerged as engines of economic growth, job creation, and prosperity in both the developed and developing world, though a clear causal link between urbanization and growth is tricky to establish. Close to 80 percent of global GDP is created in cities (Dobbs and others, 2011). Richard Florida's work suggests that about 70 percent of global GDP is produced in just forty urban megaregions, such as the Boston-New York-Washington corridor, Silicon Valley, the Pearl River Delta, and the Bangalore-Chennai cluster (Dobbs and others, 2011; Florida, Gulden, and Mellander, 2008). In the United States in 2013, metropolitan areas accounted for 90 percent of real GDP (Bureau of Economic Analysis, 2013). This spatial density is also reflected in work by Edward Glaeser (2011), which shows that five zip codes in Manhattan between 41st and 59th streets employ more than 600,000 workers, earning an average wage of $100,000 a year.

On a PPP basis, cities like New York and Tokyo are larger than major economies such as Canada, Australia, Turkey, and Spain (World Bank, 2014). The ten largest cities in the world (by GDP) all have economies of more than $500 billion, making them the economic engines of their home countries. China, of course, is where the largest economic effects of urbanization can be seen. For example, Shenzhen, China's original special zone, a small fishing town with an economy of $160 million and a per-capita income of about $760 in 1981, today boasts of a $290 billion economy and a per capita income of $27,000 (Abraham, 2016; Shenzhen Statistical Yearbook, 2016), perhaps the fastest transformation in human prosperity ever witnessed.

However, there is reason to be cautious. Duranton (2013) shows that urban systems are constantly in flux, and it is their ability to allow for creative destruction and rebuilding of their economic base that is most critical to sustained productivity and economic growth. He finds that urban systems in developing country

---

2. Bertaud (2014).

cities can often act as a "brake on growth," eroding agglomeration benefits. Urban governance is a critical component of the urban systems that enable growth.

There are few objective prescriptions one can make about an "ideal" urban governance structure. Much has already been written on the need to decentralize greater power to city governments so they can emerge as leaders in their own right (Barber, 2013; Burdett and others, 2014; Ahluwalia, 2014; Sivaramakrishnan, 2006). The literature on fiscal federalism documents a wide array of intergovernmental arrangements within countries (see Terr-Minassian, 2017a; Bahl and Linn, 2014; Bahl, Linn, and Wetzel, 2013), identifying a few key principles, including clarity, accountability, and intergovernmental coordination (Terr-Minassian, 2017b). It is difficult to tie outcomes to particular structures of government, but we can identify a few principles that work. Moreover, the local political economy remains crucial, much more so than rational arguments about appropriate scale and efficiency.

In the rest of this chapter, we discuss three considerations for the design of urban governance, with a special focus on India, for two reasons. First, we are much more familiar with the mechanics of how urban arrangements work in India and the implicit political economy of reform. Second, and more important, India alongside sub-Saharan Africa is likely to be at the vanguard of the final and biggest wave of urbanization that our planet will witness over the next forty years. Therefore, any conversation on future urbanization needs to pay careful attention to India.

Can Governance Structures Recognize and Rescale to a Changed Spatial Reality?

There is no universal definition of what it means to be urban. Some countries use only population thresholds or density criteria, while some use both. Very few, like India, also consider the primary occupation of the male population. Most often, however, the administrative boundaries of cities reflect historical or political choices and do not always correspond to the physical or economic extents of the urban area (Deuskar, 2015). As a result, people in fast urbanizing areas often deal with disastrous consequences—such as lack of basic service provision, inadequate access to transport or arterial roads—when a country is not proactive about recognizing the true extent, shape, and form of urban areas.

India is an instructive example. Here, all settlements are rural by default. They attain urban status at the discretion of the relevant state government, which then establishes an urban local body (ULB), for example, a municipal corporation, for the town. States have widely varying thresholds of what should classify as urban; for instance, the states of West Bengal and Tamil Nadu require a minimum population threshold of 30,000 people, whereas Kerala and Punjab have no set criteria. State governments also have the discretion to disregard their own benchmarks.

Taken together, by this "administrative" (or statutory) classification, India was just 26 percent urban in 2011.

The Census of India offers an alternative official estimate. Unlike the statutory classification, it applies a uniform three-part definition across the country. To qualify as urban, a settlement must have a population over 5,000 people, a density of 400 persons per square kilometer, and 75 percent of the male workforce should be engaged in nonagricultural activities. In 2011, using this census definition, India was 31.6 percent urban.

Settlements that fall in the gray area between the statutory and census definitions are called Census Towns (CTs). CTs are essentially considered urban by the census, but are still governed as rural. Between 2001 and 2011 the number of statutory towns increased by only 242. However, the number of CTs tripled, from 1,362 to 3,894. CTs range in size and include some very large settlements, for example, Bhadrachalam in the state of Telangana with a population of 42,650 people.

Why does this gray zone matter? By law, rural local bodies are not obliged to provide many of the basic services and public goods required of urban bodies. These include basic planning functions like laying of roads and sewerage lines, issuing building control regulations, and basic services like waste management, transport, and firefighting that are necessary (and viable) in high-density settlements. This severely impacts quality of life in these towns and also makes it difficult and expensive to retroactively put these services in place once haphazard development has taken place. Moreover, local taxes tend to be low to nonexistent in rural jurisdictions, and the consequent lack of a fiscal base further impedes service delivery.

Could India Be More Urban Than We Think?

An extensive policy framework—everything from health care, education, housing, public goods provision, taxation, and entitlements—has grown around this binary classification of rural and urban areas in India. Indeed, both sets of official numbers uphold a dominant political narrative that the "real" India continues to live in the villages. The vast majority of central government allocations, the primary source of funding for most state and local governments, are reserved for rural areas. State government fiscal devolution to rural versus urban areas are similarly skewed.

What if we were to change our definition of what constitutes an urban area? At IDFC Institute, we ran an exercise to test how urban India is, if we use alternate definitions.

To begin with, we used two widely used population thresholds, ignoring the density and occupation criteria used by the census. One of the most common global thresholds, used by Ghana and Qatar, is a simple minimum population threshold of 5,000 people. If we apply this definition, India would be considered 47 percent urban. Next, if we apply a more liberal threshold of 2,500 people, a definition used by Mexico and Venezuela for instance, India is as high as 65 percent urban (Tandel, Hiranandani, and Kapoor, 2016).

When applied at the state level, the difference is even starker. Take the southern Indian state of Kerala, which is just 16 percent urban under the official Indian administrative definition, but 50 percent urban under the census definition. If we apply either Mexico's or Ghana's definition, the state would be considered 99 percent urban. In effect, a state that is almost entirely urban is governed as if it were only 16 percent urban. The skew reveals itself in the pattern of fiscal devolution: the most recently available numbers, for 2008–09, show that of the total funds devolved by the Kerala state government, just 18.1 percent went to Municipalities and Municipal Corporations versus 54.4 percent to rural local bodies.[3] If we were to accept either alternate definition of urban, it would necessitate a radical shift in state policy and priorities.

Population thresholds tell us little about the density of people in a settlement. In fact, density may be a more important factor, especially for public goods provision. Jana, Sami, and Seddon (2014) apply a simple density criterion of 400 persons per square kilometer (dropping population and occupation) to all settlements in India. By this definition, India could be as high as 78 percent urban. At double the density threshold, that is, 800 persons per square kilometer, India still emerges as 55 percent urban. The findings correspond to that of the World Bank Agglomeration Index, a globally applied measure of urban concentration, that places India as 55.3 percent urban in 2010 (World Bank, 2016).

There is one key limitation to these estimates. Population and density are calculated within administrative units such as census wards or municipal boundaries. The estimates above merely apply a different threshold to numbers counted within these units. However, growth rarely limits itself to administrative boundaries. Moreover, two adjacent administrative units may individually fall under the threshold, but taken together, they may have the density and population requirements of an urban area. To relax the constraints of urban boundaries, over the past two years IDFC Institute's geospatial laboratory has mapped the urban footprint of India, using publicly available satellite data.

The city of Kozikhode (see figure 10-1) is an instructive example. Between 2000 and 2014, urban growth (depicted by the darker gray) has occurred largely out of official administrative limits. In effect, the contiguous built-up area, or what *appears* to be the functional economic unit or labor market, bears little

3. Government of Kerala (2015).

Figure 10-1. Built-Up Area Expansion in Kozhikhode, India

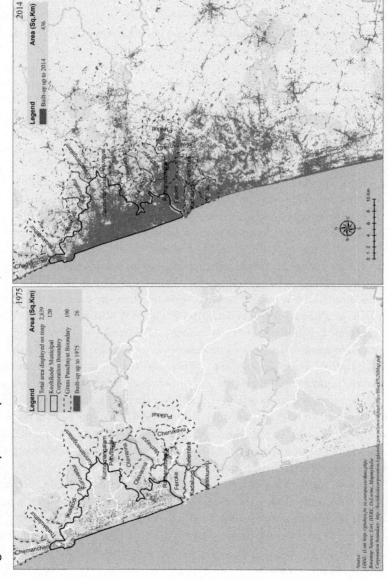

Source: Landsat data, processed by IDFC Institute Urban Expansion Obervatory.

correspondence with the administrative or municipal boundaries within which the city is managed. Most of the post-2000 growth seems to have occurred in villages that surround the municipal limits. Residents of these villages appear to be part of an urban, or urbanizing area, but their local government has no mandate to provide them with basic urban amenities or undertake basic planning functions. As a result, the quality of the urban fabric drops off sharply in these areas.

In 2014–15 New York University's Atlas of Urban Expansion used satellite data to study the quality of urban growth in 200 cities across the world, comparing pre-1990 growth with peri-urban expansion 1990–2014. To understand the degree to which new growth is planned or formally managed, they looked at indicators including the availability of open space, subdivision of plots (regular or haphazard delineation), and roads as an indicator of mobility and access within an area. The results for Kozikhode are telling. Average road width in pre-1990 Kozhikode was 9.84 meters, which falls to just 4.03 meters in the 1990–2014 expansion area. In the expansion area, the average density or coverage of arterial roads per block, which carry not only transit but also core infrastructure lines, falls to 30 percent of the 1990 road density. Similarly, the share of built-up area that is within walking distance of an arterial road falls from 98 percent to 88 percent over the same period, denoting reduced walkability (Angel and others, 2016).

This pattern plays out across India, where dense, urbanlike growth is taking place beyond city limits. For the seventeen Indian cities in the New York University study, peri-urban areas showed a high degree of informal growth, with declining access to arterial roads, open space, and formally subdivided plots. A notable exception is Navi Mumbai, the planned satellite city of Mumbai, built to accommodate the future growth in the Mumbai region. In the absence of such vision, it is often the lax regularity environment outside city limits that incentivizes unauthorized growth, as migrants move in to access the urban labor market. A 2016 World Bank study finds that for the major cities, for example, Mumbai and Hyderabad, there is a significant growth differential between the districts in which the cities are located and their immediate neighbors. For example, while the population of the district in which Delhi is located grew by just 1.6 percent per annum, the district immediately to the east saw population growth of 4.1 percent a year. Similarly, in the largest metropolitan areas, manufacturing employment seems to have dropped in the 10-kilometer radius around the city center but grown significantly in their immediate peripheries (World Bank, 2016).

Finally, satellite data has allowed us to observe emerging patterns of urban growth. A 2006 study by the Centre for Policy Research in Delhi was the first to highlight that significant shares of the population in the major industrialized states of Maharashtra, Gujarat, Karnataka, Andhra, and Tamil Nadu lived in "corrido" cities—"agglomerations [that] are long and thin stretches along a transport

artery, growing only at places without a definite pattern of core and periphery"
(Sivaramakrishnan, 2006). This pattern of growth raises an interesting governance question. These "cities" span multiple, often rural, administrations, with no
framework in place to coordinate basic services and infrastructure delivery, even as
the areas grow in size and density. Broken up into census wards or administrative
units along transit corridors, they fall prey to the measurement problem described
above—that while they individually fall under the definitional thresholds, taken
together, they may exhibit urban characteristics. Figure 10-2 illustrates one such
example of growth along the national highway leading out of the southern city
of Chennai.

Why does this matter for the SDGs? When we fail to acknowledge or plan for
inevitable urban growth for the reasons outlined above, we get poor outcomes
on virtually every measure of prosperity. There is no way a country like India can
deliver on the SDGs if more than 20 percent of the country can be characterized
as urban but without a mandate, let alone capacity, funding, or accountability, to
deliver basic urban services. We do not have corresponding data for other countries, but it is very likely other rapidly urbanizing countries have large areas caught
in similar jurisdictional mismatches as part of an expanding city but under local
governments with little authority or means to provide the needed services.

Why do countries fail to recognize and empower their cities? In the Indian
context, one reason appears to be a lack of consensus about whether and how
cities matter as drivers of growth, social mobility, or employment.[4]

A second potential explanation is perverse incentives. Being recognized as
urban not only burdens rural governments with an extensive set of responsibilities
but also deprives them of access to significant government funding and the significant discretion/system of patronage they enjoy over land use and government
programs (Lall, 2014). Another is political representation. India's electoral system
has systematically underrepresented urban areas. Constitutionally, the boundaries
of electoral constituencies for seats in the national parliament were to be redrawn
every decade to ensure proportional representation. However, after the 42nd Constitutional Amendment Act 1976, both the number of seats and the boundaries
of the constituencies were frozen for thirty years, until the census of 2001 (Lall,
2014). Put differently, constituencies that experienced rapid urbanization continued to hold the same number of seats as a more rural constituency. This underrepresentation looks set to continue. New constituencies were drawn up based on
the 2001 census, but the 84th amendment to the Constitution has frozen new

4. As the economic potential of cities becomes more clear, it may actually compound the resistance
of state governments to cede greater power to city governments.

Figure 10-2. Built-Up Area Growth Along the Chennai Sriperambadur Highway

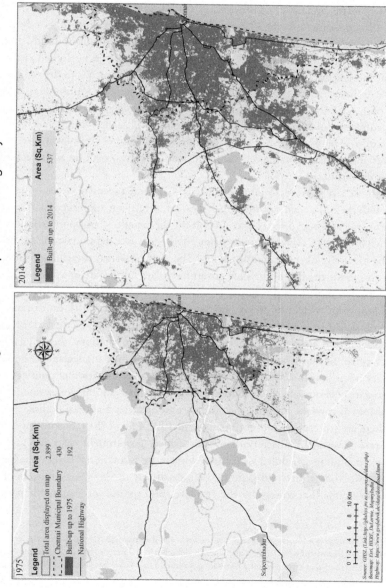

Source: Landsat data, processed by IDFC Institute Urban Expansion Obervatory.

boundaries until 2026, at which time the country will be significantly more urban that today.

State objectives, driven by a rural narrative, are rarely focused on improving the economic potential or quality of life in cities. As is well documented in the literature on devolution in India, state governments continue to exert disproportionate control over cities (Ahluwalia, 2014; Sivaramakrishnan, 2006). In 1993 the 74th amendment to the Constitution required state governments to devolve eighteen core functions to municipalities, along with the requisite funds, functional authority, and trained staff. But twenty-five years later, no Indian city has a clear mechanism of accountability and leadership or the means to deliver on its responsibilities. Service delivery remains fragmented across a multitude of agencies, both state and local, responsible for functions as diverse as police, bus transport, infrastructure planning, and waste collection and roads, with no mechanism to coordinate between them. Mumbai's transport backbone—its railway system— is built and managed by the central government railways, with no accountability to city authorities.

In most cities, de facto administrative duties and executive decisionmaking rests with the municipal commissioner, a career bureaucrat appointed by the state government and not directly accountable to the people.[5] For commissioners, a municipal posting, especially in a major city, serves as a stepping-stone to move up the hierarchy of state administration. The commissioner, therefore, has every incentive to toe the line of the state government and fulfill state objectives instead of catering to thorny local issues.

Commissioners typically serve two-year terms, giving them little time or incentive to articulate a long-term vision for the city. Moreover, given the lack of specialization in the cadre and the nature of administrative rotations, the majority of senior urban administrators have no experience in urban management. Service delivery in cities is therefore heavily dependent on a combination of political will in the state government, the incentives of the municipal commissioner, and his or her ability to convene various other critical state agencies and local bodies.

There are structural disincentives, too. Article 243T of the Constitution gives the state government discretion to reserve local government seats for various groups, including scheduled tribes and women, on a rotational basis. This helps ensure two things: first, no genuine political threat to the state government is posed from one that emerges at the city level, and second, no reasonable person

---

5. Indian mayors have largely ceremonial powers. Yet the mayoral system, whether directly or indirectly, has its own pitfalls. In the past, where a directly elected mayor has come from a different political party than that represented by the state government, the latter has abolished direct elections altogether.

will want to effectively contest from the same constituency more than once, as he or she cannot serve more than one term. This deters strong leaders from viewing local government as a path to a meaningful political career and leaves little incentive for local officials to perform well.

This is not an Indian problem alone. As Frug (2014) explains, cities' voices are inadequately represented in state legislatures in the United States as well, where electoral districts often fragment urban areas. Elected officials more often align themselves with party priorities instead of local ones (Frug and Barron, 2013; Frug, 2014). For SDG 11 to be taken seriously, we must first recognize the scale and complexity of urban growth and establish the importance of the city in the public and political imagination.

How Do We Structure Metropolitan Governance to Mediate the Tension Between the Localization Imperative and the Need for Functional Collaboration?

The emerging patterns of growth, along transit corridors and around the peripheries of cities, raises the question of how best to coordinate across adjacent jurisdictions. The question is also relevant in countries where a large share of the population and economy is also concentrated in megacities with populations greater than 10 million. Between 2014 and 2025, the number of megacities is projected to grow from nineteen to twenty-seven, of which twenty-one will be in developing countries (Bahl and Linn, 2014). National governments will have to consider the tension between the localization imperative, that is, cities managing their own affairs, and the need for functional collaboration across scales, both for technical efficiency as well as to address spatial inequities.

In theory, coordination is important when smaller cities fail to exploit economies of scale, in which case sharing public service delivery with a neighboring municipality can be more efficient. Italy is a good example, where under the Delrio reforms of 2014, named after former Italian mayor Graziano Delrio, the national government used financial incentives to encourage the creation of unions of small municipalities, coming together to jointly provide one or more public services (Ter-Minassian, 2017a). Given that 70 percent of municipal governments had fewer than 5,000 residents, there was a concern that the excessive fragmentation of local government had led to inefficiencies, which included a bloated public sector, too many levels of spending authority, and a lack of coordination between neighboring municipalities. By 2014 around 2,090 municipalities had formed permanent unions. Some municipalities have also resorted to fixed-term cooperation agreements for the provision of public goods (Ter-Minassian, 2017a).

Another reason for coordination is to "internalize" the externalities of every municipality fending for itself (Frug, 2014; Frug and Barron, 2013; Ter-Minassian,

2017b). Frug (2014) describes how the structure of incentives in the United States encourages cities to compete for resources, leading to parochialism in how they operate. City governments may take decisions for themselves that disadvantage or exclude outsiders—whether these are decisions about transport or economic development. Ng (2015) documents how the delegation of power to cities and growing intercity competition led to similar city-level "feudalism" in China. In this instance, bodies at the level of the state or region can, in theory, help balance such inequities.

Again, under the Delrio reforms, Italy established fourteen metropolitan cities, including Rome, to replace corresponding provinces (D'Antonio, 2014). The responsibilities of metropolitan cities now involve territorial planning, the organization of areawide networks for public services such as transport, utilities, telecommunications, and the promotion of metropolitan area economic development. The regions can also delegate additional functions to metropolitan cities in consultation with them. The Delrio reforms have enabled significant progress toward streamlining city administration by curtailing duplication of administrative responsibilities, giving metropolitan cities strong legal backing, and clarifying the role and scope of metropolitan cities and their powers (Ter-Minassian, 2017a). The political impetus for reform came from the election of Matteo Renzi as prime minister, who as a former mayor of Florence, placed a high priority on metropolitan area reform (D'Antonio, 2014).

Some sectors appear better suited to metropolitan-level coordination. Transportation in particular seems to lend itself to coordination across functional urban/economic areas. In Johannesburg, the metropolitan structure of local government was instituted specifically to tackle dramatic spatial inequities and a fragmented urban form resulting from the apartheid past. The Corridors of Freedom program is a transit-oriented development initiative designed to substantively link poorer neighborhoods with the rest of the city, thereby reducing structural inequities (Woldermariam and others, 2012; Pieterse, 2014). In Medellin, Colombia, city authorities invested heavily in metro and cable car systems to connect previously marginalized communities in the outskirts to the city center. This gave access to jobs and opportunity for people who previously struggled in environments facing high rates of crime and drug use (Swope, 2014; Devlin and Chaskel, 2010a, 2010b).

Ter-Minassian (2017b) documents the emerging literature on forms of metropolitan coordination, each with its own compromises between home rule and areawide governance. One model is *jurisdictional fragmentation,* where large, local governments within a metropolitan area are mainly responsible for their own affairs, such as in Paris, Mexico City, Sao Paolo, and most U.S. metropolitan areas. A second is *functional fragmentation*, where areawide public services are managed by a public company or a special government agency to unlock economies of scale and enable coordination. Third, *metropolitan governance* creates an areawide government that sits on top of several local governments and is responsible for most public services, as is the case in Toronto, London, Madrid, and Tokyo.

A variety of structures and arrangements must be coordinated across metro areas and smaller cities, each with its own drawbacks and politics. The New Urban Governance project at the London School of Economics and the Project on 21st Century Governance at Brookings are some recent attempts to map the structure and fiscal flow of urban governance arrangements across the world. Attempts to rationalize urban governance should seek both to achieve efficiency and coordination in providing public goods and to create a mechanism to facilitate dialogue and decisionmaking across neighboring areas.

Indian cities have struggled with horizontal metropolitan coordination. In the Mumbai Metropolitan Region, for example, the national government's railway department provides rail transportation. A state government–controlled body provides bus transport. The Public Works Department and local municipalities handle road building and maintenance and traffic signals. Across cities, road investments and maintenance, traffic signals, and road safety are run by a morass of overlapping agencies and jurisdictions with no clear chain of accountability or convening power. A similar fragmentation exists across services from water to education. City administration fails as a direct consequence.

When metropolitan-level coordination has been achieved, it has been transformative. In Bengaluru in the early 2000s,[6] then chief minister of Karnataka, S. M. Krishna, working with progressive bureaucrats, was able to coordinate the actions of various urban agencies and thereby significantly improve the quality of urban services. Without an institutional mechanism for coordination, these gains were short-lived when his government lost power, and the next administration abandoned this convening role and shifted its focus back to agrarian districts (Woldermariam and others, 2010).

How Do We Build Institutional Structures for Systems Integrators?

Increasingly, cities are required to coordinate across various scales and sectors to address their problems. While achieving perfect coordination is impossible, there have been efforts to prioritize sectors and rework hierarchies in a manner to reach certain goals. For instance, London and Berlin were early pioneers of an approach called *strategic spatial planning*. This model emerged in Europe in the 1990s from the realization that sectoral policies were ill suited to complex dynamics of urban

6. The information technology capital of India, known as Bangalore outside India.

growth. Strategic spatial planning seeks to create mechanisms to coordinate across sectors, time scales, and stakeholders (Rode, 2015)

In both cities, the priority was to coordinate spatial planning, city design, and urban transport. This allowed them to control their growth footprint and achieve important objectives on transport, mobility, and emissions. Both cities underwent significant and far-reaching urban governance reform to embed strategic spatial planning into institutions, policy instruments, and tools (Rode, 2015). In London this included reinstatement of citywide governance and creation of the transportation body, Transport for London, and the Greater London Authority for land use planning. Crucially, the democratically elected London mayor has the power to drive coordination across key sectors and set an overall framework for growth.

Many complex issues will necessitate this cross-sectoral, cities-based approach. On global warming, for example, cities already consume over two-thirds of the world's energy and account for more than 70 percent of global carbon dioxide emissions. Yet Edward Glaeser and Matthew Kahn (2009) found that dense urban areas have significantly lower carbon emissions than less dense suburban areas. While some decisions—for example, transport, permissible density, and zoning— may be made directly at the city level, others such as their energy mix, industry incentives, and so on, will require coordination with other levels of government.

Some countries have undertaken "vertical" reorganizations of government to bring about more clarity on accountability and responsibility. France, Italy, and Germany have in places abolished provincial-level government, created metropolitan-level authorities in their place, and further empowered city governments (Soulage, Conroy, and Sow, 2017). South Africa, under the postapartheid Constitution of 1996, designated local governments as an equal, autonomous sphere of government. In several countries, the process has been uneven, with large cities or metropolitan areas having more autonomy than smaller cities (Bahl and Linn, 2014). This has proved especially tricky in federal polities like the United States, Mexico, and India, where all powers exercised by municipal governments happen as a delegation of authority by the state.[7]

From Idea to Execution

Re-architecting structures of governance is a tall order. How do we summon the political will to recognize urban growth, especially where it threatens existing structures of power, rent, and finance? What role can outside experts, donors, and multilaterals play to move the needle on urban reform and management? How

7. Bahl, Lin, and Wetzel (2013), p. 62.

do we streamline a complicated web of agencies? How do we define clear and measurable outcomes, and with what surety of success? A few pathways of change might offer a start.

Across developing countries, one avenue may be through national political parties realizing that while the urban voter base may be unrecognized or ill-defined, it is growing and yet is largely unclaimed in full measure by any major political party. In India the urban voter is an aspirational voter trying to improve her life. Speaking to the politics of aspiration instead of the politics of the status quo has yielded electoral dividends for politicians willing to take the risk of changing the narrative. The current prime minister, Narendra Modi, has understood the changing dynamics of Indian society and has cleverly crafted an upbeat message centered on development and opportunity, a strategy that has paid off so far. Research on urban classifications, using both conventional methods as well as satellite data to document the true extent of urbanization, can play a significant role in changing the narrative. This will give cities a pivotal role in any national development agenda.

A second push may be through citizens voicing discontent about the abysmal state of public goods delivery in cities. Indeed, citizen uprisings can and have generated pressure for greater accountability and better service delivery. Decentralization in Colombia was precipitated by mass social uprisings and civic unrest. The 2017 floods that brought Mumbai to a halt have reignited calls for accountability and a directly elected mayor. In a way, the fledgling Aam Aadmi Party that swept to power in the Delhi state elections, on a platform of transparency and better services, provided an inkling that voter priorities in urban India have changed and that service delivery matters.

A third pathway may be the court system. In the United States the courts have at times curbed aggressive state power used to override local legislation. In India the states wrested power from the center in a landmark 1994 judgement, *S. R. Bommai vs. Union of India.* Prior to the judgment, the central government blatantly misused its powers to dismiss state governments that did not see eye to eye with the center's agenda. Elected state governments were removed on more than ninety occasions, in most cases with dubious constitutional cover. After the *Bommai* judgement, state governments enjoy considerable and growing autonomy from the center. The parallel with the current state control of cities is not a stretch, raising a similar option of judicial action on behalf of city governments.

Crucially though, one cannot ignore that any attempt to grant greater power to local bodies will run up against the very real problem of lack of state capacity. A senior bureaucrat once told the authors that municipal capacity in smaller Indian cities consisted of, in the main, the ability to order brooms and bleaching powder, but not much more. Whether this is true or not, it is clear that governing increasingly complex and large cities requires more specialized, strategic, and empowered roles, filled by technocrats and experts. Investing in institutions that have the capacity to manage an urban future must precede and accompany any efforts to revisit the structure of governance. Building municipal capacity is one area where international donors, universities, business schools, and even other national governments can play an important role, both in terms of financing and lending their expertise. For instance, evidence-based research on what works and what doesn't in urban governance can be as important as investing in urban management as a leadership discipline.

How we manage our cities will be critical to the next generation's sustainable development success.

References

Abraham, Reuben. 2016. "Special Governance Zones as Reform Labs." *LiveMint*, October 3 (www.livemint.com/Opinion/SJ4dAFYHlxAK0XIGt59b8K/Special-governance-zones-as-reform-labs.html).

Ahluwalia, Isher Judge. 2014. "Improving Our Cities Through Better Governance." New Urban Governance: Urban Complexity and Institutional Capacities of Cities. LSE Cities, London School of Economics (https://files.lsecities.net/files/2015/05/New-Urban-Governance_Essay03.pdf).

Angel, Shlomo, Alejandro M. Blei, Jason Parent, Patrick Lamson-Hall, and Nicolás Galarza Sánchez, with Daniel L. Civco, Rachel Qian Lei, and Kevin Thom. 2016. "Atlas of Urban Expansion—2016 Edition." Cambridge, Mass.: Lincoln Institute of Land Policy.

Bahl, Roy W., and Johannes F. Linn. 2014. "Governing and Financing Cities in the Developing World." Cambridge, Mass.: Lincoln Institute of Land Policy, May.

Bahl, Roy W., Johannes F. Linn, and Deborah L. Wetzel, eds. 2013. "Financing Metropolitan Governments in Developing Countries." Cambridge, Mass.: Lincoln Institute of Land Policy.

Barber, Benjamin R. 2013. *If Mayors Ruled the World: Dysfunctional Nations, Rising Cities.* Yale University Press.

Bertaud, Alain. 2014. "Cities as Labor Markets," Working Paper 2. Marron Institute of Urban Management. New York University, February 19.

Burdett, Ricky, and others. 2014. "Governing Urban Futures." LSE Cities conference, November (https://lsecities.net/publications/conference-newspapers/governing-urban-futures/).

Bureau of Economic Analysis. 2013. "Growth Continues across the Nation's Metropolitan Areas." *Beablog* (blog). Archive for February 2013 (https://blog.bea.gov/2013/02/).

D'Antonio, Simone. 2014. "Metropolitan Cities Are Born in Italy." *Citiscope* (http://citiscope.org/story/2014/metropolitan-cities-are-born-italy).

Deuskar, Chandan. 2015. "What Does 'Urban' Mean?" *Sustainable Cities* (blog). World Bank, February 6 (http://blogs.worldbank.org/sustainablecities/what-does-urban-mean).

Devlin, Matthew, and Sebastian Chaskel. 2010a. "Conjuring and Consolidating a
Turnaround: Governance in Bogotá, 1992–2003." *Innovations for Successful Societies.*
Princeton University (https://successfulsocieties.princeton.edu/sites/successful
societies/files/Policy_Note_ID108.pdf).

———. 2010b. "From Fear to Hope in Colombia: Sergio Fajardo and Medellin, 2004–
2007." *Innovations for Successful Societies.* Princeton University, December (https://
successfulsocieties.princeton.edu/sites/successfulsocieties/files/Policy_Note_ID116.
pdf).

Dobbs, Richard, and others. 2011. "Urban World: Mapping the Economic Power of
Cities." McKinsey Global Institute, March. (www.mckinsey.com/global-themes/
urbanization/urban-world-mapping-the-economic-power-of-cities).

Duranton, Giles. 2013. Growing through Cities in Developing Countries. *The World
Bank Research Observer* 30, no. 1: 39-73.

Florida, Richard, Tim Gulden, and Charlotta Mellander. 2008. "The Rise of the Mega-
Region." *Cambridge Journal of Regions, Economy and Society* 1, no. 3.

Frug, Gerald. 2014. "Who Decides Who Decides." LSE Cities, London School
of Economics, November (https://lsecities.net/media/objects/articles/
who-decides-who-decides/en-gb/).

Frug, Gerald E., and David J. Barron. 2013. *City Bound: How States Stifle Urban Innovation.* Cornell University Press.

Glaeser, Edward L. 2011. *Triumph of the City: How Our Greatest Invention Makes Us
Richer, Smarter, Greener, Healthier, and Happier.* New York: Penguin Press.

Glaeser, Edward L., and Matthew Kahn. 2009. "Green Cities, Brown Suburbs." *City Journal,* pp. 50–55 (www.city-journal.org/html/green-cities-brown-suburbs-13143.html).

Government of China. 2016. Shenzhen Statistical Yearbook (www.chinabookshop.net/
shenzhen-statistical-yearbook-2016-p-24471.html?currency=GBP).

Government of Kerala. 2015. Fifth State Finance Commission and Issues in Fiscal Devolution (www.sfc.kerala.gov.in/previousSfcReport.htm?pageAction=viewDocument1.pdf).

Jana, Arindam, Neha Sami, and Jessica Seddon. 2014. "How Urban Is India?" International
Growth Center (www.theigc.org/wp-content/uploads/2014/08/Arindam-Jana.pdf).

Lall, Rajiv. 2014. "AAP and the Politics of Urbanization." *Business Standard,* January
16 (www.business-standard.com/article/opinion/rajiv-lall-aap-and-the-politics-of-
urbanisation-114011501284_1.html).

Ng, Mee. 2015. "Governing China's Urban Revolution." *New Urban Governance: Urban
Complexity and Institutional Capacities of Cities.* LSE Cities, London School of Economics (https://files.lsecities.net/files/2015/05/New-Urban-Governance_Essay05.pdf).

Pieterse, Edgar. 2014. "Johannesburg: Corridors of Freedom." *New Urban Governance:
Urban complexity and institutional capacities of cities.* LSE Cities, London School of
Economics, November.

Rode, Philipp. 2015. "Integrated Governance as Privileging Key Policy Links: The Case of
Strategic Planning in London and Berlin." *New Urban Governance: Urban Governance
and Institutional Frameworks.* LSE Cities, London School of Economics (https://files.
lsecities.net/files/2016/02/Rode-P-2015-Integrated_governance_privileging_key_
policy_links-London_Berlin.pdf).

Shenzhen Statistical Yearbook. 2016. China Statistics Press.

Sivaramakrishnan, Kallidaikurichi Chidambarakrishnan. 2006. "Growth in Urban India: Issues of Governance." New Delhi: Centre for Policy Research (www.cprindia.org/research/papers/growth-urban-india-issues-governance).

————. 2015. *Governance of Megacities: Fractured Thinking, Fragmented Setup*. Oxford University Press.

Soulage, Bernard, Caroline Conroy, and Mariama Sow. 2017. "Fiscal Decentralization and 21st Century Cities in France." Brookings Institution, September.

Swope, Christopher. 2014. "How Medellín Revived Itself, Part 3: Reforms Hand Colombia Mayors and Cities More Power." *Citiscope*, April (http://citiscope.org/story/2014/how-medellin-revived-itself-part-3-reforms-hand-colombia-mayors-and-cities-more-power).

Tandel, Vaidehi, Komal Hiranandani, and Mudit Kapoor. 2016. "What's in a Definition?: A Study on Implications and Suitability of Urban Definitions in India through Its Employment Guarantee Programme." Working Paper 1. IDFC Institute Working Paper Series, July.

Ter-Minassian, Teresa. 2017a. "Local Finances in Italy." Brookings Institution, September.

————. 2017b. "Fiscal and Financial Issues for 21st Century Cities: Background and Overview." Brookings Institution, April.

Woldermariam, Michael, and others. 2012. "Restructuring Service Delivery: Johannesburg, South Africa, 1996–2001." *Innovations for Successful Societies*. Princeton University.

————. 2010. "Keeping Up with a Fast-Moving City: Service Delivery in Bangalore, India, 1999–2004." *Innovations for Successful Societies*. Princeton University, June.

World Bank. 2014. Gross Domestic Product. Online database (https://data.worldbank.org/, downloaded June 2017).

————. 2016. "Leveraging Urbanization in South Asia." World Bank (www.worldbank.org/en/region/sar/publication/urbanization-south-asia-cities).

CHAPTER ELEVEN

Protecting Half the Ocean?

Enric Sala and Kristin Rechberger

One sustainable development goal specifically targets ocean conservation: SDG 14: to "conserve and sustainably use the oceans, seas and marine resources for sustainable development." However, there is no plan yet for achieving this goal. To date, only one underlying target has a quantitative objective, which is a target of the UN Convention on Biological Diversity (CBD): "conserve at least 10 percent of coastal and marine areas" by 2020 (SDG 14.5). Yet as of May 2018, 4 percent of the ocean was under some kind of protection, and only 2 percent was fully protected from extractive activities such as fishing, oil drilling, and mining. How will the goal of SDG 14 be achieved? What would stop us from getting there?

Here we argue that the driving vision of SDG 14 should be to protect half the ocean while truly managing activities sustainably in the other half. Most other subgoals fall within this overarching vision. In this chapter we review (1) the role of the ocean and ocean life in making earth an inhabitable planet, (2) how human activities are diminishing the ability of the ocean to provide for us, (3) why we should protect half the ocean, and (4) how that can be achieved along with sustainably managing the other half. Readers already familiar with what the ocean does for us and how we are destroying it might wish to jump directly to page 246.

What Does the Ocean Do for Us?

The living layer of our planet—the biosphere—is only about 15 kilometers thick. Although microbes have been found living a couple miles deep in rocks and floating ten miles high in the atmosphere, most of earth's biodiversity is concentrated around the surface. Ninety-eight percent of that critical living space's volume is in the ocean.

The earth's ocean-atmosphere dynamic is a feedback loop. While ocean life is affected by the physical environment—temperature, depth, currents—it in turn also affects the environment. For instance, bacteria and microscopic algae in the first 100 meters below the surface use the energy of sunlight to produce organic matter like terrestrial plants, which absorb carbon dioxide and release oxygen in the process. The oxygen released into seawater will eventually reach the atmosphere, providing more than half the oxygen in it. Ocean creatures unknown and unseen by most people give us every other breath we take. The other breath comes from our forests.

A recent study indicates that during 2002–11, the ocean absorbed a quarter of all the carbon dioxide released to the atmosphere by human activities (for example, fossil fuel burning, cement manufacture, deforestation) (Le Quére and others, 2012). That's about the same amount absorbed by all terrestrial plants during that period. The ocean also has an extraordinary capacity to store heat. Since 1955 the ocean has absorbed 90 percent of the extra heat generated by our atmospheric carbon pollution.[1] If the same amount of heat had gone into the lower 10 kilometers of the atmosphere, then the earth would have seen a warming of 36°C—eighteen times more heat than the mere 2°C we don't want to exceed to avoid catastrophic consequences for life on earth. Earth would be more like Venus: life as we know it would not be possible anymore.

The white cap on top of the world, the Arctic Ocean, is also essential for making life balmy in the northern hemisphere, through a conveyor belt of ocean currents. When seawater freezes in the Arctic, it releases salt at the surface. Then the surface water, very cold and salty, becomes very dense and sinks, creating a cold undersea waterfall moving southward. The sinking water is replaced by warmer water coming from the south. That forms a loop that includes the Gulf Stream, a relatively warm current that makes the British Isles and Scandinavia temperate and inhabitable year round.

The ocean also gives us about 100 million tons of seafood every year (Pauly and Zeller, 2016a), which is the main source of animal protein for more than a billion people worldwide, mostly in developing countries. An estimated 57 million people were engaged in the primary sector of capture fisheries and aquaculture in 2014 (FAO, 2016). The global first-sale value of seafood worldwide has been estimated at over $90 billion.

Intact ocean habitats also provide other invaluable services. For example, mangroves are trees that form forests on tropical coastlines; they are the only trees growing in seawater. The UN Environment Program estimated the global economic value that can be extracted nondestructively from mangrove forests at $1.6 billion per year (UNEP, 2006). Their complex root systems are nurseries for fish. In the Gulf of California, Mexico, the annual value of the services provided to the fish and blue crab fishery by mangroves averaged $37,500 per hectare

---

1. Baxter and Laffoley (2016), p. 456.

(Aburto-Oropeza and others, 2008). Over thirty years, the destruction of each hectare of mangrove would cost local economies approximately $605,000. Mangrove forests also provide a shield against storm waves and even tsunamis. The 2004 Indian Ocean earthquake and tsunami did the worst damage in places where the natural mangrove forests had been cut and replaced by tourist resorts, shrimp farms, and industrial facilities, whereas communities sheltered behind intact mangrove forests suffered less destruction.

Healthy coral reefs also form living barriers that protect 150,000 kilometers of coastline from the power of storm waves in more than 100 countries and territories. People have been able to live on low-lying islands for millennia because coral reefs have been growing and following the natural sea level rise that occurred after the end of the last ice age (about 11,000 years ago). But these reefs might not be able to cope with the accelerated sea level rise caused by human activities.

The ocean also provides opportunities for recreation, which contributes to job creation and economic growth. Marine and coastal tourism globally employed about 7 million people in 2010, with a direct added value of $390 billion (OECD, 2016). Europe alone had 480 million international tourist arrivals and 509 million international departures (Jackson and others, 2001). The Organization for Economic Cooperation and Development estimates a growth in marine tourism employment of 122 percent between 2010 and 2030.

The above are only a few examples of what the ocean provides for us. It is clear that a functioning and healthy ocean is essential for life on our planet. But because of the world's industrial activities and accelerated human footprint, we are diminishing the ocean's capacity to provide vital resources needed by the peoples of the world: food, oxygen, and climate regulation.

How We Are Killing the Ocean—and Harming Ourselves

We are inflicting many threats to ocean life, including overfishing, polluting, destroying habitats, and causing climate change. Humans have been fishing the ocean for millennia, depleting populations of large ocean wildlife—such as the extinct giant Steller sea cow and the Caribbean monk seal, as well as whales, sea turtles, and sharks (Jackson and others, 2001). It has been estimated that 90 percent of large ocean predators—sharks, tuna, groupers—has been fished out of the ocean in the last century.[2] Sharks are particularly threatened, with some species at less than 1 percent of their original abundance (before industrial fishing).

---

2. Baum and others (2003); Ferretti and others (2008); Myers and Worm (2003).

Overfishing

Since the end of Second World War, industrial fishing has expanded from the coastal waters off the North Atlantic and West Pacific to the waters in the Southern Hemisphere and into the high seas.[3] As fish populations were depleted near shore, fishing efforts had to expand farther and deeper offshore to satisfy people's growing demand for seafood (Morato and others, 2007). By the mid-1990s, only the least productive waters in the high seas, and relatively inaccessible waters in the Arctic and Antarctic, were left as "unfished" grounds. The decline of the global fishing catch since the mid-1990s and the rapidly diminishing number of untapped fishing grounds clearly show a limit to global fisheries growth (Pauly and Zeller, 2016b). Forty percent of the world's marine fisheries are overexploited or have already collapsed. Studies estimate that if the current trends continue, most fisheries will have collapsed by 2050 (Worm and others, 2006).

The removal of species by fishing also has indirect effects, in some cases unpredictable, with the potential to create ecosystem-wide changes. For example, fur hunters killed sea otters in Alaska to near extinction in the nineteenth century, thus removing the natural predator of sea urchins. Left to their own devices, sea urchins increased dramatically and devoured their seaweed home, turning former underwater forests of giant kelp into barrens (Estes and Duggins, 1995). Without the kelp, a variety of coastal fish and many other species disappeared. This is but one instance where removal of a single keystone species changed the entire landscape, the biodiversity it harbored, and the fisheries it supported (Estes and others, 2016).

Global industrial fishing affects not only the marine environment but also coastal populations in developing countries. In West Africa, for example, foreign fishing fleets—including from Spain and China—develop access agreements with local governments in exchange for meager fishing fees. This practice, alongside illegal fishing, has resulted in depletion of local resources, and local fishers are outcompeted, driving them to fish ever-declining fish stocks more intensively. Illegal fishing in West Africa is responsible for a loss of over $2.3 billion a year that could have benefited local economies (Doumbouya and others, 2017). Moreover, almost all of the fish caught by foreign fleets is consumed in industrialized countries, thus threatening food security and biodiversity in the developing world. Studies estimate that this "ocean-grabbing" worldwide costs between $10 billion and $24 billion, mostly to developing countries. And even legal fishing is vastly mismanaged. The World Bank estimates that wise management of fisheries

---

3. Swartz and others (2010). The "high seas" are marine waters beyond national jurisdictions, that is, beyond countries' 200-nautical mile Exclusive Economic Zones (EEZs), encompassing 60 percent of the ocean.

together with a conservation approach could result in an additional global fishing revenue of $83 billion annually (World Bank, 2008).

In addition, not only fish species are taken out of the ocean faster than they can reproduce, but fragile areas of the seafloor have been destroyed through destructive fishing methods. Bottom trawling, which drags heavy nets across the seafloor, destroys everything that grows there. Often, the target species—such as shrimp or deep fish—represent only 10 percent of the catch. Whatever else is caught in the nets—unwanted species including corals, sponges, starfish, and fish without commercial value—are discarded overboard, mostly dead. The worst damage is done on seamounts—deep underwater mountain peaks—where a single trawl can destroy thousands of years of growth of deep-sea corals (Althaus and others, 2009). Because isolated seamounts harbor many species found nowhere else, deep sea trawling may be driving many species extinct even before we discover them.

Ocean Warming and Acidification

Our fossil fuel economy amplifies the problems by making the ocean warmer and more acidic. Warmer temperatures have caused a decline in permanent Arctic sea ice at a rate of 13 percent loss per decade since we started observing with satellites in 1979, and models project an ice-free Arctic Ocean in the summer as soon as 2040 (Overland and Wang, 2013). The frozen Arctic Ocean has been a planetary air conditioner of sorts, helping to regulate the climate for thousands of years. But the white cap is turning dark blue as the sea ice melts and is replaced by open water. The darker ocean surface attracts more heat, melting more ice and in turn opening up more dark surface, and so on. Retreat of sea ice and warming seawater may also cause a massive release of methane that, to date, has remained frozen in the sea floor. Methane is a more potent greenhouse gas than carbon dioxide, thus potentially accelerating warming. These feedback loops are accelerating global warming and making the Arctic the fastest warming region in the world (Bitz and others, 2012). A 2° C average change in world temperature implies a 5° C change in the Arctic. The erosion of ice shelves will eventually remove the ice stopper that prevents Antarctic glaciers from flowing faster into the Southern Ocean, which will contribute to sea level rise. The consequences of melting of sea ice have already affected local communities in the Arctic region, forcing them to relocate because of the extensive damage caused by storm waves plus sea level rise (Banerjee, 2015), but these forces will also affect the entire planet (Serreze, Holland, and Stroeve, 2007).

Warming is also killing coral reefs across the tropics. Temperatures warmer than average have caused the bleaching of corals, whereby they lose their symbiotic single-cell algae. The number of bleached corals that die depends on the severity of the warming, among other factors. In 2016 the most severe warming event caused the largest coral bleaching episode in history, killing 67 percent of the coral in the northern part of the Great Barrier Reef in Australia within just nine months (Hughes and others, 2017). Already, more than a quarter of the coral reefs of the world are unrecognizable because of warming events, as well as pollution and overfishing. Under current trends, expected further warming and acidification will result in the collapse of coral reefs globally by 2050 (Hoegh-Guldberg and others, 2007). In other words, it is likely that corals will dissolve faster than they will grow.

Acidification of the ocean results from the extra carbon dioxide that human activities put in the atmosphere and is absorbed by the ocean. Acidification affects not only corals but also any organisms with a calcium carbonate skeleton, such as oysters, mussels, and small floating snails that are the main food source for juvenile salmon (Cheung and others, 2008). The ocean is helping take our carbon pollution from the atmosphere, killing life across the food chain in the process.

In addition, warming is changing the biological productivity of many ocean areas. Excessive warming creates a thick, warm surface layer that does not mix with colder waters below—like oil on water. That means that the necessary nutrients from the deeper ocean do not reach surface waters, therefore reducing their biological productivity. At the same time, the supply of surface oxygen to the deep ocean is significantly reduced, in turn affecting life in that realm. A study found a decline of more than 2 percent in ocean oxygen content worldwide between 1960 and 2010 (Schmidtko, Stramma, and Visbeck, 2017). Warming affects the entire ocean, from top to bottom.

Seawater warming may also lead to numerous local extinctions in the polar regions and semi-enclosed seas (Jones and Cheung, 2015). As the tropics become warmer, species can move to higher latitudes; however, species in the poles have nowhere to go and will be replaced by species coming from lower latitudes. Such species turnovers could affect over 60 percent of the present biodiversity. Climate change may also lead to large-scale redistribution of fisheries productivity, which is closely related to biological productivity of the waters where these fisheries occur. Under current scenarios, the maximum catch potential may show an average of 30–70 percent increase in high-latitude regions, and a decline of up to 40 percent in the tropics (Cheung and others, 2010). Highly impacted regions in the tropics and developing countries are especially vulnerable to these changes from a socio-economic perspective.

Pollution

Pollution is another major threat to ocean life. Excessive agricultural fertilizer run-off reaches the ocean and threatens fragile ecosystems such as coral reefs. The most extreme case is the "dead zones," areas located typically off river mouths, where excess fertilizers enhance the explosive growth of microscopic plants in surface waters. This results in an accumulation of organic matter, which causes microbe populations to explode and consume all of the oxygen in bottom waters (Diaz and Rosenberg, 2008). Everything that cannot swim and escape dies, except for microbes. Currently there are more than 500 dead zones worldwide.

Another concern is the incidence of "red tides." harmful algal blooms that lead to toxicity in the environment. Although these may occur naturally, human activity can lead to their occurrence through increased coastal water pollution (for example, from untreated waste water including open sewers or fertilizer runoff) and seawater warming. Red tide toxins accumulate up the food chain, harming shellfish such as mussels and oysters. Eating contaminated seafood can produce illness and even death—in fish, birds, mammals, and humans. Impacts also include substantial economic losses to coastal communities and commercial fisheries.

Plastic trash—for example, bags, bottles, fishing gear—makes up 95 percent of trash in the ocean. Eight million tons of plastic—equivalent to dumping a garbage truck full of plastic every minute—enter the ocean annually (Jambeck and others, 2015). Some 88–95 percent of it comes from only ten rivers because of poor waste mismanagement (Schmidt, Krauth, and Wagner, 2017). Marine life—including squid, fishes, whales, and seabirds—eat pieces of plastic mistaken as food. For instance, along the coast of Brazil, 62 percent of king mackerel were found to have plastic pellets in their stomachs (Miranda and de Carvalho-Souza, 2016). Plastic contains and absorbs pollutants, including DDT, that people ingest as they eat polluted seafood. Nanoplastics are able to penetrate the blood-to-brain barrier in fish and cause behavioral disorders (Mattsson and others, 2017). We can expect similar effects on the human brain. If the rate of plastic waste continues, by 2050 plastic in the ocean may outweigh fish. The impacts on human health are obvious. We are eating the pollution that we throw in the air and the ocean, and our portions are increasing over time.

In summary, the loss of ocean biodiversity due to human activities, including exploitation, pollution, and climate change, is increasingly impairing the ocean's capacity to provide food, maintain water quality, recover from perturbations, capture carbon safely, and regulate the climate, among other stressors to the ocean environment. All of these have negative impacts on human well-being—from health issues to economic losses to human losses. Therefore, we cannot treat what happens to the ocean as an outcome independent of humanity. A healthy ocean is essential not only for sustainable development but also ultimately for human existence. This stresses the importance of connecting different SDGs. The question follows: Can we restore the former richness and productivity of the ocean, and what will be the benefits?

How to Restore the Ocean and the Services It Provides

To achieve the goals of SDG 14 and Agenda 2030, we must achieve a balance between protection and use. This is easily summarized in one simple approach: protect half the ocean and manage our activities in the other half smartly. This is the equivalent of building a giant ocean endowment that will produce compound interest that we can enjoy, instead of continuing on the current path where the ocean's natural capital is eroded, ever-decreasing its value, and its ability to produce returns degraded. We also need to dramatically reduce pollution and shift to an economy based on renewable energy—without which catastrophic climate change will hamper any gains achieved by reducing local threats to the ocean. Actions in the ocean are essential but insufficient unless the other SDGs create essential actions on land as well.

Protecting Half the Ocean

While protecting half sounds like an impossible task, steps can be taken to ensure that a good portion of the earth's water surface is safeguarded.

Marine Reserves as a Tool to Restore Ocean Biodiversity and Resilience. Better fisheries management to reduce exploitation rates of ocean life will not be enough. While reducing catch rates may help prevent the collapse of fish stocks, this does not encourage full recovery of biodiversity. No matter how well fisheries are run, biodiversity cannot be effectively restored when wildlife is removed at a commercial scale. Therefore, the world also needs strongly protected areas in the ocean, like national parks on the land.

No-take marine reserves—where fishing and other extractive activities such as mining and drilling are prohibited—can restore and preserve ocean biodiversity, from species abundance to the health of entire ecosystems (Sala and Giakoumi, 2017). On average, and typically within a decade, no-take marine reserves result in increases of 21 percent in the number of species, 28 percent in the size of organisms (Lester and others, 2009), and a remarkable 670 percent in biomass, relative to unprotected areas nearby (Sala and Giakoumi, 2017). The increase in biomass of predatory fish can be even greater. The increase in the biomass of predators has been shown to restore ocean habitats to a richer and more productive state. For example, in the Mediterranean and around New Zealand, efforts aimed at bringing back sea urchin predators reduced sea urchin density and consequently have shifted the ecosystem from a degraded state (sea urchin barren) to a complex, healthy state (algal forests with high biodiversity).[4]

4. Guidetti and Sala (2007); Shears and Babcock (2003).

These food web changes can also enhance the resilience of ocean ecosystems. For example, corals in the mid-Pacific Line Islands affected by the strong 1997–98 El Niño recovered in fully protected reefs within a decade, whereas they did not in unprotected islands (Sandin and others, 2008). In Baja California, Mexico, a mass mortality event caused by climate-driven oxygen depletion affected pink abalone populations, but they replenished faster within marine reserves because of large body size and high egg production of the protected adults (Micheli and others, 2012).

Marine Reserves Have Benefits Beyond Their Boundaries. One might worry that closing large areas to fishing will reduce the amount of food available for human consumption. But the opposite appears to be the case. Although marine reserves were not initially conceived to fix the problems of mismanagement of fisheries, they can help improve local fisheries around their boundaries.[5] The increase in the biomass of commercial species inside marine reserves increases reproductive output. Simply put, if we do not kill the fish, they grow larger and produce an exponentially greater amount of eggs and larvae. Areas outside reserves show a significant increase in biomass after the reserve is in place, through the spillover of adults or the export of larvae, or both (Lester and others, 2009). Well-enforced marine reserves can increase adjacent fishery catches. One study showed that local fisheries would not be sustainable without the reserves in some cases, while in other cases spillover offsets potential losses in catch (Halpern, Lester, and Kellner, 2009). In addition to enhancing or ensuring sustainable yield, well-designed marine reserves with proper business plans can start benefiting fishers in the short term and increase the long-term profitability of fisheries.[6] Recreational fishing outside reserves may also benefit from spillover. In Florida, the no-take areas in the Merritt Island National Wildlife Refuge have supplied increasing numbers of world record–sized fish to adjacent recreational fisheries since the 1970s (Roberts and others, 2001).

Some opponents to ocean protection argue that because creating marine reserves will displace fishing effort outside the reserves, unprotected areas would be depleted faster,[7] and fishers displaced by protection would suffer economic losses. As of May 2018, however, only 2 percent of the ocean was fully protected from fishing; thus, the displacement and the economic loss issues are currently insignificant. And as we'll see later, creating large fishing closures, reducing fishing effort, and reforming fisheries management can be a better solution for fisheries than the way they are managed currently (Barner and others, 2015).

5. Halpern, Lester, and Kellner (2009); Sala and others (2013); Sala and others (2016).
6. Sala and others (2013); Sala and others (2016).
7. Dinmore and others (2003); Hiddink and others (2006).

Marine reserves can also provide economic benefits through tourism and other services, some of which are difficult to quantify (for example, insurance value, local amenity value, storm protection, political value, and intangible capital such as spiritual beauty) (Sala and others, 2013). The increase in marine life inside marine reserves, in particular large fish, is the main attraction for divers and other tourists, which can bring revenue disproportionately higher than fishing. In the wider Caribbean and Pacific coast of Central America, for instance, 50 percent of all dives (7.5 million dives annually in 2003) took place within marine protected areas (Green and Donnelly, 2003). In the Galápagos Islands, a live shark brings in $5.4 million over its lifetime through "shark diving," whereas a shark killed for its fins brings only $200 (Lynham and others, 2015). Globally, almost 600,000 divers expend $314 million per year to dive with sharks (Cisneros-Montemayor and others, 2013). In contrast, the landed value of shark fisheries is $630 million and falling because of overexploitation. The number of shark watchers could more than double within the next twenty years, generating $780 million in tourism revenue annually. Sharks and other large fish are worth more alive than dead.

Why Do We Need to Protect Half the Ocean? The specific guidelines of SDG 14 include a target of setting aside 10 percent of the ocean into "protected areas" (without specifying the level of protection), but this target needs to be understood as only an interim milestone en route to more extensive and sustainable ocean conservation. A recent review of 144 studies indicated that, on average, at least 37 percent of the ocean should be protected in marine reserves to achieve, maximize, or optimize conservation and sustainability objectives (O'Leary and others, 2016). An analytical model also indicated that closing half the ocean to fishing would result in equivalent yields to those under good fisheries management (Hastings and Botsford, 1999). E. O. Wilson argues that to preserve 75 percent of species, half the planet (including the ocean) should be protected.[8] All of those studies recommend that between 40 and 50 percent of the ocean must be protected as a reasonable way to restore ocean biodiversity, its resilience, and all the services it provides to humanity—including helping to replenish fisheries in the half that would remain unprotected.

Currently, the world's 4 percent of protected ocean is spread across more than 10,000 marine protected areas (MPAs) of different sizes.[9] Their geography is highly skewed. Most protection occurs within a couple dozen very large MPAs, located within fewer than twenty countries' exclusive economic zones (EEZs).[10] Meanwhile, less than 1 percent of the high seas is protected.

8. Wilson (2016), p. 276.
9. Spalding, Fish, and Wood (2008). Also mpatlas.org.
10. Lubchenco and Grorud-Colvert (2015); Wood and others (2008).

Figure 11-1. Fish Biomass in Marine Protected Areas Relative to Nearby Unprotected Areas

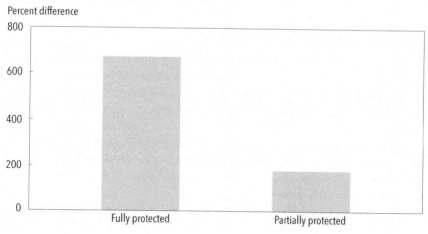

Source: Sala and Giakoumi (2017).

It is important to note that there are many types of MPAs. At the most protective end of the spectrum are no-take "marine reserves"—areas where extractive activities are prohibited (reviewed above). The rest are partially protected MPAs that allow extractive activities to different degrees. Recent meta-analyses show that no-take marine reserves are far more effective than partially protected MPAs in protecting and restoring ocean biodiversity. See figure 11-1, which shows the total biomass of fish (a strong indicator of the maturity and health of the entire fish assemblage) is, on average, 670 percent greater within marine reserves than in unprotected areas, and 343 percent greater than in partially protected areas. The effectiveness of partially protected areas presented high variability, however, and often fish biomass was barely different from unprotected areas nearby. Partially protected MPAs are very useful for managing conflicting ocean uses in specific areas, but they are not truly protected.

Calling a marine area that allows fishing "protected" is like calling a logging concession (no matter how well managed) a "protected forest." Therefore, no-take marine reserves are the most appropriate and effective type of protected area in the ocean. This is no trivial clarification: little is accomplished if countries rush to label areas as simply "protected"—without implementing any real protective measures—before the 2020 United Nations deadline for protecting 10 percent of the ocean. The "Natura 2000" sites in the Mediterranean are a great example of how countries claim they have protected so much of their waters without actually protecting anything.[11]

Changing the Way We Obtain Food from the Ocean

To achieve ecological sustainability while providing food for more than 9 billion people by 2050 under the half-ocean-protected scenario, we will need to change the way we obtain food from the other half that is unprotected. Some even argue that the world need not increase the extraction of food from the ocean, because global food production globally could increase by a third just by reducing the current massive food waste (Shafiee-Jood and Cai, 2016). Regardless of how much food comes from the ocean, food production relying on the ocean must change, and that means basically reforming fisheries management and transforming aquaculture in a sustainable way.

Fixing Fisheries. Currently, fishing exploitation rates are not controlled in vast ocean areas, including the high seas. Only a small fraction of the fisheries of the world are managed and science-based, and they mostly concern single species targeted by industrial fleets in developed countries (Mora and others, 2009). Of those assessed fish stocks, 63 percent are overexploited and require rebuilding (Worm and others, 2009). Fisheries that target multiple species in developing countries are mostly unsustainable. Currently, there is overcapacity of fishing; too many vessels after too few fish—encouraged by government subsidies to the tune of $35 billion per year (Sumaila and others, 2016).

The fishing industry applies, at best, a disingenuous argument for the need to continue maximizing the catch to feed the world—one based largely on overcapacity of the global fishing fleet and inefficient use of resources. As mentioned earlier, the fisheries of the world have expanded farther offshore and into deeper waters because fish populations have collapsed in fishing grounds along the continental shelf.[12] Only a few select fisheries in a few countries such as the United States are sustainable (Worm and others, 2009). A World Bank report suggested that cutting fishing effort by 40 percent would increase the efficiency and profitability of fishing (World Bank, 2017).

11. UNEP-MAP-SPA/RAC M, "The 2016 Status of Marine Protected Areas in the Mediterranean," 2017 (http://d2ouvy59p0dg6k.cloudfront.net/downloads/medpan_forum_mpa_2016___brochure_ a4_en_web_1_.pdf). Natura 2000 is a network of nature protection areas in the territory of the European Union. It is made up of Special Areas of Conservation and Special Protection Areas designated respectively under the Habitats Directive and Birds Directive.

12. Swartz and others (2010); Morato and others (2007).

To effectively regulate fishing, end overfishing and illegal fishing, and make fisheries more sustainable and profitable while fishing in only half the ocean, the following must occur:

—A new regime of rights-based fisheries (RBF) management is required.[13] RBF assigns fishers and communities clearly defined rights to each fishery, as opposed to open access regimes that result in overfishing. If properly implemented, RBF gives fishers a vested interest in preventing overfishing and increasing compliance with catch limits (Barner and others, 2015).

—Fishing capacity needs to be reduced: boats need to be taken out of the water.[14] It would probably be self-regulated and reduced in a well-implemented RBF scheme. That would also reduce the issue of displacement of effort to unprotected areas after creation of large no-take marine reserves.

—Subsidies that perpetuate overcapacity and overfishing need to be eliminated. That would also save the world over \$35 billion annually (Sumaila and others, 2016), which could be used to restore artisanal fisheries within countries' EEZs.

—National and global catch statistics need to be corrected. The Sea Around Us project at the University of British Columbia has reconstructed all catches reported to the Food and Agriculture Organization (FAO). The university researchers found that reconstructed global catches between 1950 and 2010 were 50 percent higher than reported to FAO and are declining more strongly since catches peaked in the 1990s (Pauly and Zeller, 2016b). FAO should not accept vastly underreported data anymore.

—Regional Fisheries Management Organizations (RFMOs) need to be reformed (Gjerde and others, 2013) and made accountable to a new independent global fisheries agency, one that oversees fisheries on the basis of science and sustainability rather than national interests. The high seas (over 60 percent of the ocean) are still largely unmanaged. Fishing of migratory species that migrate between countries, such as tuna and sharks, are managed by RFMOs, known, with some exceptions, to be ineffective in conserving the wildlife they exploit and driven by short-term gain and political pressure, while ignoring scientific advice on fishing quotas. Two-thirds of stocks fished on the high seas under RFMO management are either depleted or overexploited (Cullis-Suzuki and Pauly, 2010).

Farming Seafood the Right Way. As of 2017 aquaculture—fish and shellfish farming—provides about half the ocean food the world eats (FAO, 2016), and its yield is increasing fast, whereas the global wild fisheries catch has been declining since the mid-1990s and without hope of recovering anytime soon unless strong conservation measures are put in place (Pauly and Zeller, 2016b). Many view

13. Costello and others (2016); Worm (2016).
14. World Bank (2017); Barkin and DeSombre (2013).

aquaculture as the future of food production from the sea, but currently most aquaculture practices are not sustainable because, ironically, they depend on fish feed, which only exacerbates the pressure on wild fish populations (Diana, 2009).

Aquaculture also has enormous negative impacts by polluting the coastal environment, spreading disease, and depleting local fish populations through introduced farmed species (Diana, 2009). Therefore, aquaculture needs to (i) abandon its current dependence on fish feed, (ii) enhance the production of seaweed and filter feeders (for example, mussels and oysters), and (iii) close its production cycle as to avoid environmental impacts (Duarte and others, 2009). A recent study suggests that nearly every coastal country has large areas that are suitable for aquaculture and that those exceed the space required to meet forecasted seafood demand (Gentry and others, 2017). In fact, the current total catch from wild fisheries could be replaced totally by aquaculture, using less than 0.015 percent of the global ocean area. These results suggest that sustainable aquaculture alongside reduction of food waste could help feed the growing human population, thus eliminating the need for many industrial fisheries.

Let's Not Forget the Climate and Pollution

The only solution to reverse global warming and acidification of the ocean is to reduce our carbon emissions beyond the commitments of the 2016 Paris Climate Agreement. Even the commitment to limiting the average worldwide temperature increase to only 2° C by 2025 still will result in the loss of coral reefs and the melting of Arctic sea ice, among other ecological tragedies. To avert the worst disasters, rapid decarbonization of our human society is required (Rockström and others, 2017). Meanwhile, we can buy time by reducing local threats such as conserving fishing grounds and limiting pollution, to increase the resilience of ocean ecosystems.

To achieve the SDG target to "prevent and significantly reduce marine pollution" by 2025, the world needs to move from our current "linear economy" (make, use, dispose) to a circular economy in which resources do not become waste but instead are recovered and regenerated at the end of each service life.[15] Some companies are pioneering this approach. For example, Patagonia, a U.S. outdoor apparel company, has embedded the principles of the circular economy into its business strategy. By extending the usable life of its products, Patagonia can reduce the amount of carbon, waste, and water used by up to 20–30 percent per person, and it has diverted about 82 tons of gear from landfill in the United States.[16] But companies cannot be expected to voluntarily adopt such strategies.

15. Webster and MacArthur (2016), p. 210.
16. Chouinard and Stanley (2012), p. 160.

Government should embed the circular economy into national strategies. For instance, Scotland has already placed the circular economy at the core of its own economic strategy and manufacturing plan; China also has adopted a national circular economy strategy (Geng and others, 2013). In addition to current marine pollution regulations, governments should put a price on waste, including plastic, and use market incentives to foster innovation among businesses. Some enterprising companies, from carpet to sock manufacturers, are harvesting marine litter to upcycle for products.

How to Make Protection Happen?

To summarize the above proposition: in order to truly achieve global ocean sustainability goals, we need (a) a world where half the ocean is protected from direct human threats, while the other half is fished and farmed sustainably and (b) an economy based almost fully on renewable energies. The decarbonization needed to prevent catastrophic and irreversible climate change is detailed in Rockström and others (2017). The basic principles for fixing the way we fish are outlined above. But how to protect half the ocean? And what should be protected? We propose the following strategy.

The first step is to identify which areas to protect. Under the assumption that little of our ocean will be protected, what are the most critical areas for ensuring survival of as many species as possible? An example is the academic concept of "biodiversity hotspots," which aims to protect the smallest needed surface of the planet to preserve a large fraction of earth's biodiversity.[17] But such attempts to identify an optimal area are frequently overtaken by opportunities in the real world (such as the presence of an enlightened leader in a specific country), and hence not fruitful. Moreover, recent evidence suggests a need to think beyond species numbers, because entire ecosystems provide services key to our survival (Worm and others, 2006). Species numbers are key, of course, but the ecosystems they live in help us avert catastrophic climate change by capturing carbon from the atmosphere and seawater.

Through National Geographic's Pristine Seas project, which aims to save the wildest places in the ocean, we have learned that simply protecting as large an area as possible in as many places as possible is the most practical rule of thumb to ensure the protection of a representative sample of the ocean's major ecosystems and all the biodiversity within.[18] This broad approach to geographical representation would achieve goals for conservation of biodiversity and would also help

17. Roberts and others (2002); Myers and others (2000), p. 853.
18. See www.nationalgeographic.org/projects/pristine-seas/.

replenish local fisheries and help sequester some of our carbon pollution (Spalding and others, 2007).

How can we ensure that marine protected areas are evenly distributed so they will cover 50 percent of the ocean? If fishing were excluded from the high seas, about 60 percent of the ocean in spatial terms would form a giant savings account for those species that migrate between exclusive economic zones and the high seas, potentially increasing yield of these species by 30 percent (if caught only within EEZs) and aggregate profits by more than 100 percent.[19] A total high seas closure would also be easier to enforce than a mosaic of smaller protected areas. But it would not fulfill global conservation goals, because EEZs contain most of the biodiversity and currently account for 95 percent of the global fish catch.

Different approaches are required to create marine reserves in countries' exclusive economic zones, compared to the high seas. First, action can be more easily taken and is more practical within EEZs than in the high seas, because coastal countries have full jurisdiction to create protected areas within their 200-mile waters. How much of the economic exclusive zones of the world should be protected? Start with the 30 percent target as a milestone agreed on by most conservation groups worldwide.[20] While not every country can or will protect 30 percent of their own territory, several nations have already implemented no-take marine reserves covering more than 10 percent of their EEZs, including through large reserves as the most efficient path to protection: Palau (80 percent), United Kingdom (32 percent), Chile (24 percent), Gabon (26 percent), United States (23 percent), and Kiribati (12 percent). These examples show that the 30 percent EEZ target is politically feasible.

Not all coastal countries, as noted, have the ability or space to create large marine reserves. And not all reserves should be large. While reserves greater than 100,000 square kilometers, for example, are necessary to protect large ecosystems and have regional benefits, small reserves have local benefits for coastal communities too. Many governments do not have sufficient staff and resources to create and finance small marine reserves, so new business models are needed whereby a local enterprise could invest in the reserve and reap the economic benefits from increased tourism and better fishing around the reserve.[21] That will require governments to pass legislation empowering local communities to manage their local reserves.

If 30 percent of the aggregate EEZs are protected, this translates to about 12 percent of the global ocean. In turn, to reach fully half the ocean under protection, at least 80 percent of the high seas need full protection, as shown in figure

19. Sumaila and others (2015); White and Costello (2014).
20. International Union for Conservation of Nature (2016).
21. Sala and others (2013); Sala and others (2016).

Figure 11-2. Schematic Representation of the Strategy
to Protect Half the Ocean in Marine Reserves

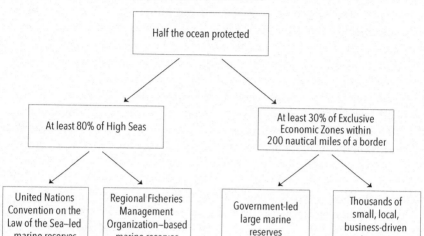

11-2. This high seas target is consistent with a study that showed that the more of the high seas under protection, the greater the ecological and economic benefits (White and Costello, 2014).

For the high seas, the question is how to protect 80 percent of something that no country owns? They are governed by the UN Convention on the Law of the Sea (UNCLOS) but when the convention concluded in 1982, there was little concern about deep sea trawling or mining, and no attendees realized that Atlantic bluefin tuna was on its way to commercial extinction. The agreement reached by countries involved in UNCLOS dealt mostly with fishing, with only vague references to conservation in the high seas: "Necessary measures shall be taken . . . with respect to activities in the Area to ensure effective protection for the marine environment from harmful effects which may arise from such activities" (Article 145). But there were no specifics on what "effective protection" meant, and no mention of the need for marine protected areas or a mechanism to implement them. In other words, governance to ensure biodiversity conservation in the high seas is absent.

To remedy this, on June 21, 2017, 193 countries agreed at the United Nations to begin negotiations on a legally-binding instrument for on the conservation and sustainable use of biological diversity beyond national jurisdiction (BBNJ). This will likely be a slow process (formal negotiations are to commence only at an Intergovernmental Conference in September 2018) and will encounter resistance by the key countries conducting high seas fishing—China, Taiwan, Korea,

Japan, and Spain (Sumaila and others, 2015). The BBNJ process is necessary to establish a mechanism for creation of MPAs in the high seas, but to be successful, it cannot be subordinated to the special interests within Regional Fisheries Management Organizations (RFMOs). It will also be essential that China, Taiwan, Korea, Japan, and Spain take a leadership role in high seas protection. They are taking more than 75 percent of the aggregate catch in the high seas and have a responsibility to ensure the integrity of the ecosystems they exploit.

Despite their shortcomings, regional organizations can be a solution to conservation of biodiversity in waters beyond national jurisdiction. A great example is the 2016 agreement to create the largest MPA in the ocean (at 1.5 million square kilometers) in the Ross Sea in Antarctica.[22] It required consensus among twenty-four nation states and the European Union and did not require a United Nations–led process. This shows that while the BBNJ instrument is developed, RFMOs could propose and implement marine protected areas on their own accord.

The final question is whether these large areas far from shore can be effectively enforced. The answer is yes, through a combination of remote surveillance and enforcement at port. Recent interest in the enforcement of marine protected areas has resulted in an unprecedented burst of innovation, including well-established satellite tracking and imagery, and drones, among other technologies.[23] Satellite technology is already being used by countries, or can be accessed at increasingly reduced costs through commercial applications. Citizens can also monitor illegal fishing using some of these tools through internet browsers.[24] The Food and Agriculture Organization of the United Nations promulgated in 2009 the Port State Measures Agreement to prevent, deter, and eliminate illegal, unreported, and unregulated (IUU) fishing. Once illegal fishing vessels are detected by competent government agencies, enforcement can be implemented at sea or at port with the aim "to prevent, deter and eliminate illegal, unreported and unregulated fishing." This means that parties to the agreement will apply it to foreign vessels when seeking entry to ports or while they are in port.[25] As of November 2017, fifty countries and the European Union had already joined the agreement.

What would be the timeline for protecting half the ocean? Currently there is no intergovernmental agreement beyond the CBD (adopted by SDG 14) target of 10 percent of the ocean to be protected by 2020. Because of the slow accretion of ocean protection to date, it might be impractical to expect 50 percent of the ocean protected by the SDG 2030 deadline. A more feasible timeline may be 30 percent

22. Commission for the Conservation of Antarctic Marine Living Resources (2016).
23. See secureoceans.org for more details.
24. See, for example, Global Fishing Watch at globalfishingwatch.org.
25. See www.fao.org/fishery/psm/agreement/en for details concerning this agreement.

by 2030—as recommended by the 2016 World Parks Congress[26]—and 50 percent by 2050.

Conclusion

Ocean protection and management require a radical new approach, a more ambitious scale of thinking based on science already available. Marine protection understood as a mosaic of small-scale uses seems appropriate in theory, but in practice it is much easier to enforce large no-take areas. Half the ocean needs to be protected from fishing, and the other half needs to be managed responsibly. In practical terms the protection requirement can only be achieved by protecting at least 80 percent of the high seas and 30 percent of countries' exclusive economic zones—by 2050 if not earlier.

It is key that countries that are leading in ocean conservation actively inspire other countries to follow suit. For example, high-level peer pressure at the "Our Ocean" conferences that U.S. Secretary of State John Kerry initiated in 2014 helped to double the total ocean area protected within three years. This is a clear example of how mutually reinforcing actions at the country level can facilitate a wave of action internationally.

Moreover, the challenges of protecting the ocean include integrating all the Sustainable Development Goals and not treating them within silos. For instance, industrial waste and agricultural runoff affect ocean life and end up polluting humans. And if the world does not shift away from fossil fuels soon, the ocean will be exceedingly warm and acidic, absorb less and less carbon, and could produce less oxygen. Without a healthy ocean, human life will suffer, through direct and indirect effects not always predictable. Let us imagine a day when the health of our ocean improves through better governance, and with this improvement come more business opportunities through sustainable tourism inside marine reserves; sustainable fisheries outside marine reserves; and other enterprises that restore our ocean, including sustainable aquaculture and agriculture, and management of waste, water, and energy. Our choice and path forward are clear.

References

Aburto-Oropeza, O., and others. 2008. "Mangroves in the Guld of California Increase Fishery Yields." *Proceedings of the National Academy of Sciences* 105, no. 30: 10456–59.
Althaus, F., and others. 2009. "Impacts of Bottom Trawling on Deep-Coral Ecosystems of Seamounts Are Long-Lasting." *Marine Ecology Progress Series* 397: 279–94.
Banerjee, S. 2015. "In the Warming Arctic Seas." *World Policy Journal* 32, no. 2: 18–27.

26. International Union for Conservation of Nature (2016).

Barkin, J. S., and E. R. DeSombre. 2013. *Saving Global Fisheries: Reducing Fishing Capacity to Promote Sustainability*. MIT Press.

Barner, A. K., and others. 2015. "Solutions for Recovering and Sustaining the Bounty of the Ocean: Combining Fishery Reforms, Rights-Based Fisheries Management, and Marine Reserves." *Oceanography* 28, no. 2: 252–63.

Baum, J. K., and others. 2003. "Collapse and Conservation of Shark Populations in the Northwest Atlantic." Science 299, no. 5605: 389–92.

Baxter, J. M., and D. Laffoley, eds. 2016. *Explaining Ocean Warming: Causes, Scale, Effects, and Consequences*. Gland, Switzerland: International Union for Conservation of Nature.

Bitz, C. M., J. K. Ridley, M. Holland, and H. Cattle. 2012. "Global Climate Models and 20th and 21st Century Arctic Climate Change." In P. Lemke and H. W. Jacobi, eds. *Arctic Climate Change*. Atmospheric and Oceanographic Sciences Library, vol. 43, pp. 405–36. Dordrecht: Springer.

Cheung, W., C. Close, V. Lam, R. Watson, and D. Pauly. 2008. "Application of Macroecological Theory to Predict Effects of Climate Change on Global Fisheries Potential." *Marine Ecology Progress Series* 365: 187-197.

Cheung, W. W., and others. 2010. "Large-Scale Redistribution of Maximum Fisheries Catch Potential in the Global Ocean under Climate Change." *Global Change Biology* 16, no. 1: 24–35.

Chouinard, Y., and V. Stanley. 2012. *The Responsible Company: What We've Learned from Patagonia's First 40 Years*. Ventura, Calif.: Patagonia Books.

Cisneros-Montemayor, A. M., M. Barnes-Mauthe, D. Al-Abdulrazzak, E. Navarro-Holm, and U. R. Sumaila. 2013. "Global Economic Value of Shark Ecotourism: Implications for Conservation." *Oryx* 47, no 03: 381–88.

Commission for the Conservation of Antarctic Marine Living Resources (CCAMLR). 2016. Conservation Measure 91-05: Ross Sea Region Marine Protected Area (www. ccamlr.org/sites/drupal.ccamlr.org/files//91-05_4.pdf).

Costello, C., and others. 2016. "Global Fishery Prospects under Contrasting Management Regimes." *Proceedings of the National Academy of Sciences* 18 (2016): 5125–29.

Cullis-Suzuki, S., and D. Pauly. 2010. "Failing the High Seas: A Global Evaluation of Regional Fisheries Management Organizations." *Marine Policy* 34, no. 5: 1036–61.

Diana, J. S. 2009. "Aquaculture Production and Biodiversity Conservation." *BioScience* 59, no. 1: 27–38.

Diaz, R. J., and R. Rosenberg. 2008. "Spreading Dead Zones and Consequences for Marine Ecosystems." *Science* 321, no. 5891: 926–29.

Dinmore, T., D. Duplisea, B. Rackham, D. Maxwell, and S. Jennings. 2003. "Impact of a Large-Scale Area Closure on Patterns of Fishing Disturbance and the Consequences for Benthic Communities." *ICES Journal of Marine Science* 60, no. 2: 371–80.

Doumbouya, A., and others. 2017. "Assessing the Effectiveness of Monitoring Control and Surveillance of Illegal Fishing: The Case of West Africa." *Frontiers in Marine Science* 4, no. 50.

Duarte, C. M., and others. 2009. "Will the Oceans Help Feed Humanity?" *BioScience* 59, no. 11: 967–76.

Estes, J. A., and D. O. Duggins. 1995. "Sea Otters and Kelp Forests in Alaska: Generality and Variation in a Community Ecological Paradigm." *Ecological Monographs* 65, no. 1: 75–100.

Estes, J. A., M. Heithaus, D. J. McCauley, D. B. Rasher, and B. Worm. 2016. "Mega-faunal Impacts on Structure and Function of Ocean Ecosystems." *Annual Review of Environment and Resources* 41, no. 1: 83–116.

FAO. 2016. "The State of World Fisheries and Aquaculture." Rome: Fisheries and Aquaculture Department, FAO (www.fao.org/3/a-i5555e.pdf).

Ferretti, F., R. A. Myers, F. Serena, and H. K. Lotze. 2008. "Loss of Large Predatory Sharks from the Mediterranean Sea." *Conservation Biology* 22, no. 4: 952–64.

Geng, Y., J. Sarkis, S. Ulgiati, and P. Zhang. 2013. "Measuring China's Circular Economy." *Science* 339, no. 6127: 1526–27.

Gentry, R. R., and others. 2017. "Mapping the Global Potential for Marine Aquaculture." *Nature Ecology and Evolution* 1, August 14 (doi:10.1038/s41559-017-0257-9).

Gjerde, K. M., D. Currie, K. Wowk, and K. Sack. 2013. "Ocean in Peril: Reforming the Management of Global Ocean Living Resources in Areas beyond National Jurisdiction." *Marine Pollution Bulletin* 74, no. 2: 540–51.

Green, E., and R. Donnelly. 2003. "Recreational Scuba Diving in Caribbean Marine Protected Areas: Do the Users Pay?" *Ambio* 32: 140–44.

Guidetti, P., and E. Sala. 2007. "Community-Wide Effects of Marine Reserves in the Mediterranean Sea." *Marine Ecology Progress Series* 335: 43–56.

Halpern, B. A., S. E. Lester, and J. B. Kellner. 2009. "Spillover from Marine Reserves and the Replenishment of Fished Stocks." *Environmental Conservation* 36, no. 04: 268–76.

Hastings, A., and L. W. Botsford. 1999. "Equivalence in Yield from Marine Reserves and Traditional Fisheries Management." *Science* 284, no. 5419: 1537–38.

Hiddink, J., T. Hutton, S. Jennings, and M. Kaiser. 2006. "Predicting the Effects of Area Closures and Fishing Effort Restrictions on the Production, Biomass, and Species Richness of Benthic Invertebrate Communities." *ICES Journal of Science* 63, no. 5: 822–30.

Hoegh-Guldberg, O., and others. 2007. "Coral Reefs under Rapid Climate Change and Ocean Acidification." *Science* 318, no. 5857: 1737–42.

Hughes, T. P., and others. 2017. "Global Warming and Recurrent Mass Bleaching of Corals." *Nature* 543, no. 7645: 373–77.

International Union for Conservation of Nature. 2016. "Increasing Marine Protected Area Coverage for Effective Marine Biodiversity Conservation. WCC-2016-Res-050-EN (https://portals.iucn.org/library/sites/library/files/resrecfiles/WCC_2016_RES_050_EN.pdf).

Jackson, J. B., M. X. Kirby, W. H. Berger, and others. 2001. "Historical Overfishing and the Recent Collapse of Coastal Ecosystems. *Science* 293, no. 5530: 629–37.

Jambeck, J. R., and others. 2015. "Plastic Waste Inputs from Land into the Ocean." *Science* 347, no. 6223: 768–71.

Jones, M. C., and W. W. Cheung. 2015. "Multi-Model Ensemble Projections of Climate Change Effects on Global Marine Biodiversity." *ICES Journal of Marine Science* 72, no. 3: 741–52.

Le Quéré, C. and others. 2012. "The Global Carbon Budget 1959–2011." *Earth System Science Data Discussions* 5, no. 2: 1107–57.

Lester, S. E., and others. 2009. "Biological Effects within No-Take Marine Reserves: A Global Synthesis." *Marine Ecology Progress Series* 384: 33–46.

Lubchenco, J., and K. Grorud-Colvert. 2015. "Making Waves: The Science and Politics of Ocean Protection." *Science* 350, no. 6259: 382–83.

Lynham, J., C. Costello, S. D. Gaines, and E. Sala. 2015. "Economic Valuation of
    Marine and Shark-Based Tourism in the Galápagos Islands." Pristine Seas Report to
    the Galápagos National Park. Washington: National Geographic Society.
Mattsson, K., E. V. Johnson, A. Malmendal, S. Linse, L. A. Hansson, and T. Cedervall.
    2017. "Brain Damage and Behavioural Disorders in Fish Induced by Plastic Nanopar-
    ticles Delivered through the Food Chain." *Scientific Reports* 7, no. 1: 11452.
Micheli, F., and others. 2012. "Evidence That Marine Reserves Enhance Resilience to
    Climatic Impacts." *PLoS One* 7, no. 7: e40832.
Miranda, D. de A., and G. F. de Carvalho-Souza. 2016. "Are We Eating Plastic-Ingesting
    Fish?" *Marine Pollution Bulletin* 103, no. 1: 109–14.
Mora, C., and others. 2009. "Management Effectiveness of the World's Marine Fisheries."
    PLoS Biol 7, no. 6: e1000131.
Morato, T., R. Watson, T. Pitcher, and D. Pauly. 2007. "Fishing Down the Deep." *Fish
    Fish* 7: 24–34.
Myers, N., R. A. Mittermeier, C. G. Mittermeier, G. A. Da Fonseca, and J. Kent. 2000.
    "Biodiversity Hotspots for Conservation Priorities." *Nature* 403, no. 6772.
Myers, R. A., and B. Worm. 2003. "Rapid Worldwide Depletion of Predatory Fish Com-
    munities." *Nature* 423, no. 6937: 280–83.
OECD. 2016. *The Ocean Economy in 2030.* Brussels: OECD Publishing.
O'Leary, B. C., and others. 2016. "Effective Coverage Targets for Ocean Protection."
    Conservation Letters 9, no. 6: 398–404.
Overland, J. E., and M. Wang. 2013. "When Will the Summer Arctic Be Nearly Sea Ice
    Free?," *Geophysical Research Letters* 40, no. 10: 2097–101.
Pauly, D., and D. Zeller. 2016a. *Global Atlas of Marine Fisheries: A Critical Appraisal of
    Catches and Ecosystem Impacts.* Washington: Island Press.
————. 2016b. "Catch Reconstructions Reveal That Global Marine Fisheries Catches
    Are Higher Than Reported and Declining." *Nature Communications* 7, January 19
    (doi:10.1038/ncomms10244).
Roberts, C. M., J. A. Bohnsack, F. R. Gell, J. P. Hawkins, and R. Goodridge. 2001.
    "Effects of Marine Reserves on Adjacent Fisheries." *Science* 294: 1920–23.
Roberts, C. M., and others. 2002. "Marine Biodiversity Hotspots and Conservation
    Priorities for Tropical Reefs." *Science* 295, no. 5558: 1280–84.
Rockström, J., and others. 2017. "A Roadmap for Rapid Decarbonization." *Science* 355,
    no. 6331: 1269–71.
Sala, E., and S. Giakoumi. 2017. "No-Take Marine Reserves Are the Most Effective Pro-
    tected Areas in the Ocean." *ICES Journal of Marine Science* (https://doi.org/10.1093/
    icesjms/fsx059).
Sala, E., and others. 2013. "A General Business Model for Marine Reserves." *PLoS One* 8,
    no. 4: e58799.
————. 2016. "Fish Banks: An Economic Model to Scale Marine Conservation." *Marine
    Policy* 73: 154–61.
Sandin, S., and others. 2008. "Baselines and Degradation of Coral Reefs in the Northern
    Line Islands." *PLoS One* 3: e1548.
Schmidt, C., T. Krauth, and S. Wagner. 2017. "Export of Plastic Debris by Rivers into
    the Sea." *Environmental Science & Technology* 51, no. 21: 12246–53.
Schmidtko, S., L. Stramma, and M. Visbeck. 2017. "Decline in Global Oceanic Oxygen
    Content during the Past Five Decades." *Nature* 542, no. 7641: 335–39.

Serreze, M. C., M. M. Holland, and J. Stroeve. 2007. "Perspectives on the Arctic's Shrinking Sea-Ice Cover." *Science* 315, no. 5818: 1533–36.

Shafiee-Jood, M., and X. Cai. 2016. "Reducing Food Loss and Waste to Enhance Food Security and Environmental Sustainability." *Environmental Science and Technology* 50, no. 16: 8432–43.

Shears, N. T., and R. C. Babcock. 2003. "Continuing Trophic Cascade Effects after 25 Years of No-Take Marine Reserve Protection." *Marine Ecology Progress Series* 246: 1–16.

Spaulding, M. D., L. Fish, and L. J. Wood. 2008. "Toward Representative Protection of the World's Coasts and Oceans—Progress, Gaps, and Opportunities." *Conservation Letters* 1, no. 5: 217–26.

Spaulding, M. C., and others. 2007. "Marine Ecoregions of the World: A Bioregionalization of Coastal and Shelf Areas. *BioScience* 57, no. 7: 573–83.

Sumaila, U. R., and others. 2015. "Winners and Losers in a World Where the High Seas Is Closed to Fishing." *Scientific Reports* 5: 8481 (doi:10.1038/srep08481).

Sumaila, U. R., V. Lam, F. Le Manach, W. Swartz, and D. Paul. 2016. "Global Fisheries Subsidies: An Updated Estimate." *Marine Policy* 69: 189–93.

Swartz, W., E. Sala, S. Tracey, R. Watson, and D. Pauly. 2010. "The Spatial Expansion and Ecological Footprint of Fisheries (1950 to Present)." *PLoS One* 5, no. 12: e15143.

Tomberlin, J. K., and others. 2015. "Protecting the Environment through Insect Farming as a Means to Produce Protein for Use as Livestock, Poultry, and Aquaculture Feed." *Journal of Insects as Food and Feed* 1, no. 4: 307–09.

UNEP. 2006. "Marine and Coastal Ecosystems and Human Well-Being: A Synthesis Report Based on the Findings of the Millennium Ecosystem Assessment." Nairobi: UN Environment Program.

Webster, K., and E. MacArthur. 2016. *The Circular Economy: A Wealth of Flows*. Isle of Wight: Ellen MacArthur Foundation Publishing.

White, C., and C. Costello. 2014. "Close the High Seas to Fishing?" *PLoS Biology* 12, no. 3: e1001826.

Wilson, E. O. 2016. *Half-Earth: Our Planet's Fight for Life*. New York: Liveright (W. W. Norton).

Wood, L. J., L. Fish, J. Laughren, and D. Pauly. 2008. "Assessing Progress towards Global Marine Protection Targets: Shortfalls in Information and Action." *Oryx* 42: 340–51.

World Bank. 2008. "The Sunken Billions. The Economic Justification for Fisheries Reform." Washington: World Bank (https://siteresources.worldbank.org/EXTARD/Resources/336681-1224775570533/SunkenBillionsFinal.pdf).

———. 2017. "The Sunken Billions Revisited: Progress and Challenges in Global Marine Fisheries." Washington: World Bank (https://openknowledge.worldbank.org/handle/10986/24056).

Worm, B. 2016. "Averting a Global Fisheries Disaster." *Proceedings of the National Academy of Sciences* 113, no. 18: 4895–97.

Worm, B., and others. 2006. "Impacts of Biodiversity Loss on Ocean Ecosystem Services." *Science* 314, no. 5800: 787–90.

———. 2009. "Rebuilding Global Fisheries." *Science* 325, no. 5940: 578–85.

PART III
Updating Governance

CHAPTER TWELVE

A Canadian North Star
Crafting an Advanced Economy Approach to the Sustainable Development Goals

Margaret Biggs and John W. McArthur

C anada enjoys some of the world's highest average living standards. The country is widely admired for its natural beauty, and its cities rank among the most livable in the world. Not surprisingly, outside observers look at Canada with admiration, and Canadians themselves are proud of their natural riches and the society they have built. But below the surface, Canada, like other countries, faces profound challenges. Many segments of the population face economic and social exclusion. Inequality is creeping upward. And the country's environment faces risks—from depleted fisheries to loss of biodiversity and the effects of climate change, most conspicuously in the Arctic.

At the same time, forces on the horizon threaten to create new challenges and compound existing ones. Large numbers of jobs are at risk of disruption from technological change. Fewer than half of Canadians are estimated to have trust in public institutions (Edelman, 2018). Canada is also challenged outside its borders. As a middle-sized open economy, the country is deeply invested in the postwar norms of international cooperation. But the rules of the international order are in flux, and protectionist forces are on the rise. Canada cannot be complacent. It needs to update its approaches to confront intersecting challenges at home and abroad.

Canada is not the only country grappling with these domestic and international challenges. Quite the opposite: developed and developing economies alike

We are grateful to many colleagues for helpful comments and suggestions at various stages of drafting, including Kaysie Brown, Raj Desai, Kate Higgins, Christine Hogan, Homi Kharas, Naheed Nenshi, Tony Pipa, Julia Sanchez, Khalil Shariff, and Scott Vaughan. We further thank Krista Rasmussen for fantastic research support.

are confronting the need to promote prosperity that is both socially inclusive and environmentally sustainable. It is the common nature of these issues that led all 193 UN member states in 2015 to adopt the Sustainable Development Goals as universal objectives for 2030.

But advanced economies such as Canada are unaccustomed to tracking their progress against comprehensive international benchmarks like the SDGs—let alone organizing policy efforts to achieve them. This chapter presents a framework for doing so. Throughout, we aim to present concepts to inform strategies instead of delving into specific policy details. As part of this, we differentiate between issues to be tackled at home, those to be tackled abroad, and those on which domestic actions contribute to collective global outcomes. Throughout, we emphasize the difference between issues that are currently "on track" for success and those that need a breakthrough. This informs a subsequent distinction between where "business as usual" might be satisfactory and where new approaches are required.

In situations where accelerated progress or breakthroughs are needed, many forms of action tend to be required, spanning business practices, citizen action, public policy, and technical or scientific innovation. In a complex federation like Canada, multiple levels of government need to be engaged, as do indigenous people and communities. Thus any Canadian "national approach" to the SDGs in fact needs to be a constellation of approaches. Each sector in society and each community, province, and territory will need to identify their own priorities for shifting from business-as-usual. And everyone will need to be able to track progress against a common set of outcome measures.

Why Do the SDGs Matter to Canada?

In Canada as in other countries, many expert communities and policymakers are already working on—and often making progress against—each of the economic, social, and environmental problems embedded in the SDGs. This is important context when considering the common critique that the goals are an excessive list of topics or commandments decreed by the UN. The goals are instead best understood as a distillation of what people around the world already care about and have told the global community to care about. In turn, the SDGs are commitments that all governments have made to their own people and hence have a responsibility to deliver.

The SDGs are not perfect. In some areas, for example, the official wording is vague or imprecise. But the fundamentals of the goals help crystallize a common, multidimensional definition of societal success. This multidimensional nature can help specialist communities map how their priorities—ranging from healthy aging to quality jobs to biodiversity to sustainable infrastructure—can interconnect as part of the same agenda. The common reference point allows diverse constituencies to compare approaches, align efforts, and monitor outcomes. It also opens up possibilities for new forms of collaboration, enterprise, and civic action. The SDGs can provide an opportunity to fight joint battles—across business, science, civil society, and all orders of government.

In short, the SDGs offer a tool for putting everyone on the same page, literally and figuratively. This "North Star" function offers the SDGs' greatest opportunity—a common guidepost that everyone can see, regardless of initial vantage point. The 2030 horizon can serve as a guiding light that endures beyond short-term headlines and political cycles. A deadline still a dozen years out is far enough away to offer space for organizing new approaches, yet near enough to rally widespread societal efforts.

In public debates, the goals offer a neutral set of outcome metrics against which everyone can assess progress. Fortunately, Canada signed on to the goals under a government led by one political party and has begun to pursue the goals under a government led by another party. This provides a helpfully nonpartisan political anchor to underpin the necessary national policy debates. In the best cases, a common set of future-oriented aspirations can even expand the political space to break long-standing policy logjams, where the cumulative strains of past arguments might otherwise inhibit progress.

Crucially, the SDGs' focus on "leave no one behind" speaks to the needs of millions of Canadians struggling with poverty and exclusion. The theme is of greatest significance for the challenges faced by many of the country's approximately 1.7 million indigenous people. In this respect, the timing of the SDGs could not be more critical in the wake of the 2015 final report of the Truth and Reconciliation Commission. That body chronicled the history of residential schools in Canada—the decades-long forced removal of indigenous children from their homes, the abuse they suffered, and the multigenerational social and economic impacts that resulted. The commission's calls to action seek both to redress past harms and open a new chapter in relations between indigenous and non-indigenous Canadians. The norms and human rights standards embedded in the United Nations Declaration on the Rights of Indigenous Peoples (UNDRIP) are seen as the framework for reconciliation.

The SDGs can help Canada move forward in this broader effort of reconciliation. The goals' foundation in human rights principles and connections to UNDRIP can provide a common language to facilitate conversations among Canada's diverse indigenous communities and non-indigenous people. Moreover, the principles outlined in the UN declaration, combined with the focus on outcomes emphasized by the SDGs, can help forge a shared agenda and new mutual accountability framework with federal and provincial governments.

Figure 12-1. Distinguishing Between Domestic, Collective, and External Objectives

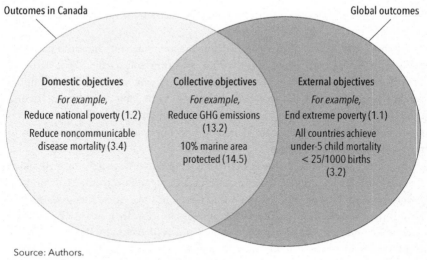

Source: Authors.
Note: Numbers in parentheses indicate SDG targets.

Canada's need to address these and other domestic challenges while helping address global priorities reflects the universal nature of the SDGs. In that regard, the goals offer an interface for connecting local and international challenges. To start, Canadians can benchmark their own outcomes against peers on common problems—in other cities, provinces, and countries. This can foster global communities of practice, whereby local experts share and learn with groups working on similar challenges in other parts of the world.

Ultimately, Canada's dedication to tackling all the SDGs will affect the country's standing on the world stage. The goals are becoming a lingua franca of international cooperation both inside and outside of government: major economies such as China, India, and Germany are making high-profile commitments to implementation, and major global associations of scientists, business leaders, and civil society champions are beginning to organize their own actions around the SDGs. To be credible and have influence across a range of geopolitical priorities, Canada needs to model progress on its own internal problems, while carrying an adequate share of the burdens of global problem solving. In the long term, Canada's demonstrated commitment to the goals will foster alliances that can be leveraged on many other geostrategic issues down the road.

Figure 12-1 presents a schematic diagram to help distinguish between the different types of objectives embedded in the SDGs. The left circle represents outcomes most pertinent within Canada's own geography. The right overlapping circle represents outcomes that are most pertinent at a global scale. On the left, the non-overlapping part represents SDG "domestic objectives." This includes issues like domestic poverty as nationally defined, where SDG target 1.2 calls for every country to cut its domestic poverty rate by half by 2030, or noncommunicable disease, where SDG target 3.4 calls for every country to cut its premature mortality by one-third by the same year. On the right, the non-overlapping part refers to global SDG challenges that will be achieved entirely outside of Canada's geography, even if Canada has a direct interest in seeing the issue succeed. Each country will lead on its own objectives, but in some cases the targets will only be met with international cooperation—for instance, eliminating the most extreme form of dollar-a-day-type poverty (SDG target 1.1) or ensuring child mortality falls below twenty-five deaths per 1,000 live births in every country (SDG target 3.2). These are standards that Canada has already achieved and where it can help support implementation elsewhere. As one of the world's more advantaged societies, Canada has special responsibility to contribute at least its share toward these external objectives.

The overlapping part of the two circles in the middle represents SDG "collective objectives" across countries, where Canada's domestic actions will contribute directly to global outcomes. For example, global problems defined by externalities—like cross-border tax cooperation, climate change mitigation, or pandemic disease preparedness—drive the need for each country to contribute its part. In addition, the world can properly protect its maritime areas only if all countries protect their maritime areas, especially large countries like Canada with significant coastal zones. In some cases, Canada also still grapples with domestic challenges that other advanced economies consider solely external problems.

In that context, the next section presents an approach for assessing where Canada is on track to meet the SDGs domestically and where there is the greatest need for change. This informs the subsequent section's focus on Canada's contributions to global outcomes.

How Is Canada Doing on the SDGs at Home?

To consider SDG trajectories within Canada carefully, a first step is to diagnose the issues on which the country is off track, either as a whole or in part—which outcomes, by how much, where, and among whom? Answers to these questions will provide essential evidence about where improvement is needed, at what scale, and at what pace. This information can then inform decision-making about where business-as-usual might suffice, and where new approaches are required. The following suggests a basic approach.

Where Are Breakthroughs Needed?

In principle, there are two ways to assess a country's status with regard to the SDGs. One is to track relative standing compared to other countries. Another is to compare against absolute standards. Both offer important insights, but from the SDG perspective of "no one left behind," absolute standards are most salient for understanding Canada's SDG challenges. In a country of 36 million people, for example, even achieving 97 percent access to a basic service might rate better than many countries, but it still implies more than 1 million people without access, which is simply too large a number for most Canadians to accept. Even 99 percent still means hundreds of thousands left out. Moreover, peer comparisons are inadequate on absolute global challenges. On greenhouse gas emissions, for example, the standard that ultimately matters is an absolute biophysical one: the global carbon budget consistent with a specific ceiling for global warming.

McArthur and Rasmussen (2017a) present a framework for how to benchmark advanced economies' trajectories against SDG outcome targets. It assesses Canada against both SDG targets framed in absolute global terms—like eliminating hunger, achieving safe drinking water for all, and protecting 10 percent of the ocean—and those framed in relative national terms—like reducing the domestic poverty rate by half, cutting national noncommunicable disease mortality by one-third, or meeting the nationally defined commitment for reducing greenhouse gas emissions. In cases where the formal SDG language is quantitatively vague, the framework assesses trajectories against existing national targets or proxy benchmarks.[1]

The framework classifies each SDG outcome target under one of four categories:

- *On track*: where the target is already achieved or on course for success by the relevant deadline—usually 2030, although 2020 or 2025 in select instances.
- *Acceleration needed*: where the indicator is on course to close at least half the distance to the target, but not yet the whole way.
- *Breakthrough needed*: where the indicator is on course to cover somewhere between 0 to 50 percent of the distance to the target.
- *Moving backward*: where recent trends are moving in the wrong direction.

Conceptually, these classifications emphasize the rate of progress required to succeed more than they do the absolute distance to the finish line. To illustrate, if an indicator for access to an essential service has been stuck at 99 percent for a decade then it rates as "breakthrough needed," even though only a small distance

---

1. McArthur and Rasmussen (2017a) includes a detailed description of proxy targets, many of which can be framed by translating nonspecific SDG target wording such as "substantially reduce" into a more measurable "cut by half."

Table 12-1. Summary of Canada's Domestic Status on Seventy-Three SDG Indicators

Sustainable Development Goal	Moving backwards	Breakthrough needed	Acceleration needed	On track
1 Poverty		•	•	•••
2 Hunger and food systems	•••			
3 Good health and well-being	•	••	••••••	•••
4 Quality education	••	•		•••
5 Gender equality	•	••••••		
6 Clean water and sanitation	••	••	•	
7 Affordable and clean energy	•	•	•	•
8 Decent work and economic growth		••	•	•
9 Industry, innovation, and infrastructure	•	••		
10 Reduced inequalities	•	•		
11 Sustainable cities and communities	•••			•
12 Responsible consumption and production		•••		
13 Climate action		•		
14 Life below water	•		•	••
15 Life on land		•••		•
16 Peace, justice, and strong institutions	••	••	•	••
	18	26	12	17

Source: McArthur and Rasmussen (2017a).

remains to the 100 percent target. Meanwhile, an indicator stuck at only 40 percent coverage would also be deemed in need of a breakthrough. Thus "breakthrough needed" might imply either a systematic gap or last-mile challenge of reaching marginalized populations.

Table 12-1 applies this performance framework to summarize how Canada currently measures up against the SDGs. It assesses sixty-one outcome targets through seventy-three indicators with available data as of mid-2017. (Detailed results for each underlying indicator are available in the appendix.) The table shows that the country is not yet wholly on track for any SDG, although the right-side column highlights Canada's existing success on many targets and indicators, ranging from eliminating dollar-a-day-type extreme poverty (SDG target 1.1) to reducing child mortality (SDG 3.2) and premature mortality from cardiovascular disease (SDG 3.4). In a less positive vein, more than half the indicators—forty-four in total—are either moving backward or need a breakthrough. Clearly, even Canada needs to do better in order to achieve the SDGs.

A handful of specific indicators helps to illustrate where Canada has overall challenges. Starting with domestic poverty, although Canada does not have an official poverty line, the share of people living below the low-income cut-off (after tax) dropped only slightly, from 10.8 percent in 2005 to 9.2 percent in 2015—not yet fast enough to achieve a 50 percent reduction by 2030. Perhaps surprisingly, Canada is not on track for any of the indicators under SDG 2 (hunger and food systems) or SDG 5 (gender equality), the latter of which includes indicators ranging from pay equity to representation in parliament and reported violence against women. Nor is the country on track for any of the indicators under SDG 6 (clean water and sanitation), SDG 9 (industry, innovation, and infrastructure), SDG 10 (inequality), SDG 12 (responsible consumption and production), and SDG 13 (climate action).

Diving a layer deeper, issues framed under the "acceleration needed" column help prompt questions of where each stakeholder community might need to improve its approaches. For example, on target 14.5 for the protection of oceans and marine-protected areas, the federal government reports that around 5 percent of the country's marine areas were protected as of the end of 2017 (DFO, 2017). This is a significant increase relative to the previous level of 0.9 percent in 2015, but far shy of a pledge to reach 10 percent by 2020. Meanwhile, greenhouse gas emissions are currently on a trajectory to fall only around 8 percent by 2030, if recent policies are fully implemented, compared to a promised 30 percent reduction. Acceleration is also needed to halve traffic deaths by 2020 (target 3.6). On issues like these, subject specialists, stakeholders, and policymakers will need to make concerted efforts to drive faster progress.

The most fundamental challenges raised in table 12-1 are those falling under the left-side columns of "Moving backward" and "Breakthrough needed." These are the issues on which Canada most needs new trajectories—again, due either to society-wide challenges or shortfalls in reaching specific populations. To illustrate the range of issues at stake, table 12-2 provides quantitative details for a cross-section of indicators that have been moving in the wrong direction. Examples of systemic challenges include increasing rates of food insecurity, child obesity, and substance abuse, alongside declines in the share of teenagers showing core competencies in numeracy and potentially also in literacy. The latter comes in a context where more than 3 million Canadian adults might already lack crucial literacy skills and 5 million might lack relevant numeracy skills. Meanwhile, reported sexual violence against children has been rising, as has the number of unsentenced detainees as a share of the prison population. As of 2014, the most recent year available, aggregate public and private spending on research and development was also declining as a share of GDP, reducing Canada's long-term capacity for innovation. All of these indicators reveal areas where business-as-usual approaches are clearly not working.

Table 12-2. Cross-Section of Indicators "Moving Backward" in Canada

SDG	Indicator	Initial value	Most recent value	Trajectory for 2030
2.1	Food insecurity: not enough money to buy food, some point in last 12 months	9.0% (2007)	9.9% (2016)	11.2%
2.2	Malnutrition: children overweight, aged 2–4 (%)	38.4% (2000)	42.3% (2015)	46.2%
3.5	Substance abuse: alcohol consumption per capita (liters)	9.8 (2005)	10.3 (2015)	11.1
4.6	Numeracy: <2 on PISA in 15-year-olds	11% (2006)	14% (2015)	20%
6.1	Drinking water: Lacking access to improved water	0.6% (2000)	1.6% (2015)	2.6%
9.5	Scientific research: R&D expenditures as share of GDP	2.0% (2004)	1.6% (2014)	1.0%
16.2	Violence against children: sexual violations per 100,000 population (police reported)	10.8 (2010)	19.1 (2016)	38.3
16.3	Justice for all: unsentenced detainees as share of prison population	29.0% (2005)	33.8% (2015)	41.0%

Sources: Food insecurity, Carol Graham (2017). Other indicators based on McArthur and Rasmussen (2017a).

The Importance of Unpacking the Numbers

Canada is defined by its diversity and vast geography, so each relevant SDG indicator needs to be considered by province, municipality, or community; gender; age; indigenous status; disability status; immigration status; and so forth. On many indicators, some groups in Canada are on track while others are falling behind (see McArthur and Rasmussen, 2017a, for details). On the positive side of the ledger, for example, all ten provinces and three territories are currently on track to achieve a one-third reduction in the major cardiovascular disease mortality rate by 2030, a key part of SDG target 3.4 on noncommunicable diseases.

Other indicators point to more fundamental challenges. Figure 12-2, for example, shows gender-disaggregated information on food insecurity across Canada's ten provinces and three territories as of 2011–12, the most recent year with relevant available information. Two aspects of the data stand out. One is that women register higher estimated food insecurity than men in almost all regions. Another is that food insecurity is by far highest in Nunavut, a northern territory with a population of around 36,000 people, the large majority of whom are indigenous. The next highest measure of food insecurity is in the Northwest Territories, where more than half of the population of around 42,000 people are also indigenous.

Figure 12-2. Moderate and Severe Food Insecurity,
by Gender and Geography, 2011–12

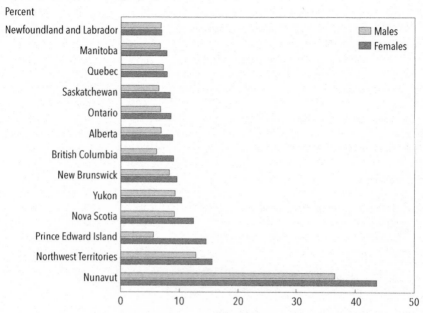

Source: McArthur and Rasmussen (2017a), based on Statistics Canada CANSIM 105-0547.

This offers a window into the much larger challenge of inequities and histor-ical injustice faced by many of Canada's indigenous people, as referenced ear-lier. For instance, estimated rates of child poverty, food insecurity, and violence against women are more than twice as high among Canada's indigenous compared to non-indigenous people. Indigenous people also have considerably lower life expectancy and average measures of access to essential health services and learning outcomes, in addition to lower confidence in the justice system and courts.[2] Even on access to drinking water (SDG target 6.1), Canada is off track on universal access (see tables 12-1 and 12-2), largely because more than ninety First Nations communities remain subject to long-term drinking water advisories as of early 2018 (Indigenous and Northern Affairs Canada, 2018). Against this backdrop, one sine qua non measure of Canadian progress on the SDGs will be whether indigenous people's outcomes can be dramatically improved across the board.

2. Anderson and others (2016) compare a variety of health-related outcomes for indigenous and non-indigenous people in Canada, alongside other countries. McArthur and Rasmussen (2017a) pres-ent comparisons for several other SDG-relevant indicators.

Identifying Priorities for New Approaches

When considering how best to pursue the SDGs domestically, decision-makers in Canada (and likewise other countries) need to resist false choices among individual goals. The operative question is not whether any single goal is more important than another. One citizen's problem of food insecurity, for example, is not more or less important than another citizen's problem of domestic violence. The key question is which issues are on track for success and which require better trajectories. Priorities should not be identified by pitting goals against each other in terms of importance, but instead by pitting trajectories against each other—to identify where business-as-usual most needs change.

Fortunately, an advanced economy like Canada clearly has the bandwidth to tackle the entire SDG agenda. Each target already falls within the explicit mandate of at least one ministry. The Canadian federal cabinet, for example, had thirty-one members as of the beginning of 2018, and provincial government cabinets commonly have twenty to thirty members or more. In the simplest logic, it is not too complicated for every minister to have responsibility for her or his own goal. Of course, in the Canadian context, issues might well touch on multiple officials' responsibilities, spanning multiple levels of government. Health outcomes, for example, are a product of everything from food and drug regulation (federal), to health and educational services (provincial, territorial), to urban design and recreational opportunities (local). In these cases, the responsibilities for SDG puzzle pieces all need to connect across jurisdictions.

Nonetheless, governments still need to make choices, especially at the level of top political leaders, who often need to focus on three to five overarching priorities for change. An SDG trend diagnosis can inform assessments of where current approaches are working and where better approaches need to be developed. On some issues, focused improvements are required to accelerate progress. On others, a wholesale renewal in approach might be necessary. The domestic SDG meta-question therefore becomes, on which issues should new approaches be prioritized? Six component questions can help inform that analysis.

First, where are breakthroughs needed? Where are targeted changes required to reach populations persistently excluded, and where are more systemic shifts needed across society? Which people and issues are getting left behind?

Second, where could other countries' experiences inform breakthroughs? Can Canada learn from other countries in areas where they have performed well? Are there case studies to learn from in bending curves toward longer-term progress? A nuanced cross-country analysis can help uncover relevant insights.

Third, where will near-term decisions drive outsized long-term effects? Some policy decisions are inherently long term in nature, lasting for decades or generations.

For example, every major piece of public energy or transport infrastructure is likely to last for forty years or more, so long-term effects need to be consistent with medium-term SDG outcomes, and vice versa. Similarly, today's educational systems will shape a generation's labor market opportunities over the course of several decades to come. Policies need to consider multiple decades when evaluating trade-offs.

Fourth, where are innovations required, because current approaches won't solve the problem? Some problems require profound science-based disruption, new market-based systems, or new policy approaches. The challenge of decarbonizing economies, for example, will not be achieved with existing technologies. In a different vein, the national challenge of ensuring safe drinking water for First Nations reserves has persisted for many, many years, due to deep institutional issues rather than a lack of technology. In the broadest sense of the term, innovation is essential in both situations.

Fifth, what actions could have big multiplier effects across issues, positive or negative? Progress will ultimately be interconnected across the SDGs—few goals can be achieved without mutually supportive progress on others. It might be that early advances on one issue lead to faster subsequent progress on another. Quick wins might also be possible, either within or across issue domains, such that rapid deployment of known interventions could help generate broader policy momentum and public understanding. Any of these scenarios would imply a need for strategic sequencing.

Sixth, where are current trajectories most at risk of disruption? Some issues, like artificial intelligence and extreme weather events, present a possibility of rapid shifts to existing norms and trends. Resilience strategies need to anticipate emergent risks. Educational systems need to foster technologically relevant skills across the working lifecycle, for example. Likewise, cities and ecosystems need investments to adapt to changes in the physical environment.

Applying these questions to a quantitative assessment of domestic trajectories can help Canadian decision-makers hone in on priorities for change. A strength of this framework is that it can be applied at any scale—by all levels of government and equally across business, civil society, or the scientific community—and equally by actors in other countries.

How Best to Support the SDGs Globally?

Whereas all countries have a domestic duty to ensure, as a guiding principle, that all of their citizens and communities can achieve all the SDGs, a country such as Canada needs to make strategic choices on external issues. The country represents only 0.5 percent of total world population, 2.2 percent of world income, and

3.7 percent of OECD donor country annual income, so it cannot solve all the world's problems on its own. Instead, Canada needs to consider where global needs are greatest and then decide how its resources and comparative advantage can be deployed to best effect. Here we present a logic to guide those questions.

Where Are Global Breakthroughs Needed?

The UN (2017) provides the most comprehensive update on global SDG trends to date. However, no single consolidated assessment has yet been published to map 2030 SDG trajectories or to identify which issues might need "breakthroughs" or "acceleration." Nonetheless, a basic assessment offers a sense of where the world is off track for achieving SDG success.

Among external objectives, the first among equals is to end extreme poverty by 2030. Recent estimates suggest that the number of people living in extreme poverty is on course to decline from around 630 million people as of early 2018 to around 440 million by 2030 (World Data Lab, 2018). By that time, under business-as-usual, more than half the people in extreme poverty will be concentrated in just six sub-Saharan countries, most prominently Nigeria.[3] In these and other geographies, the challenge of ending extreme poverty will be deeply interconnected with the challenge of promoting sound institutions and mitigating political fragility and conflict.

Shortfalls are also projected for universal access to basic needs. For instance, the number of people living with food insecurity in developing countries has recently been stuck at more than 800 million people. Dozens of countries are off track for meeting the targets for universal access to safe drinking water, sanitation, child mortality, maternal mortality, and even primary school completion by 2030.[4] Distressingly from the vantage point of gender equality and broader development outcomes, around 130 million girls and young women are still out of school, a number not on track to shrink to anywhere near zero by 2030 (UNESCO, 2016).

Among the world's collective objectives, greenhouse gas emissions (GHG) were still growing as of 2017, en route to increase by another 10 to 20 percent by 2030 (UNEP, 2017). However, to meet the Paris Agreement, the world needs to *decrease* GHGs by nearly 20 percent by 2030 (Ibid.). Meanwhile, only 3.6 percent of the world's oceans are estimated to be protected as of early 2018 (Marine

3. On current trajectories, Nigeria will have the largest estimated number of people in extreme poverty in 2030, at approximately 100 million. The countries with the next five largest estimated numbers are Democratic Republic of the Congo (around 60 million), Madagascar (22 million), South Sudan (14 million), South Africa (14 million), and Mozambique (13 million).

4. See FAO and others (2017); McArthur and Rasmussen (2016); McArthur, Rasmussen, and Yamey (2018).

Conservation Institute, 2018). This is far short of the SDGs' 10 percent protection target for 2020 and a growing scientific consensus around the need to protect half the ocean.[5] There are also now 500 oxygen-free dead zones linked to fertilizer run-off, especially in fast-growing economies (Breitburg and others, 2018). Some scientists are warning of "planetary boundaries" being crossed (Steffen and others, 2015).

At the same time, the changing nature of the global economy is transforming the nature of global challenges. Perhaps most prominent, many fast-growing economies require urgent investments in energy, transport, and housing in order to underpin their own inclusive prosperity (UNIDO, 2014; Schmidt-Traub, 2015). But the most affordable investments often have high carbon intensity, so countries like Canada need to find ways to support other countries' sustainable infrastructure through both public and private investment tools.

Emerging threats lurk across the global horizon too. Fast-spreading pandemic disease, for example, presents a growing risk, as do antimicrobial resistance and noncommunicable diseases. Political systems are also at risk of disruption everywhere, as digital technologies are increasingly deployed both to expand and inhibit civil society efforts around the world.[6]

It is no small task, therefore, for Canada to contribute to the new global agenda, and many societal ingredients need strengthening (Biggs and others, 2015). Nonetheless, Canada has many strengths to tap—from its democratic institutions and civil society, to its high average level of education, to its extensive scientific capabilities, and beyond. The rest of the world also sees Canada as one of the most trusted and positive forces in the world (Ipsos, 2017; Edelman, 2018). The country therefore needs to be as strategic as possible in leveraging its assets in service of addressing shared global challenges.

Identifying Priorities for New Approaches

We suggest seven questions that can help Canada—or other countries in similar situations—assess strategic opportunities to fulfill global responsibilities. We start with questions most relevant to collective objectives:

First, where do domestic actions disproportionately affect global outcomes? For example, Canada has 17 percent of the world's maritime coastline, 4 percent of all countries' national maritime areas, and 9 percent of all forests, so any domestic action it takes in these realms—irrespective of other countries' choices—will have disproportionate consequences in determining global outcomes. On SDG target

5. See chapter 11 by Sala and Rechberger in this volume.
6. See chapter 13 by Sriskandarajah in this volume.

14.5, for example, to conserve at least 10 percent of coastal and marine areas by 2020, Canada is among the world's top seven countries in terms of national marine area that needs to be protected.[7]

Second, where are "fair share" commitments most crucial? On which issues do the country's contributions per capita simply need to align—for political, strategic, or moral reasons—with its share of the collective solution? Here the underlying issues are to ensure international political legitimacy and avoid the costs of being dubbed a free-rider. Climate change and GHG emissions frame a classic example, whereby each country needs to show its own long-term pathway to decarbonize each unit of economic output by at least 90 percent by 2050. If Canada meets its own target for 2030, this will account for 2.4 percent of the global objective— arguably a modest share in overall global terms but an essential share in light of the "swing voter" role that Canada has recently played in galvanizing global coalitions for climate action (McArthur, 2016).

Third, where do collective outcomes disproportionately affect domestic interests? For instance, as a modest-sized open economy with significant dependence on trade, Canada is considerably affected by any risks or changes to the rules-based, multilateral trading system, and likewise to changes in international banking regulations that might affect the rules for cross-border private finance. Canada always needs to prioritize contributions to such essential global systems.

Turning to external objectives:

Fourth, where do external outcomes disproportionately affect domestic interests? On some issues, Canada simply has a vested interest in promoting other countries' sustainable development. For example, the SARS and Ebola crises vividly displayed how strong health systems in all corners of the world have direct consequences for Canadian communities. In parallel, Canada has strong interests in promoting prosperity and stability in places that might otherwise harbor conflict and sources of geopolitical volatility. These issues always merit strong strategic investment.

Fifth, where could national assets make distinctive global contributions? Are there areas where the country has distinctive expertise or political leadership with the potential to make disproportionate global contributions? For example, Canada has uncommon technical expertise in natural resource management, including regulatory frameworks, governance, and technologies. Many citizens and public leaders have also developed unique global political capital by emphasizing refugee settlement and gender equality as priorities for concerted domestic and international action. An additional benefit here is that when properly managed,

---

7. Countries like the United States and France with distant island territories have larger absolute marine areas.

Figure 12-3. Official Development Assistance as
Share of Gross National Income, 2016

Percent GNI

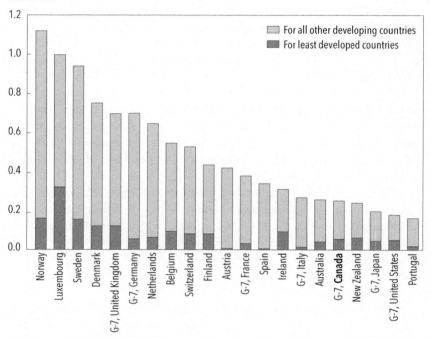

Source: Authors' calculations using data from OECD (2018a, 2018b).

earned political influence in areas of comparative advantage can translate to
substantial agenda-setting influence across multilateral policy forums.

Sixth, what is an objective standard of burden sharing? Depending on the nature of
the issues at hand, Canada can compare its burden-sharing contributions against
objective benchmarks. One measure is to compare investments relative to the
country's share of OECD donor-country income (as a measure for humanitarian
and development issues). As one reference point, Canada's contributions to grant-
based multilateral finance are roughly equivalent to its share of donor-country
income (McArthur and Rasmussen, 2017b). Contributions can also be measured
relative to capacity to contribute, such as the internationally affirmed benchmark
of 0.7 percent of gross national income (GNI) for official development assistance
(ODA) to developing countries, and 0.15 to 0.2 percent of GNI for ODA targeted
to the least developed countries. On these measures Canada is trailing well behind
its peers, as indicated in figure 12-3, and also well behind its own historical trends

(Greenhill and Wadhera, 2017). Figure 12-3 highlights how Canada compares to other G-7 countries in particular.

Seventh, what issues remain unaddressed or loom on the horizon? Policymakers need to review the global landscape constantly: are there major problems, either known or newly emerging, that simply are not being adequately addressed? For instance, antibiotic resistance might need anticipatory systems for surveillance, prevention, and rapid response. Meanwhile, secondary education for girls has long been understood as a high-impact investment for societies as a whole, but huge global resource gaps persist (Summers, 1992; Sperling and Winthrop, 2016).

All seven of the above questions need to be constantly revisited, especially as new issues and actors evolve on the global stage. In some instances, Canada might have an outsized comparative advantage to step up in moments when another country steps back, and vice versa. For example, the current government has prioritized issues of sexual and reproductive health when other countries expressed reservations. In other instances, such as the recent Ebola crisis, Canada was able to play a leading role in the rapid development of a vaccine. Global issues need to be constantly reassessed in terms of where progress is lagging, where leadership is required, and which resources Canada can best bring to bear.

Moving to Action

We have seen how the SDGs can be used to identify where Canada needs to accelerate progress and achieve major breakthroughs. We have seen how Canadians can determine where best to target efforts to address critical collective and external challenges. Now we turn to questions of action. How can Canada best fulfill its SDG commitments—at home, to the world, and on collective challenges?

Part of the answer will be driven by official processes. As a signatory to Agenda 2030, the government of Canada has committed to formal international reporting and peer review on its progress. This will need to include some form of "voluntary national review" presented to the UN's High-Level Political Forum in mid-2018, and public indicators will need to be tracked all the way up to the 2030 deadline. But Canada's complex federal structure makes it difficult to forge top-down national strategies, and it would be politically fraught to try to do so. Unlike many of its European peers, including federations like Germany, Canada does not have a history of national planning, nor does it have a track record of integrating sustainable development priorities into national policy frameworks.

Fortunately, there are advantages in being a decentralized federation, unencumbered by entrenched policy processes for sustainable development. A lack of structures can allow leap-frogging into new forms of problem solving. Moreover, Canada's foremost SDG challenges are too complex to be addressed by any single actor, sector, or action plan. Domestic issues like childhood obesity and collective issues like greenhouse gas emissions require innovation across public, private, and scientific sectors, alongside strong community-level mobilization. Meanwhile, external challenges like ending extreme poverty and promoting sustainable infrastructure in emerging markets will require leadership from the federal government, backed by strong academic, civil society, and private sector champions.

Toward a "Whole of Canada Approach"

As noted above, to achieve the breakthroughs and accelerations required for SDG success, Canada will need many actors to adopt new roles, new actors to be brought into problem-solving processes, and new ways of working together to find solutions and accelerate progress. This will hinge on active experimentation and engagement between scientists, companies, indigenous communities, civic leaders, and people from all walks of life. Amid the complexity, a few key ingredients can help guide new approaches:

A consistent focus on 2030 outcomes. All major Canadian actors can agree to assess societal success against domestic, collective, and external SDG targets.

A commitment to measurement and reporting. All major actors—government, the private sector scientific communities, and civil society—can commit to regular public reports and databases that inform learning and decision-making across Canada's diverse constituencies.

Locally defined targets. On issues where the official SDG language is unclear, federal, provincial, territorial, and community leaders can coordinate relevant stakeholders to establish specific 2030 outcomes objectives.

Shared scorecards. Provinces, cities, universities, and industry associations can each agree to track progress among peer entities on a common set of indicators out to 2030.

Sustained public spotlights. The SDGs will matter in Canada once enough people believe they matter; leaders in politics, business, and civil society can all use their public platforms to draw consistent attention to the goals.

Against that backdrop, here we describe some key ways in which different actors can help spur needed SDG progress across Canada.

Indigenous People and Communities: Front and Center

As already mentioned, a cornerstone for Canada's SDG success will be to ensure the engagement and leadership of indigenous people and communities, and for indigenous community outcomes to improve dramatically across a wide range of indicators—from access to clean water, to child health, to productive employment, and more. While increased investments are no doubt part of the answer, these need to be anchored in broader reconciliation efforts that ensure indigenous people are leading the development and implementation of their own plans on issues that affect them and their communities. Although it is early days, there are signs the SDGs are in fact already providing much-needed common ground for a new relationship between First Nations and government (AFN and GoC, 2017), something that could be sustained and replicated with all indigenous communities.

Federal Government: Leader, Convener, and Catalyst

The government of Canada has a unique responsibility to help drive the national SDG enterprise forward, playing an instrumental role in setting the conditions for societal breakthroughs. To start, the federal government can lead by example in embracing and articulating the SDG framework and 2030 outcomes as guideposts for federal policymaking—as baseline standards, as a platform for reporting, and as a basis for building coherence across the federal portfolio. The country's political leadership has a particularly special role to play in helping to set reference points for public debate. The "federal throne speech," for example, is the government's foremost agenda-setting policy statement. On each delivery through to 2030, the speech could include specific forthcoming priorities for domestic, collective, and external SDG breakthroughs, followed by annual updates on progress.

More broadly, the federal government can be the "systems architect" that leads by example and facilitates the connectivity and capacities of other societal actors. Among other responsibilities, this includes taking a lead in incorporating the SDGs into the broader agenda of reconciliation with indigenous peoples and communities in Canada. All of this will require new mindsets and roles in order to nurture, but not control, innovative networks. It will also call for regulatory, legal, and administrative improvements to enable new partnerships to form, for example, between private foundations, civil society organizations, and the private sector. Below we outline some pillars for this multidimensional government role.

Harnessing the whole-of-government. The SDGs offer an opportunity for the government of Canada to break down silos—across ministries and between domestic and external policies—while stressing the collective global challenges that overlap. On the external side, an important step could be a first ever, whole-of-government strategy for mobilizing Canadians' external and collective commitments to tackle clear global SDG gaps. This would require an initial objective assessment of global trends and shortfalls. It should then include an assessment of Canada's comparative advantages in tackling the same gaps, followed by an objective evaluation of the burden-sharing responsibilities to fill those gaps, relative to objective benchmarks like Canada's share of OECD donor countries' total annual income. Most important, a coherent external strategy would need to incorporate multiple policy domains such as health, environment, trade, public finance, and private finance—including market and institutional investors.

Similarly, the SDG framework can be used to forge connections on domestic priorities. For example, the goals of halving poverty and reducing inequality on the one hand, and promoting sustainable growth and productive work on the other, require economic and social ministries to collaborate on inclusive growth strategies. Status of Women Canada, the federal ministry, will need to be engaged across the board to advance gender-equal outcomes on all issues.

Integrating strategies. The existing Federal Sustainable Development Strategy (FSDS) on environmental issues (ECCC, 2016) offers a potential entry point for a broader federal government approach. It has been driven by Environment and Climate Change Canada and has many excellent attributes, including some targets aligned with global SDG standards, some nationally defined targets, and some targets aligned with highly localized environmental problems. It also commits to being a living document to be updated on an ongoing basis as new policy learning takes shape.

The FSDS's environmental approach could be expanded across the Canadian government's vast policy realms to integrate the economic prosperity and social inclusion dimensions of the SDGs. It could develop an overall framework that is SDG consistent and tied to a full suite of SDG outcome metrics and reporting regimes. Ideally, it could also identify which policy issues are mutually reinforcing and where they are in conflict (ICSU, 2017), providing an objective basis for government and public debate on how to optimize the interactions.

An augmented FSDS could further build on the Advisory Council on Economic Growth's recommended up-front criteria for government action by proposing a three-part test for assessing any policy initiative's contribution to the SDGs. That is, (i) will the initiative move the relevant SDG needle; (ii) will its benefits persist; and (iii) will it leave no one behind.[8] This would provide a framework to evaluate, during the design phase, major federal interventions like infrastructure investments, tax policy, and innovation policy. It could also help guide public sector procurement and thereby help align a large share of the country's market supply chains to the SDGs.

---

8. The Advisory Council on Economic Growth recommendations are tested along three dimensions: "will it 'move the needle' on income growth," particularly real household income; "will it drive economic growth consistently over time"; and "will it drive inclusive growth, i.e. not just for the most advantaged?" (ACEG, 2017).

Building the integrated public SDG database and information platform. If the SDGs are to be adopted as a national outcome framework, then public data systems will play an outsized role. This implies a key role for Statistics Canada to present a unified SDG database, similar to the U.S. portal (sdg.dta.gov), alongside annual reports tracking progress and countdowns by indicator. Fortunately, Canada has tremendous strengths in one of the world's strongest statistical agencies. Wherever feasible, data need to disaggregated by gender, indigenous people, age group, and geography. Ideally, Canadians will be able to track progress not just by province and territory but also at the community level. With regard to indigenous people and communities, the government will need to bolster information systems while taking into account the principles of ownership, control, access, and possession (FNIGC, 2018) of information, in order to ensure that indigenous people and communities agree on the approach to the collection of data affecting them.

Spurring innovation on grand challenges. On issues where breakthroughs are required, the federal government can galvanize research, innovation, and local action on two types of grand challenges: those faced uniquely at home and those shared with the rest of the world. Invariably, these challenges, such as obesity or sustainable food systems, cut across specialist disciplines. Canada has deep endowments of research and scientific expertise in many areas—global health, renewable energy, water management, and sustainable agriculture, to name just a few. However, prevailing incentive structures and legacy research networks need updating to realign with the cross-disciplinary nature of contemporary global challenges.

There are prototypes to build on. The Canada First Excellence Research Fund invests in research initiatives with the potential for breakthrough discoveries and global leadership. In the United Kingdom, the Global Challenges Research Fund supports "challenge-led" research on global problems and interdisciplinary research hubs. Meanwhile, the multicountry, multipartner Future Earth consortium seeks to promote a new type of science that "links disciplines, knowledge systems and societal partners" in order to achieve the SDGs. One of Future Earth's global hubs is in Montreal, backed by Quebec's universities.

Eliciting community-level inspiration. The federal government can also challenge Canadians directly to find innovative solutions to local and national problems. The Impact Canada Initiative is a step in this direction, beginning with the new Smart Cities Challenge, which is itself all about measuring and reporting outcomes, building new partnerships, finding new solutions to "wicked" problems, and dispersing results across Canada. What this kind of initiative needs, however, is an outcome framework directly linked to the SDGs—to provide coherence across the various activities, a consistent set of benchmarks, and a platform for sharing results across the country and with the global community. At a practical level, this will require a creative focus on things like convening Canadians from across the country and around the world to facilitate and jump-start problem solving, as well as to foster world-class expertise within government and in relevant nodes across the country.

Tasking accountability. At an operational level, the federal government will need to define how ministers and departments take responsibility, both individually and jointly, for SDG-focused strategies at home and abroad, especially where new approaches are needed. Other peer countries are pursuing a wide range of organizational models. Some are quite centralized (for example, coordination in Germany takes place in the office of the chancellor, and in Colombia at the level of the prime minister), others more disaggregated (in Norway each minister is assigned lead responsibility for a SDG), and others a mix (in Italy the environment and foreign ministers have shared the lead).

In Ottawa there would ideally be multiple ministerial SDG champions, with departments mandated by the prime minister to work collectively and with a diverse range of stakeholders. The federal cabinet could review progress periodically, either on a rolling basis by issue or on a collective basis perhaps once or twice per year. Parliament could also pass legislation requiring annual federal SDG updates on domestic, collective, and external SDG targets through to 2030. Meanwhile, opposition critics should feel encouraged to use the SDGs as neutral reference points for promoting government accountability and proposing alternative strategies to achieve the same outcomes.

Provincial and Territorial Governments: Leaders Across the Full SDG Landscape

Many of Canada's most important SDG decisions will be taken by provincial and territorial government policymakers and regulators. Constitutionally, Canada's provinces are lead actors in numerous policy areas such as education, skills development, health care, road safety, affordable housing, environmental protection, and sustainable infrastructure. They also have primary responsibility for postsecondary education, are important investors in research and development, and act as lead regulators of market exchanges. Canada's three territories have many of the same responsibilities with respect to social services, the administration of justice, and, increasingly, land and natural resource management.

In this respect, the political leadership of each province and territory has a special role to play in setting the terms of SDG debate, including targets and reporting within their areas of responsibility. Provinces and territories will also need to embrace the agenda of reconciliation with indigenous people, as many of them are already doing, and ensure that indigenous communities lead or co-develop approaches aimed at improving the outcomes for their people.

Many of the federally focused recommendations above will apply similarly at this subnational level. For example, each province and territory has its own throne speech tradition, which could be used to articulate SDG priorities, but with emphasis on areas of provincial or territorial responsibility. Each province and territory will also need to establish its own mechanisms for interministry collaboration and its own reporting and accountability measures. A number of provinces and territories have already developed long-range sustainability-linked strategies, but most of these were drafted before the launch of the SDGs and require more explicit alignment with the SDGs (McArthur and Rasmussen, 2017a).

Across relevant indicators, provinces and territories could agree to a framework for common annual SDG reports, enabling citizens to track and compare progress between their own provinces and their peers. These reports could be produced in collaboration with civil society, building on partnership efforts like those already developed by local leaders in Alberta and British Columbia. Joint SDG action plans could be discussed at annual meetings of the provincial-territorial Council of the Federation.

Cities and Communities: Front Lines for Citizen Feedback and Solutions

Cities are not included in Canada's formal intergovernmental machinery and constitutional division of powers, but the country can only meet its national SDG challenges if municipal actors are centrally involved in the solutions. The official SDG framework highlights the importance of cities and communities in growth, inclusion, and sustainability. This is fitting for Canada, since more than 80 percent of Canadians live in large or medium-sized cities, and more than a third reside in the three metropolitan areas of Toronto, Montreal, and Vancouver alone. Cities are epicenters for jobs, growth, and innovation. They are also the locus for many of Canada's most serious social and environmental challenges—poverty, homelessness, crime, and pollution, to name just a few.

The SDG framework provides an explicit entrée for cities through the articulation of issues like transportation, housing, and waste management embedded under SDG 11 for Sustainable Cities and Communities. But cities play important broader roles across the economic, social, and environmental dimensions of all the other goals too. They often offer the most direct public interface with citizens on the ground. They also have many relationships with peer cities and local governments around the world, largely unencumbered by state-to-state politics, thus amplifying Canada's ability to form purpose-built alliances for innovation, such as those that have taken shape around climate change.

Through the Federation of Canadian Municipalities (FCM) and global partners, Canada's cities worked hard to ensure that urban issues and local government found pride of place in the SDG agenda. Now they need to integrate the SDGs into their own strategic plans and accountability frameworks.[9] Joint reporting is also crucial for consolidating data and providing context to citizens and municipal decision-makers. To that end, the FCM could work with its member cities to establish a common suite of SDG-relevant indicators and outcome targets for 2020, 2025, and 2030. These could build on the Canadian Municipal Benchmarking Network's reporting effort (MBNC, 2016), perhaps packaged as an annual "Canadian SDG Cities Report." These could also be informed by the International Institute for Sustainable Development's recently initiated SDG monitoring effort for thirteen Canadian cities (Bizikova and Pinter, 2017; Temmer, 2017).

Coordinated reporting would enable all Canadians living in municipalities to benchmark their local living standards and rates of progress against comparator communities and, in turn, promote collaboration and peer-learning across regions. Municipal reporting efforts could partner with city-led efforts in other countries, where appropriate. For example, Baltimore, New York, and San Jose have all initiated their own SDG-focused initiatives. Los Angeles Country has partnered with Measure for America to create a local dashboard tracking SDG indicators disaggregated by race and ethnicity. Other cities have collaborated with the Sustainable Development Solutions Network to benchmark status against an integrated index of SDG-relevant measures. Canadian cities and research partners could pursue similar exercises together.

Business: Leading the Shift from Compliance to Performance

The private sector, Canada's central economic driver, creates the vast majority of jobs, accounts for a large share of Canadians' international activities, and profoundly impacts the country's environmental footprint. Absent the crucial drivers of private sector investment, innovation, and public advocacy, SDG efforts will fall short, so market actors need to be part of the SDG solution at every step. At the global level, businesses like Unilever and Aviva have already dedicated considerable attention to the SDGs. In September 2017 the World Economic Forum launched an inaugural Sustainable Development Impact Summit in New York, timed purposely to coincide with major UN General Assembly events and aimed at promoting public-private partnerships for the SDGs.

Some major Canadian firms like Agrium (now part of Nutrien) and Suncor have already begun to engage actively and publicly on the goals. They have gone

---

9. McArthur and Rasmussen (2017a) examined recent municipal strategies for Calgary, Montreal, Toronto, Vancouver, and Winnipeg and found that some have well-defined targets, but none yet aligns fully with the SDGs.

beyond traditional "ESG" (economic, social, and governance) compliance to link explicitly to the SDGs, receiving recognition from the Canadian chapter of the UN Global Compact, which has been working to build private sector awareness of the SDGs and promote opportunities for multistakeholder collaboration. Much broader private sector engagement will be needed across industries and different-sized business in order to fulfill the country's promise on the goals. Part of this will hinge on Canadian businesses spotting the self-interest in doing so and aiming to outperform competitors in addressing the SDGs. In 2017 the Business and Sustainable Development Commission (2017) outlined a $12 trillion SDG market opportunity embedded in four industry segments alone: food and agriculture; cities and urban mobility; energy and materials; and health and well-being.

The flipside of the business opportunity equation lies in managing the risk of SDG inaction, especially material risks that companies might need to disclose to their investors. These include regulatory risks, market disruptive risks, socio-economic risks, and the risk of declining social license to operate. Many of these risk issues have already started to arise in the context of climate change, due in part to prominent global voices, including Mark Carney, governor of the Bank of England and chairman of the G-20's Financial Stability Board, and Michael Bloomberg, chair of the Task Force on Climate-Related Financial Disclosures. Risk profiles linked to other SDG-related issues like food security and global health are still being explored.

On the investment side, many of the world's foremost institutional investors are beginning to call for alignment with the SDGs.[10] Canada is home to some of the world's most respected institutions in this domain, including Canada Pension Plan Investment Board, Ontario Teachers' Pension Plan, and La Caisse de dépôt et placement du Québec, all of which have been active in global discussions of sustainability and the need to avoid excess short-termism. Through their public statements and private actions, these major institutions send influential signals to private and public actors around the world. Alberta Investment Management Corporation has already made major public commitments to the SDGs. If all of Canada's major institutional investors can explicitly support SDG-consistent outcomes while ensuring competitive returns for their shareholders—Canadian pensioners—they can play a decisive role in helping to move markets toward the goals.

National SDG business efforts will require a constellation of action, including personal leadership from corporate chief executives, SDG-consistent incentives

---

10. For example, Temasek, the Singaporean sovereign wealth fund, has strongly signaled its alignment with the SDGs as part of a call for collective action to achieve the goals (see *Temasek Review*, 2017); several major European pension investors have committed to use the SDGs as an investment framework (Rust, 2016); and the California Public Employees' Retirement System (CalPERS) has started to map its investment portfolio to the SDGs to find points of connectivity as an "economic necessity" (Baker, 2017).

from policymakers, strong demand for SDG-consistent performance metrics from major investors, and a clear commitment to industry-smart scorecards from industry regulators (Kharas and McArthur, 2016). Consumers, of course, always have a major say in guiding final market demand too. As Jane Nelson outlines in chapter 4 in this volume, pre-competitive alliances are required in which industry leaders and independent experts define performance standards for a level competitive field. In Canada an umbrella entity like the Business Council of Canada or the Canadian Chamber of Commerce could help to promote such alliances, partnering with organizations like the World Business Council on Sustainable Development or global industry associations to identify SDG-consistent approaches most pertinent to Canadian business.

To match this private sector action among public sector players, a combination of provincial and federal leadership is required, since, as noted earlier, Canadian securities regulators and other key market oversight bodies are generally structured at the provincial level, while banking regulations are generally governed at the federal level. Much of this will hinge on the establishment of SDG-relevant reporting standards that speak to the industry-specific playing field in which each company competes. Building on initiatives like the World Benchmarking Alliance, the Sustainability Accounting Standards Board, and other relevant bodies, Canada's political leadership could call on provincial regulators to develop, by a target deadline like 2025, a common North American approach to SDG-consistent reporting for each industry. Canada could potentially even play a leadership role to promote alignment between American, Asian, and European efforts on private sector SDG reporting.

The launch of Canada's new development finance institution, FinDevCanada, also provides a major opportunity to tie Canadian private businesses to the achievement of SDG-consistent breakthroughs abroad. Part of this will hinge on the new institution publicly measuring its progress against contributions to development outcomes. This could build on evolving practices at the International Finance Corporation, the New Development Bank, and other development finance institutions like the CDC Group (formerly Commonwealth Development Corporation) in the United Kingdom to develop common standards for aligning investment processes with the SDGs.

Universities and Colleges: Hubs for Intergenerational Collaboration

Much of Canada's emerging SDG leadership is being fostered on university and college campuses. Tertiary institutions are explicitly meant to be places where young people learn about the world's challenges and cultivate new approaches to solve them. They are also places where researchers create the insight and innovation for taking on those same challenges. In these respects, universities are naturally poised to promote nexus explorations and collaborations across disciplines, sectors, and generations—all of which are essential for achieving the SDGs.

Each Canadian university and college will bring its own strengths to tackling local, national, and international SDG challenges. The Waterloo Global Science Initiative, for example, is convening multidisciplinary and cross-generational efforts to identify solutions to advance the SDGs. Institutions across the country can partner with provincial and federal counterparts to identify SDG targets where breakthroughs are required. Ideally, they can also work together on issues of common concern, potentially by collaborating through purpose-built research collaborations or new joint ventures sponsored by the research granting councils. These could be bolstered by developing a common benchmarking framework for tracking progress through to 2030.

Another potential avenue is through the Association of Public and Land Grant Universities (APLU), which convenes institutions from around North America, including Canada and Mexico.[11] Eight major Canadian universities are already part of this association, which has been exploring ways to promote widespread university-level collaboration around the SDGs. Opportunities could include activities focused on developing students' global competencies, conducting relevant research, exchanging scholars and ideas, and operating in a manner consistent with supporting SDG priority outcomes.

Philanthropy and Community-Level Action: Kick-Starting Collaboration and Innovation

Many of Canada's most important innovations for the SDGs will be initiated through either direct community-level work, social entrepreneurship in the private sector, or new efforts that provide proof of concept for the public sector to take up at scale. Philanthropy can play a crucial role in all of these processes, whether focused on domestic, collective, or external objectives. Canada is estimated to have more than 10,000 public and private foundations managing more than C$69 billion in assets and allocating roughly C$6 billion in annual giving (PFC, 2017). The MasterCard Foundation, a major and relatively new international entity based in Toronto, is by far the largest of these organizations and could be a major source of learning and insight among other Canadian actors.

The country's local foundations meanwhile play a crucial role in supporting community-level action and innovation. The Community Foundations of Canada

---

11. The Canadian members of APLU are Dalhousie University, Queen's University, University of Alberta, University of British Columbia, University of Calgary, University of Guelph, University of Saskatchewan, and Western University.

(CFC) is a national network of 191 community foundations, which together serve more than 90 percent of Canadian communities and jointly manage more than C\$5 billion of assets. CFC has already taken the SDGs on board as a central pillar of its work and is actively collaborating with other community foundation networks in the United States and Mexico. It is taking steps to connect the CFC's own indicators of community resilience—the Vital Signs Framework—to SDG outcomes (Ross, 2018). CFC members could also partner with local universities and industry associations to generate active community-level consultations, reporting, and collaborative problem-solving initiatives across the country. They could expand to include local researchers working alongside the Federation of Canadian Municipalities and the Canadian Municipal Benchmarking Network to develop common indicators for tracking outcomes.

Such cross-country collaborations could naturally feed in to the global work of the SDG Philanthropy Platform, which has established itself as the leading collaborative network to promote partnerships between philanthropic organizations and diverse global public and private SDG stakeholders. As of early 2018 the platform had begun working in eight pilot countries to identify how philanthropy could best contribute to the SDG planning and implementation process, ranging from Brazil to Ghana to India to the United States. With leadership from Canadian community foundations, some major institutional philanthropies, and potentially the federal government, Canada could commit to being a ninth pilot country focused on pioneering new strategies for jointly seeding domestic, collective, and external SDG breakthroughs.

SDG Forums: Convening Practitioners and Problem Solvers

We have argued above that Canada's approach to achieving the SDGs cannot be pursued via a single national plan but rather through the concerted efforts of diverse actors, problem solving at all levels—community, national, and international—and new solution-focused partnerships. The impetus and glue for this national enterprise can be the SDGs themselves—as shared goals for benchmarking and regular reporting of actions and outcomes. But the ultimate power will come through human connections—the learning, cooperation, and problem solving generated in an SDG-focused societal ecosystem.

The most innovative partnerships cannot be planned, but environments for creating them can be fostered. There has already been movement in this direction. For example, the Alberta SDG initiative (Wilson, 2016) has convened provincial leaders from business, government, and civil society to advance the SDGs as a common framework for measuring economic, social, and environmental progress across the province, and the Alberta Council for Global Cooperation convened the Together2017 symposium to "set the foundation for how government, business, and civil society can work together to use the SDGs as a framework and common language" (ACGC, 2017). Similar 2030-focused conversations are taking shape in each province and territory, on university and college campuses, and by citizen-led groups across the country.

New forms of partnership are being formed too. For example, the Canadian Council for International Cooperation traditionally focuses on mobilizing civil society efforts to advance global sustainable development abroad and the Community Foundations of Canada traditionally focuses on the country's local community development. These two organizations are joining forces to advance an integrated national conversation on the SDGs. This is just one powerful example of how the goals are already prompting unexpected forms of partnership among diverse constituencies.

For Canada as a whole, an annual pan-Canadian SDG forum could provide a much-needed focal point for diverse activities across the country, as a venue to draw disparate sectors and regions together. The government of Canada, in keeping with its role as SDG systems architect, could collaborate with partners to convene this annual SDG forum in a different city each year. The forum could adopt a three-pronged approach: advancing each of the seventeen SDGs across the country, tackling cross-cutting priorities across issues (for instance, measurement or gender equality), and addressing critical nexus issues that can only be achieved through action on multiple fronts. Each province and municipality could convene similar forums of its own, perhaps feeding into the national forum, which could have opportunities for municipalities, provinces, and territories to showcase their community-level innovations for peer learning.

An annual Canada SDG forum could also expand to include a complementary global SDG forum. Canada has unique convening ability, and its proximity to UN headquarters offers distinct geographic advantages. Canada could convene SDG-focused practitioners across all seventeen substantive goal areas, while taking a specific interest to help guide multistakeholder progress on its own global priorities. Partner countries could be invited to play a similar role, driving progress on issues where they are taking a leadership mantle. Such a convening would not just help ensure Canada's domestic SDG communities are connected to peer leaders from other countries but could also help foster new bottom-up forms of collaboration on problems of shared global interest.

Conclusion

This chapter has focused on the nature of opportunity presented by the SDGs for Canada and countries like it. The foremost offering is a shared sense of direction, a North Star around which diverse constituencies can rally collective efforts. Although the notion of global goals originally took hold around ambitions to support the poorest nations, today such goals offer a tool for all nations to do better on issues of common importance. The SDGs offer a remarkably useful shorthand for what matters. As neutral outcome benchmarks, they can help guide societal efforts across a highly diverse and geographically expansive country like Canada.

By assessing trajectories out to 2030—by issue, geography, and segment of the population—Canadians can foster a shared understanding of where current approaches are on track and where new approaches are needed. The simple exercise of rating all seventeen goals on the same page provides an important tool for identifying shared domestic priorities for change. By doing the same for collective external global challenges, Canada can then map its own strengths against global needs to assess how its global priorities should shift or be amplified.

The final major offering of the SDGs is to prompt new forms of collaboration to find solutions and accelerate progress. While some issues can be addressed through targeted policy changes, many will require systemic innovations that draw from the best of business, science, civil society, and government in concert. In many cases, the role of government will be to foster experimentation and innovation across other sectors. A data-driven outcome framework can inform public debate on which approaches are making the right dent in the relevant problems.

Despite their imperfections, the SDGs represent the best means the world has yet crafted for defining successful societies in which no person or major issue is left behind. If Canadians embrace them as an outcome framework for measuring success—compared to both local benchmarks and global standards—they can help ensure Canada achieves the social, economic, and environmental breakthroughs that it and other countries need most. Done right, Canada can frame a model approach for the world.

Appendix 1. Assessment of Canada's status on domestic SDG targets

Target	Proxy target	Indicator used	Moving backwards	Breakthrough needed	Acceleration needed	On track
1.1 End extreme poverty		Share in extreme poverty				•
1.2 Reduce national poverty by 50%		Share in low income—low income cutoffs			•	
		Share in low income—market basket measure		•		
1.3 Implement social protection		Share of poor covered by social protection				•
1.5 Build resiliency of poor to climate events	P	Mortality rate from disasters				•
2.1 End hunger/food insecurity		Moderate + severe food insecurity	•			
2.2 End malnutrition		Children overweight, aged 2–4	•			
2.4 Ensure sustainable food production systems	P	Nutrient balance—nitrogen, kg/ha	•			
3.1 Maternal mortality < 70 per 100,000 births		Maternal mortality ratio				•
3.2 Child and newborn mortality (< 25 and < 12 per 1,000 births)		Neonatal mortality rate				•
3.3 End AIDS/TB/Malaria epidemics		TB incidence rate		•		
3.4 Reduce premature mortality from noncommunicable diseases (NCDs) by 1/3		Mortality rate attributed to NCDs			•	
		Cancer mortality rate			•	
		Major cardiovascular disease mortality rate				•
		Suicide mortality rate		•		
3.5 Strengthen prevention/treatment of substance abuse	P	Annual alcohol per capita consumption	•			
3.6 Halve traffic deaths by 2020		Mortality rate due to road injuries			•	
3.7 Universal access to sexual and reproductive services		Women with family planning needs satisfied			•	
3.8 Universal health coverage (UHC)		Population with coverage of 7 UHC tracer interventions			•	
3.9 Reduce deaths due to pollution & chemicals	P	Mortality rate from household/ambient air pollution			•	

(continued)

	Target	Proxy target	Indicator used	Moving backwards	Break-through needed	Accel-eration needed	On track
4.1	Ensure all complete primary/secondary education		Upper-secondary graduation rate				●
4.2	Universal access to early childhood education		Early childhood education net enrollment				●
4.5	Eliminate gender disparities in education		Gender differences in mean reading PISA scores		●		
			Gender differences in mean math PISA scores				●
4.6	Achieve literacy and numeracy		Literacy: 2+ on PISA in 15-year-olds	●			
			Numeracy: 2+ on PISA in 15-year-olds	●			
5.1	End discrimination against all women/girls		Gender wage gap in full-time employees		●		
5.2	Eliminate violence against women/girls		Women experiencing intimate partner violence		●		
			Female victims of police-reported violent crime	●			
5.3	Eliminate harmful practices such as child, early and forced marriage, and female genital mutilation		Share of 15- to 17-year-old females who are married		●		
5.4	Recognize and value unpaid care and domestic work	P	Gender disparity in hours of unpaid work		●		
5.5	Ensure women's full participation in leadership	P	Share of seats held by women in national parliament	●			
6.1	Universal access to safe drinking water		Access to improved water		●		
6.2	Access to adequate and equitable sanitation for all		Access to sanitation facilities	●			
6.3	Improve water quality and halve untreated wastewater		Wastewater treated		●		
6.4	Increase water-use efficiency	p	Freshwater sites rated good or excellent			●	
		p	Annual freshwater withdrawals		●		
7.1	Universal access to modern energy services		Access to electricity				●
7.2	Increase share of renewable energy	P	Renewable electricity consumption	●			
		N	Electricity generated from renewable and nonemitting sources		●		
7.3	Double global rate of improvement in energy efficiency		Energy intensity level of primary energy			●	

Target	Proxy target	Indicator used	Moving backwards	Break-through needed	Accel-eration needed	On track
8.4 Improve resource efficiency in consumption and production	P	Domestic material consumption per unit of GDP			•	
8.6 Reduce share of youth not in employment, education, or training by 2020	P	Youth not in education or employed (age 15–29)		•		
8.8 Protect labor rights, promote safe working environments	P	All-cause DALY rate attributable to occupational risks		•		•
8.10 Strengthen capacity of domestic financial institutions to expand access to banking for all	P	Share of adults with account at bank, financial institution, or mobile money				
9.4 Upgrade infrastructure and retrofit industry to make sustainable	N/P	Emissions of CO_2 per unit of GDP PPP		•		
9.5 Enhance scientific research and increase no. of R&D workers & public-private R&D spending	P	R&D expenditures as share of GDP	•			
		Full-time researchers per million inhabitants		•		
10.1 Achieve and sustain income growth of bottom 40% higher than national average		Palma Ratio	•			
10.4 Progressively achieve greater equality	P	Gini coefficient, adjusted after-tax income		•		
11.1 Access to adequate, safe, and affordable housing for all		Households spending 30%+ of income on shelter	•			
11.5 Decrease deaths and economic loss from disasters	P	Cost from natural disasters, share of GDP	•			
11.6 Reduce adverse per capita environmental impact of cities	P	PM2.5 annual average concentration	•			
11.7 Universal access to safe, inclusive green and public spaces	P	Share with park or green space < 10 minutes from home				•
12.3 Halve per capita food waste		Food waste		•		
12.5 Reduce waste generation through prevention, reduction, recycling	P	Solid waste diversion rate		•		
	P	Solid waste per capita		•		
13.2 Integrate climate change measures into nat. policy	N	GHG emissions total		•		

(continued)

Target	Proxy target	Indicator used	Moving backwards	Break-through needed	Accel-eration needed	On track
14.1 Prevent and reduce marine pollution		Volume of spills detected / Number of spills detected				•
14.4 Regulate harvesting and end overfishing by 2020		Major fish stocks harvested above approved levels				•
14.5 Conserve at least 10% of coastal and marine areas by 2020		Share of marine area protected			•	
15.1 Ensure conservation of terrestrial and inland ecosystems by 2020	N	Share of terrestrial area protected				•
15.2 Sustainably manage forests by 2020	N	Volume of wood harvested relative to sustainable wood supply		•		
15.4 Ensure conservation of mountain ecosystems	P	Share of important sites protected		•		
15.5 Reduce degradation of national habitats, halt loss of biodiversity, protect threatened species by 2020	N	Species at risk showing trends of recovery		•	•	
16.1 Reduce all forms of violence and related deaths	P	Rate of homicides	•			
16.2 End abuse, exploitation, trafficking, and violence against children		Rate of sexual violations against children per 100,000 population	•	•		
16.3 Promote rule of law, ensure access to justice for all	P	Unsentenced detainees as share of overall prison population	•	•		
16.5 Reduce corruption and bribery	P	Control of corruption		•		
16.6 Develop effective, accountable, and transparent institutions at all levels	P	Confidence in institutions—justice system and courts		•		
16.9 Provide legal identity for all		Proportion of births registered with a civil authority				•
16.10 Ensure public access to information & protect fundamental freedoms	P	Killing, kidnapping, arbitrary detention, and torture of media, unionists, and human rights advocates				•

Source: McArthur and Rasmussen (2017a).

Note: P indicates proxy target, N indicates Canadian national target.

References

ACEG (Advisory Council on Economic Growth). 2017. "Executive Summary." *The Path to Prosperity*. Ottawa: Department of Finance Canada.

ACGC (Alberta Council for Global Cooperation). 2017. "About Together2017" (www.together2017.ca/about/).

Anderson, Ian, Bridget Robson, Michele Connolly, Fadwa Al-Yaman, and others. 2016. "Indigenous and Tribal Peoples' Health (*The Lancet*-Lowitja Institute Global Collaboration): A Population Study." *The Lancet* 388: 131–57.

AFN and CoC (Assembly of First Nations and the Government of Canada). 2017. A New Approach: Co-development of a New Fiscal Relationship between Canada and First Nations. Ottawa: AFN.

Baker, Sophie. 2017. "Asset Owners Push to Satisfy U.N. Goals." *Pensions & Investments*. October 16 (www.pionline.com/article/20171016/PRINT/171019887/asset-owners-push-to-satisfy-un-goals-esg-institutions-making-major-effort-to-use-investment-acuity-to-make-world-better).

Biggs, Margaret, John W. McArthur, Kate Higgins, David Moloney, Julia Sanchez, and Eric Werker. 2015. *Towards 2030: Building Canada's Engagement with Global Sustainable Development*. Ottawa: Centre for International Policy Studies.

Bizikova, Livia, and Laszlo Pinter. 2017. "Cities—The Engines for Implementing the Sustainable Development Goals." International Institute for Sustainable Development Briefing Note. June (www.iisd.org/sites/default/files/publications/cities-the-engine-for-Implementing-sdgs.pdf).

Breitburg, Denise, Lisa A Levin, Andreas Oschlies, and others. 2018. "Declining Oxygen in the Global Ocean and Coastal Waters." *Science* 359, no. 6371 (doi: 10.1126/science.aam7240).

Business and Sustainable Development Commission. 2017. *Better Business, Better World*. London.

Edelman. 2018. *2018 Edelman Trust Barometer: Global Report* (http://cms.edelman.com/sites/default/files/2018-01/2018_Edelman_Trust_Barometer_Global_Report_Jan.PDF).

ECCC (Environment and Climate Change Canada). 2016. *Achieving a Sustainable Future: A Federal Sustainable Development Strategy for Canada 2016-2019*. Gatineau, Quebec.

FAO, IFAD, UNICEF, WFP, and WHO. 2017. *The State of Food Security and Nutrition in the World 2017. Building Resilience for Peace and Food Security*. Rome: FAO.

FNIGC (First Nations Information Governance Centre). 2018. "The First Nations Principles of OCAP®" (http://fnigc.ca/ocap.html).

DFO (Fisheries and Oceans Canada). 2017. "Canada Reaches 5% Marine Conservation Target." Updated as of October 27, 2017 (www.dfo-mpo.gc.ca/oceans/publications/mct-ocm/five-cinq-eng.html).

Graham, Carol. 2017. Mimeo. Brookings calculations based on Gallup World Poll.

Greenhill, Robert, and Celine Wadhera. "Assessing Canada's Global Engagement Gap: Second edition—January 2017." Global Canada.

Indigenous and Northern Affairs Canada. 2018. "Ending Long-Term Drinking Water Advisories in First Nations Communities." Updated as of January 23, 2018 (www.aadnc-aandc.gc.ca/eng/1506514143353/1506514230742).

ICSU (International Council for Science). 2017. *A Guide to SDG Interactions: From Science to Implementation.* Paris.

Ipsos. 2017. "Dangerous World" (www.ipsos.com/sites/default/files/2017-06/Dangerous_World-2017.pdf).

Kharas, Homi, and John W. McArthur. 2016. "Links in the Chain of Sustainable Finance: Accelerating Private Investments for the SDGs Including Climate Action." Brookings Global Views No. 5. September. Brookings Institution.

Marine Conservation Institute. 2018. "Atlas of Marine Protection" (http://mpatlas.org/map/mpas/).

McArthur, John W. 2016. "It's Canada's Moment to Seize." *Toronto Star.* August 3.

McArthur, John W., and Krista Rasmussen. 2016. "How Close to Zero? Assessing the World's Extreme Poverty-Related Trajectories for 2030." Brookings Global Views No. 6. November. Brookings Institution.

———. 2017a. "Who and What Gets Left Behind? Assessing Canada's Domestic Status on the Sustainable Development Goals." Global Economy and Development Working Paper 108. October. Brookings Institution.

———. 2017b. "Who Funds Which Multilateral Organizations?" Brookings Global Views No. 8. December. Brookings Institution.

McArthur, John W., Krista Rasmussen, and Gavin Yamey. 2018. "How Many Lives at Stake? Assessing 2030 Sustainable Development Goal Trajectories for Maternal and Child Health." *The BMJ* 360: k373.

MBNC (Municipal Benchmarking Network Canada). 2016. *2016 MBNCanada Performance Measurement Report.* Dundas, Ontario.

OECD (Organization for Economic Cooperation and Development). 2018a. "Net ODA (indicator)" (doi: 10.1787/33346549-en).

———. 2018b. "Distribution of Net ODA (indicator)" (doi: 10.1787/2334182b-en).

PFC (Philanthropic Foundations Canada). 2017. *Snapshot of Foundation Giving in 2015.* Montreal.

Ross, Natalie. 2018. *Local Leadership, Global Impact: Community Foundations and the Sustainable Development Goals.* Council of Foundations.

Rust, Susanna. 2016. "Major European Pension Investors Commit to UN Development Goals." *Investment and Pensions Europe.* September 7 (www.ipe.com/news/esg/major-european-pension-investors-commit-to-un-development-goals/10015051.fullarticle).

Schmidt-Traub, Guido. 2015. "Investment Needs to Achieve the Sustainable Development Goals." Working Paper. New York: Sustainable Development Solutions Network.

Sperling, Gene, and Rebecca Winthrop. 2016. *What Works in Girls' Education: Evidence for the World's Best Investment.* Brookings Institution Press.

Steffen, Will, Katherine Richardson, Johan Rockstrom, Sarah E. Cornell, Ingo Fetzer, and others. 2015. "Planetary Boundaries: Guiding Human Development on a Changing Planet." *Science* 347 (6223): 1259855.

Summers, Lawrence H. 1992. "Investing in All People: Education Women in Developing Countries." *Pakistan Development Review* 34, no. 4: 367–404.

Temmer, Jennifer. 2017. "Tracking the SDGs in Canadian Cities: SDG 1." Briefing Note. October. International Institute for Sustainable Development.

United Nations. 2017. *Progress towards the Sustainable Development Goals: Report of the Secretary-General.* E/2017/66. New York.

UNESCO (United Nations Educational, Scientific, and Cultural Organization). 2016. "Leaving No One Behind: How Far on the Way to Universal Primary and Secondary Education." Policy paper 27 / Fact sheet 37. July. Paris.

UNEP (United Nations Environment Program). 2017. *The Emissions Gap Report 2017*. Nairobi.

UNIDO (United Nations Industrial Development Organization). 2014. *World Investment Report 2014. Investing in the SDGs: An Action Plan*. Vienna.

Wilson, Mel. 2016. "The Alberta SDG Initiative." September 24 (www.linkedin.com/pulse/alberta-sdg-initiative-mel-wilson).

World Data Lab. 2018. "World Poverty Clock" (http://worldpoverty.io/).

CHAPTER THIRTEEN

A People's Agenda
Citizen Participation and the SDGs

Dhananjayan Sriskandarajah

The Sustainable Development Goals (SDGs) will not be achieved without significant public awareness and engagement. It is citizens who will hold governments accountable to the promises they made in 2015, and we need to find innovative ways of raising public pressure to deliver a more just and sustainable world by 2030. Only through such an "accountability revolution" will we have any chance of achieving the commitments made in the SDGs, and the lynchpin for that revolution is citizen participation.

Citizens and civil society have been actively involved in the SDGs since long before the goals existed in any formal way. They have raised awareness about the importance of the "post-2015" process through nongovernmental organizations (NGOs) and actively contributed to the drafting of the goals through the Open Working Group.

As Secretary General of CIVICUS—a global civil society alliance actively involved in the post-2015 process—I have participated in countless United Nations meetings about the SDGs and their predecessor, the Millennium Development Goals. Often at these meetings, I would make a half-tongue-in-cheek remark that the problem with the MDGs was that no one ever lost their job for failing to meet an MDG target. This comment always made the officials in the room shift uneasily in their seats, especially when I would ask why, if we truly want the SDGs to be a success, would we not hold accountable those of us in governments, intergovernmental agencies, global business, or civil society organizations (CSOs) responsible for achieving them, even to the point that our jobs would depend on it.

If such an argument seems absurd, it is because we do not (yet) see the SDGs as having real political bite. They are not legally binding, their complexity and interconnectedness makes apportioning blame (or credit) difficult, and they arise out of an intergovernmental system that is losing credibility among activists.

When local and national leaders and institutions make promises, almost all societies, both democratic and undemocratic, have fairly sophisticated ways of holding them to account. If the SDGs are a set of global promises—made by our leaders and institutions—then it should follow that we have at least *some* ways of ensuring these leaders are held accountable.

However, I recognize that the accountability revolution will only be possible if civil society also adapts to the evolving development agenda. We will need to re-evaluate our strategies for cooperation and funding as well as for accountability and communication. We will also need to continue to defend and promote the civic space that citizens rely on to hold decision-makers to account. Despite their potential, the SDGs have arrived at a worrying time for civic freedoms. The civil society institutional landscape does not seem ready to channel citizen voices adequately toward the goals. The rising tide of populist politics across the globe poses a massive threat to the values that underpin the SDGs and internationalism more broadly. Meanwhile, there are not enough people thinking about innovative ways of promoting citizen participation in the SDGs or the global governance mechanisms that are their guardians. With all this in mind, this chapter explores some of the challenges and opportunities facing civil society's role in implementing the SDGs.

The MDGs Versus the SDGs

One key distinction between the SDGs and their pre-2015 predecessor, the Millennium Development Goals (MDGs), emerges as being of critical importance. Where the MDGs were narrow in focus—aimed specifically at boosting policy attention, especially donor attention, in particular sectors—the SDGs represent a much broader agenda. The new goals are about many things at once. They tackle a nexus of interconnecting global public goods—a comprehensive framework for ending poverty and a system that provides humanitarian relief reduces inequality and fights climate change.

They are about the quality of life everyone should enjoy by 2030: the right to a minimum standard of living, that is, a global social floor below which no one should be allowed to fall. They are about the right to be protected from extreme poverty, the right to food and clean water, the right to education and to protection from the effects of environmental degradation.

The SDGs move us toward a more universal vision. As such, they require the involvement of all stakeholders: the governments of rich and poor countries, the private sector, civil society organizations (CSOs), and, perhaps most important, people. They represent a people's agenda: a vision for improving societal behaviors and a means of holding the 193 governments that have committed to achieving the goals to account. They offer a potential tool for ensuring that failure to meet their commitments will come with a political price.

The goals represent a global power shift—not rich countries promising to fix the problems of the poor, but all of us changing our behaviors in order to achieve common objectives. The SDGs are an opportunity to usher in a new age of mutual accountability. No longer can accountability just be about what Western governments or donors demand of recipients, but policy coherence and behavior changes everywhere. Given the universal and thorny nature of the challenges covered by the SDGs, we may need to find inspiration and solutions from all over the world. It may be that Ugandans hold lessons for how to reduce consumption in the United States, or that Rwandans can provide a model for improving gender equality or finding solutions to plastic waste in Romania.

As such, the role the SDGs require of civil society also goes far beyond the oversight, or watchdog, function of previous years. True, civil society still has a critical role to play by ensuring that these ambitious goals are not watered down or cherry picked and that states embrace the new universalist, human rights–based approach that is required of them. Holding governments and the private sector to account will be essential. But civil society has a significant role to play in the practical implementation of this new agenda as well. Should civil society fail to understand, and embrace, this necessary shift to include the politics *and* practicalities of Agenda 2030, our new global framework may not transport us very far from where the MDGs dropped us off.

The State of Civil Society

Civil society, the arena outside of the family, the state, and the market, where people associate to advance common interests and come together to influence broader society, has no specific organizational form. It amounts to more than just NGOs or individual CSOs; its defining feature is that it involves collective citizen action of some form, organized or spontaneous.

Playing a crucial role in instigating social and political change, promoting good governance and people-centered development, civil society often acts as the catalyst for altering deeply entrenched societal power structures. Its role is to speak unpalatable truths to power—to amplify the voices of the marginalized, to tackle the causes of discrimination, and to promote equal rights and access to services.

In the last few years, rising inequality, insecurity, and a sense of political disenfranchisement have fueled an uprising of public anger. We have seen citizens take to the streets to demand change in countries all over the world—from Chile to South Africa, Armenia to South Korea, and Guatemala to Romania. Protests have led to high-level political change, and in the United Kingdom and United States, citizens have caused seismic political disruptions in the form of Brexit and the election of President Donald Trump.

A functioning civil society relies on three fundamental rights: the freedoms of association, assembly, and expression. Together, these freedoms define the parameters of civic space: the arena in which civil society can exist and act and the bedrock of any open and democratic society. When civic space is open, citizens and CSOs are able to organize, participate, and communicate without hindrance; they are able to claim their rights and to influence the political and social structures around them. A free, vibrant civil society, operating within open civic space, plays a critical role in stemming tides of extremism, intolerance, and exclusion, yet often it is something we appreciate only when it starts to disappear.

Worryingly, in far too many countries—and in all global regions—civic space has worsened appreciably in recent years. The freedom of citizens to protest, to mobilize, and to speak out is being contested and restricted. Data from the CIVICUS Monitor (CIVICUS, 2017) shows that more than 3.2 billion people now live in countries where civic space is repressed or closed, and in 2015 serious violations of civic space were recorded in 109 countries.

The sources and methods of restriction are manifold. Attacks on civil society are being made by political leaders, government agencies, state and private sector security forces, corporations, organized crime cells, and extremists. Most recently, methods of restriction include legislation to constrain how civil society can organize, what it can act on, how it must account for itself and how it can be funded, verbal attacks and hate speech, arbitrary detention and disappearances, criminalization of activists through biased judicial proceedings, restrictions on travel, as well as physical attacks and assassinations. In the last year, peaceful protests have often been met by a violent state response; civil society personnel have been targeted in conflict settings; international humanitarian law has routinely been flouted; and civil society activists have been violently attacked, jailed, or detained in numerous contexts. Governments are brutally silencing dissent by cracking down on protest or by intimidating and murdering human rights defenders, lawyers, and journalists.

These threats to democracy are no longer limited to authoritarian regimes. Citizen-led disruption driven by deepening economic inequality—from the radical mass movements of Occupy to the kind of anti-establishment populism that fueled Trump's insurgency in the United States and the Brexit "leavers" in the United Kingdom—has brought with it a new era of messy, unpredictable democracy, increasing the tendency for authoritarian reflexes. In the face of such disruption, democratic governments are taking increasingly drastic steps to curtail the ability of citizens to criticize authority or even to call for their basic social and economic needs to be met. Restriction of online freedom of expression, including the targeting of social media commentators and restriction of content, is now a marked trend, not only in China, Thailand, and Turkey, but also in mature democracies. The traditional institutions of formal democracy might no longer be sufficient to guarantee civil society's rights and people's participation. Civil society actors who work to question the power of political and economic elites, to expose corruption or poor governance, and to realize human rights are facing the strongest restrictions. Within the last year alone, assassinations and violent attacks in Brazil, Colombia, Honduras, Peru, the Philippines, and South Africa show the dangers faced by those CSOs, activists, and investigative journalists who challenge corporations linked to economic and political elites—often those with extractive or agribusiness concerns.

When civil society actors challenge dominant narratives, they risk being accused of promoting terrorism, sedition, or instability. Indeed, recent attacks on civil society in Jordan, Saudi Arabia, and Sudan have all been made with reference to upholding national security and combating extremism. Since civil society is often the target of threats from extremist and terrorist forces, this seems particularly ironic.

Despite these myriad challenges, civil society has also seen significant success—not least on the global stage—in the past two years. Playing an important role in the processes to develop the major international commitments of 2015—the Sustainable Development Goals and Paris climate change agreement—civil society successfully advocated for both to be more comprehensive, ambitious, inclusive, and rights-oriented than any previous agreements. Civil society contributed to the formal negotiation process through, for example, formal contributions to the Open Working Group on the Sustainable Development Goals. It also mobilized like never before through platforms such as Action/2015, where more than 2,200 organizations from 157 countries joined forces and took actions to demand that world leaders play their part in delivering an ambitious Agenda 2030 (CIVICUS, 2016). Indeed, civil society is mentioned, in different ways, ten times in the Agenda 2030 resolution (UN, 2015).

Civil society must build on these successes to contribute to the realizing of Agenda 2030. It must continue to play its important watchdog function, speaking truth to power and holding governments and the private sector to account for their commitments. But we must also be ready to roll up our sleeves and contribute to SDG implementation—continuing the important work we have done for decades but also forging new alliances with each other and with others and experimenting with new ways of contributing to social change. To do this, we need to adapt to a new development landscape and engage with and push this landscape in directions that still align with our core values.

Adapting to a New Development Landscape

The development landscape is shifting dramatically as it re-orients itself around the SDGs and adapts to rapid global socioeconomic changes. As such, civil society must also begin to think and behave in radically different ways. Sustainable development is not simply about how much aid should be provided, or about what the rich world can do for the poor; it is about our shared responsibility to achieve a more sustainable future for everyone. A useful, universal tool for holding governments—but also businesses and CSOs—to account, the SDGs empower people to question what progress has been made and to demand further action.

Helping to construct this new development landscape—and learning to operate within it—will be crucial to successfully implementing the SDGs. And the importance of civil society's role in this endeavor cannot be underestimated. We must seek to protect the core values at the heart of the development project as a global public good. We must call for governments and other major donors to remain true to the essence of aid, maintaining existing commitments to a minimum 0.7 percent of gross national income (GNI) spending on development. We must safeguard all that is good in the current system and ensure that the development sector's foundational principles are not lost.

Charting this middle ground, between protecting what is good about our existing system and branching out into new territory, will not be easy. Tensions are already clear and the challenges many and varied.

Much of the critical role that civil society will need to play in implementing the SDGs depends on our ability to push back against the narrowing of civic space around the world. In recognition of this, a broad global movement to defend civil society rights is beginning to form. This emerging movement will need to develop strong, more accessible messaging around why civic space matters and the roles citizens can play in defending it. It will need to engage in international processes to foster norms and structures that uphold civic space and work to see the same standards applied at national levels. Equally, civil society will need to maintain the highest standards of integrity, developing its own capacity to demonstrate transparency and accountability, so that it is in a position to rebut any criticisms that undermine its legitimacy.

In the context of this new development landscape, civil society will have to engage simultaneously in multiple functions—accountability, implementation, engagement, advocacy; at multiple levels—local, national, regional, global; and on multiple fronts—with the public, the media, governments, and the corporate world. More actors from across civil society will need to be encouraged to take sustainable development and the SDGs seriously, ranging from CSOs in the

Global North, which work on domestic issues and don't see the SDGs as relevant, to the Southern activists who still see the SDGs as a UN-led, top-down process.

There are at least four things civil society will need to do collectively to ensure we are able to make our rightful contribution to the achievement of the SDGs. First, we will need to engage honestly with the problems of our existing funding models and contribute to building more sustainable and fair resourcing methods. Second, we will need to navigate blurring boundaries on what constitutes development partnerships, engaging with the corporate sector while also maintaining our independence and ability to challenge the status quo. Third, we need to put citizens at the heart of the data revolution, to ensure that people and their organizations are central to measuring and driving progress on the SDGs. And fourth, we will need new, accessible narratives that localize this global agenda and genuinely represent, resource, protect, and engage those that are most affected by global injustice. Making these things happen will not always be comfortable. But it is crucial if civil society is to have the legitimacy it needs to drive the change we want to see.

Changing Funding Models

Introducing new sources of funding, and diverting existing flows, will be critical to constructive disruption of the current system. Moving more money through direct funding to civil society in the Global South must be a priority. The development sector's existing dominant funding model, which sees money channeled through chains of "fundermediaries" in the Global North (agencies that receive large grants and pass them on to local partners), has one major flaw: funding may trickle down, but power does not. It remains concentrated in the hands of a relatively small number of big players, predominantly in the Global North. In recent years only about 1 percent of all official aid, and an even smaller portion of humanitarian assistance, has gone directly to civil society in the Global South (OECD, 2013). And research into private foundations suggests that they too channel the majority of their giving through Northern-based fundermediaries.

If we are to have any hope of achieving the SDGs in the Global South, a fundamental transfer of power must be the defining feature of our new development landscape. Northern civil society has a continuing role to play, but not in its current organizational form, dominated by massive, competitive, service-delivery-focused NGOs. These organizations will need to move back toward something more closely resembling their original identities as membership networks, social movements, and powerful voices for change. They will need to abandon their overriding commitment to the science of delivery and instead rediscover the art of social transformation and disruptive change. Civil society actors have a responsibility to kick-start this fundamental shift in the power hierarchy and, in the process, to construct a truly multipolar civil society sector, more suited to the universalist demands of the SDGs.

When it comes to this rebalancing of civil society's role in the art of social transformation versus the science of delivery, local resourcing has the potential to tick both boxes. Local actors offer more efficient sustainable development solutions, so supporting local CSOs, based in the communities they seek to serve, satisfies many of the technical efficiency criteria that are so important to the allocation of development resources. But going local is also about more than technical efficiency and development impact; it's about a political, transformative power shift.

The power imbalances perpetuated by the dominant development modalities of the last two decades have actively contributed to worrying global restrictions of civil society's core freedoms. Certainly, they have made civic freedoms more difficult to fight for. Our funding models have nurtured a cadre of contracted, professionalized CSOs who excel at "accounts-ability" but struggle to catalyze disruptive social change. Advocating for human rights and sustainable social justice is an awkward fit with most donors' insistence on short-term, discrete, measurable projects, leaving the very organizations that may be best positioned to fight back against closing civic space severely underresourced and struggling for survival.

The dominance of official development assistance (ODA) and high-level, large-scale funding in many developing countries has also facilitated the ongoing trend for politicized government regulation and the imposition of barriers to what is commonly termed the "foreign funding of dissent." Even as we begin to see official government donors withdraw, for example, from countries recently designated as middle income, the dependence they have created, at the expense of homegrown resource bases, leaves a gaping hole, often quickly filled by repressive governments, intolerant of civic activism and dissent. These governments then choose only to fund CSOs that will deliver against the government's own agenda—some openly using the threat of funding cuts to silence critical voices—leaving the independence of the civil society sector dangerously compromised.

The public in many countries now view CSOs with suspicion—as self-serving, corrupt agents of external forces. In recent years, a rapid rise in engagement with charitable activities in some countries in the Global South—many home to exploding middle-class populations—raised hopes of a global surge in private donations. But the relationship between in-country wealth and the proportion of people giving money to charity has been shown to be weak. Deeper, underlying conditions and narratives drive or restrict a culture of giving. Widespread campaigns of vilification against civil society, and all the more subtle ways in which civic space is being restricted, are a real problem.

The SDG agenda will never be anything more than aspirational unless we are prepared to build a more diverse and resilient civil society. To do this, we need practical measures that have a chance of early impact.

One example will be a greater role for community foundations. There has already been a significant increase in the number of community foundations around the world in recent years, but a further investment in these mechanisms could help build community assets, support sustainable development, and change the power dynamics within the development sector—all at once. A well-resourced, established community philanthropy sector would entail our sustainable development efforts being grounded in strong relationships of trust, responsive to the evolving needs of communities, as well as to local political and social dynamics. Because of their independence, the financial backers of this kind of philanthropy—social investors and grant makers—are empowered to take risks, to seed-fund new ideas, to test innovation, and to tolerate a degree of failure. Perhaps most important—by supporting communities' efforts to gain control of their own development future, this kind of philanthropy is inherently sustainable.

Another area for potential action is around localization, defined as distributing a greater share of resources to local actors and giving them greater control over how those are spent. There has been no shortage of commitments to localization in recent years. For example, in 2010 the U.S. government announced the USAID Forward initiative that promised to promote sustainable development through greater investment in local solutions, including support to civil society organizations that serve as engines of growth and progress for their own nations. More recently, participants at the World Humanitarian Summit in 2016 agreed to a "Grand Bargain" that included a commitment to more direct resourcing of local actors and first responders in humanitarian emergencies.

Yet despite these commitments, we have seen very few concrete measures that have made a difference. We need to find new mechanisms for channeling resources from international donors, UN agencies, and international NGOs quickly and flexibly to national and local actors. One set of actors that will play a critical role will be a new generation of Southern institutions that will be able to deal directly with Northern donors and be more grounded in the communities they serve. In some cases, these will take the form of dedicated Southern funder-mediaries that allow Northern donors to devolve funding decisions closer to the ground. Examples like the African Women's Development Fund and the newly formed NEAR initiative on humanitarian assistance are likely to hold a key to localization, which in turn, will have a positive impact on supporting a more diverse and resilient civil society.

Indeed, if traditional donors and international actors are interested in building local capacity and long-term impacts, investing in new development modalities like community philanthropy and local fundermediaries should be at the top of their list. This will require a nuanced approach and an honest acknowledgment of the politics embedded in their funding decisions. Above all, it will require a willingness to use their power to shift unequal power structures on the ground.

Navigating Blurred Boundaries

As major donor governments in the Global North seek to adapt to the new development era, many are placing a new emphasis on the importance of market-based solutions. In many ways, this is understandable: if the resourcing challenges around the MDGs were huge—and ultimately not achieved—then the funds and structural changes needed to achieve the SDGs are eye watering. As a result, the private sector, philanthropic foundations, and social enterprises are being expected to play a greater role in sustainable development, and an increasing proportion of ODA is also being channeled through or in partnership with these actors.

In many ways, the multistakeholder approach to Agenda 2030 is reflective of broader trends around the changing nature of traditional "sectors" around the world. Seismic shifts are already taking place in the balance between the traditional functions of each sector, as we know them. Businesses no longer exist solely to make profits: many see themselves as social enterprises, pursuing more than just monetary profits. Governments no longer hold a monopoly on providing public services: many such services are being delivered by the private sector, civil society organizations, or community actors. And civil society organizations are themselves changing rapidly: many of the largest NGOs have multibillion-dollar annual incomes and an equivalent global reach. Previously distinct sectors are undergoing a process of hybridization: a transformative shift from competition to collaboration that will need to be a defining feature of the new SDG landscape.

Yet civil society must also be careful to safeguard its ability to stand beyond the market and the state in order to question the fundamentals of the status quo. Should we fail to maintain this degree of independence, as we collaborate—and as the private sector plays an ever-increasing role in development—we risk simply working toward a perpetuation of the dominant capitalist system and a naturalization of neoliberal market fundamentalism. The SDGs are about tackling the drivers—the root causes—of poverty, inequality, and climate change. And as such, civil society must secure its ability and impetus to criticize the current economic system and to challenge dominant powers.

As we move into the implementation phase of the SDGs, civil society has a role to play in counterbalancing the influence of the private sector in development. Left unchecked, this growing influence threatens to privilege those parts of the global agenda that most closely connect with private sector interests and to downplay those that do not. The role that large, transnational corporations are being asked to play in funding UN agencies and other international initiatives risks creating opportunities for corruption, reducing accountability, and substituting corporate charity for citizens' rights. When the institutions of global governance begin to be used to advance corporate agendas and to launder the reputations of private sector corporations, we are entering dangerous terrain.

Finally, amid this growing "multistakeholderism" and collaboration, it is also important to recognize and protect the special role that civil society needs to play in achieving sustainable development. A resilient, independent, and effective civil society is both a means and an end in itself when it comes to the SDGs. Successful implementation of the SDGs will require strong and efficient civil society institutions that can help deliver programs and interventions, but a vibrant and vocal civil society is also critical to achieving the just, inclusive, peaceful, and democratic societies envisioned in Goal 16.

Putting Citizens at the Heart of the Data Revolution

Another way in which we will need to redistribute power closer to the ground—if we are to achieve the SDGs—will be by altering the way we produce and use data. In this respect, the MDGs achieved something remarkable by entrenching the idea of measuring progress through robust metrics, partly to measure effectiveness for donors, but more importantly to promote greater accountability on international development objectives.

The SDGs may follow in the tradition of the MDGs, but their requirements in terms of volume, complexity, and breadth of data go far beyond anything previously attempted in the development sector. SDG metrics may still be in their infancy, but already there is widespread consensus that significant investment in the capacity of all development actors— including citizens—to generate, use, and curate data will be crucial. If we are to have any hope of achieving the new vision, robust new metrics, fed by nothing less than a data revolution, will be essential.

When citizens wanted to understand a country's performance in relation to a particular MDG target, the only information available was official, often patchy, government data or academic research. Indeed, the first countries to present their SDG plans to the UN in 2016 all said they would require better data in terms of geographical coverage, frequency, and specificity. Some official data are only collected once every five to ten years, making it very difficult to track change. The quality of rural and urban data often differs hugely, with metropolitan areas benefiting from much better data coverage and rural areas often being omitted from datasets or included only in a limited capacity. Women and indigenous communities are among the large demographics less likely to be represented in traditional household surveys and data collection techniques. With 230 distinct indicators to quantify, measuring progress toward the SDGs is a daunting task, but one that comes with opportunity: the opportunity to create a new approach to monitoring and accountability that puts citizens at its core.

New forms of citizen-generated data—produced by people, or their organizations, to monitor, demand, or drive change on issues that affect them—will revolutionize the successful implementation of this agenda (see Lämmerhirt, Jameson, and Prasetyo, 2017). New technologies offer exciting new ways for citizens to generate and use data democratically and creatively. Data disaggregated by age, gender, disability, and so on cannot be considered an expensive, optional add-on to the SDG framework. Citizen-generated data can monitor commitments made by governments (for example, Promise Tracker in Brazil) and feed evidence from the ground up into higher-level policy debates (for example, the ocean litter program Dive Against Debris). Importantly, data can also be used to verify official narratives and datasets, empowering people and giving them a way to actively engage with political processes that might otherwise seem far removed (for example, Float Beijing in China).

Work is under way on connecting these efforts with SDG monitoring subnationally, nationally, and globally. Everyone Counts, for example, is an initiative building on the success of community scorecards as accountability tools to monitor SDG progress. In this case, Care International, World Vision, and the social enterprise Kwantu are working to connect and aggregate citizen-generated and community-level service delivery data to monitor and hold power holders to account for commitments made on the SDGs.[1]

Of course, citizen-generated data does not come without challenges. While there are some encouraging examples of citizens already generating new data on important aspects of development, these initiatives, thus far, remain scarce, of mixed quality and sophistication, and unable to be compared within and across countries. Most CSOs lack the capacity and confidence to use new technology to generate data, or to use it in ways that can support their decision-making and bolster their campaigns. At the global level, while the role of national statistics and big data in driving the data revolution has gained considerable traction since the launch of the SDGs, less attention has been paid to the role that citizens and citizen-generated data could play in monitoring progress and supporting accountability.

More citizen-generated data initiatives across the world, particularly in the Global South, and greater complementarity and comparability of these datasets

---

1. See UN, "Everyone Counts," SDGAction 11910 (https://sustainabledevelopment.un.org/partnership/?p=11910).

will be crucial to ensuring that citizen-generated data comes to be widely accepted as credible, reliable, and valuable. This kind of more timely, nuanced, and comprehensive data collection will also need to be at the very heart of any decision-making if we're to succeed in ensuring that the sustainable development agenda truly leaves no one behind.

Developing New, Accessible Narratives

An additional challenge facing those who would like to see the SDGs become "famous," and therefore a popular and frequently used tool in the advocacy strategies of those campaigning for sustainable development, is to come up with a new strategy for communicating them. At one level, this will mean finding new ways to raise awareness in a shallow sense among the largest possible population—something we failed to do for the MDGs. In a more important sense, it will mean finding effective ways of bringing these "global goals" to life in the local context. For example, this could include showing a community activist working on gender equality or children's rights how the SDGs could become a useful tool. Initially and primarily, this would drive accountability at their local or national level, but would also help contribute to a global accountability strategy. Recent experience in Lanet Umoja Location, Nakuru County in Kenya, through a collaboration between the Open Institute, Chief Francis Kariuki, and DataShift, has demonstrated the power of "domesticating" the SDGs.[2] Indeed, this experience has demonstrated the utility of the SDGs as a framework for measuring progress and demanding accountability on sustainable development at the local level—in this case SDG 5 on achieving gender equality and empowering all women and girls.

The commitment to "leave no one behind" appears no less than six times in the declaration made by world leaders when they announced the 2030 Agenda for Sustainable Development (UN, 2015) and has quickly emerged as one of the most powerful means of framing our new approach to inclusivity: a means of engaging and motivating people in a way that a list of seventeen goals and 169 targets cannot. Civil society must be at the vanguard of shaping and delivering this agenda. When we signed up for the SDGs, we committed to reach the furthest behind first, to listen to their voices, to involve them in designing policies that promote inclusion, and challenge the social barriers that deny or limit potential. We signed up to ensure that our new approach to development will address all forms of discrimination and exclusion, including on the basis of gender, age, location, caste, religion, disability, or sexual identity.

2. See "Global Goals for Local Impact," Open Institute, June 22, 2016 (www.openinstitute.com/global-goals-for-local-impact-lanet-umoja-community-leaders-meeting/).

The MDGs' inadequate attention to inequality and the most marginalized emerged as one of the earlier goals' key weaknesses. The MDGs' focus on aggregate figures and overall progress failed to take into account growing social and economic disparities, while incentivizing states and large NGOs to prioritize big-picture wins. Even as overall poverty levels fell, inequality often increased, and the standard of living for the poorest and most marginalized sometimes worsened significantly. Take India, often held up as an exemplar of economic growth and poverty reduction using basic income-level measures. Research shows that, in fact, India has not kept pace with progress in other large countries; the proportion of the Indian population that falls within the poorest 20 percent of all people globally has grown from 16 to 38 percent in the last twenty-five years (Development Initiatives, 2017). In the same period, the absolute gap between the poorest 20 percent globally and the rest of world has widened significantly. Indeed, only *eight* individuals now own as much wealth as the poorest half of the world's population (Oxfam, 2017).

The SDGs call on us to tackle social and political marginalization, as well as economic, to amplify the voices of those who are not ordinarily heard and to create a system in which people are empowered to shape their own communities. Civil society has a critical role to play in mobilizing to make these global goals relevant, useful, and powerful for local actors.

Interestingly, the SDGs may offer a way of connecting progressive and populist political agendas. In most cases, recent moves toward populist and anti-establishment movements around the world are in response to poor people being pushed further to the margins of society and middle-class people feeling left behind. This deepening of social and economic marginalization is perceived to be a by-product of globalization, privatization, and power captured by established elites. The universal nature of the SDGs could in fact be a vehicle for uniting grassroots civil society actors across the political spectrum who are concerned with rising economic inequality. This would require bold leadership as well as humility, but the SDGs could in fact become a framework for constructively bringing together civil society actors who typically don't collaborate, all in an effort to see governments deliver in tangible ways on commitments that they have made.

Within this radically changed development context, civil society must embrace a new way of working. Our old, or perhaps existing, global campaigns were largely Northern-led, dominated by international NGOs, and aimed at influencing global targets and Northern governments with top-down, centralized messaging. Our new models of campaigning—if they are to align with the SDG era—will need to be networked, bottom-up, decentralized, and, more often than not, designed, led, and owned by actors in the Global South.

A sustained, coordinated, collective, radical effort on the part of a global community of active, engaged citizens committed to the creation of a more just and equitable world can enable us to meet the most pressing global challenges of our time. This will need to encourage and rely on cooperation between networks of CSOs in countries around the world, be based on common objectives and coordinated and aligned activities, and involve sharing knowledge, skills, and other resources. It will need to create a space for organizations that may ordinarily have differing areas of focus and agendas to cooperate and, where appropriate, to campaign under one global brand.

There are reference points to draw from. In the 1970s and 1980s, nuclear disarmament and anti-Vietnam war movements in the West birthed a new kind of public consciousness around the value of peace and tolerance. The anti-apartheid movement managed to deliver a peaceful transition in South Africa. More recent movements such as the women's marches of 2017 give us hope that we will find the techniques and tools to build a similarly powerful, constructive, social movement around sustainable development.

Conclusion

It is positive that civil society was involved in creating the Sustainable Development Goals. But this is a far cry from what will be needed in order to ensure that the goals are achieved. Involving civil society in implementing the SDGs will be essential. And it will also be necessary to address the negative trends in civic space that harm people, planet, and prosperity. We need to find ways to reverse these trends and the legal and regulatory restrictions that hamper civil operations.

We will also need to encourage healthier democracies, characterized not just by the absence of violations but by those in power taking proactive steps to safeguard citizen action, tolerate dissent, and provide platforms for meaningful dialogue. We need fewer governments fearing people power and instead more governments nurturing active citizenship (something that will be critical to achieving Goal 16 on the promotion of peaceful and inclusive societies). More open spaces—online and offline—are also needed to channel citizen voice and dissent in meaningful ways without dismantling open and democratic societies.

The civil society sector itself also faces its own challenges. It needs to find ways of building resilience, voice, and independence. It must make sure to model good practice in addressing inclusion, rather than reproducing the exclusionary attitudes and practices of the societies around it. Civil society must lead the way in creating new, progressive, peace-building tactics to convince a radicalizing world of the need for reconciliation and constructive dialogue.

For CSOs involved in sustainable development, the SDGs present some significant challenges and opportunities. In an era of disintermediation and disruption of existing power dynamics, no longer can it be assumed that a few, relatively well-resourced international NGOs will form the leading edge of citizen action around sustainable development. We need a new set of change agents, including many more grounded in local action—whether it is the soup kitchen in the Global North or the women's rights organization in the Global South—who can effectively translate a global agenda to local issues and, in turn, feed local concerns into global monitoring frameworks. Promoting this sort of translocal action will increase the chances of civil society raising political pressure on both local actors (who will feel the power of locally led mobilization) and global actors (who will see evidence grounded in local realities). Indeed, broadening participation in this process beyond the relatively few CSOs who are currently active around the SDGs to a wider set of civil society actors will be critical to delivering any sort of accountability revolution.

Successfully implementing the seventeen SDGs will require a new way of working with more meaningful multistakeholder partnerships. Civil society needs to play its rightful and multifaceted role—not just as campaigners pointing out shortcomings but also as innovators leading delivery. The SDGs themselves should become the crucible in which new state-society and local-global dynamics are forged. Ultimately, if a local public official somewhere is held accountable for delivering Agenda 2030—and even loses his or her job for not meeting an important SDG target—it will mark a breakthrough for ensuring that this agenda has traction and that power answers to the people who matter most: citizens themselves.

References

CIVICUS. 2016. *CIVICUS Annual Report 2015-16.* Johannesburg (www.civicus.org/ documents/reports-and-publications/annual-reports/annual-report-2016-en.pdf).
————. 2017. CIVICUS Monitor (https://monitor.civicus.org/).
Development Initiatives. 2017. *The P20 initiative* (http://devinit.org/post/ ending-poverty-by-focusing-on-the-poorest-20-of-people-globally/).
Lämmerhirt, D., E. Jameson, and E. Prasetyo. 2017. *Acting Locally, Monitoring Globally? How to Link Citizen-Generated Data to SDG Monitoring.* Open Knowledge International and DataShift (http://civicus.org/thedatashift/wp-content/uploads/2015/07/ Acting-locally-monitoring-globally_Full-Report.pdf).
OECD. 2013. *Aid for CSOs* (www.oecd.org/dac/peer-reviews/Aid%20for%20CSOs%20 Final%20for%20WEB.pdf).
Oxfam. 2017. *An Economy for the 99 Percent* (www.oxfam.org/en/research/economy-99).
United Nations. 2015. *Transforming Our World: The 2030 Agenda for Sustainable Development.* A/RES/70/1. October 21 (www.un.org/ga/search/view_doc.asp?symbol=A/ RES/70/1&Lang=E).

CHAPTER FOURTEEN

Safeguarding Our Global Commons

Naoko Ishii

The world achieved a milestone to build a common vision of development and sustainability in 2015 when Agenda 2030 was adopted universally. The resolution adopting the goals of Agenda 2030 stated: "We are determined to protect the planet from degradation, including through sustainable consumption and production, sustainably managing its natural resources and taking urgent action on climate change, so that it can support the needs of the present and future generations" (United Nations, 2015). The sustainable development goals link core issues of human welfare with sustaining a healthy planet. They reject the idea of trade-offs between economic, social, and environmental dimensions of sustainability, arguing that these are "integrated and indivisible." They seek to bring together the previously separate agendas of Rio+20 and the Millennium Development Goals into a single framework.

This chapter argues that urgent action is needed to safeguard the global commons—the Earth's shared resources such as ecosystems, biomes, and processes that regulate the stability and resilience of the Earth system. It posits that multistakeholder coalitions are needed at global, regional, national, and subnational levels to manage key economic systems that currently threaten our global commons in a new way. It suggests that a systems approach can offer a framework for action. Armed with such understanding, there is an opportunity to provide lasting prosperity—a new growth model that provides faster increases in living standards, to more people, in a sustainable manner.

The four key economic systems that must change are the food and agriculture system, the energy system, the cities and urban system, and the global production/consumption system. This chapter explores the process through which change can come about.

The Science of Global Commons

Almost a decade ago—in 2009—renowned scientists warned that the processes and biomes that regulate the stability and resilience of the Earth system were reaching a tipping point (Rockström and others, 2009).[1] The groundbreaking planetary boundaries framework they developed clearly showed nine Earth systems processes whose thresholds ought not to be crossed in order to keep our planet in a safe operating space for humanity: (1) stratospheric ozone depletion, (2) loss of biosphere integrity, (3) chemical pollution and the release of novel entities, (4) climate change, (5) ocean acidification, (6) freshwater consumption and the global hydrological cycle, (7) land system change, (8) nitrogen and phosphorus flows to the biosphere and oceans, and, finally, (9) atmospheric aerosol loading. Crossing these boundaries could generate abrupt and irreversible environmental changes.

According to the latest planetary boundaries assessment in 2015 (Steffen and others, 2015), four of these systems have already been transgressed, including climate change, biodiversity integrity, land-use change (deforestation), and biogeochemical flows (mainly overuse of phosphorus and nitrogen in fertilizers). In September 2016 at the International Geological Congress in Cape Town, geologists from all over the world concluded that our planet had left the Holocene epoch abruptly and unexpectedly and entered a new geological epoch, the Anthropocene. In this new epoch, the stability of the Earth system cannot be taken for granted.

The message from science is clear. We are at a defining moment for the future of the planet and for the well-being of all humanity. Our planet is reaching the limits of what it can provide for all living creatures in a sustainable manner. The global environmental commons that support life on Earth, meaning our collectively shared planetary resources, such as clean air and water, biodiversity, healthy forests, land, and oceans, as well as a stable climate, are facing overexploitation and exponential degradation.

The nations of the world have recognized the importance of global environmental stewardship at least since June 1972 with the Conference on the Human Environment, followed by a series of world environmental conferences and various international conventions, the promulgation of national legal frameworks and multilateral funding. However, the significant acceleration of our global economy and human footprint on Earth in the last fifty years has outpaced the efforts to protect our planet, leaving us a narrow window of opportunity and an

---

1. The framework was developed by twenty-eight scientists led by Johan Rockström of the Stockholm Resilience Centre and Will Steffen of the Australian National University.

unprecedented, urgent need to adopt new safeguards and to find ways that the global community can stop the potential further damage to the Earth's systems.

In parallel, the business community is increasingly recognizing that a deteriorating global environment poses significant risks to the prospects for future economic growth. In the World Economic Forum's 2017 Global Risks Report, environment-related risks feature among the highest-ranking global risks.[2] Four of the top-five perceived risks in terms of impact were environmental risks. Ten years ago, none of the top-five risks was related to the environment. Moreover, environmental risks are closely interconnected with other risk categories, so there is a strong correlation between ineffective management of the global environment and adverse local and global consequences in other areas, such as increased migration and unrest in fragile states.

Fundamentally, the underlying driver of continued environmental degradation is a "tragedy of the commons" phenomenon on a global scale. The global commons can be regarded as a global natural capital—but a sort of capital that is not accounted for in monetary value. Our economic and political systems have failed to price nature and the services we obtain from it adequately. Instead of maintaining and increasing our natural capital, we have depreciated it, pushing our Earth systems to their limits. Given that no global accountability system exists, there is no mechanism to sensibly manage provision of the global commons. For that reason, we need to address the perverse incentives that are embedded in our economic and political systems. Since the expansion of the Industrial Revolution, fossil fuels and an ever-growing extraction of natural resources have powered our economic activities. The incentives and decisionmaking frameworks at global and national levels have led to an impressive accumulation of wealth but have also caused our environmental footprint to grow exponentially.

Looking Ahead: Fundamental Transformation in Key Economic Systems Required

In the next few decades, the pressure on the global environment is set to grow stronger due to rapid population growth, a booming middle class, and exploding urbanization. Global megatrend projections show the dimensions of change. Less than 4 billion people inhabited the world in 1970. By 2050 that number will be more than 9 billion. An estimated 6.3 billion—practically 70 percent of the global population—will be living in cities (United Nations, 2014). The global middle class could triple, reaching nearly 5 billion people by 2030. Accordingly, demand for food, water, and energy is expected to grow drastically.

2. The report is available at http://reports.weforum.org/global-risks-2017/.

In order to sustain a larger, urbanized, and more prosperous global population, there is a need to reconcile our economic and social development with the health of our global commons. To "decouple" the impact of these megatrends, we must fundamentally transform our key economic systems. We need to change the systems that support how we live, how we eat, how we move, and how we produce and consume. In other words, four revolutionary shifts in social and economic life are needed: rethinking food and agriculture, decarbonizing energy systems, transforming cities, and investing in the circular economy.

Food and Agriculture System

Food and agriculture's impact on the global commons is extensive. Historically, the expansion of agriculture is a dominant driver of land-use change, nutrient pollution, and biodiversity loss. Currently, 37 percent of the Earth's landmass is used to produce food.[3] Agriculture accounts for 70 percent of freshwater consumption (Pimentel and others, 2004) and 24 percent of global greenhouse gas—GHG—emissions (Smith and others, 2014). It also contributes to land degradation through the overuse of fertilizers and pesticides.

The world will require about a 70 percent increase in food production to meet dietary demands from a world population of nine to 10 billion by 2050 (World Resources Institute, 2013)—and those of the approximately 700 million malnourished people today. Producing enough food in a sustainable way while dealing with land use and degradation will be essential. A concentrated focus on global commodities with a significant deforestation footprint, on food security goals in areas of rapid agriculture expansion, on restoration of fisheries, and to a certain extent, on expanded efforts on land restoration will contribute significant environmental gains while reversing the negative effects of land and coastal habitat degradation.

Energy System

Decarbonization of the global energy system is of critical importance for a 1.5–2°C future global temperature increase, in line with the Paris Agreement. The energy system represents 68 percent of global GHG emissions, and despite recent improvements, only 23 percent of energy is provided by renewables as of today (International Energy Agency, 2016); 1 billion people still lack access to electricity (United Nations, 2016c). By 2040 energy demand is projected to increase

---

3. For percent of land area used for agriculture, see https://data.worldbank.org/indicator/%20AG.LND.AGRI.ZS.

by 30 percent (International Energy Agency, 2016). In the face of these trends, deployment of renewable energy needs to accelerate sharply, as do energy efficiency improvements, all while increased energy demand is being met—including from what is needed to close the electricity gap, especially in sub-Saharan Africa and South Asia. As suggested recently by Rockström, carbon emissions must peak no later than 2020, and we must reach a fossil fuel–free world economy by 2050 to avoid catastrophic consequences (Rockström, 2017).

Cities and Urban System

During the coming decades, the planet will face the largest and fastest urban growth in human history. In the next fifteen years, 70 percent of new infrastructure will be built in urban areas (United Nations, 2014). Currently, cities emit more than 70 percent of global GHGs (Seto and others, 2014) and are also particularly vulnerable to climate change (rising sea levels, storms, floods, heat waves). Low-carbon and resilient infrastructure could make a significant contribution to the global reduction of GHG emissions, while enhancing urban development. Such investments could generate annual GHG savings of 3.7 gigatons (Gt) by 2030, a significant share (perhaps 15 to 20 percent) of the overall contributions to the Paris Agreement (New Climate Economy, 2015). Also, low-carbon infrastructure—particularly in the buildings-efficiency, public transportation, and waste-management sectors—could save cities an estimated U.S. $17 trillion globally by 2050 (New Climate Economy, 2016).

Rapidly growing cities will need to make room to accommodate their urban populations and their increasing demands for electricity networks, sanitation systems and sewers, public transit, new housing, and waste management, among other large-scale projects. As evidence shows, when cities grow in population and wealth, they expand in area as well (Angel and others, 2016). How cities plan their land use, design, and new infrastructure will determine their share and contribution to the global sustainability efforts. Their potential is large.

Circular Economy (Global Production/Consumption System)

Today's economies are dominated by linear approaches to the way products are manufactured, used, and disposed. As a consequence, the rates of extraction of natural resources—such as industrial and construction minerals, fossil fuels, biomass (from agriculture, forestry, and fishery), and metal ores—have expanded quickly. In the last four decades, global materials use has tripled, from 23.7 billion tonnes in 1970 to 70.1 billion tonnes in 2010 (United Nations, 2016b). What results from our linear "take-make-waste" industrial production and consumption systems is immensely unsustainable material resource use and accumulation of waste and toxic materials in the environment.

A circular economy framework offers a more sustainable alternative. The objective is to keep resources in the economy for as long as possible. "Circular economy" refers to the decoupling of economic growth from the extraction and consumption of constrained natural resources such as fossil fuels, metals, and minerals (Lacy and Rutqvist, 2015). By designing out waste from products, increasing sharing business models, and changing behavior of consumers and companies, we can make a more long-lasting use of our limited natural resources.

A Systems Approach Is Needed

Environmental challenges are connected and interdependent within themselves and are linked with social and economic issues. Solutions for one environmental problem could lead to unintended negative consequences or create new environmental or socioeconomic challenges. Moreover, science has shown us that it is possible to have synergistic solutions that can help solve two or more environmental challenges. For example, actions to mitigate climate pollutants will help mitigate global warming while also providing health, agricultural productivity (and thus food security), as well as economic benefits (Scientific and Technical Advisory Panel, 2017).

A common element in each of the four systems identified above as being in need of transformational change is that they are indeed complex systems with multiple interactions and interconnections across various levels and scales. Understanding them with a view to change is best done through application of systems thinking (Arnold and Wade, 2015).

As has been highlighted in recent scientific literature (Scientific and Technical Advisory Panel, 2017), the application of systems integration methods can assist in bringing together different environmental objectives in a more holistic approach to planning and management and deliver multiple benefits. It can also assist in enhancing synergy while managing trade-offs across scales (local, subnational, and national) and sectors (for example, increasing food production without degrading land, increasing greenhouse gas emissions, or polluting water resources). Systems integration methods can also untangle complexity between interactions, so that root causes can be identified and managed through focused interventions, while also anticipating feedbacks and building resilience.

Systems thinking has many definitions but can be boiled down to a few concepts. Systems are bounded by what is needed to achieve a given purpose. In a world where many things are connected to each other, it is tempting to overdefine systems and incorporate many elements. The risk is that this results in a degree of complexity that inhibits action. A well-designed systems approach narrows the field to include only a subset of elements and relationships that are required to achieve a given objective.

Because Agenda 2030 has laid out a consensus for goals and targets that are shared by all governments and that provide a focus for nonstate actors, it is conducive to systems thinking. For each of the four systems described, the actual objective is well specified in the SDGs, permitting the purpose of each system to be described and quantified in a way that is acceptable to all potential actors in the system.

Another feature of systems thinking is that it starts by considering the system structure—the way in which different components interact with each other. In the case of economic systems, this system structure includes the price, tax/subsidy, and regulatory incentives that guide private actors—both businesses and consumers—and the bureaucratic processes (and civil service incentives) that determine government interventions (Hasnain, Manning, and Pierskalla, 2014).

In each of the four economic systems mentioned earlier, it is clear that a major market failure has been the zero pricing of environmental externalities. A carbon price is the obvious economic answer, but an explicit price faces practical issues with implementation in many country situations. The reality is that 85 percent of global emissions come from countries where carbon is currently not priced at all. Nevertheless, even in the absence of an actual carbon price, it is possible to simulate the effect through other instruments, including cap-and-trade systems, carbon markets, and shadow pricing of carbon in public investments. The key is to arrive at an appropriate "shadow" price.

This has been the subject of work by the High-Level Commission on Carbon Prices, a group of experts on economics, climate change, and energy that was tasked at the 2016 United Nations Climate Change Conference (COP22) meetings in Marrakech to identify indicative corridors of carbon prices. The commission concluded that the explicit carbon-price level consistent with achieving the Paris targets for climate change is at least $40–80/tCO2 by 2020 and 25 percent higher by 2030 (Stiglitz and others, 2017). Price levels within this corridor would give incentives for innovating with technology, help introduce new business models, stimulate learning, and minimize adjustment costs.

Other dimensions of sustainability are also not properly valued. As Ahmad and Viscarra (2016) show, an economy-wide set of shadow prices reflecting spatial and income inequalities can be used to identify priorities for public investments. Simply managing public investments well, in the sense of implementing effectively, is necessary but not sufficient for sustainability. When the investments help improve connectivity and integration across space, they only yield maximum benefit when complemented by appropriate tax regimes that create the right incentives for private business. Absent this, spatial interventions can even worsen inequality by lowering the cost of movement from lagging areas to more efficient urban hubs. The feedback loop in the systems approach can help policymakers identify whether a public intervention is generating the right kind of change or if it is worsening existing problems.

Each of the four systems display significant nonlinearities. They are subject to tipping points. For example, when value chains in a particular commodity take hold in a country, many producers and cooperatives are able to join; the value chain gets strengthened by these numbers and sustainable growth occurs. But getting the value chain started can be difficult because quality control, guaranteed supplies, storage and logistics, and other parts of the system are underdeveloped and costly. As another example on the energy side, the demand for electric cars will only take off once charging stations become ubiquitous.

Large-scale systems, like the ones identified above, operate on many different levels: global, national, and subnational. The action on the ground is often at the subnational level. Think of land use or city development. But the scope for such actions depends importantly on actions at the national level (the policy and enabling environment and often large-scale public investments) and even at the global level where knowledge-sharing partnerships and other mechanisms for understanding systems can accelerate the pace of innovation and learning.

Understanding these core features of a systems approach helps to determine how to build a multistakeholder coalition, the actionable tool that is most likely to drive the transformation that is needed. This is discussed in the next section.

An Action Path: Building Multistakeholder Coalitions to Safeguard Our Global Commons

To trigger transformational changes in each of the four key economic systems is far from easy, because the very nature of the global environmental commons—as mentioned above—suffers from the tragedy of the commons: natural capital is not monetized, and perverse incentives are embedded in current economic systems. Moreover, a key factor that distinguishes environmental problems is that they are inevitably tied to the complex structures and processes of boundary-spanning ecosystems (Bodin, 2017).

However, it is encouraging that in the past few years a proliferation of coalitions among stakeholders from governments and international institutions, business, academics, and CSOs have formed to solve environmental problems. The number of such coalitions suggest that leaders of these institutions believe that they can be triggers to achieve the needed system change (Steer and others, 2016). For the most part, these coalitions are horizontal and cut across the traditional boundaries of interest, expertise, and nationality. Their defining feature is that they are characterized by goals and objectives.

By building multistakeholder coalitions around common principles, commitments, and targets, we can accelerate change in our economic systems. Through multistakeholder coalitions, we can create platforms that convene multiple actors to jointly overcome obstacles. Such an effort is critical to change the prevailing incentive structure and to create critical mass moving beyond tipping points.

The benefits of collective leadership are increasingly being recognized in the efforts to address global challenges. These have encouraged the private sector and civil society organizations to play a prominent role at, and following, the Rio+20 Conference on Sustainable Development in 2012. Additionally, the global results achieved by the Lima-Paris Action Agenda for Climate Change are also due to the active participation of nongovernmental actors such as cities, civil society, indigenous peoples, and the private sector.

It is worthwhile mentioning a few examples of multistakeholder coalitions that are particularly relevant to safeguarding the global commons.

In food and agriculture systems, there has been a flowering of new initiatives with at least twenty major entities created since 2008 (Kharas and others, 2014). For instance, the Tropical Forest Alliance 2020 (TFA, 2020) is a global umbrella partnership that brings together governments and private sector and civil society organizations to eliminate deforestation practices in the production of palm oil, beef, soy, pulp, and paper by 2020. As global supply chains involve a large and complex variety of actors, TFA is comprised of companies, traders and producers, developing nation governments, donors, NGOs, and indigenous peoples groups working together as a community of purpose on this collective goal. TFA 2020 aims to collaboratively improve planning and management related to tropical forest conservation, agricultural land use, and land tenure. Also, TFA aims to share best practices for tropical forest and ecosystem conservation and commodity production.[4]

Another interesting example of a multistakeholder coalition emerges in the area of the circular economy. The New Plastics Economy (NPE) is a three-year initiative to build momentum toward a sustainable plastics system. Applying the principles of the circular economy, the initiative brings together key stakeholders to rethink and redesign the future of plastics, starting with packaging. NPE is led by the Ellen MacArthur Foundation in collaboration with a broad group of leading companies, cities, philanthropists, policymakers, academics, students, NGOs, and citizens. The initiative aims to 1) create a shared direction, 2) spark innovation, and 3) move the plastics value chain into a positive spiral of value capture, stronger economics, and better environmental outcomes.[5]

---

4. Objectives of the Tropical Forest Alliance, see www.tfa2020.org/en/about-tfa/objectives/.
5. About the New Plastics Economy, see https://newplasticseconomy.org/about.

Through a cross-value chain collaboration, NPE brings together global consumer goods companies, retailers, plastic producers and packaging manufacturers, cities, and businesses involved in collecting, sorting, and reprocessing to drive collaborative demonstration projects and shape the initiative.

In the area of city systems, the C40 Cities Climate Leadership Group (C40) is a network of the world's megacities committed to addressing climate change.[6] The group supports cities to collaborate, share knowledge, and drive effective action on climate change. Connecting more than eighty of the world's largest cities, representing over 600 million people and one-quarter of the global economy, C40 has had a global impact in reducing both greenhouse gases emissions and climate risks and brings together a unique set of assets, while creating shared purpose. For example, C40's "Deadline 2020" maps routes to transform the Paris Agreement aspirations to the city level. It outlines a set of specific common actions to be delivered by C40 cities by 2020. Beside cities, C40 is a forum for all actors, including international organizations, the private sector, think tanks, and financial institutions, to work collaboratively to bring about change in the world's largest cities.

Taking Charge of Multistakeholder Coalitions

The examples above of a new and growing generation of partnerships show that there is a demand for action and a willingness among key actors to engage. The question, however, is whether the system will self-adjust, as more and more players join, or if more needs to be done. Given the urgency of the situation, a more proactive stance is needed at a minimum in the following areas:

1. Set goals and targets for each system. For food and agriculture systems, outcome indicators in the SDGs are mostly well developed (United Nations, 2016b), although actual metrics continue to be a challenge to compile. For example, indicator 2.3.1 calls for productivity data by farm size, and indicator 2.3.2 calls for measures of the average income of small-scale producers, but neither indicator is currently available on a global scale. Similarly, for energy, there are well-developed indicators, but some, such as 7.a.1 ("mobilized amount of USD per year accountable towards the $100 billion commitment"), are not yet well defined. For cities and the circular economy (Goals 11 and 12), the suggested indicators are far more vague with considerable scope for judgment. Examples include "proportion of population that has convenient access to public transport"; "the global food loss index"; and "number of countries implementing sustainable public procurement." In these examples, work remains to define terms such as "convenient," "food loss," and "sustainable procurement." The point is, simply, that without more specific

6. About C40 Cities Climate Leadership Group, see www.c40.org/about.

work on these metrics, it is impossible for multistakeholder coalitions to form themselves into vehicles for overall system change.

2. Generate the right incentives. A recurring theme is that incentives for both the public sector and for private business are currently misaligned. Governments in the multistakeholder coalitions have yet to take on responsibility for putting in place the range of implicit shadow prices discussed above. Some countries, like Chile, have a system of national investment where environmental, social, and governance considerations affect public investment choices. Most governments, however, do not, and international organizations are not propagating such methods. Meanwhile, business responsibilities for sustainable production are also unclear. In certain areas, such as the Principles for Responsible Investment in Agriculture and Food Systems (Food and Agriculture Organization, 2014) and the New York Declaration on Forests (2016), global norms have been spelled out.[7] But in most areas, norms remain weak and underdeveloped. Additionally, in most developing countries, business investments are primarily financed by banks. The criteria banks use to judge risk, therefore, and the way they are required to set aside capital by regulators can affect the cost of capital and hence the composition of investment. As Kharas and McArthur (2016) show, reorienting private investment toward more sustainable practices is critical to generating the volume of sustainable production that is needed to reach scale.

3. Enhance disclosure and transparency both in private and public sectors. Authorities in several countries are starting to require large companies to disclose material nonfinancial aspects of their operations, including such items as carbon emissions, use of natural resources, and social indicators like gender equity in pay and benefits. Disclosure, by itself, may be necessary but not sufficient to drive behavioral change in firms. But if institutional and other investors start to use sustainability comparisons to drive their allocations, then firms will have an incentive to pay more attention to these issues. Moreover, in the public sector there is also an emerging recognition that transparency is fundamental to achieve global sustainability goals. For instance, as part of the Paris Agreement, all countries agreed to an enhanced transparency framework for action and support and therefore agreed to establish an initiative to strengthen the institutional and technical capacities of developing countries to meet the enhanced transparency requirements of the Paris Agreement.[8] The information reported under this enhanced transparency

7. See http://forestdeclaration.org/summary/.
8. See more on this initiative at www.thegef.org/topics/capacity-building-initiative-transparency-cbit.

framework will inform the global inventory to assess collective progress toward achieving the purpose of the agreement.

The point being made is that multistakeholder coalitions that are narrowly focused on specific topic areas, as is the case now, will not be enough to achieve scaled-up transformations in the key systems identified in this chapter. More far-reaching changes are also required. One way of encouraging these changes is to systematically organize multistakeholder coalitions at the global and national level that address the issues of large-scale system change. These coalitions should be addressing questions such as are governments orienting their investments so as to encourage sustainable development by using tools and metrics to build sustainable national investment plans; are regulators requiring banks to consider sustainability practices when evaluating business risk; and are corporates providing adequate information on their sustainability practices to allow investors and consumers to judge whether to support them.

Conclusion

For too long, the world economy has operated under two parallel systems. Our planetary system provides foundational services of clean air, habitable temperatures, fresh water, and nutrient rich soil. Our economic system attempts to provide wealth and prosperity to a growing number of people. For centuries, these systems have successfully cooperated without much disruption, and our approaches to managing the one in relation to the other have accordingly also been separate. But today, the connections are too tight. We cannot operate two systems independently. We must develop mechanisms for integrating the two.

Our planetary systems that support life on Earth are facing a downward spiral of environmental degradation. The window of opportunity is narrow and we need to act urgently. Incremental changes are not enough. We need a radical transformation of key economic structures: the food and agriculture system, the cities and urban system, the energy system, and the production/consumption system. These arrangements have the largest impact on our global commons, and therefore they also offer the highest potential for change.

Nonetheless, designing and implementing transformative solutions that achieve the leverage to cause transformative change is not a simple task. There are structural barriers that explain why our economic systems operate in the way they do. Our market and political frameworks are attached to the idea of constant growth and short-term gains. Our global commons are subject to the classic tragedy of the commons, where individual behaviors lead to overuse and degradation. Our natural resources and the services they provide are not valued in monetary terms. Prices of products and services do not reflect the negative externalities on the environment, and business models do not concern themselves with the associated costs of pollution, degradation, or waste.

This chapter suggests that multistakeholder coalitions can be an effective tool to devise and implement solutions that catalyze transformational change in our key economic systems. By designing solutions from a "system view," where every actor is involved, we can achieve a larger impact and leverage the comparative advantage of every actor for the same common objectives. Also, multistakeholder coalitions facilitate synchronization of efforts, collaboration, and bold action where all actors committed go forward at the same time to multiply our chances of success. Only through the combined effort of a wide range of stakeholders—from local to national governments, from entrepreneurs to large private corporations, from the financial institutions to the multilateral organizations and from NGOs and academia to civil society—can we achieve the scale and speed we need to safeguard our global commons before the window of opportunity is closed.

Building multistakeholder coalitions is not an easy process. It requires every participant to move out of their comfort zone under current incentive systems. It requires consultation, negotiation, and a shared long-term view. Once the coalition is designed, it is crucial to keep actors working together and to monitor progress and results. By leveraging the comparative advantage of every stakeholder and strengthening and fostering collaboration, we can achieve larger and more transformative results than if we were to act independently. As the old Sufi proverb says: "The behavior of a system cannot be known just by knowing the elements of which the system is made."

Multistakeholder coalitions are emerging across different dimensions of the economy—global, regional, national, and local—and are leading to new public-private alliances, disruptive innovation, new investment flows, and civil society engagement. While each of these multi-actor activities may be specific to an issue, sector, or place, in aggregate the sum impact of these initiatives is disruption and a redefinition of the way our economic systems interact and how we use, protect, and manage our global commons (Steer and others, 2016). Topic-specific multistakeholder coalitions will only be able to work if their activities are supported by processes that support a change towards sustainable systems.

But we need higher-level coalitions to succeed, ones that address the basic incentives that drive government and business investments. We need organizations that combine protection of the planet's health with expansion of economic opportunities. Such organizations can bring together others in a multistakeholder coalition for sustainability to build political support for deep-seated change.

References

Ahmad, E., and H. Viscarra. 2016. "Public Investment for Sustainable Development in Chile." IDB Discussion Paper IDB-DP-469. Washington: Inter-American Development Bank (https://publications.iadb.org/bitstream/handle/11319/7842/Public-Investment-for-Sustainable-Development-in-Chile-Building-on-the-National-Investment-System.pdf?sequence=1&isAllowed=y).

Angel, S., A. Blei, P. Lamson-Hall, N. Galarza Sanchez, P. Gopalan, A. Kallergis, D. L. Covco, S. Kumar, M. Madrid, S. Shingade, and J. D. Hurd Jr. 2016. "Atlas of Urban Expansion." New York: New York University, Lincoln Institute of Land and Policy, and UN Habitat (www.atlasofurbanexpansion.org/data).

Arnold, Ross D., and Jon P. Wade. 2015. "A Definition of Systems Thinking: A Systems Approach." *Procedia Computer Science* 44: 669–78.

Bodin, Orjan. 2017. "Collaborative Environmental Governance: Achieving Collective Action in Social-Ecological Systems." *Science* 357, no. 6352 (August 18) (http://science.sciencemag.org/content/357/6352/eaan1114).

Food and Agriculture Organization. 2014. "Principles for Responsible Investment in Agriculture and Food Systems." Rome: Committee on Food Security, FAO.

Hasnain, Z., N. Manning, and J. H. Pierskalla. 2014. "The Promise of Performance Pay? Reasons for Caution in Policy Prescriptions in the Core Civil Service." World Bank Research Observer 29, no. 2 (August 1) (https://doi.org/10.1093/wbro/lku001).

International Energy Agency. 2016. "World Energy Outlook 2016." Summary (www.iea.org/newsroom/news/2016/november/world-energy-outlook-2016.html).

Kharas, H., and J. McArthur. 2016. "Links in the Chain of Sustainable Finance." Global Views, No. 5. Washington: Global Economy and Development, Brookings Institution.

Kharas, H., J. McArthur, G. Gertz, S. Mowlds, and L. Noe. 2014. "Ending Rural Hunger: Mapping Needs and Actions for Food and Nutrition Security." Washington: Global Economy and Development, Brookings Institution (https://assets.contentful.com/5faekfvmlu40/3QhEcuQRO8OACqIWKMi6CK/cd474f0e01a1170a07581346597666d9/ERH_Full_Report.pdf).

New Climate Economy. 2015. "Accelerating Low-Carbon Development in the World's Cities." Working Paper (http://newclimateeconomy.report/workingpapers/wp-content/uploads/sites/5/2016/04/NCE2015_workingpaper_cities_final_web.pdf).

New Climate Economy. 2016. "The Sustainable Infrastructure Imperative" (http://newclimateeconomy.report/2016/wp-content/uploads/sites/4/2014/08/NCE_2016Report.pdf).

Lacy, P., and J. Rutqvist. 2015. *Waste to Wealth: The Circular Economy Advantage*. Basingstoke, Hampshire, UK: Palgrave MacMillan.

New York Declaration on Forests. 2016. New York: United Nations Climate Summit.

Pimentel, D., B. Berger, D. Filiberto, M. Newton, B. Wolfe, E. Karabinakis, S. Clark, E. Poon, E. Abbett, and S. Nandagopal. 2004. "Water Resources: Agricultural and Environmental Issues." *BioScience* 54, no. 10 (October 1): 909–18 (https://academic.oup.com/bioscience/article/54/10/909-918/230205).

Rockström, J. 2017. "Why the World Economy Needs to Be Carbon Free by 2050." *New York Times*, March 23.

Rockström, J., W. Steffen, K. Noone, A. Persson, F. S. Chapin, E. F. Lambin, T. M. Lenton, M. Scheffer, C. Folke, H. J. Schellnhuber, B. Nykvist, C. A. de Wit, T. Hughers, S. van der Leeuw, H. Rodhe, S. Sörlin, P. K. Snyder, R. Costanza, U. Svedin, M. Falkenmark, L. Karlberg, R. W. Corell, V. J. Fabry, J. Hansen, B. Walker, D. Liverman, K. Richardson, P. Crutzen, and J. A. Foley. 2009. "A Safe Operating Space for Humanity." *Nature* 461: 472–75.

Scientific and Technical Advisory Panel (STAP). 2017. "Why the Scientific Community Is Moving toward Integration of Environmental, Social, and Economic Issues to Solve Complicated Problems." Working Paper. Washington: Global Environment Facility. October (www.thegef.org/council-meeting-documents/draft-stap-working-paper-why-scientific-community-moving-toward).

Seto, K. C., S. Dhakal, A. Bigio, H. Blanco, G. C. Delgado, D. Dewar, L. Huang, A. Inaba, A. Kansal, S. Lwasa, J. E. McMahon, D. B. Müller, J. Murakami, H. Nagendra, and A. Ramaswami. 2014. "Human Settlements, Infrastructure and Spatial Planning." In *Climate Change 2014: Mitigation of Climate Change. Contribution of Working Group III to the Fifth Assessment Report of the Intergovernmental Panel on Climate Change*, edited by O. Edenhofer, R. Pichs-Madruga, Y. Sokona, E. Farahani, S. Kadner, K. Seyboth, A. Adler, I. Baum, S. Brunner, P. Eickemeier, B. Kriemann, J. Savolainen, S. Schlömer, C. von Stechow, T. Zwickel, and J. C. Minx. Cambridge University Press (www.ipcc.ch/pdf/assessment-report/ar5/wg3/ipcc_wg3_ar5_chapter12.pdf).

Smith, P., M. Bustamante, H. Ahammad, H. Clark, H. Dong, E. A. Elsiddig, H. Haberl, R. Harper, J. House, M. Jafari, O. Masera, C. Mbow, N. H. Ravindranath, C. W. Rice, C. Robledo Abad, A. Romanovskaya, F. Sperling, and F. Tubiello, 2014. "Agriculture, Forestry and Other Land Use (AFOLU)." In *Climate Change 2014: Mitigation of Climate Change. Contribution of Working Group III to the Fifth Assessment Report of the Intergovernmental Panel on Climate Change*, edited by O. Edenhofer, R. Pichs-Madruga, Y. Sokona, E. Farahani, S. Kadner, K. Seyboth, A. Adler, I. Baum, S. Brunner, P. Eickemeier, B. Kriemann, J. Savolainen, S. Schlömer, C. von Stechow, T. Zwickel, and J. C. Minx. Cambridge University Press (www.ipcc.ch/pdf/assessment-report/ar5/wg3/ipcc_wg3_ar5_chapter11.pdf)

Steffen, W., K. Richardson, J. Rockström, S. E. Cornell, I. Fetzer, E. M. Bennett, R. Biggs, S. R. Carpenter, W. de Vries, C. A. de Wit, C. Folke, D. Gerten, J. Heinke, G. M. Mace, L. M. Persson, V. Ramanathan, B. Reyers, and S. Sörlin. 2015. "Planetary Boundaries: Guiding Human Development on a Changing Planet." *Science* 347, no. 6223 (accessible at DOI: 10.1126/science.1259855).

Steer, A., D. Waughray, G. Ellison, M. McGregor. 2016. "The Great Decoupling: Our Human Economic Footprint and the Global Environmental Commons." Gland, Switzerland: International Union for Conservation of Nature. October (www.iucn.org/sites/dev/files/the_great_decoupling_10_10_16.pdf).

Stiglitz, Joseph E., and others. 2017. "Report of the High-Level Commission on Carbon Prices." Carbon Prices Leadership Coalition. May 29 (https://static1.squarespace.com/static/54ff9c5ce4b0a53decccfb4c/t/59244eed17bffc0ac256cf16/1495551740633/CarbonPricing_Final_May29.pdf).

United Nations. 2014. "World Urbanization Prospects: The 2014 Revision, Highlights" (ST/ESA/SER.A/352). Department of Economic and Social Affairs, Population Division (https://esa.un.org/unpd/wup/Publications/Files/WUP2014-Highlights.pdf).

United Nations. 2015. "Transforming Our World: The 2030 Agenda for Sustainable Development." Resolution adopted by the General Assembly on September 25 (www.un.org/ga/search/view_doc.asp?symbol=A/RES/70/1&Lang=E).

United Nations. 2016a. "Global Material Flows and Resource Productivity." Environment Program (http://web.unep.org/documents/irp/16-00271_LW_GlobalMaterial-FlowsUNE_SUMMARY_FINAL_160701.pdf).

United Nations. 2016b. "Report of the Inter-Agency and Expert Group on Sustainable Development Goal Indicators (E/CN.3/2016/2/Rev.1). Annex IV."

United Nations. 2016c. "Affordable and Clean Energy: Why It Matters" (www.un.org/sustainabledevelopment/wp-content/uploads/2016/08/7_Why-it-Matters_Goal-7_CleanEnergy_2p.pdf).

World Resources Institute. 2013. "Creating a Sustainable Food Future. World Resources Report 2013–2014: Interim Findings" (www.wri.org/sites/default/files/wri13_report_4c_wrr_online.pdf).

CHAPTER FIFTEEN

Unity in Diversity
Reshaping the Global Health Architecture

Ikuo Takizawa

To promote healthy lives and "well-being for all, at all ages," the third of the Sustainable Development Goals includes targets that are challenging for many countries. Making progress in this regard, therefore, will require globally coordinated efforts while respecting the legitimacy of the national governments and autonomy of the various actors involved. It will require, in other words, a global architecture that can address new challenges to health while managing differences, or *unity in diversity*, between players.

SDG 3 comprises a diverse set of targets. Four of the targets are essentially extensions of Millennium Development Goals focusing on maternal health (target 3.1), newborn and child health (target 3.2), infectious diseases (target 3.3), and reproductive health (target 3.7). To these longstanding agendas, new targets were added for noncommunicable diseases (target 3.4), substance abuse (target 3.5), traffic accidents (target 3.6), illnesses from hazardous chemicals and environmental pollution (target 3.9), and universal health coverage (target 3.8).

The constellation of players is diverse. Aside from national governments, a number of other transnational actors are associated with each target. In addition to the World Health Organization (WHO)—the only organization designated for health matters in the UN system—other specialized United Nations agencies such as the UN Population Fund (UNFPA) (targets 3.1 and 3.7), the UN Children's Fund (UNICEF) (targets 3.1 and 3.2), and the Joint United Nations Program on HIV and AIDS (UNAIDS) (target 3.3) are involved. Organizations created to mobilize resources for specific health issues include Gavi, the Vaccine Alliance (target 3.2), and the Global Fund to Fight AIDS, Tuberculosis and Malaria (the Global Fund) (target 3.3). The World Bank and other multilateral development banks also play an important role as a major source of global health financing, as do private philanthropic organizations—notably the Bill & Melinda Gates Foundation.[1] Many donor countries, such as Canada, France, Germany, Japan, Norway, the United Kingdom, and the United States, are contributing significantly to global health, through both multilateral and bilateral channels (Dieleman and others, 2016). Non-OECD donors, international NGOs, and a variety of private sector organizations and corporations, finally, round out the lengthening list of actors increasingly engaged in global health.

Meeting the challenges in achieving the 2030 targets will require a renewed effort to resolve coordination problems across governments and transnational actors so that the international health community can reconcile diverse agendas and constituencies in order to improve the global governance of health. This chapter reviews the global efforts to promote collective actions for health in recent years and identifies three thematic areas, namely, health security; reproductive, maternal, neonatal, child, and adolescent health; and universal health coverage, for which extensive mobilization at the global level is being pursued through global health initiatives. This chapter seeks to identify—however preliminarily—a set of criteria by which the activities of existing alliances, partnerships, and other international health regimes can be evaluated for a better global collective action for health under the SDGs.

Global Health Governance

Governance in general is defined as the actions and means adopted by a society to promote collective action and deliver collective solutions in pursuit of common goals (Dodgson, Lee, and Drager, 2002). A central question to the study of global governance is how to deal with issues that require concerted behaviors of both state and nonstate actors transcending national governments while respecting the legitimacy of those governments as well as the autonomy of various public and private actors. The Commission on Global Governance in 1995 defined global governance as the "sum of the many ways individuals and institutions, public and private, manage their common affairs. It is a continuing process through which conflicting or diverse interests may be accommodated and co-operative action may be taken. It includes formal institutions and regimes empowered to enforce

---

1. These health-related international organizations (WHO, UNICEF, UNFPA, UNAIDS, Global Fund, Gavi, Gates Foundation, and the World Bank) organized themselves into an informal group called Health 8 (H8) in 2007 to stimulate a global sense of urgency in achieving the health-related MDGs through better ways of working together and robust knowledge management. H6 formed around the health of women, children, and adolescents by UNAIDS, UNFPA, UNICEF, UN Women, WHO, and the World Bank Group.

compliance, as well as informal arrangements that people and institutions either have agreed to or perceive to be in their interest."

Global governance for health has emerged as an area for policy analysis, as decisions affecting population health are increasingly made beyond the borders of national governments and national health systems (Kickbusch, Marianna, and Szabo, 2014; Frenk and Moon, 2013). Fidler (2010) defines global health governance as the "use of formal and informal institutions, rules, and processes by states, intergovernmental organizations, and non-state actors to deal with challenges to health that require cross-border collective action to address effectively."

In recent years two phenomena have catalyzed growing interest in the global health governance. First, global health initiatives have proliferated since 2000, many of which were created as the platforms to coordinate the actions of a large number of players in specific health areas (WHO Maximizing Positive Synergies Collaborative Group, 2009; Hoffman, Cole, and Pearcey, 2015).[2] Prompted by the Millennium Development Goals, many of these initiatives were undertaken by organizations with dedicated funding mechanisms (such as Gavi and the Global Fund) that have emerged as influential actors. Others were a result of looser, voluntary networks of member countries and organizations connected by shared visions or principles, typically with a relatively small secretariat often hosted by an existing international organization such as the WHO and the World Bank. Second, recent epidemics—SARS, H1N1, Ebola, MERS, and Zika—have highlighted the shortcomings of the existing system of transnational health governance in preventing some infectious diseases from spreading across borders. The Ebola outbreak of 2013–16 in West Africa, for example, claimed the lives of more than 11,000 people across the three hardest-hit countries and spread as far as Italy, Spain, the United Kingdom, and the United States (Undurraga and others, 2017). The growth in global health initiatives with an intention to promote collective actions for specific health issues—coupled with the inability of the world to mitigate transnational threats to health security through globally coordinated efforts—prompted a new debate over the effectiveness of the global architecture for health, as well as its capacity to address global public health crises (Bill & Melinda Gates Foundation and McKinsey & Company, 2005; WHO Maximizing Positive Synergies Collaborative Group, 2009; Mackey, 2016; Global Health Working Group, 2016).

There is, consequently, a continuing need to revise the structures of global governance that affect health in light of new global targets, changing disease

2. They are also called global health partnerships and may be considered as a form of public-private partnership. Some have solid organizational structure and funding sources, but many are looser, voluntary networks of member countries and organizations.

burdens, and funding constraints. An important step in this regard is a better global health architecture that is able to coordinate responses, policies, and decisions across countries.

The Governance of Global Health: A Recent History

The global commitment to the Millennium Development Goals coincided with a growing recognition that global health systems of the past, in which nation-states had been the primary actors, were ill equipped to deal effectively with some current global health issues. Intensified cross-border health risks, a growth in the number and degree of influence of nonstate actors in health governance, along with the need for greater financing to sustain health care for aging populations—all served to highlight the often-limited capacity of national governments to care for the health of their citizens (Dodgson, Lee, and Drager, 2002).

The ability of international institutions to fight diseases has also been hindered by their fragmentation. Growing discontent with the conventional *inter-national* governance for global health issues, together with the growing body of evidence on a set of cost-effective interventions, increased funding commitments not only from donor countries but also from private philanthropic organizations, and increased engagement of the private sector, has created new momentum for global health initiatives involving multiple partners, which numbers around 100 (WHO Maximizing Positive Synergies Collaborative Group, 2009).

Proliferation of new global health initiatives yielded two important changes in global health governance. First, some of the recent global health initiatives instituted more inclusive models of governance (Szlezak and others, 2010). One of the most successful initiatives established in the MDG era after 2000, the Global Fund, channeled some U.S. $3.3 billion to developing countries, representing 9 percent of total development financing for health disbursed in 2015 (Dieleman and others, 2016). The Global Fund's board has twenty voting members, with equal representation by both funders and implementers. Civil societies including NGOs and communities affected by HIV/AIDS, tuberculosis, and malaria, along with private foundations and the private sector, are also represented. The representatives of the partner organizations, including the WHO and the World Bank, participate in the board as nonvoting members. Inclusive governance is also ensured at the country level through country coordination mechanisms. Gavi, which channeled U.S. $1.6 billion in 2015, or 4 percent of total development assistance for health (Dieleman and others, 2016), has a similar board composition: out of twenty-seven seats, ten are equally allocated to both recipient and donor countries, and nine are for nonaffiliated independent individuals. The rest are allocated to partner institutions such as WHO, UNICEF, World Bank, Gates

Foundation, civil society organizations, research and technology institutions, and players in the vaccine industry. As with the Global Fund, Gavi's inclusivity in terms of its country operations is ensured through an interagency coordination committee. There are positive lessons we can learn from this new style of governance, even though they are adding another layer of planning and monitoring associated with the funded programs at the country level.

Second, creation of new global health initiatives has resulted in the mobilization of greater resources around globally agreed health goals. Overall development assistance for health between 1990 and 2015 increased fivefold, from U.S. $7.2 billion to U.S. $36.4 billion, while financing for MDG health targets increased eightfold, from U.S. $3.2 billion to U.S. $25.4 billion in real terms, resulting in an increase in the share of the total from 43.7 percent to 70.1 percent (Dieleman and others, 2016). A significant portion of these increased funds are spent to scale up the proven and selective interventions associated with certain health goals. These global health initiatives made a significant impact in improving the health of the people, even though its predictability and sustainability is often questioned (Dodd and Lane, 2010).

The increase in global financing for health over a relatively short period also had unintended consequences. As the number of initiatives proliferated, and as their resources grew, the potential areas of duplication and overlap also increased. There is evidence, moreover, that the presence of global health initiatives created its own distortions: agenda setting and resource allocation, for example, would skew in the direction of these initiatives as domestic health-sector actors began to chase international funding, resulting in imbalances in the development of health systems in recipient countries. Indeed, the proliferation of initiatives is perceived by some as one of the major challenges in international development assistance for health (Action for Global Health, 2008; Sridhar, 2010).

The question of how much consolidation of existing global partnerships and initiatives is needed to reform the architecture for global health, and whether it is possible, is paramount. It may be the case that some rationalization of global initiatives is necessary to reduce transactions costs, duplication, distortion, and other inefficiencies. Without the presence of a strong gatekeeping function in the existing international institutions such as the WHO and its World Health Assembly, it is inevitable at least for the near future that global health initiatives will continue to be created as people see the need for collective action at the global level for specific health issues. It is imperative for countries and organizations, therefore, to recognize global health initiatives as an integral part of the global health architecture and to understand their implications, potential benefits, and costs.

Emerging International "Regimes" for Global Health

The current structure of global health governance with multiple initiatives resembles the depiction by Inada (2013) of the international development aid regime among a multitude of regimes. In the classic definition, international regimes are the "principles, norms, rules, and decision-making procedures around which actor expectations converge in a given issue-area," according to Krasner (1983). The global health initiatives can be systematically assessed by applying those factors of international regimes.

There are three issue areas in global health around which significant mobilization on a global scale is being pursued at the start of SDG era, through the creation of platforms for better coordination and collective actions among countries and development partners. These are (i) global health security; (ii) reproductive, maternal, newborn, child, and adolescent health; and (iii) universal health coverage.[3] It is essential for the low- and middle-income countries and other global health actors to know what these initiatives entail and what they can expect from them.

Health Security

The Global Health Security Agenda (GHSA) was launched in February 2014 by twenty-nine countries along with the WHO, the Food and Agriculture Organization (FAO), and the World Organization for Animal Health (OIE).[4] Since then, membership has expanded to sixty-two countries.[5] This was intended to become a multisectoral partnership, involving not just the health sector but specialized organizations and constituencies from agriculture and animal/livestock sectors, on the premise that epidemic preparedness requires coordinated actions across these sectors. Involvement of actors from the security sector, such as the participation of Interpol, is also a prominent feature of this partnership in order to prevent access of criminal organizations to dangerous pathogens and to mobilize

---

3. These are in addition to the preceding global mobilization around infectious disease control through the Global Fund and Gavi, which is not included in a detailed analysis here.

4. It is coordinated by a steering group made up of ten countries (Canada, Chile, Finland, India, Indonesia, Italy, Kenya, Kingdom of Saudi Arabia, Republic of Korea, United States), and eight international organizations as advisers (Permanent: WHO, FAO, OIE, and Cooperative: Interpol, African Union, European Union, Economic Community of West African States, World Bank Group). Finland and Indonesia played major roles in its establishment by hosting preparatory meetings and taking on the responsibility of steering group chair and the GHSA secretariat, together with the United States, which played the leading role, with President Obama hosting the 1st High Level Meeting at the White House and in obtaining endorsement from G-7 countries in Brussels.

5. See www.ghsagenda.org/members.

an interconnected global network that can respond effectively to limit the spread of infectious disease outbreaks.

GHSA can be perceived as a partnership formed around management of externalities.[6] The failure of a country to manage properly the outbreak of infectious diseases, and the failure to report such incidents to the global community, can pose significant transnational threats to other countries. These principles and norms are reflected in the stated purpose of the initiative as follows: 1) to advance a world safe and secure from infectious disease threats, 2) to bring together nations from all over the world to make new, concrete commitments, and 3) to elevate global health security as a national leaders-level priority.

Threats from infectious diseases are often considered threats to national security.[7] The nexus between national and health security is one of the oldest unifying norms in global health governance. In 1851 the first International Sanitary Conference was held in Paris to address quarantine practices and to help coordinate responses against outbreaks of infectious diseases (Dodgson, Lee, and Drager, 2002).

Health security is highly effective in mobilizing citizens and governments in the shadow of disease outbreaks, even though such mobilization can be short-lived when the memories of epidemics recede, often limiting the sustainability of global efforts to coordinate responses. International Health Regulations (IHR)—the set of principles that were guided by the Paris conference—were adopted in 1969 as a globally agreed framework to define WHO member countries' obligations for the control of the international spread of diseases. The World Health Assembly of the WHO called for its revision in 1995, but it was only after the SARS pandemic of 2003 that the revisions to IHR were completed in 2005 (WHO, 2008).

The revised rules stipulate a set of core capacities for the countries to equip themselves to prevent and combat outbreaks, with a time frame for fulfillment. Yet only two-thirds of the member countries complied.[8] Again, it was only after the Ebola outbreak that renewed attention turned to the shortcomings of rule

6. Frenk and Moon (2013) identified management of externalities across countries and mobilization of global solidarity as functions of global health systems, along with production of global public goods and stewardship, including consensus building and priority setting. Management of externalities and mobilization of global solidarity are two major norms that prompt collective actions for health and creation of global health partnerships. The production of global public goods is more relevant for R&D partnerships, while stewardship is relevant for all kinds.

7. The Global Health Security Initiative—established as an informal network of like-minded countries in 2001 based on the suggestion from the then U.S. secretary of health and human services after 9/11—has a clearer focus on the threats from infectious diseases on national security such as biological terrorism. Membership includes Canada, European Commission, France, Germany, Italy, Japan, Mexico, United Kingdom, United States, and WHO. The group continues to hold an annual health ministerial meeting.

8. This figure is from the self-reporting of each country; therefore, actual compliance could be much lower.

implementation. Recently, heightened awareness of vulnerabilities to health security have resulted in various attempts to improve global health governance for infectious disease control (Commission on a Global Health Risk Framework for the Future, 2016; Mackey, 2016; Moon and others, 2015; UN High-Level Panel on the Global Response to Health Crises, 2016). Whether the global community can maintain current political momentum to deliver envisioned changes in global health governance and country health systems remains to be seen.

Being a partnership built on voluntary membership, GHSA does not have, in a strict sense, rules and procedures with which participating members are obligated to comply. There are, still, several general guidelines for members, one of which is the prevent-detect-respond "Action Package," described as a five-year framework for joint action.[9] Member countries with adequate willingness and capacity are encouraged to choose the areas in which to lead the process either as lead or contributing countries.[10] Another common procedure is the Joint External Evaluation, developed as a tool for objective surveillance of countries' preparedness to meet IHR requirement and Action Package guidelines. The process involves self-assessment by the countries followed by external assessment by a group of international experts. By the beginning of 2018, sixty-eight countries have completed evaluations, and thirty-one more are in the pipeline.[11]

What does the establishment of GHSA imply to the existing international institutions responsible for global health security, namely, IHR and the WHO? The WHO, in particular, is the main, specialized health agency for health within the UN system and is charged with leading and coordinating global efforts to prevent and respond to infectious diseases. When it comes to preparedness, all WHO member countries are obligated to follow IHR based on Articles 21 and 22 of the WHO Constitution. That countries and organizations have fashioned a new framework for globally concerted actions regarding pandemics suggests a degree of discontent with the existing apparatus. Despite the WHO's participation in GHSA, there are legitimate concerns about duplication and inefficiency. More recently, GHSA has been framed as purely an initiative to promote capacity development of the countries in line with IHR so as to harmonize old and new regimes. The joint evaluation tool has also been revised in order to assess the

9. The three broad areas are "prevent" (antimicrobial resistance, zoonotic disease, biosafety and biosecurity, immunization), "detect" (national laboratory system, real-time surveillance, reporting, workforce development), and "respond" (emergency operations centers, linking public health with law and multisectoral rapid response, medical countermeasures, and personnel deployment).

10. Interestingly, non-OECD countries such as Georgia, Indonesia, Jordan, Kenya, Malaysia, Peru, South Africa, Thailand, and Vietnam have volunteered themselves to be a leading country in some of the Action Package areas. All participating countries are encouraged to come up with a five-year action plan at the country level, using the same framework as the Action Packages.

11. WHO Strategic Partnership Portal (https://extranet.who.int/spp/jee-dashboard).

whole spectrum of IHR compliance. Still, it is plausible that relationships between similar regimes will remain a source of occasional confusion in global health governance today.[12]

Women and Children

The UN–World Bank Global Financing Facility in Support of Every Woman Every Child (GFF) was launched in 2015 as a partnership for mobilization of global solidarity around reproductive, maternal, newborn, child, and adolescent health. It was established to accelerate global efforts to end preventable maternal and child deaths and improve the health and quality of life of women, children, and adolescents by 2030. Of the sixty-three eligible countries with high maternal and child mortality and substantial funding gaps, four were identified initially to receive direct support. By November 2017 the list of countries to receive direct support had expanded to twenty-six, still representing only 40 percent of all eligible countries. GFF launched replenishment, aiming to enroll fifty countries within five years.[13]

The health of mothers and children has always been at the center of global health, as seen in the promotion of the "Child Survival Revolution" in the 1980s and global mobilization around reproductive health in the International Conference on Population and Development in the 1990s. Significant inequality in the distribution of maternal and child health outcomes has been documented across groups within countries, and across countries, with the most vulnerable populations being the most adversely affected (Graham and others, 2016; Liu and others, 2016). A focus on mothers and children who suffer high mortality due to mostly preventable diseases is appealing to people across the political spectrum and regardless of sociocultural beliefs.[14] The unifying norm of the women-child health regime, therefore, is mobilization of global solidarity based on its appeal to equity, social justice, and human rights. In contrast to the global health security regime, management of externalities plays a limited role, even as some may link limited access to reproductive health services with issues of environmental degradation, vulnerability to disease transmission, or other spillovers.

---

12. One apparent complication is the increase in the number of international conferences on similar topics. One of the participants in a recent conference described it as an "epidemic of meetings."

13. Global Financing Facility (2017).

14. Issues around abortion and family planning, however, can be highly contentious in certain circumstances.

GFF, like GHSA, does not have an extensive list of its own rules and procedures, but several principles function as general guidelines for member practices.[15] By aligning itself with the Every Woman Every Child (EWEC) initiative of
the United Nations, GFF is positioned within the "Global Strategy for Women's,
Children's, and Adolescents' Health (2016–2030)."[16] At the country level, GFF
promotes the development of "investment case," which is used to align country
priorities and donor assistance related to women's and children's health. Activities of member countries and the so-called investors' group donors are regularly
updated and shared for better coordination through regular meetings held twice a
year, as well as other forms of communications.

GFF is funded from three major sources: (i) contributions to the trust fund
managed by the World Bank (and linked to the World Bank's concessional funding); (ii) parallel funding from development partners in the investors' group; and
(iii) domestic resources of the engaged countries. Designated funding streams,
including donor resources, give GFF a solid core. But with the gap between the
number of countries designated for support and the universe of countries that
need it, there is little expectation that donor resources alone will meet the need.

Incentivizing countries to develop the "investment case" focused on wom-
en's and children's health priorities and encouraging donors to increase support
in accordance with it may yield undesirable effects, depending on the extent to
which the case is aligned with overall health priorities. If properly aligned, the
investment case can serve as a mutual signal for both countries and donors to
invest collectively in these health areas that have seen less funding compared to
other globally prioritized areas. Without these alignments to existing national

15. GFF has three levels of governance structure. The first one is the Investors Group, which is
a group of representatives from the countries to be supported, bilateral and multilateral donors that
are contributing either through the GFF Trust Fund hosted in the World Bank or through parallel
financing, civil society, the private sector, and private foundations. The members as of November 2016
include DRC, Ethiopia, Kenya, Liberia, Senegal, Canada, Japan, Norway, the United Kingdom, the
United States, GAVI, GFATM, BMGF, the Office of the UN Secretary-General, PMNCH, UNICEF,
UNFPA, WBG, WHO, and others. The second level is the GFF Trust Fund Committee, with membership from those who are contributing to the trust fund. The third one is the GFF Secretariat housed
in the World Bank. Norway and Canada played leading roles in the establishment of GFF through
setting up of a trust fund in the World Bank, joined by BMGF and the United States. As it is linked
to the networks of wider constituencies related to reproductive, maternal, newborn, child, and adolescent health (RMNCAH), such as Every Woman Every Child (EWEC) and Partnership for Maternal,
Newborn and Child Health (PMNCH), the potential constituency is much larger than those directly
involved currently.

16. See www.who.int/life-course/partners/global-strategy/globalstrategyreport2016-2030-lowres.
pdf.

health development strategies and overall investment plans, funding can result in the usual problems of confusion and inefficiency.

Over the decades, scientific knowledge and evidence have grown over on what works cost-effectively to promote the health of mothers and children (PMNCH, 2011). Even in the MDG era, population coverage of such essential interventions has been regularly monitored and publicized by the Countdown to 2015, a joint effort by more than forty academic, international, bilateral, and civil society institutions (Victora and others, 2016). It was these monitoring activities that revealed the lagging progress in maternal and child health relative to global targets. Resource mobilization was also behind compared to health measures for responses to infectious diseases. In fact, while donor financing for AIDS, tuberculosis, and malaria control increased thirty-four-fold in real terms, from U.S. $0.4 to U.S. $14.3 billion between 1990 and 2015, financing for maternal, newborn, and children's health merely quadrupled, from U.S. $2.6 to U.S. $10.0 billion (Dieleman and others, 2016).

One important mechanism for global mobilization by the women-child health regime will continue to be institutionalization of a strong accountability framework. The Countdown (now renamed the Countdown to 2030) will continue to serve the same function in the SDG era.[17] The EWEC initiative has established an independent group to monitor the implementation of the Global Strategy for Women's, Children's, and Adolescents' Health.[18] Although it is difficult to prove the direct attribution of GFF or any related partnerships to the improvement of women-child health, even by such strong monitoring and accountability frameworks, the knowledge and evidence produced can only benefit the regime.

Universal Health Coverage

Formally announced by the director-general of the WHO in September 2016, the International Health Partnership for Universal Health Coverage 2030 (UHC2030) is now taking shape. The former International Health Partnership Plus (IHP+), which served as a predecessor for UHC2030, had a membership of fifty-three countries (of which thirty-seven are low- and middle-income countries, the others being donor countries), thirteen donor organizations (including WHO, World Bank, UN specialized agencies such as UNFPA and UNICEF, Gavi, Global Fund, USAID, and Gates Foundation), and civil society organizations. Agreement was made among all the signatories of IHP+ to transform the partnership to include promotion of coherent activities for health systems strengthening, leading to universal health coverage as a new mission. The former members of IHP+ will remain

17. See http://countdown2030.org/.
18. See www.everywomaneverychild.org/2016/07/28/independent-accountability-panel/.

with the new initiative, while the membership is expected to be broadened further to include additional stakeholders.[19]

Japan and Germany, in line with their commitment to promote universal health coverage as a global agenda, provided political leadership in the transformation of IHP+ to UHC2030. It was endorsed by the G-7 in 2016 with adoption of the Ise-Shima Vision for Global Health, under the Japanese G-7 presidency. Germany, which in 2015 announced an initiative for coherent health systems strengthening called "Healthy Systems—Healthy Lives," supported the move as well. Both countries advocated a mechanism for better coordination of global support to universal health coverage, yet there was a general sentiment against adding a new initiative in the global health landscape. The proposal from the WHO to transform IHP+ to meet the purpose was deemed a practical option, though it might not have been the optimal one. Enthusiasm of some middle-income countries such as Thailand and South Africa for active engagement, and the active engagement of civil society organizations from the very beginning, provides UHC2030 with an opportunity for a pluralistic model of governance.

UHC2030 seeks global solidarity around two distinct, yet interrelated, issue areas. First, it promotes effective development cooperation. The IHP+ was originally created out of the recognition that health should showcase the effective development cooperation advocated through the Paris Declaration on Aid Effectiveness ahead of other sectors, as there had been dire need for donor coordination in light of increased vertical funding and the fragmentation of aid money. Second, it promotes universal health and coherent health systems strengthening. Universal health coverage calls for widespread access to essential health services and extensive coverage with financial protection schemes. Achievement of universal health coverage requires coherent investments on health systems, which calls for effective development cooperation. Furthermore, achievement of universal health coverage requires conscious efforts to reach the poor and the vulnerable, something that is only possible with redistribution of resources to remedy the inequality and promote social justice. By addressing risk of ill-health and impoverishment,

---

19. The governance structure of the UHC2030 has four tiers, with the steering committee as the highest decisionmaking body with balanced representation from low-, middle-, and high-income countries, multilateral organizations, philanthropic foundations, civil society, and the private sector. The WHO and the World Bank, which will continue to jointly host the core team for the operation of the initiative, are allocated with permanent seats in the steering committee. Representatives from the related global health initiatives are encouraged to join as observers, for better coordination of the activities. The Reference Group is composed of any interested technical representatives from the signatories and the related global health initiatives to support the steering committee and the core team. The Working Groups are to be organized with technical personnel to carry out collective actions identified as a priority in the work plan. In addition to these structures, an arrangement for promoting civil society engagement is also being proposed.

universal health coverage entails human security as a fundamental principle for unity among the actors.

One of the first collaborative efforts by UHC2030 was to develop a "consensus document," to elaborate guidelines for both national governments and donors, to help ensure a coordinated approach toward universal coverage and health systems strengthening. The guidelines (WHO and World Bank, 2017) highlighted equity, together with quality, responsiveness, efficiency, and resilience,[20] as one of the core features that all health systems should pursue. The document incorporates the preceding efforts to develop a framework for joint action leading to coherent health systems that can establish and strengthen universal health coverage. Chief among the models are a German initiative on "Healthy Systems—Healthy Lives" and the "UHC in Africa" announced at the Sixth Tokyo International Conference on African Development (TICAD VI) in 2016 (World Bank and others, 2016).[21] Nevertheless, the diversity of countries involved requires a delicate balance between overarching principles for unity and prescriptive rules and decisionmaking procedures. Each country must make its own informed decisions as to which path to take toward universal health coverage, considering not only technical and economic feasibility, but political viability.

UHC2030 is unique from the governance perspective because it envisions itself as "a network of networks," by incorporating existing and related global health initiatives into its governance structures.[22] Considering the potential complexities and transaction costs at the country level that an increasing number of global health initiatives may pose, there is a good reason to demand a traffic control function. As universal health coverage is an overarching target among various health targets in the SDG 3, and reflecting on the transformation of IHP+ to UHC2030, UHC2030 seems to be best positioned to take on responsibility in the current global health landscape. What the network of networks entails in reality and how effective it can be as an overarching initiative to link various initiatives toward the common goal remains to be seen.

20. Health security had come to be regarded as one of the indispensable features of universal health coverage, which resulted in the inclusion of *resilience* in the guidelines.

21. UHC in Africa was jointly developed by the World Bank, Japan International Cooperation Agency (JICA), Global Fund, African Development Bank, and WHO as a common framework and endorsed by fifty-three African countries and other development partners.

22. The initiatives include Alliance for Health Policy and Systems Research, P4H Network for Health Financing and Social Health Protection, Global Health Workforce Alliance, Global Service Delivery Network, Health Data Collaborative, Health Systems Global, Health Systems Governance Collaborative, Inter-agency Pharmaceutical Coordination Group, Inter-agency Supply Chain Coordination Group, Joint Learning Network for UHC, Primary Health Care Performance Initiative, and Universal Health Coverage Partnership.

Sharing of knowledge as global public goods will play an important role in the promotion of universal health coverage. Unlike the other regime areas for which a repertoire of effective interventions and frameworks for capacity development are available, universally effective interventions to push country health systems toward embracing universal health coverage do not exist. One mechanism may be to support knowledge spillovers across borders; numerous initiatives, in fact, currently promote this idea of horizontal learning. UHC2030 may be able to excel in knowledge management by functioning as a network of networks. In addition, having a solid accountability and monitoring framework will increase the credibility of globally concerted efforts. UHC2030 can benefit from the work on UHC monitoring already under way by the WHO and the World Bank. Since the work is focused on quantitative analysis on equity in service coverage and financial protection at the global level, UHC2030 may be able to enrich this work through case studies on the experience of each member country looking at the other aspects of universal health coverage as well, that is, quality, responsiveness, efficiency, and resilience.

Conclusions and Recommendations

Global health governance in the MDG era was mainly characterized by the proliferation of global health initiatives. Some of them presented alternative, more inclusive models for governance, compared to the traditional intergovernmental (or *inter-national*, as opposed to *global*) system. These initiatives also helped mobilize global resources for health, with a clear focus on globally agreed targets. These global health initiatives helped to scale up essential health services related to the specific targets, expanding access to health for vulnerable populations, much of which resulted in significant reductions in morbidity and mortality in many developing nations.

In the SDG era, however, such initiatives may become less successful even though there will be continued interest in creating new ones reflecting the diversification of globally agreed health targets and the actors involved. It is because health systems constraints, such as availability of essential health workers, will become more prominent as a common bottleneck to deliver health services to the harder-to-reach populations. It can create more problems if the initiatives focused on specific health issues continue to grow in numbers unchecked. As each initiative tends to be organized around different principles and a different set of rules and procedures, the interface between global health initiatives and country health systems can be more complex. Inconsistent or duplicated rules and procedures can create confusion and inefficiency in developing country health systems, unless each initiative undertakes a deliberate effort to align its operations to the country system and not vice versa.

Global efforts toward broad-based health systems strengthening must be converged, and any traffic control function should reconcile the rules and procedures that are brought into country health systems by different initiatives. As described in the preceding analysis, UHC2030 is uniquely positioned to respond to such needs as it promotes the overarching target of universal health coverage and the concept of the network of networks. It remains to be seen whether it can meet the expectation in reality.

The proliferation of global health initiatives requires us to broaden our vision of global health governance, to focus not only on the individual initiatives but also their interactions. This chapter argues that it is instructive to examine global health initiatives as international regimes, focusing on the actors involved, norms and principles that unite the actors, and rules and procedures applied for collective actions. Knowledge and evidence for informed decisionmaking may be added to these factors. Systematic assessment of individual initiatives will help to identify opportunities for positive interactions.

The analysis of actors reveals a shift toward a more pluralistic and inclusive system of governance within each initiative. Health security, for example, is unique not only for its multisectoral membership but also for the leadership role of countries beyond the conventional global health donors. UHC2030, similarly, is elaborating an inclusive model of governance that has attracted middle-income countries with hands-on experience in pursuing and achieving universal health coverage. Both GFF and UHC2030 consciously ensure the active engagement of civil society organizations in their governance structures. The challenge, however, is the exclusion of nonmembers. Even though the membership is voluntary and often open to anyone interested, membership is required to join and understand what is going on in each initiative. As these initiatives tend to have multiple layers of governing bodies, the countries and the organizations need to consider in which level to engage in order to benefit the most.

There are two prominent norms uniting actors involved in the global health initiatives examined here: the management of externalities and the mobilization of global solidarity.[23] While GHSA is an example of an initiative geared toward the management of externalities, GFF and UHC2030 represent initiatives created for the mobilization of global solidarity. The management of externalities can

---

23. Adopting the framework of Frenk and Moon (2013), the third one may be production of global public goods, which is more relevant for the initiatives focused on research and development. The discussion here is focused on those dealing with health systems strengthening and capacity development of countries. The impact of proliferation of the initiatives with an R&D focus is another interesting area of study on global health governance.

appeal to the national security constituencies, leading to wider political mobilization, even for a short period of time, prompted by a certain shock event. By contrast, mobilization of global solidarity is anchored in human rights, social justice, human security, and other values appealing to the compassion of citizens. Just as global health governance needs to embrace both in order to achieve the diverse health targets in SDG, the global community needs to pay attention to the underlying norms and principles of the initiatives. Why we unite is as important as how in order to shape a better future for us all.

Global health initiatives, like international regimes, interface with country systems through rules and decisionmaking procedures specific to each one. Even though the initiatives do not tend to have an overabundance of rigid procedures, all of them promote some kind of standard procedures, or tools, as the basis for collective actions. Examples include the Joint External Evaluation (JEE) for GHSA, the Investment Case for GFF, and the Country Compact and Joint Vision for UHC2030. Caution is warranted, therefore, in excessively relying on those tools, as they can be a source of confusion when introduced to the countries with different contexts and backgrounds. It is important to modify procedures and tools to suit country systems, not the other way around. Careful analysis of rules and procedures will also help to identify opportunity to find synergies among the initiatives. For example, findings from JEE and other diagnostic tools can reinforce each other for holistic assessment of country health systems and policies. Investment cases should be produced in alignment with other related national plans and policies. A clearinghouse for such rules and procedures may be helpful for countries and donors to find opportunity for convergence.

Production of public goods in the form of knowledge and evidence may not be the primary focus of the global health initiatives analyzed here, but the effective use of information is important for global advocacy and mobilization, as well as for strengthening the accountability framework and monitoring progress. It is worth noting that intellectual resources will become more important in international cooperation for health as countries' dependence on foreign financial resources decreases. However, how to translate knowledge into actions will continue to be a challenge for many countries. There is a need to coordinate knowledge management as well to avoid duplication and inconsistencies in what is promoted by different initiatives.

What can we do to ensure more coordinated and coherent actions by the global health actors, including various initiatives? It is highly unlikely that the landscape of multiple initiatives can be rationalized or consolidated, particularly where strong constituencies are created by the issues. Some of the initiatives, such as the Global Fund and Gavi in particular, have proven to be effective in mobilizing resources and producing results. It would be wise not to lose their momentum by radical restructuring. However, there is a strong imperative to manage complexity and potential confusion associated with multiple initiatives. The best we can do, at least for the moment, is to assess carefully the governance of each initiative by viewing critically each set of rules and procedures to ensure all are compatible with each other and with different country systems and contexts. By aspiring to be a network of networks for coherent health-systems strengthening, UHC2030 has a potential to perform such a function, if the members see a value in the endeavor and are willing to work together—even though there is a risk for it to become another initiative to produce a different set of rules and procedures.

What is more important, finally, is to strengthen each country's leadership, encouraging a more inclusive style of governance within each country. Even with the proliferation of global health initiatives, a country's autonomy in decision-making and responsibility to strengthen its own health systems for the benefit of its people will not be undermined. At the same time, with more exposure to and involvement in global health initiatives by civil society organizations and other nonstate actors, citizens' expectation and demand for better health systems will increase. In the end, the benefit of different global initiatives needs to be viewed through the prisms of country health systems. Countries should be able to manage the initiatives effectively, by understanding the actors involved, the norms and principles, rules and procedures, and their implications.

Deliberate collaboration at the global level, as well as informed and inclusive leadership at the country level, is what it takes for unity in diversity as required for global health governance under the SDGs.

References

Action for Global Health. 2008. "Healthy Aid: Why Europe Must Deliver More Aid, Better Spent to Save the Health Millennium Development Goals." Brussels.

Bill & Melinda Gates Foundation and McKinsey & Company. 2005. "Global Health Partnerships: Assessing Country Consequences." New York.

Commission on Global Governance. 1995. *Our Global Neighbourhood: The Report of the Commission on Global Governance.* Oxford University Press.

Commission on a Global Health Risk Framework for the Future. 2016. "The Neglected Dimensions of Global Security: A Framework to Counter Infectious Disease Crises" (http://nam.edu/GHRFreport) (doi: 10.17226/21891).

Dieleman, Joseph L., and others. 2016. "Development Assistance for Health: Past Trends, Associations, and the Future of International Financial Flows for Health." *Lancet* 387: 2536–44.

Dodd, Rebecca, and Christopher Lane. 2010. "Improving the Long-Term Sustainability of Health Aid: Are Global Health Partnerships Leading the Way?" *Health Policy and Planning* 25: 363–71.

Dodgson, Richard, Kelley Lee, and Nick Drager. 2002. "Global Health Governance: A Conceptual Review." Centre on Global Change and Health Discussion Paper No. 1. London: London School of Hygiene and Tropical Medicine and WHO.

Fidler, David P. 2010. "The Challenge of Global Health Governance." New York: Council on Foreign Relations.

Frenk, Julio, and Suerie Moon. 2013. "Governance Challenges in Global Health." *New England Journal of Medicine* 368: 936–42.

Global Financing Facility. 2017. "Ten Countries Join Global Financing Facility to Save the Lives of Millions of Women, Children and Adolescents," Press Release. November 9 (www.globalfinancingfacility.org/ten-countries-join-global-financing-facility-save-lives-millions-women-children-and-adolescents).

Global Health Working Group. 2016. "Protecting Human Security: Proposals for the G7 Ise-Shima Summit in Japan." *Lancet* 387 (10033): 2155–62.

Graham, Wendy, and others. 2016. "Diversity and Divergence: The Dynamic Burden of Poor Maternal Health." *Lancet* 388: 2164–75.

Hoffman, Steven J., Clarke B. Cole, and Mark Pearcey. 2015. "Mapping Global Health Architecture to Inform the Future." Research Paper. Centre on Global Health Security. London: Chatham House.

Inada, Juichi. 2013. *Kokusai Kyoryoku no Regime Bunseki: Seido, Kihan no Seisei to Sono Katei* [The International Aid Regime: The Dynamics of Evolution of Institutions and Norms]. Tokyo: Yushindo Japan.

Kickbusch, Ilona, Martina Marianna, and Cassar Szabo. 2014. "A New Governance Space for Health." *Global Health Action* 7: 23507 (http://dx.doi.org/10.3402/gha.v7.23507).

Krasner, Stephen D. 1983. "Structural causes and regime consequences: regimes as intervening variables" in Stephen D. Krasner, ed. *International Regimes.* Cornell University Press.

Liu, Li, and others. 2016. "Global, Regional, and National Causes of Under-5 Mortality in 2000–2015: An Updated Systematic Analysis with Implications for the Sustainable Development Goal." *Lancet* 388: 3027–35.

Mackey, Tim K. 2016. "The Ebola Outbreak: Catalyzing a 'Shift' in Global Health Governance?" *BMC Infectious Diseases* 16: 699 (doi 10.1186/s 12879-016-2016-y).

Moon, Suerie, and others. 2015. "Will Ebola Change the Game? Ten Essential Reforms before the Next Pandemic. The Report of the Harvard-LSHTM Independent Panel on the Global Response to Ebola." *Lancet* 386: 2204–21.

PMNCH (Partnership for Maternal, Newborn, and Child Health). 2011. "A Global Review of the Key Interventions Related to Reproductive, Maternal, Newborn and Child Health (RMNCH)." Geneva.

Sridhar, Devi. 2010. "Seven Challenges in International Development Assistance for Health and Ways Forward." *Journal of Law, Medicine & Ethics* (Fall): 2–12.

Szlezak, Nicole A., and others. 2010. "The Global Health System: Actors, Norms and Expectations in Transition." *PLoS Medicine* 7(1): e1000183 (doi: 10.1371/journal.pmed.1000183).

UN High-Level Panel on the Global Response to Health Crises. 2016. "Protecting Humanity from Future Health Crises" (www.un.org/News/dh/infocus/HLP/2016-02-05_Final_Report_Global_Response_to_Health_Crises.pdf).

Undurraga, Eduardo A., and others. 2017. "Potential for Broad-Scale Transmission of Ebola Virus Disease during the West Africa Crisis: Lessons for the Global Health Security Agenda." *Infectious Diseases of Poverty* 6: 159 (doi 10.1186/s40249-017-0373-4).

Victora, Cesar G., and others. 2016. "Countdown to 2015: A Decade of Tracking Progress for Maternal, Newborn and Child Survival." *Lancet* 387: 2049–59.

World Bank, JICA, Global Fund, African Development Bank, and WHO. 2016. "UHC in Africa: A Framework for Action." Nairobi: World Bank.

WHO. 2008. "International Health Regulations (2005) Second Edition." Geneva.

WHO Maximizing Positive Synergies Collaborative Group. 2009. "An Assessment of Interactions between Global Health Initiatives and Country Health Systems." *Lancet* 373: 2137–69

WHO and World Bank. 2017. "Healthy Systems for Universal Health Coverage—A Joint Vision for Healthy Lives." Geneva.

CHAPTER SIXTEEN

Crowding-In Private Finance
What Multilateral Banks Can Do Differently

Mahmoud Mohieldin and Jos Verbeek,
with Nritya Subramaniam

P rivate sector financing and investments are vital for the implementation of the 2030 Agenda and achievement of the Sustainable Development Goals (SDGs). Approximately, U.S. $3.5 to $4.5 trillion in financing is required annually to attain the SDGs by 2030 (UNCTAD, 2014). Financing at this scale is far beyond the ability of official institutions, including multilateral development banks (MDBs). They must shift from a resource transfer mentality to a resource mobilization mind-set.

One challenge is to divert the U.S. $22 trillion of annual global savings into investments for the implementation of the 2030 Agenda. An opportunity now exists because alternative investments are unattractive: currently, there are U.S. $8 trillion in bonds yielding negative real interest rates.[1] By the same logic, some of the savings managed by institutional investors, which stood at over U.S. $80 trillion as of 2016 (and are growing steadily), could be funneled into long-term investments in developing countries.[2]

The paper benefited from the comments and suggestions of Caroline Heider, Mike Kelleher, Homi Kharas, Marilou Uy, and participants at the workshop organized by Brookings Institution in February 2017 in Washington, D.C. We gratefully acknowledge the research assistance of Farida Abdoulmagd and Mariam El Maghrabi and the editorial assistance of Tochi Nwokike. The findings, interpretations, and conclusions expressed in this paper are entirely those of the authors. They do not necessarily represent the views of the International Bank for Reconstruction and Development (World Bank) and its affiliated organizations, or those of the executive directors of the World Bank or the governments they represent.

1. See Chanda (2017).
2. Based on OECD data for total financial assets held by investment funds, insurance corporation funds, and pension funds, respectively.

The private sector is not apprehensive about investing in sustainable development. However, private sector participants often lack the expertise to prepare and implement development projects and lack the instruments to mitigate political and regulatory risks that arise from long-term investing in developing countries. They prefer to fund brownfield investments that have already dealt with land acquisition, permitting, construction, and other project implementation risks.

We argue that the MDBs are well suited to intermediate between countries that need to invest in development projects and private finance. MDB staff are skilled in preparing, implementing, and supervising projects. The MDBs have a positive track record in assisting countries to improve their national capabilities for project and public investment management, and they provide some assurance that any disputes that arise will be handled in a technical and apolitical manner.

This chapter focuses on the work that MDBs must do to engage the private sector in financing investments needed to attain the SDGs. It elucidates an ex-ante and ex-post engagement that brings the private financial sector on board as financier or cofinancier of a project and is transaction-intensive since it requires investors to be involved in the various processes of project preparation, implementation, and supervision, but there is also a long history of public-private partnerships in infrastructure financing on which to draw.

An ex-post engagement involves selling assets from the MDBs' portfolio to private investors (mostly institutional investors such as pension funds and insurance companies) with an appetite for long-term investments. Such an approach would create portfolios that are tailored by sector and/or region to meet investor preferences. It would require MDBs to implement the projects themselves and have initial resources to finance the projects from their own means or through a designated project preparation facility in which the private investors participate, before selling them to the private financial investor.

MDBs do have asset sales programs, just as the International Finance Corporation's Managed Co-Lending Portfolio Program and its Asset Management Corporation have pools of debt and equity finance that they manage. But these programs are not the main focus of MDBs' engagement, and scaling them up would pose challenges to their administrative capacity to prepare, implement, and supervise projects. The MDBs will need to develop standard asset classification of their loans and equity, as well as address pricing so as to recover their administrative costs to prepare and implement projects.

Both the ex-ante and ex-post approaches require innovative and new forms of partnerships between MDBs, the private sector, and governments. For the MDBs to be successful in this endeavor, they will have to transform and adjust their operational approaches as well as internal staff incentive structures.

The Evolving Landscape for Development Financing

The global economy has transformed significantly since the establishment of the MDBs, mainly due to globalization and the malfunctioning statist models of development. These transformations have led to the acceptance of private sector and private international finance as key to economic development.

However, two global megatrends require substantial investments that will significantly influence implementation of the SDGs: urbanization and climate change. These megatrends have implications for the development challenges that the MDBs are helping to address. In some cases, they may present an opportunity to pursue more sustainable and inclusive development paths.

Urbanization, if well managed, can help lower poverty rates, improve health outcomes, and increase prosperity. A focus on proper planning, connecting, and financing of a growing urban area in a sustainable manner will enhance implementation of the SDGs. On the other hand, if poorly managed, urbanization can result in the emergence of slums, rising unemployment, and inadequate access to basic services. Meeting the challenge of urbanization requires an enhancement of both the breadth and the magnitude of investments in infrastructure, and this should happen fast. For the next two decades, urbanization will occur at a very rapid pace. Cities will expand from housing 4 billion residents today to 5 billion by 2030. At that time, urbanization will slow, as most residents will already be urban. Thus the nature of urban investments in the medium term will lock in the shape of urban environments and the way cities function for the foreseeable future.

The second megatrend is climate change and its effects, which is a defining challenge of this century. The MDBs have committed to work together to support efforts at the local, country, regional, and global levels. As with urbanization, investments made over the next decade will determine whether the temperature increase can be kept below 2° C. If countries fail to invest adequately in low-carbon pathways, the effects of climate change will be felt long into the future.

It is the urgency of action and the risks of inaction that make MDBs so important for implementing Agenda 2030. The MDBs must also adapt to make an impact. The MDBs were established at a time when private capital was not flowing to developing countries. Historically, their engagement has focused on avoiding crowding-out of private capital flows. In the current context, this is not sufficient. The MDBs must strive to encourage the crowding-in of private capital to generate sufficient funding for infrastructure and other investments.

Third International Conference on Financing for Development

As institutional stakeholders participating in the Third International Conference on Financing for Development, the MDBs and the International Monetary Fund (IMF) prepared a guidance note, titled "From Billions to Trillions," which provided options on the various modes of financing for development and the implementation of the 2030 Agenda (African Development Bank and others, 2015). It recommends actions to mobilize and deploy resources from international sources for global public goods, domestic public resources, and private sources (see figure 16-1).

International Public Resources and Global Public Goods

The MDBs have long focused on the implications of global policies for developing countries in areas such as trade, aid, debt relief, financial stability, and public health. The International Financial Institutions (IFIs), including the IMF and the MDBs, play a seminal role in promoting economic and financial stability, and advocate for global public goods in various forums such as the Group of 20 (G-20) and the Group of 7 (G-7). The 2008 financial crisis and current global developments such as climate change, migration and the refugee crisis, natural disasters, and pandemics provided impetus to the MDBs to proactively engage with the UN and other actors to ensure effective delivery of finance and support to affected countries.

The MDBs play a critical role in adaptation, mitigation, and climate finance. They are scaling up activities to strengthen policy, build institutional capacity, provide access to finance, and deliver technical support to client countries and their private sector partners. In 2015 the MDBs collectively committed more than U.S. $25 billion for climate finance and have financed more than U.S. $131 billion

Figure 16-1. Key Components of Financing for Development

1. International public resources	–Provide better and smarter aid –Ensure resources to tackle global public goods
2. Domestic public resources	–Improve domestic resource mobilization (DRM) –Promote domestic credit and capital markets
3. Domestic and international private resources	–Unlock private investment for development –Attract foreign direct investment, remittances, and philanthropic finance

Source: Authors.

in climate action since 2011. Furthermore, the MDBs have been applying methods for climate finance accounting, thus adding transparency to the efforts to track global development finance flows that deliver climate cobenefits.

Domestic Public Resources

The MDBs are committed to assisting developing countries to increase domestic resource mobilization. The critical hurdles that developing countries face in increasing their domestic revenues include compliance, weak revenue administration, underutilization of financial institutions, low taxpayer morale, weak governance, and corruption. Tax avoidance activities of international corporations present a major challenge, and this is being addressed by the G-20–OECD Action Plan on Base Erosion and Profit Shifting (BEPS), which contains a new standard for information and reporting. Also, current international initiatives to promote exchange of information between tax administrations can strengthen the enforcement capacity of national tax administrations, including taxing residents' holdings of assets abroad.

While there is no agreed definition of illicit financial flows (IFF) or a method for measuring them, IFFs entail cross-border movement of financial assets, international trade fraud (mis-invoicing), criminal activities, and corruption. Measuring and tracking IFFs is challenging since these financial flows are opaque and not recorded. Presently, a few methods are being utilized to estimate IFFs, but they do not portray a global perspective of the size and nature of IFFs. The World Bank Group's "residual model" methodology for measuring IFFs assumes that all funds not recorded officially are "illicit."

Private businesses and governments often rely on local currency financing to avert the risks that can occur with borrowing in a foreign currency. Many developing countries have underdeveloped local currency and corporate bond markets. The MDBs provide local currency finance to vulnerable borrowers and their intermediaries through swap markets, or local currency bonds issuance. The MDBs champion participation in domestic capital markets by providing technical and policy advice on institutions and regulations, offering credit improvements and structured finance, and hedging solutions for bond offerings. In certain circumstances, the MDBs develop regional bond funds, tackle information asymmetry with market data, and enhance the investor base by augmenting the domestic insurance and pension funds.

Domestic financial intermediaries (banks and nonbank financial institutions) play a pivotal role in financing but are restricted in their ability to lend to the real economy, especially to marginalized individuals and Micro- and Medium-Sized Enterprises (MSMEs). The MDBs support financial inclusion through MSME finance and strengthening the domestic financial sector. They assist unregulated financial institutions to become regulated banks, promote innovative capital-boosting debt-funding structures, stimulate the use of new lending methodologies to increase funding availability to MSMEs, provide equity disbursements to banks and insurance companies, support regional private equity funds, and offer specific credit lines.

Role of MDBs in Catalyzing the Private Financial Sector

Since the 1980s, private capital flows to developing countries have increased while net official flows have steadily declined. There is mounting evidence that foreign direct investment (FDI) has contributed positively to growth and development. Evaluating financial flows to developing countries by income groupings shows a remarkable upturn since the early 1990s in FDI, followed by large increases in remittances and private lending to governments or related entities with a guarantee. Breaking the flows down by low-income countries (LICs) and middle-income countries (MICs), it becomes clear that much of the increased private financial resources are flowing to MICs and that LICs still depend heavily on multilateral and bilateral assistance for development.

An interesting observation is that MICs and to a much lesser extent LICs received significant inflows from the private sector before the various debt crises in the 1980s and 1990s. This was in the form of lending from commercial banks. The upsurge in lending from the private sector to developing countries since the early 2000s is mostly due to the issuance of government bonds.

Traditionally, the MDBs have focused on poverty alleviation, economic growth, and environmental protection, promoted by working directly with governments and government agencies. The MDBs achieved these objectives by providing loans to public sector projects, technical assistance, and policy-based lending. MDB loans have generally been guaranteed by the borrowing states. Since the role of the private sector has gained momentum in the past three decades, a core challenge for the MDBs is to foster opportunities for the private sector. The two channels that the IFIs can use to enhance the role of the private sector are to:

—Assist governments to create conditions for the right kind of market oriented growth—this entails macroeconomic stability and assistance with tax, legal, and sectoral reform, and creation of a social safety net through policy-based lending.

—Collaborate with the private sector and increase private capital flows by becoming participant investors. This approach requires sovereign guarantees, but governments are often reluctant to provide these to private lenders because they do not want to subsidize the private sector.

If MDBs are to partner successfully with the private sector, they must develop expertise in various aspects of international banking, adapt to the flexibility and confidentiality required of private sector operations, and develop a new risk culture and the knowledge base for commercial risk analysis. The comparative advantage of the MDBs in this partnership is that they possess a capital structure that allows them to operate in high-risk environments, and their relationship with developing-country governments enables them to reduce political risks in a manner that the private international financial sector cannot do. Governments will often have more faith in a project when there is a partnership between the private sector and an MDB, which is duty bound to protect its members' interest.

The collaboration of the MDBs with the private financial sector involves various financial interventions ranging from equity to quasi-equity instruments and debt, underwriting, guarantees, and syndication. Interventions can also entail introducing new financial instruments, such as green bonds, to capital markets through MDB treasury departments. In addition, MDBs can play a role in nonbank financial institutions, such as insurance and mutual funds. The MDBs can promote access to equity and venture capital by small and medium-sized enterprises. Additionally, the MDBs can develop opportunities that allow the private financial sector to buy part of its portfolio by sector or by region.

The MDBs are well positioned to assist in attracting institutional investors, such as pension and mutual funds, into developing countries. Thus they can bolster fledgling capital markets. The MDBs have been focusing on infrastructure financing for decades. However, as infrastructure becomes commercially oriented, it creates opportunities for partnering with private finance. The success of MDB collaboration with the private sector involves judicious design, utilization of various instruments, and allocation of the intertwined risks (political, regulatory, and commercial), which creates scope for valuable contributions by the institutions.

Practical Financial Interventions: The Cascade

There also must be a realization that different investors—including institutional, impact, and project investors—all have different needs and requirements. Various approaches need to be put in place to attract them to invest in development. Most recently, the World Bank Group (WBG) has pioneered an approach of pursuing private sector solutions for attaining development goals while reserving public finance for critical areas where private sector involvement is not optimal or available. The approach is based on the "Principles of MDBs Strategy for Crowding-In Private Sector Finance for Growth and Sustainable Development (the "Hamburg

Figure 16-2. The Cascade Approach to Development Finance

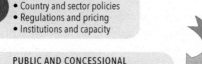

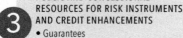

1 COMMERCIAL FINANCING

Can commercial financing be cost-effectively mobilized for sustainable investment? If not …

2 UPSTREAM REFORMS AND MARKET FAILURES
• Country and sector policies
• Regulations and pricing
• Institutions and capacity

Can upstream reforms be put in place to address market failures? If not …

3 PUBLIC AND CONCESSIONAL RESOURCES FOR RISK INSTRUMENTS AND CREDIT ENHANCEMENTS
• Guarantees
• First loss

Can risk instruments and credit enhancements cost-effectively cover remaining risks? If not …

4 PUBLIC AND CONCESSIONAL FINANCING, INCLUDING SUB-SOVEREIGN
• Public finance (including national development banks and domestic SWF)
• MDBs and DFIs

Can development objectives be resolved with scarce public financing?

Source: World Bank (2017a).

Principles"),[3] the Addis Ababa Action Agenda, and the Joint MDB Statement of Ambitions for Crowding in Private Finance, which commit the MDBs to collectively increase private financing by 25–35 percent over the next three years.[4]

With a view to enhancing its commitment to Maximizing Finance for Development (MFD), the WBG introduced in March 2017 the "cascade approach," a concept that the WBG could utilize to leverage private sector financing and solutions (see figure 16-2). If public debt and contingent liabilities are limited, then private solutions are promoted, and if not, then the option of public finance is pursued while upholding environmental, social and fiscal standards, and good governance criteria. The cascade approach serves as a complement to domestic resource mobilization and enhances the effectiveness of public finance.

---

3. The Hamburg Principles elucidate the importance of country ownership in determining its investment priorities and the role of the private sector in providing solutions. They also emphasize the pivotal role of the government to improve the investment climate, bolster domestic financial markets, promote sound and sustainable financing practices regarding debt sustainability, improve governance, and strengthen project pipelines, based on robust public investment planning to accommodate expanded financial resources.

4. See "Joint MDB Statement of Ambitions for Crowding In Private Finance" (www.bundesfinanzministerium.de/Content/DE/Downloads/G20-Dokumente/Hamburg_Genannte_Berichte/Joint-MDB-Statement-of-Ambitions.pdf?__blob=publicationFile&v=1).

The WBG provides support for policy and regulatory reforms and conducts risk assessment at the country and sectoral level to bolster the enabling environment for private sector solutions, which in turn can increase the supply of local currency financing that can be tapped for development purposes. The WBG will assist clients to ensure that costs and benefits of public versus private financing are adequately assessed and incorporate lessons and sound practices, while considering equity and affordability.

The MFD approach hones the WBG's spectrum of experience and expertise in working with governments to harness private sector financing and solutions to achieve development goals in collaboration with development partners. The MFD complements the IFC's strategy to "create markets" and the Multilateral Investment Guarantee Agency's 2020 strategy by reinforcing regulatory or policy frameworks, championing competition, and developing local capital markets. Applying this approach will also provide opportunities to utilize the IFC-MIGA Private Sector Window created as a result of the International Development Agency's eighteenth replenishment to help mobilize private investment. The Concessional Finance Strategy for Climate Change and green bonds are examples of the MFD at the global level.

Operationalization of the cascade approach requires effective cross-WBG coordination and systematic efforts to equip staff with guidance, resources, training, and monitoring progress to scale up and integrate MFD into the WBG's operations and in its engagement with clients. Advisory capability, knowledge sharing, and capacity building in governments are critical. The WBG Corporate Scorecard tracks private finance mobilized in compliance with the MDB-agreed-on methodology. Developing these metrics is vital for implementing the MFD approach.

The MFD approach has been piloted in nine countries—Cameroon, Côte d'Ivoire, Egypt (see box 16-1), Indonesia, Iraq, Jordan, Kenya, Nepal, and Vietnam. The WBG's assistance has been provided in these countries to attract private solutions for development. Building on these initial pilots, the implementation of the MFD will be scaled up geographically and in various sectors. As mentioned earlier, successful implementation of the MFD requires collaboration with development partners. Examples of this collaboration of the MDBs is the establishment of the Global Infrastructure Forum and the Global Infrastructure Facility. MDBs' interface with the private sector at the sector level requires more effort to incorporate standardized approaches that can be replicated to achieve scale.

Practical Financial Interventions: The Portfolio Approach

The cascade approach, if implemented across all MDBs, will facilitate a paradigm shift in the way the MDBs operate. Staff will be expected to always look

Box 16-1. Reform of Egypt's Power Sector

Egypt has embarked on a program to reform its power sector by harnessing private investment in renewables. The World Bank Group is providing coordinated support in collaboration with development partners. Investment is implemented systematically and in conjunction with other MDBs. With cofinancing from the African Development Bank, the International Bank for Reconstruction and Development's development policy finance instrument has supported crucial policies such as an adjustment to electricity tariffs; elimination of fuel subsidies; revision of the feed-in-tariff policy; and the introduction of a renewable energy law and a regulatory framework for competitive bidding mechanisms for independent power producers. The International Finance Corporation and IBRD jointly designed the Solar Feed-in Tariff, or FiT, program, which is expected to attract sufficient private investment. Multilateral Investment Guarantee Agency is providing political risk insurance of up to $400 million for solar projects under the program. The European Bank for Reconstruction and Development (EBRD) has approved thirteen solar power projects in Egypt.

The EBRD, the Agence Française de Développement, the European Investment Bank, and the European Union have also launched a €140 million Green Economy Financing Facility to enable Egypt to "provide loans for small-scale renewable energy investments by private companies through a group of participating banks." The Asian Infrastructure Investment Bank, Islamic Development Bank, African Development Bank, and bilateral partners are also engaged in reform of the renewable sectors. Lower costs of technology make renewable energy solutions commercially viable for investors and attractive for Egypt's consumers.

Source: Authors, based on World Bank-International Monetary Fund, "Maximizing Finance for Development: Leveraging the Private Sector for Growth and Sustainable Development," Development Committee, DC2017-0009, Washington, 2017.

for financing from the private financial sector when preparing a project. Staff will have to develop structures that are appealing to institutional investors, who in general do not engage at an individual project level and do not have the expertise to analyze the merit of a project, the appropriateness of its design, its economic rationale, or its implementation risks.

The margins with which the institutional investor operates are often so thin that the cost of acquiring the knowledge and relevant expertise to analyze and evaluate developmental projects might render financing development less attractive, if not impossible. Hence, to ensure that institutional investors will take part in financing development, the cascade approach needs to be complemented by an approach that does not require institutional investors to obtain detailed knowledge about viability of individual development projects. The MDBs provide this function; they are the institutions with project management expertise that can be provided as a public good for those that want to finance development.

There is an increased awareness and interest by the private financial sector to provide resources for sustainable development. Sustainable investing in which environmental, social, and governance issues are taken into account is increasingly gaining momentum. The United Nations supported the launch of the six Principles for Responsible Investing (PRI) in 2006. Since then, more than 1,800 companies have become signatories, up from 100 at the principles' inception and double the number reached in 2010. The resources under management by financial intermediaries has increased nearly fourfold since 2010 and is reported to be close to U.S. $70 trillion (PRI, 2017). At the same time, evidence is emerging that investing in companies that adhere to the PRI is more profitable than investing in those that do not (Barclays, 2016).

The MDBs, with their acquired skill sets and expert knowledge on how to prepare, implement, monitor, and evaluate projects, are well placed to tap into this growing market and direct those resources to high value for money investments that assist developing countries to attain the SDGs. For this to become a reality, the cascade approach needs to be complemented with an approach that allows the private financial sector to buy into the portfolio of the MDBs, ex-ante, or prior to the preparation and implementation of the project, and/or ex-post, or after the project has been fully disbursed.

The approach we would like to label the "portfolio approach" is one way through which the MDBs can mobilize and catalyze financial resources from institutional investors. It contains the following characteristics:

1. It will rely on the MDBs to prepare and implement projects as they do now, drawing on their expertise. (To scale this up, additional expertise will be needed as resources will flow in multiple amounts through the MDBs.)

2a. The MDBs will seek ex-ante financing from institutional investors for a portfolio of projects in the pipeline, that is, in the early stages of preparation. This portfolio can be by narrow sector, for example, health, water, and sanitation, and/or a broader infrastructure category, or by region or grouping of countries. The institutional investor is requested to pool money in a project preparation and implementation facility. The MDBs identify, prepare, and manage the projects themselves and potentially cofinance a part of the portfolio.

2b. The MDBs will ex-post (that is, after the loan has been fully disbursed) sell their existing portfolio of loans to institutional investors. A project fully disburses between one to ten years, with shorter periods for development policy lending and longer disbursement periods for traditional investment loans. At the same time, maturities are often close to twenty years. Under the ex-post approach, the MDBs could sell their loans by sector or by region and/or country grouping directly to institutional investors, thereby receiving fresh resources for a new cycle of project preparation and implementation. Such an ex-post approach would benefit from a capital injection into MDBs for the initial syndication of the existing portfolio of loans.[5]

3. In principle, the loan conditions of MDB lending could be kept the same in the portfolio approach, even though some adjustments to pricing might be needed. However, as long as the net present value of the loan remains below that of commercially available instruments such as bonds or commercial bank credit, the borrower is better off. The maturity of the loans could be adjusted to better match the need of the institutional investor.

Various critical issues will have to be resolved going forward, such as pricing, impact on preferred creditor status, and credit-worthiness of the MDBs. But given the serious resource constraints faced by developing countries in implementing the 2030 Agenda, the MDBs have ample incentives to seek practical solutions to move a portfolio-based approach forward (box 16-2).

Some Critical Underlying Success Factors

A systematic analysis of projects implemented by MDBs and assessed using common standards reveals that eventual project outcomes are correlated with country-level macro-institutions and economic conditions.[6] Research reveals that macro- and micro-correlates of successful implementation of a project hinge on institutional resource allocation decisions regarding aid that are based on project characteristics and country-level policies and institutions. Among country-level factors, GDP growth and a sound policy environment are positively correlated with the success of a project. Actual and early stage planned funding is also positively correlated with project outcomes. In addition, shorter project duration and surge financing are markedly correlated with enhanced project outcomes. Complex projects and those that face glitches during implementation are associated with lower success rates. Also, detailed project designs and procurement packages should be prepared in advance of implementation. At the same time, projects that have warning ratings should be truncated since they are unlikely to succeed.

Project Preparation and Implementation

The track record of the project manager of the MDB involved strongly correlates with the project outcomes. If the MDBs judiciously select the project manager

5. The MDBs could even consider designing derivatives that they sell directly to institutional investors or through secondary markets.

6. Based on research of a significant number of projects of the Asian Development Bank and the Word Bank; see Bulman, Kolkma, and Kraay (2015) for detail.

Box 16-2. Various Instruments in Support of Portfolio Approach at the World Bank Group

1. Asset Management Company (AMC)

The International Finance Corporation's AMC mobilizes and manages third-party funds for investment in high-potential companies and infrastructure projects in emerging markets across Latin America and the Caribbean, Africa, the Middle East, Eastern Europe, and Asia. The AMC allows the IFC to achieve one of its core development mandates—mobilizing additional capital resources for investment in productive private enterprise in developing countries—by managing funds on behalf of institutional investors such as sovereign funds, pension funds, and development finance institutions. As of 2016 the fifty-four investors in the AMC fund have raised a total of U.S. $9.8 billion.

2. Managed Co-Lending Portfolio Program (MCPP) Infrastructure

To address emerging-market infrastructure challenges, the IFC developed the MCPP as a solution to scale up IFC's debt mobilization from institutional investors and demonstrate a path for more investors to invest in such markets. The aim is to unlock capital flows to infrastructure from new sources. In sum, MCPP Infrastructure is designed for institutional investors seeking to increase their exposure to emerging-markets infrastructure. Through the program, IFC originates, approves, and manages a portfolio of loans that mirrors IFC's own portfolio in infrastructure. The MCPP seeks to raise U.S. $5 billion by 2021, and this year has raised U.S. $1.1 billion from Allianz, Eastspring Investments, and the Asian asset management business of Prudential.

3. IFC Syndication

Through syndication loans, the IFC acts as a catalyst for raising capital from foreign and domestic sources, in both private and public markets, for projects in the private sector of its member countries. The IFC has mobilized over U.S. $9.5 billion from parallel lenders, including Development Finance Institutions and local commercial banks for borrowers, globally.

Source: Authors, based on IFC documents. See www.ifcamc.org/; www.ifc.org/wps/wcm/connect/corp_ext_content/ifc_external_corporate_site/solutions/products+and+-services/syndications/mcpp; www.ifc.org/wps/wcm/connect/CORP_EXT_Content/IFC_External_Corporate_Site/Solutions/Products+and+Services/Syndications.

and provide the requisite training and supervision, then it results in improved development outcomes and aid effectiveness. This points to a critical issue for the MDBs in scaling up—they will need to develop an adequate number of experienced project task managers. Finally, allocation of aid on project-level indicators is critical since it provides countries with more incentives to ensure project success and scale up projects in those countries that have subpar policy and institutional environments.

The MDBs could focus more on identifying additional within-country project-level correlates of success and discuss further the importance of institutional rules and implementation agency quality. The MDBs on their own, or in partnership, could evaluate each developing country's policy and institutional assessment (World Bank, 2017b), public expenditure and financial accountability performance (PEFA, 2016), and potential to manage public investments (Rajaram and others, 2014). They should use these assessments more systematically to design country programs that improve capabilities at the country level.

Public Investment Management

In order to use supplemental fiscal space for investment effectively, it is vital to carry out an assessment on the efficiency of public investment and determine specific weaknesses that contribute to poor outcomes so that appropriate institutional and technical measures are undertaken to correct failures. The eight key "must-have" features of an effective public investment system are (1) investment guidance, project development, and preliminary screening; (2) formal project appraisal; (3) independent review of appraisal; (4) project selection and budgeting; (5) project implementation; (6) project adjustment; (7) facility operation; and (8) project evaluation.

In this framework, the basic processes and controls are linked at relevant stages to wider budget processes to yield the greatest assurance of efficiency in public investment decisions. In principle, the identification of weaknesses enables reforms to focus scarce managerial and technical resources where they will yield the greatest impact. The approach is based on a meticulously defined institutional framework and underscores the role of institutions, their capacity, and incentives. It also adheres to the Public Expenditure and Financial Accountability program initiative that addresses public investment management (PIM). Additionally, the approach endeavors to catalyze governments to undertake periodic self-assessments of their public investment systems and design reforms to enhance the productivity of public investment.

Another aspect of this pragmatic approach is to use diagnostic indicators of inputs, processes, and outputs to assess the functioning of actual public investment systems and also provide objective measures of inefficiency supplemented by a "gap analysis" to identify which processes may be failing. The framework recognizes that data collection capacity, accounting, auditing, and oversight are critical features of an efficient public management investment system. PIM reforms require the alignment of incentives to improve project design and selection, as well as additionally reliable commitments and investments in administrative capacity to boost project implementation. Thus this indicator-based approach provides a basis both for objective assessment and highlights gaps that should be addressed if the use of additional fiscal resources is to improve public sector assets and economic growth.

Risk Management

The partnerships that the MDBs seek with the private financial sector to implement the 2030 Agenda and attain the SDGs come with fiscal risks. For example, in the context of Public Private Partnerships (PPPs), fiscal risk can emerge through weaknesses in a country's legal and institutional frameworks, and/or through inadequate policy formulation. Risks can be of a technical, financial, or political nature or can be beyond control of all partners. In practice, the fiscal consequences of such risks are either direct or contingent and result in implicit or explicit fiscal liabilities (IMF, 2005).

The MDBs need to work with their client countries to mitigate these risks effectively. While some of these risks can be mitigated through improved PIM, a strong institutional framework will also be needed that provides a thorough understanding of how risks are shared across partners and how disputes are managed. The legal framework should set the parameters for assurances to the private sector that contracts will be honored. Moreover, a framework that calculates the fiscal implications of these partnerships needs to be in place and embedded in government budgets. Notwithstanding these challenges, a body of literature housed at the MDBs and the IMF explains how to incorporate risk from PPPs (Irwin, 2007; Farquharson and others, 2011; Nose, 2017).

The MDBs have various guarantee instruments, such as political risk insurance, and ongoing initiatives, such as blended finance or first loss provisions, which can be expanded or adjusted to help countries navigate the risk associated with increased private sector involvement in development. In addition, the IMF in collaboration with the MDBs and, in particular, in partnership with the World Bank has initiated a comprehensive technical assistance program to assist countries in managing their public debt better. Further adjustments to this program might be needed to enhance a government's capabilities to manage the fiscal risk of private participation in development finance.[7]

---

7. In 2009 the Boards of the WB mad IMF jointly endorsed a capacity-building program to help developing countries strengthen their public debt management. Various tools were developed, and the latest addition, the PPP Fiscal Risk Assessment Model (PFRAM), helps countries assess the potential fiscal costs and risks arising from PPP projects. References and tools by IMF and WB can be found at http://pubdocs.worldbank.org/en/982261479317855835/InfrastructureToolkit-Booklet-FINALWEB.pdf and at www.imf.org/external/np/fad/publicinvestment/pdf/PFRAM.pdf.

Different Capabilities, Different Challenges, and Opportunities

A country's ability to manage its economy and development process correlates with its income level. Consequently, MDBs need to take potential institutional and policy weaknesses into account when interacting with a country. Each year, the World Bank undertakes an assessment of countries' policies and institutions, also referred to as the Country Policy and Institutional Assessment (CPIA). For African countries, this is done in collaboration with the African Development Bank. The CPIA assesses the quality of a country's present policy and institutional framework. "Quality" refers to how conducive that framework is to fostering poverty reduction, sustainable growth, and the effective use of development assistance.

A look at the ratings for low-income (LICs) and middle-income countries (MICs) indicates that the ratings in all clusters of the CPIA are lower in LICs than in MICs. The gap is largest in the cluster of public sector management and institutions. Hence capacity-building efforts to improve public institutions, especially those dealing with public expenditure management and investment preparation and implementation, must be a priority.

Given that some countries have a lower ability to effectively manage development resources, it will be important to realize that different sustainable finance approaches will be needed for them. A good starting point will be to use income per capita as a gradient and complement this with country-specific information that can be distilled from various tools and assessments that evaluate and analyze a country's capacity to manage its macroeconomy, development process, and public finances.

Conclusion

The MDBs were set up to address the failure of financial markets to provide long-term finance, initially for the rebuilding of Europe after the World War II and later to make available resources for developing countries. While initial focus was mostly on providing funding, the MDBs have evolved into institutions that also provide knowledge products about development at the global, regional, country, and local level, and help build capacities to manage interrelated development processes. Consequently, the MDBs are well positioned to address the challenges posed by the 2030 Agenda and the SDGs.

Market-oriented economic development has gained momentum, and it behooves the MDBs to form partnerships with the private sector to complement and catalyze private finance well into the twenty-first century. It is a great opportunity for the MDBs to harness the potential of the private sector and facilitate these processes to achieve development gains. For this partnership to flourish, the

MDBs must continue to adapt their mode of operations, not only continuing to work with governments but also participating in private investment processes. MDBs can help to strengthen a country's ability to prepare, implement, and monitor projects in a manner conducive to private financial sector participation.

To mobilize the private financial sector, the MDBs will also need to develop the right internal incentive mechanisms for staff to embrace the cascade and portfolio approaches, that is, to move away from designing and implementing projects funded by themselves to facilitating the financing by others. For the portfolio approach to succeed, various additional steps are needed, for example, in classifying portfolios to meet market needs. The pricing formula for MDB projects will need adjusting in such a way that the private financial sector, in particular institutional investors, is incentivized to provide resources and client countries are interested, able, and willing to take on the projects and any financial budgetary implications.

Developing countries should not underestimate the risks associated with the cascade and portfolio approaches. Therefore, the MDBs should actively assist developing countries with (i) project management, including preparation, implementation, and supervision of projects; (ii) public investment management with a focus on the planning and effectiveness and affordability of projects; and (iii) risk management, including guarantees and implications of public private partnerships for debt management.

In addition, the MDBs also need to take the lead in preparing the classes of assets that can be offered under the portfolio approach to the financial markets. This is a global public good the MDBs are well positioned to deliver on and is at the heart of the promise to increase the availability of development finance from the billions to the trillions. Unless the MDBs collectively own the 2030 Agenda to mobilize private finance for development, achieving the SDGs will not be possible.

References

African Development Bank, Asian Development Bank, European Bank for Reconstruction and Development, European Investment Bank, Inter-American Development Bank, International Monetary Fund, and World Bank. 2015. "From Billions to Trillions: Transforming Development Finance." Development Committee Discussion Note, April 2. Washington: International Monetary Fund and World Bank (http://siteresources.worldbank.org/DEVCOMMINT/Documentation/23659446/DC2015-0002(E)FinancingforDevelopment.pdf).

Barclays. 2016. "Sustainable Investing and Bond Returns—Research Study into the Impact of ESG on Credit Portfolio Performance." London: Barclays Bank PLC.

Bulman, D., W. Kolkma, and A. Kraay. 2015. "Good Countries or Good Projects? Comparing Macro and Micro Correlates of World Bank and Asian Development Bank Project Performance." Policy Research Working Paper 7245. Washington: World Bank.

Chanda, Sukanto. 2017. Global Positive and Global Negative Yielding Debt (table). Unpublished. London: Deutsche Bank, Bloomberg Barclays indexes.

Farquharson, E., C. Torres de Mästle, E. R. Yescombe, and J. Encinas. 2011. "How to Engage with the Private Sector in Public-Private Partnerships in Emerging Markets." Report. Washington: World Bank.

IMF (International Monetary Fund). 2005. "Government Guarantees and Fiscal Risk." Washington.

Irwin, T. C. 2007. "Government Guarantees: Allocating and Valuing Risk in Privately Financed Infrastructure Projects." Directions in Development—Infrastructure (series). Washington: World Bank.

Nose, M. 2017. "Enforcing Public-Private Partnership Contract: How do Fiscal Institutions Matter?" Working Paper 17/243. Washington: IMF.

Rajaram, A., T. Minh Le, K. Kaiser, J.-H. Kim, and J. Frank. 2014. "The Power of Public Investment Management: Transforming Resources into Assets for Growth." Directions in Development—Public Sector Governance (series). Washington: World Bank.

PEFA (Public Expenditure and Financial Accountability). 2016. "Framework for Assessing Public Financial Management." Washington: PEFA Secretariat.

PRI (Principles for Responsible Investment). 2017. "Delivering an Ambitious Agenda Annual Report." London.

UNCTAD. 2014. Investing in the SDGs: An Action Plan. World Investment Report. Geneva.

World Bank. 2017a. "Maximizing Finance for Development: Leveraging the Private Sector for Growth and Sustainable Development." Washington: Development Committee, International Monetary Fund and World Bank.

———. 2017b. CPIA Criteria. Washington: World Bank.

Contributors

Editors

Raj M. Desai: Walsh School of Foreign Service, Georgetown University, and Brookings Institution

Hiroshi Kato: Japan International Cooperation Agency

Homi Kharas: Brookings Institution

John W. McArthur: Brookings Institution and United Nations Foundation

Contributors

Reuben Abraham: IDFC Institute, Mumbai

Margaret Biggs: Queen's University School of Policy Studies

Olha Danylo: International Institute for Applied Systems Analysis

Ann Florini: Singapore Management University and the University of Maryland School of Public Policy

Steffen Fritz: International Institute for Applied Systems Analysis

Pritika Hingorani: IDFC Institute, Mumbai

Naoko Ishii: Global Environment Facility

Jeni Klugman: Harvard Kennedy School and Georgetown Institute for Women, Peace and Security

Noriharu Masugi: Japan International Cooperation Agency

Amina Mohammed: Former Minister of the Environment, Nigeria

Mahmoud Mohieldin: World Bank Group

Inian Moorthy: International Institute for Applied Systems Analysis

Jane Nelson: Harvard Kennedy School and Brookings Institution

Bettina Prato: International Fund for Agricultural Development

Kristin Rechberger: Dynamic Planet

Barbara Ryan: Group on Earth Observations

Enric Sala: National Geographic Society

Linda See: International Institute for Applied Systems Analysis

Dhananjayan Sriskandarajah: CIVICUS

Rogério Studart: Federal University of Rio de Janeiro (formerly) and Brookings
  Institution

Nritya Subramaniam: World Bank Group

Ikuo Takizawa: Japan International Cooperation Agency

Ryuichi Tomizawa: Japan International Cooperation Agency

Laura Tyson: University of California, Berkeley, Haas School of Business and Blum Center for Developing Economies

Michiel van Dijk: International Institute for Applied Systems Analysis

Jos Verbeek: World Bank Group

Simon Zadek: United Nations Development Programme

Index

WHO (World Health Organization), 334, 336–37, 339–41
Widerburg, Oscar, 108
Wilson, E. O., 248
WOEs (women-owned enterprises), 32–34, 54, 56, 59
Women: child care and elderly care responsibilities and, 14; Convention for the Elimination of All Forms of Discrimination Against Women (CEDAW), 58; education and, 26, 30, 53, 111–12, 277, 281; employment and, 14; empowerment, cross-sector collaborations in, 110–12; financial inclusion and, 41–42, 46–50, 111, 156; food security and, 273; household surveys and, 312; of indigenous populations, 273–74; maternal and reproductive health initiatives, 334, 342–44; maternal mortality rates, 3, 277; maternity leave for, 39–40, 53; #MeToo movement and, 4; rural areas, poverty and, 156, 158, 164; SDG inclusiveness and, 14; underrepresentation in data collection, 312–13. *See also* Credit access; Financial sector; Gender gap in employment; Gender norms
Women-owned enterprises (WOEs), 32–34, 54, 56, 59
Women's World Banking, 45
World Bank (WB): Agglomeration Index, 225; Collaborative Leadership for Development, 119; Country Policy and Institutional Assessment (CPIA), 368; on discriminatory gender laws, 34; Enterprise Survey (2010), 129–30; financial inclusion goals of, 41; on fishing industry, 242–43, 250; Global Financing Facility in Support of Every Woman Every Child (GFF), 342–43, 348–49; green bonds of, 73; health

initiative financing of, 336–37; illicit financial flows, measuring, 357; on infrastructure in Brazil, 136; poverty evaluations, 3; public debt assistance from, 367; Public Private Partnerships in Infrastructure Resource Center (PPPIRC), 121; on subsidized child care, 38; *World Development Report,* 162
World Bank Group (WBG), 359–61
World Benchmarking Alliance (WBA), 102
World Business Council for Sustainable Development (WBCSD), 81–82, 96, 290
World Data Lab, 184–85
World Economic Forum: 2014 report on infrastructure, 129; Center for the Fourth Industrial Revolution, 94; Partnership Brokers Association courses, 120; Shaping the Future of Food Security and Agriculture System initiative, 112; Sustainable Development Impact Summit (2017), 288
World Economic Outlook (2016), 164
World Health Organization (WHO), 334, 336–37, 339–41
World Humanitarian Summit (2016), 310
World Organization for Animal Health (OIE), 339
World Parks Congress, 257
WorldPop (gridded global population product), 180, 186, 188
World Resources Institute, 192
World Vision International, 119, 313

Youth population. *See* Children

Zadek, Simon, 15, 67
Zambia, public procurement practices and gender in, 57
Zeckhauser, Richard, 114